ALSO BY NOAH FELDMAN

After Jihad:
America and the Struggle for Islamic Democracy

What We Owe Iraq:
War and the Ethics of Nation Building

Divided by God:
America's Church-State Problem—and What We Should Do About It

The Fall and Rise of the Islamic State

Scorpions:
The Battles and Triumphs of FDR's Great Supreme Court Justices

Cool War:
The United States, China, and the Future of Global Competition

The Three Lives of James Madison:
Genius, Partisan, President

The Arab Winter:
A Tragedy

The Broken Constitution:
Lincoln, Slavery, and the Refounding of America

TO BE A JEW TODAY

TO BE A
JEW
TODAY

A New Guide
to God, Israel, and
the Jewish People

NOAH FELDMAN

Farrar, Straus and Giroux
New York

Farrar, Straus and Giroux
120 Broadway, New York 10271

Printed in the United States of America
First edition, 2024

Library of Congress Cataloging-in-Publication Data
Names: Feldman, Noah, author.
Title: To Be a Jew Today : a new guide to God, Israel, and the Jewish
   people / Noah Feldman.
Description: First edition. | New York : Farrar, Straus and Giroux, 2024.
Identifiers: LCCN 2023038955 | ISBN 9780374298340 (hardback)
Subjects: LCSH: Judaism—21st century. | Judaism—Doctrines. |
   God (Judaism) | Israel—History. | Jews—Identity.
Classification: LCC BM562 .F48 2024 | DDC 296.3—dc23/eng/20230918
LC record available at https://lccn.loc.gov/2023038955

Designed by Patrice Sheridan

Our books may be purchased in bulk for promotional, educational, or business use.
Please contact your local bookseller or the Macmillan Corporate and Premium Sales
Department at 1-800-221-7945, extension 5442, or by email at
MacmillanSpecialMarkets@macmillan.com.

www.fsgbooks.com
Follow us on social media at @fsgbooks

1 3 5 7 9 10 8 6 4 2

In memory of Rabbi Ben-Zion Gold

CONTENTS

PART III: OF THE JEWISH PEOPLE

Note on Translation and Transliteration

Unless otherwise noted, translations in the book are my own. Transliteration follows standard academic practice, with the Hebrew letter *het* represented as the letter *h*. Proper names are spelled according to Western convention when one exists.

TO BE A JEW TODAY

INTRODUCTION

What's the point of being a Jew? And, really, aside from Jews, who cares? There are 7.6 billion people on earth. We're all hurtling toward climate disaster. Politics has rarely been more polarized. A global pandemic is barely behind us. Artificial intelligence is coming, ready or not. Fundamental questions of racial justice and of the rights of indigenous peoples remain unresolved in the United States and elsewhere. Meanwhile there are perhaps 16 million Jews in the world, depending on how you count, of whom some 7.6 million live in the United States. What they believe or don't believe, how they relate to Israel, a country of 9.7 million people (among them 7.1 million Jews), and whether they feel like part of a Jewish people, can seem like trivial questions when seen in this global context.

Yet somehow, the question of the Jews (not the Jewish question, which is something else) remains pressing to many people, not only to those who identify as Jewish. Young Jews—Jews of all ages, really—are trying to figure out whether to think of themselves as Jewish, and if so how and how much. They're trying to figure out if they should marry Jews, or only marry Jews. They want to know if they have to believe in God to be good Jews, and if so, what God. They are exploring wide-ranging spiritual paths, Buddhist and Hindu-Yogic and New Age, and wondering how their journeys through consciousness might draw on

Kabbalah, the ancient and also not so ancient Jewish mystical way. Non-Jews who are encountering these Jews (and their issues—oy, their issues) care about the same things.

Perhaps most pressing to Jews and non-Jews alike in the current moment is the matter of how Jews understand their relationship to Israel. For a country with fewer citizens than Sweden or Tunisia, Israel garners an extraordinary amount of attention in the world press, on social media, and in the minds of people almost everywhere. Its conflict with the Palestinian nation inspires not only rage but fellow feeling around the world, some of it reserved for each side. The latest manifestation of this intense global focus began on October 7, 2023, when Hamas launched terrorist attacks against Israel, killing some 1,200 people, mostly civilians, and taking 240 hostages. Israel responded by besieging, bombarding, and entering Gaza, precipitating a humanitarian crisis and killing thousands of Palestinians, including, inevitably, civilians who were not Hamas fighters. As I write these words, the war is ongoing, as are the expressions of both anger and sympathy from governments, groups, and individuals globally. Most Jews, wherever they are, care deeply about Israel, as do millions of American evangelical Christians. Many of the world's 1.8 billion Muslims care deeply about the Palestinian struggle, as do many left-leaning people of varied backgrounds who are influenced by anti-colonial ideas that, they believe, apply to the Israeli-Palestinian situation.

And of course Jews still seem to be represented disproportionately in fields from finance to film and comedy to constitutional law, not to mention Jewish accomplishments in science, medicine, and scholarship. Jews helped shape worldviews as divergent as communism and capitalism, psychoanalysis and physics. The earliest standardized intelligence tests identified Jews of European origin as some of the dumbest people measured.[1] More recent iterations of the same tests rank European-origin Jews at the top of the table. It seems almost inevitable that outlier status finds the Jews, or they find it. The systematic destruction of the Jews during the Holocaust was an outlying historical case. So was the building of the state of Israel, complete with its displacement of a potential Palestinian state along the way.

For myself, I don't need an excuse to engage with Jewish belief, Jewish meaning, and Jewish identity. I was born to it, or at least educated to believe that I was born to it. I had Hebrew tutors from the age of four and started full-time Jewish study at six. My parents, thoughtful keepers of their own brand of semi-progressive Modern Orthodox Jewish practice, embraced intellectualism, liberalism, and serious religious observance all at the same time. Our holiday trips to visit family and friends encompassed Afghan Jews who sprinkled us with rosewater, and Yeshivish (to use a word that didn't then exist), black-hat wearing ultra-Orthodox cousins who embraced us with love and curiosity. Since we didn't drive on the Sabbath, we walked two miles to synagogue every Saturday morning. After services, we had formal Shabbat lunch at our house with the students, professors, and hangers-on whom my parents invited spontaneously to join us. Then, on Sunday mornings, my same parents would drink Bloody Marys with their sophisticated graduate school friends, looking for all the world like ordinary denizens of Cambridge, Massachusetts.

Figuring out how it all fit together—if it did—has been a life project for me. I studied Judaism in college and graduate school and, if I'm honest, ever since. From the Bible to the Talmud to the medieval rabbis and philosophers and mystics and poets to modern reformers and Zionists to the new formations of today, there's no area of Jewish thought that's been alien to me. I love them all. And they all make me crazy.

But in nine previous books, I barely touched the Jews. I wrote about contradictions in search of resolutions, like those between Islam and democracy, or American slavery and the constitutional ideals of freedom and equality. Yet I tried to keep the contradictions of the Jews off the page.

For me to write about the Jews, therefore, I must ask your permission to be personal while still speaking historically and analytically. You, my readers, may each hate a different part of what I have to say, and perhaps you will also each love something different. I hope you will allow me to be mystical and rational, traditionalist and progressive, conservative and revolutionist. In my defense I can offer nothing but the truth that Jews, now and always, have occupied all of these different positions, often at the same time.

That's not all, though. I must also ask you to accept, for the sake of this book, that the many struggles and arguments and debates and exchanges at the heart of this story matter. They matter to me—that goes without saying. But they also matter to other people, Jews and non-Jews and those in between.

Maybe they shouldn't matter. Nothing in this book will in any immediate sense preserve a verdant earth or establish justice or create the conditions of permanent happiness for us and our posterity. This book won't solve the Israel-Palestine conflict, nor even offer an adequate account of its intricacies and moral weight.

Nevertheless, the ideas I hope to expound here do have the potential to help humans make meaning. They have that potential for people who think of themselves as Jews, Christians, Muslims, Buddhists, Hindus, atheists, spiritual believers, or nothing at all. They are meant to help all of us navigate where we come from and where we're going, and to illuminate the paths we might take to get there.

In what follows, I'm going to start from scratch. I'm going to lay out a range of beliefs that Jews have today, and have had in the past, about God and faith and how we should live our lives in accordance with both of those, or their absence. I plan to show how the existence of the modern state of Israel, and the movement of Zionism that created it, has utterly transformed Jewish life and thought over the past century—and the consequences of that transformation for us all, including for those who worry that eternal Judaism should not be so intertwined with an actually existing nation-state. I plan, too, to explore what Jewishness can mean for our world, as identity, as belief, as family, and as a state of being.

I will be making a number of new arguments here, which will be evident to anyone who has delved into these questions before. To name just a few primary ones: My presentation of how Jewish beliefs should be understood and organized—based on how God and spiritual morality are conceived internally—differs markedly from the standard sociological account of the different movements of contemporary Jews, such as ultra-Orthodox, Modern Orthodox, Religious Zionist, Conservative, Reconstructionist, Reform, and Humanist.[2] My claims about how the idea of Israel has fundamentally transformed all strands of Jewish belief are, I think, new in substance and form compared to the claims of others. My account of Jewish peoplehood as family—real and imagined,

solid and evanescent, connected and conflicted—will sound different from
other familial descriptions of the Jews. The hint of theology I offer, a
theology of struggle, contention, connection, embrace, and capability
that is available as much to nonbelievers as to the faithful, also departs
in certain respects from other Jewish theological approaches with which
I am familiar. In addition to these, on nearly every page I make small or
middle-sized new arguments about Jewish history, contemporary Jewish
faith, and what one might want to think about God or the Jews.

   In the course of writing the book, I intentionally have not flagged
what I think is new in it. My goal in that isn't to make what I write seem
obviously true. It's to allow you, the reader, to use your own reaction to
gauge and solidify what you think, not what I think. You can certainly
read this book by arguing with it. I read a lot of books that way, and it
often works for me. If you want, however, you can also read this book
not argumentatively but introspectively—the way I wrote it.

   If I accomplish what I am setting out to accomplish, with the help of
God or without it, then I will not have told you what to believe. Moses
Maimonides (1135–1204), by many measures the greatest Jewish thinker
ever to have lived, wrote an Arabic book called the *Guide of the Perplexed*.
It was a work of philosophy, in the usual sense of the term. It described,
accounted for, explained, and amplified the beliefs of many different people: Greek philosophers, Islamic schoolmen, ancient idolaters whose attitudes Maimonides sought to reconstruct from the best historical sources
available to him, and Jewish rabbis. Maimonides had strong views about
what Jews should believe, to say the least. His goal was to nudge careful
readers to beliefs he considered true. Yet in the *Guide*, to achieve that
objective skillfully, he mostly avoided telling his audience directly what
they must think. He spent a long time describing the kinds of contradictions that can occur within a book, no matter when written. As a result,
no two interpreters of the *Guide* have ever really agreed on precisely what
Maimonides himself believed. In this, if in nothing else, I seek to follow
his model: to illuminate for you, the reader, the multiplicity of different
possible viewpoints and ideas, and to let you decide for yourself.

   Maimonides would never have considered himself a bad Jew. To
the contrary, whatever his exact beliefs were—and I will return to them

often in these pages—he clearly thought he had ascertained the true inner meaning of the Torah to a degree not achieved by many of his predecessors. To his admirers, he was nothing less than a second Moses. They captured their adulation in an aphorism: "From Moses to Moses, there arose no one like Moses."[3]

The sad truth, however, is that to some who read Maimonides's work in his lifetime and in the centuries after, this great master of Jewish law, this innovator in the use of the Hebrew language, this towering genius, was in fact a bad Jew, one whose philosophical beliefs ought to be suppressed. In a series of pan-European controversies, leading rabbis called for bans on reading or teaching the *Guide of the Perplexed*. In the midst of one of these episodes, in 1232 or 1233, Dominican inquisitors in France, presumably inspired by the internal Jewish controversy, seized and publicly burned copies of the *Guide*.[4] The event may have set the stage for a more famous book burning, a tragedy still acknowledged in Jewish tradition and liturgy: the burning of the Talmud in Paris in 1242.[5]

The takeaway is that if Moses Maimonides could be denounced as a bad Jew, anyone can be. Which brings me to an important aspect of my argument, one that feels especially pressing in a moment when Jews are experiencing anguish, fear, pain, and anger. It makes me sad when, often in rueful, gentle self-mockery, Jewish friends of mine say of themselves, "I'm a bad Jew." They aren't. You aren't. There are so many ways to be Jewish, so many beliefs and practices and worldviews consistent with sincere and conscientious Jewishness, that we should avoid calling anyone a bad Jew, seriously or even in jest.[6]

This impulse to include, not exclude, and to embrace, rather than condemn, can be traced back to the medieval rabbis. Faced with mass baptism of Jews, they fell back on a maxim of Talmudic origin that they made into a principle of Jewish law: "An Israelite, though he has sinned, is an Israelite."[7] Even a Jew who goes so far as to embrace a competing religious tradition remains a Jew. According to this perspective, a Jew can do wrong. But by wrongdoing he does not cease to be a Jew. In fact, I know of no expression in the whole vast sea of Jewish teaching that corresponds precisely to the phrase "bad Jew." According to classical Jewish thought, one may become a bad person by doing bad deeds. But the sinner is not defined as a bad Jew. The biblical commandment to love your fellow applies with equal force to the Jew who disidentifies with the Jewish community to the point of becoming an apostate.

I've had my days of feeling like a bad Jew. Probably I will have more. So much of the Jewish tradition is framed in terms of obligations and commandments and prohibitions that it would be almost impossible never to feel that you are a bad Jew for failing to observe the law—or even rejecting it outright. And because Judaism is also an embodied, living tradition, there are always communities of Jews more than willing to tell you that you are a bad Jew. I can pretty much guarantee that someone will read this very paragraph and say, "Yes, Noah. You have felt like a bad Jew because you are a bad Jew—and here's a list of your transgressions to prove it." The ability to judge others has never been lacking in the Jewish tradition. The Jesus who said "Judge not, that ye be not judged" was speaking to fellow Jews.[8] Not for nothing did his aphorism become central to the Christian religious tradition that grew from his example, not to normative Judaism.

The feeling of being a bad Jew is therefore archetypally Jewish—and simultaneously a misreading of the Jewish way of engaging the world. A Jew can sin and repent, depending on your conception of sin and repentance. A Jew can judge and be judged, regardless of what conception of judging you hold. A Jew should not, however, slot herself or himself into the category of bad Jew. Nor should Jewish communities, however defined, define others as bad Jews. A bad Jew is just a Jew expressing irony and self-skepticism and maybe a little guilt. In other words, a Jew.

GOD, COUNTRY, FAMILY

One initial aim of this book is to chart a map of contemporary Jewish lives and ideas, a map the reader can use not to identify bad Jews but to explore and appreciate the many different ways Jews can be and think and experience. It can be used as a field guide to Jewish people and ideas as they exist today, and as they are being transformed for the future. The purpose of the map, however, isn't just to know what's where. It's to achieve a deeper aim: to help you chart your own journey, or to understand the journey of someone you know or love or don't like very much at all. It's to help my children chart their paths and to help me chart my own.

We need a new map today because we are, globally, in the midst of a series of significant transformations in Jewish life and thought. A map from thirty years ago, roughly when I graduated from college, would be surprisingly outdated. Time and again, in writing this book, I have been astonished by how beliefs and attitudes have shifted in a period of time that is historically very short—and how my own views have been changing alongside them, often without my fully noting it.

The book follows, roughly, a three-part plan: God, country, and family. Part I addresses Jewish beliefs about God and the nature of religious faith. It does so by introducing and describing four Jewish belief patterns that crosscut the existing Jewish movements. Unlike the movements, which are best identified and described sociologically via their leaders, members, synagogues, schools, publications, and other institutional accoutrements, these belief patterns are best identified as types of interior experiences or beliefs about who God is and what God wants, however conceived.

I call these belief patterns the Traditional, the Progressive, the Evolutionist, and the Godless. I'm limning these patterns, instead of using the more familiar terminology of Orthodox, Reform, Conservative, and so forth, because the old group descriptions are not the right tools to use in deciding what to believe for yourself, if they ever were. I'm encouraging you to figure out what you believe not by asking where you belong but rather by asking what you think, and from there seeing what kind of belonging might appeal to you. This might not fully solve your perplexity, but it should help you determine what you are perplexed *about*, assuming you are.

As for Jewish mysticism, it is less a belief pattern than an experiential mode of engagement with the divine. For that reason, it can (and does) coexist with any of the four belief patterns. There is a modest amount of mysticism in the book, as in me, even if it is not always labeled as such. You may sometimes notice it peering through the cracks in the wall, especially when I touch on matters of theology.

Jewish beliefs about God have actually changed less in recent decades than have Jewish beliefs and experiences connected to Israel and Jewish

peoplehood, the subjects of parts II and III of the book. That's not because faith always changes more slowly than other kinds of belief. There
have been times in Jewish history when stunning shifts in fundamental
beliefs about God occurred in just a few decades. Rather, the reason for
the comparative stability of these beliefs in the current moment lies in the
nature of what most Jews today spend most of their time thinking about:
not God so much as politics, morals, family, and community.

For this reason, some readers may want to go straight to the discussions of Godless Jews, Israel, and peoplehood. If that is what moves you,
please read that way—or any way you choose.

My reason for starting with God, not Israel, is that the divine has
become a too-much-neglected topic in Jewish thinking of all kinds. It's
not that God isn't there at all. Many Jews, whether personally traditional
or progressive, believe that God exists and shape their religious lives
accordingly. For Jewish atheists, God's nonexistence is a starting point.
And yet for the large number of Jewish agnostics, as well as for lots of
other Jews across the belief spectrum, the most efficient way to engage
Jewish life and thought is usually to get on with it and leave God to one
side. You can, it turns out, pray to a God who may or may not exist. You
can live in community with others without spending too much time
asking whether they believe you are united as a community because of a
covenant with the maybe-there, maybe-not God. Trust me, I know. For
much of my own religious life, I too slighted basic questions about God,
not because I knew what to think but because I had no idea. Judaism is
well set up to allow God to be kept in the margins.

This setup has some advantages. It can enable various kinds of cooperation, for example. Different Jewish communities disagree strongly
about who should be able to marry whom and how inclusive Jewish life
should be. But they mostly avoid framing their positions by saying explicitly that they know what God wants. Zionism, the movement that has
influenced global Jewish thought more than any other in the past century,
is avowedly agnostic. You can be an atheist Zionist or a Religious Zionist
or neither. The big-tent character of Zionism has helped it infuse Jewish
spaces that resisted its point of view for generations before succumbing,
consciously or unconsciously.

The drawback of Jewish religious structures that can operate independent of whether God exists, and in what form, is that they lend themselves to action and practice without reflection. That works just fine provided you never pause to ask yourself exactly why you are doing what you are doing. The moment you do, you will find yourself disastrously lost if you haven't built your practices on a foundation of belief that you can hold with confidence.

To be clear, I'm not saying that a meaningful Jewish life requires either total belief or nonbelief. It can also stand on uncertainty about the nature of the divine, as does an enormous amount of rich Jewish life. But that uncertainty must be earned by thoughtful consideration if it is going to underpin a meaningful life. It must be *conscious* uncertainty, not the uncertainty that comes from trying to avoid the hardest questions of all. At the end of part I, I will offer a glimpse of what a conscious uncertainty might look like in the light of a Jewish theology of struggling or contending with God.

By engaging some of the toughest and most stark problems of God and faith in Jewish life, I hope to lay a groundwork for my discussions of Israel and Jewish peoplehood. Arguments about national and communal and familial belonging look very different when they can be connected to questions of ultimate belief. That might make compromise and cooperation harder. But it will also unveil moral answers to moral questions that deserve a hearing. It is, in the end, odd to talk about issues like the rights of women to become rabbis or LGBTQ people to marry as Jews without talking about the moral foundations of equality and dignity themselves. And it is almost impossible to take a coherent stand on Israel, democracy, and the state of the Israeli-Palestinian conflict without relying on a moral framework, whether derived from faith or reason or a combination. By figuring out where you lie on the map of Jewish beliefs about God and religion, you will be able to understand much more clearly where you stand on Israel and Jewish peoplehood. Ideally, those position points should converge.

When it comes to Israel, the subject of part II, we desperately need a new account because of how Israel has been evolving in recent decades—and because of how Israel has come to assume a substantially different place in Jewish thought over that time frame. Zionism, the movement that imagined and produced the state of Israel, began as a development within the history of Jewish thought. It aspired to be more than that, however: Zionism aspired to *become* the history of the Jews, and to transmute historical Judaism into a modern nationalism that would transcend the specifically Jewish experience of life in the Diaspora.

Zionism created a Jewish state. It did not achieve the related ambition of replacing Jewishness with a new, national identity based solely on Israel and not at all on Jewish religion. At the same time, over the past roughly thirty years, Zionism did accomplish something transformative in the history of Judaism. It made the state of Israel—and a contested set of ideas about that state—into a fundamental component of Jewish life, thought, and experience, even for Jews who might prefer it otherwise. When the 2023 Hamas-Israel war broke out, Jews everywhere, whether sympathetic to Israel or critical or some combination, had to deal with its impact and significance. Like it or not, they found themselves reacting intensely and emotionally and spiritually *as Jews*. Nonreactivity was not a realistic option. Israel and Jewishness were thus interwoven to an unprecedented degree, complete with traumatic intergenerational resonances of European pogroms and the Holocaust.

This gradual development, made suddenly and dramatically visible by recent events, has been epochal for all Jews and for their ways of engaging the world. Part II explains how it happened—very differently, it turns out, for Jews with different belief patterns. It describes what various Jews' current beliefs about Israel look like today, not just in relation to Israel's complicated and controversial place in global politics but in relation to God and Jewish theology, especially Jewish thought about the messianic age. And it explores the challenges, difficulties, and crises that Jews of different belief patterns face today and will face in the future with respect to the idea of Israel and its place in their thoughts and lives.

There is always a great deal to argue about when it comes to Israel, and the claims I make in part II are no exception to that rule. The point of my discussion of Israel, however, isn't to give you the right answers, assuming such right answers exist. It's to help you work through the interaction between your thinking about Israel and your thinking about

God and Jewishness. It's to explore whether Israel necessarily must play the central role in constructing Jewish thought and identity that it presently plays, and to ask if there are other options. It's to try to figure out where Israel is going today and where it is taking Jewish thought and Jewish life in the future.

In this spirit, at the end of part II, I offer some reflections on the resources Jewish thought has for the moral aspects of a Jewish state in Israel, seen in the light of the theology of struggle. I draw attention to the biblical theology of covenant, collective sin, and collective punishment, and to the Deuteronomic warning against saying, "My strength and the power of my hand has made me this wealth."[9]

Part III of the book looks beyond the existing state of Israel and its meaning for Jews to what is perhaps an even more difficult problem: What, today, is the nature of Jewish peoplehood? Or better yet, whatever Jewish peoplehood looks like now, what should we want it to look like? These questions are, naturally, intertwined both with Jewish ideas about God and Godlessness and with ideas about Israel; that's why this part of the book comes last. The problem of Jewish peoplehood has pressing practical aspects, like the recurring question of whom Jews should marry and the even more fundamental question of who should be considered a Jew, on which the marriage question ultimately rests. And the problem of Jewish peoplehood has crucial definitional sides, too. What is a Jew? Who are the Jews? What is the Jews' role in history, if the question even makes sense? Who cares? *Should* we care? And if so, why?

To address these questions, I will survey several attempts at answering them, both past and present. Although I don't claim to have definitive answers, I will, as I'm trying to do throughout this book, suggest some advantages and disadvantages of each possible approach—and some directions that seem attractive to me. I will offer an extended comparison of the Jewish people to a family: not the simplistic family structure of birth parents and biological offspring but the real-world, complex structures of attachment by adoption, accident, choice, creativity, friendship, love, hate, and, above all, imagination. Family is not inevitable, nor is family always an unmitigated good in our lives. It can be self-chosen and self-created. At the same time, family necessarily exists in relation to other people whose own experiences we do not and cannot fully control. We can walk away from existing families and form new ones based on our ideals and aspirations and loves. Regardless of how we engage our various families, family remains (for all humans, I suspect) a crucial archetype for how we experience the world.

Ideally, we should each be able to find an understanding of Jewish peoplehood that corresponds to our beliefs about God and Israel. Ideally, too, our understandings of the three topics corresponding to the three parts of this book would hold together in some loosely defensible fashion. In a perfect world, our beliefs about each of these topics would affect our beliefs about the others.

If Jewish peoplehood is familial in a key sense, that also should help explain why this book includes its fair share of internal disagreement within the framework of familial love. This isn't a novel, but the famous opening line of Tolstoy's *Anna Karenina* still applies: "All happy families are alike; each unhappy family is unhappy in its own way." A book about an idealized happy family wouldn't be true, and it wouldn't be interesting to read or write. Real family means real love and real struggle. Both give our lives meaning.

I don't take it as given, in part III of the book or any part of it, that the Jews as a people must continue to exist. That is a conclusion that must be supported by good reasons, some of which I hope to provide. Not all families last forever, whether understood biologically or conceptually. Not all families should. Like any other human phenomenon, we should hope to preserve Jewishness only if doing so reflects our deepest values and beliefs. So if Jews are to experience peoplehood in an era of religious disagreement, intense controversy over Israel, and uncertainty about what being Jewish even means, it will require new resources of creativity. Like experiencing family, it will take work: emotional, spiritual, and intellectual. I am setting out to suggest some ways in which that work might be worthwhile. That's all I can do—maybe all anyone can.

At the end of part III, I connect the idea of peoplehood as family to the theology of struggle and connection. I suggest that Jews struggle with God together, as a family, finding in the divine, as in one another, love and embrace along with contention. Indeed, I suggest that for Jewishness, the two intertwined aspects of struggle and love may be inextricable. For readers who find the love of God too oblique in the theology of struggle as I sketch it in parts I and II, I promise that love will become manifest by the conclusion.

A note on what I do and don't believe: Some early readers of the book told me they were sure they knew exactly where in the book I was writing about my own chosen beliefs and where not. Maybe they were right. But as it happens, each of these readers picked a different viewpoint as the one that must be mine. The reason, I suspect, is that I have had the fortune or misfortune to identify with nearly every view I lay out here at one time or another in my life. I have tried to write about (nearly) all with sympathy and empathy, including those with which I disagree at the moment of writing. If, then, the book sometimes seems to contain contradictions, the contradictions may be my own.

Am I writing this book for my kids? Yes and no. I'm not *not* writing it for them. Whenever you write a book, it's helpful to have an intended audience in mind. My teenagers have been the intended audience for much of this one. At the same time, the genre of a book containing a message to one's kids might be misleading. I am not trying to inculcate one specific lesson but to model a method of thinking and offer it for reflection.

"Hear, my son, your father's instruction, and do not forsake your mother's teaching."[10] That line from the book of Proverbs relies on both the similarity and the distinction between "instruction"—in Hebrew, *musar*—and "teaching"—in Hebrew, *torah*. *Musar* is ethical or moral instruction, associated with parental education. *Torah* is that and also much more. *Torah* is the most protean word in the Jewish vocabulary, meaning the law that must be followed and God's ultimate Law and also authoritative teaching and guidance and worldview, to describe just some of its semantic field. In this verse, which differs from the Freudian picture of parent-child relations, the father instructs through his model and his ideas, but the mother lays down the law.

This book isn't Torah. It doesn't lay down any laws. It might be *musar*, however. I hope it is. Unlike Maimonides, I do not have all the answers, not even answers I might be hiding from you. This book is more a guide to living with perplexity than a guide for the perplexed.

The one thing I can say with confidence is that, having immersed myself in Jewish tradition and thought, and having occupied the position of bad Jew to some observers and commentators some of the time, I have come to learn that the tradition, in all its multifarious guises and unexpected manifestations, will never abandon *me*. That's something.

PART I

OF GOD

I:1

THE GOD OF BLACK
AND WHITE

Jewish ultra-Orthodoxy—its adherents prefer the term "Haredi"*—
has an identifiable, branded color scheme: black hats, black suits, and
white shirts. To watch Netflix, you would think its adherents were the
only Jews on earth. The miniseries *Unorthodox* (2020) and reality show
My Unorthodox Life (2021) were both about women who had left Haredi
communities. The Israeli series *Shtisel* (2013–2021) is a more positive
depiction: a soap opera–cum–allegory about a gentle, dreamy Israeli
Haredi who is a gifted painter. The shows' popularity reflects enduring,
if cyclical, audience interest in Haredi Jews. Those Jews look (to the
uninitiated) like throwbacks to the eastern European shtetl, and so are
well suited to serve as canvases for modern impulses of revulsion and
nostalgia.

The Haredi color scheme could hardly be more symbolically perfect.
The black and white hark back to nineteenth-century Europe, a time

---

* The Hebrew word means to tremble or quake with fear. It comes from Isaiah 66:5,
which reads, "Hear the word of the Lord, you who quake at his word." And yes, it's the
same verse that named the Society of Friends, the Quakers, who brought you Pennsyl-
vania, abolitionism, and Quaker Oats.

before color photography. Poetically, they conjure up the Haredi vision of God: a God of right and wrong, of permitted and forbidden, a God whose Torah records and commands bright-line rules that are written in black ink on white parchment and that lay out a black-and-white morality without shades in between or room for updated modernization.

I can remember the appeal of that black and white when, as a child, I visited my Haredi cousins in Borough Park, Brooklyn. I could already make out that the way they dressed stood for Jewish authenticity: the idea that there was a right and a wrong way to be Jewish and that theirs was the right way. In particular, I envied the crisp black fedoras the boys were given to wear when they became bar mitzvah. My own family identified as Modern Orthodox, which meant that we followed the law fairly rigorously but didn't wear the black-and-white uniform.

I lobbied my father, then as now a model of traditional Ivy style, to buy me a fedora. He didn't want to, realizing, I am sure, that I would have no occasion to wear it back in Cambridge. But when he visited his Brooklyn family, he himself would break out a natty soft blue fur-felt number from Worth & Worth. So somehow he relented, buying thirteen-year-old me a child-sized fedora. It was manufactured by a company called Kova Hats, "Hat Hats," since *kova'* means hat in Hebrew. (I looked it up online: Hat Hats still exists, appropriately enough in Lakewood, New Jersey, the home of the largest yeshiva in the United States.)

The hat my father let me get wasn't black, however. It was gray, as if to say to my relatives, and the world, that we weren't fully with the program, but somewhere betwixt and between. Authenticity eluded me. I am pretty sure I didn't wear the fedora in public more than a few times.

The God of black and white is the right starting place for making sense of the beliefs and lives of the Haredim. There are numerous subgroups of Haredim—so many, in fact, that almost no Haredi would ordinarily use the term to describe himself or herself, preferring a much more specific designation. What almost all Haredim share is a common and complete inner commitment to what they consider the unbroken tradition of Jewish belief and practice. This can be summarized neatly by the first teachings found in the *Ethics of the Fathers*, a compilation of wise aphorisms by rabbis who lived roughly from 200 BCE to 200 CE:

> Moses received the Torah at Sinai and transmitted it to Joshua; and Joshua to the elders; and the elders to the prophets; and the prophets transmitted it to the men of the Great Assembly. They said three things: Be patient in doing justice; raise many students; and make a fence round the Torah.[1]

The main point of the passage is to establish the chain of custody of the Law from God to Moses on down to the sages and rabbis, who have authoritatively borne the tradition ever since. The secondary points are that the Law governs in the real world (it does "justice"); that it is to be studied by the many students of the rabbis; and that the rabbis must protect the observance of the Law by making new, more restrictive rules to assure no one comes close to violating the rules laid down by God.

To Jews whose beliefs belong to this pattern, God is the ultimate authority. His will can be known through the living tradition: the binding, definitive body of interpretation that tells them what God requires of His people. Jews who believe in this God may justly be named "Traditionalists."[2] They know God through His Torah. They know His Torah is true because the tradition teaches them that it is. And they are certain that the tradition to which they belong goes straight back to the revelation at Mount Sinai.[3]

Traditionalists believe that God requires a totalizing envelopment of purely Jewish spiritual and communal life. For them, the authority of the rabbis does not stop at the outer boundary of what the Torah requires nor even at the fence that extends around the Law. To be precise, they do not think the Torah's requirements delineate a boundary at all: every aspect of human life is to be integrated into a single Torah worldview that is articulated by the rabbis and obeyed by everyone else.

To historians, whose job is to chart the development of human ideas and religious movements from outside rather than from within, ultra-Orthodox Traditionalism is not actually a seamless continuation of unbroken Jewish historical practice. To the historians, Haredi thought

is a product of the modern age, a reaction to the ideas of the Jewish Enlightenment.* The Traditionalist insistence on an absolutist Torah worldview is, to the historical eye, a cousin of the other totalizing worldviews
that emerged in the modern era, including the totalizing commitment to
reason or science. In other words, from the standpoint of academic history, what I am calling Traditionalism isn't inherently traditional at all.†

To the Traditionalists themselves, however, who conceive even their
innovations as part of unbroken tradition, this set of external observations is basically irrelevant. Hasidim, one of the two major groups
of Haredim, symbolically trace their old-Polish-style fur hats and long
black coats back to ancient Israel and its priestly and royal garments.
They revere their founder, Rabbi Israel Baal Shem Tov (c. 1698–1760),
not only as the creator of *devekus*, a radical mystical practice of cleaving
to God, but as a lineal descendant of the royal House of David. The
other major Haredi group, today often called Yeshivish after the yeshivas
that form the heart of its community, understand themselves as the inheritors of a continuous chain of intellectual-spiritual-legal Torah study
going back to the beginning, even though in the past only a small number of intellectually qualified young men studied in the great yeshivas.

In their daily lives, Traditionalist Jews seek to operationalize the Torah in every moment, waking or sleeping. They pray three times daily,
the men always in conjunction with a quorum of at least ten, whether

---

* The *Haskalah*, as it is called in Hebrew, followed the broader Enlightenment, lasting a
bit more than a century from its beginnings in the 1770s. Its proponents, many of them
skeptical critics of religious traditionalism, combined dedication to reason and modernity with renewed interest in Hebrew language, Jewish history, and Jewish culture.

† Some sociological scholars of religion consider Haredim to be religious fundamental-
ists. The monumental Fundamentalism Project devoted five chapters of one of its major
volumes to them. See The Fundamentalism Project, vol. 4: *Accounting for Fundamentalisms: The Dynamic Character of Movements*, ed. Martin E. Marty and R. Scott Appleby
(Chicago: University of Chicago Press, 1994), 173–357. Its editors defined fundamentalism as a modern strategy whereby "beleaguered believers attempt to preserve their
distinctive identity . . . by selective retrieval of doctrines, beliefs, and practices from a
sacred past." The "fundamentals" so "retrieved and updated" are "accompanied . . . by
unprecedented claims and doctrinal innovations" intended "to regain the same charismatic intensity today by which they forged communal identity . . . long ago." Marty
and Appleby, *Accounting for Fundamentalisms*, Introduction, 1.

in synagogues or at work or at the study house. They marry young and have many, many children in fulfillment of the divine command to be fruitful and multiply. Everyone studies Torah full-time until around the age of eighteen in schools that teach either the bare minimum of legally required secular knowledge or, sometimes, less than that. After eighteen, almost all men continue to study Torah as a profession for roughly another decade, sometimes longer. Women may obtain college and professional degrees and might work in non-Haredi jobs, but men generally do neither. Traditionalists live in big, like-minded, highly supportive, and highly insular communities where they can be close to their extended families and participate in their own institutions of education, prayer, and even health care. They read newspapers and books aimed at their communities. They speak to each other either in Yiddish, a language they have lovingly preserved from pre-Holocaust Europe, or else in distinctive dialects of English or Hebrew that are shot through with Jewish words and ideas. Those dialects are pronounced and intoned a lot like Yiddish and can sound strikingly different from conventional English or Hebrew.

From these distinctive aspects of Traditional Judaism, it is possible to begin to glimpse the extremely attractive aspects of its lived reality for those who choose it, and perhaps for some others who appreciate it from a distance. Traditionalism offers that most elusive, rare phenomenon in our contemporary fragmented world: total, comprehensive belonging in an environment of total, comprehensive belief. Traditionalists, at their best, can experience lives of divinely driven purpose, enmeshed in the love and unwavering support of families and communities that share the same sense of meaning and the same ethical framework.

All this is, for Traditionalists, warmed by the comforting, nurturing flame of authenticity. For hundreds of years now, since the start of the modern age, self-questioning and self-doubt have informed or defined many people's spiritual lives. The postmodern worldview is, if anything, more troubled by uncertainty than the modern. Traditionalists are living out a kind of solution to this doubt. They can take refuge in their confidence that they are doing what God wants, in the way God wants them to do it. They are, in short, living their spiritual and familial lives in perfect alignment with how they believe things ought to be. From their perspective, they are being authentic not merely to themselves but to the divine order of the universe.

The model of authenticity, collective commitment, and a high birth rate has translated into a communal flourishing and growth that was all but unimaginable after the devastating losses of the Holocaust. Today there are well over 1.5 million Haredi Jews in the world, with about two-thirds in Israel, one-third in the United States, and a smattering elsewhere. That accounts for perhaps 7 percent of American Jews[4] and 12.5 percent of all Israelis.[5]

Measured in institutional terms, the Traditionalist resurgence is even more stunning. More people study in yeshivas today than at any time in Jewish history. Greater wealth and changing social norms have created enormous yeshivas of unprecedented size. In eastern Europe, a large yeshiva might have had a couple hundred students. Today the largest yeshiva in the United States, Beth Medrash Govoha in Lakewood, New Jersey, known colloquially as BMG or Lakewood, has roughly eight thousand students, ranging in age from eighteen into their thirties.[6] The Mir Yeshiva in Jerusalem has some nine thousand students.[7]

GOD'S COMMANDMENTS, GOD'S AUTHORITY

The success and sustainability of the Traditionalist way of life begins with God. He (gendered in the Hebrew language but genderless according to most Jewish theology, because God has no body) is not just any God. He is a God of law and of love whose ways can be known. His gracious commandments can be satisfyingly followed. His prescribed rituals of worship are meant to sustain human beings through joy and sorrow, all the while reminding us that the divine Presence is near. Awesome as this God is, Traditionalists often experience Him as caring and present. He even has an affectionate Yiddish nickname, *der Aibishter* (literally, "the Uppermost"), which conjures up a God who is aware of humans and the details of their lives.*

---

* Sholem Aleichem's Tevye addresses God a bit more familiarly still. After formulaically thanking God for a year of flourishing crops, he tells his Maker as an after-

A life lived in accordance with God's requirements and rituals can be a life infused with a near-constant connection to the spiritual plane. The family lies close to the heart of this Traditionalist life, and ideally, family life is constantly reinforced and elevated by the shared sense of holiness that comes with fulfilling God's plan. The highest individual value is the nourishment of the soul, whether understood as the mind (in Yeshivish circles) or as the spirit (in mystical Hasidism). The service of God—the *love* of God—consists in connecting the individual soul to the collective soul. And what, really, could be more beautiful than that?

The challenges of creating and sustaining this kind of total spiritual community in the context of late consumer capitalism—a shorthand for the background social conditions of life in contemporary America, Israel, and Europe, where Traditionalists live—are as obvious as they are overwhelming. Our contemporary societies are, to a great degree, places of dissociation, disunity, and difference. Lots of people today experience connection, community, and even spiritual transcendence. But almost by definition, those parts of our lives are partial, not total. Sometimes we are in community; sometimes not. Sometimes we worship—or meditate, or do yoga, or drink in sports bars—with others; sometimes not. Almost never do we find ourselves in the setting of total community among people who share essentially *all* our deepest commitments and beliefs. You might even say that our societies are designed to accommodate our many different overlapping selves and identities and group attachments.

Traditionalists want to achieve a state of being that is almost the opposite of our background conditions of freedom and multiplicity. They might want to be free to choose the lives they lead, but that is where the freedom ends. In fact, Traditionalists are even ambivalent about whether we are free to choose to worship God or whether that choice is forced upon us.

Consider the pivotal moment depicted in the Bible in which the children of Israel enter into covenant with God at Mount Sinai. Accord-

---

thought: "As I think of it, what good will all that flourishing do for a *shlimazel* like me? Does my horse care whether oats are expensive or cheap?" "The Great Windfall," in Sholem Aleichem, *Tevye the Dairyman and Motl the Cantor's Son*, trans. Aliza Sevrin (New York: Penguin Books, 2009).

ing to the book of Exodus, God offers the Israelites an if-then agreement: "Now if you will surely listen to my voice and keep my covenant, then you shall be my treasure from among all the peoples, for all the earth is mine."[8] Faced with this opportunity, "All the people answered together, and said, 'All that God has spoken we will do.'"[9]

The literal meaning of the text seems to be that the covenant with God is accepted freely by the Israelites. For most modern Jews, influenced by the structures of classical liberal political thought, the voluntary choice to enter into the covenant is central to what makes Jewish faith and practice appealing: to worship God is to make a free choice to do so. Seen this way, the good and just God of the Bible does not mandate obedience. He offers the Law to those who choose it.*

The earliest rabbis sometimes embraced a version of this notion of free choice at Sinai. But the Talmud also records a very different viewpoint, which begins with the Bible's innocuous-sounding statement that the Israelites at Sinai "stood at the bottom of the mountain."[10] One rabbi, Avdimi bar Hama, suggested taking this phrase literally: the children of Israel stood *beneath* the bottom of the mountain. "This teaches," Avdimi said, "that the Holy One, Blessed be He, overturned the mountain above them like a cask, and said to them: 'If you accept the Torah, excellent; and if not, there will be your burial place.'"[11]

In Avdimi's version, God did not offer the Israelites a truly free choice to enter the covenant. Instead God made them an offer they couldn't refuse: accept the Law or die right here, right now. The rabbis of the Talmud understood that Avdimi was contradicting the notion that the Israelites accepted the covenant voluntarily. Another rabbi, Aha bar Ya'akov, is recorded as noting that Avdimi's story creates a "great caveat" to the Torah. By implication, based on Avdimi's account, the

---

* For a subtle, important discussion, see Rabbi Irving Greenberg, "Voluntary Covenant," *Perspectives* (National Jewish Center for Learning and Leadership, 1982). I will say more about this voluntarism in the next chapter. For now, note that the voluntary reading of the covenant isn't merely a result of liberal ideals. Those liberal ideals themselves were influenced originally by a (Protestant) voluntary reading of the very same biblical covenant that was itself influenced by some rabbinic readings of the same story.

Israelites would be able to say they were coerced into accepting the Law and therefore are not truly bound by it.

The Talmud offers a weak response to Rabbi Aha's worry, suggesting that the Israelites later reaccepted the Law voluntarily in the time of Queen Esther.[12] To my mind, the weakness of the response reflects and even acknowledges that Avdimi's authoritarian version of the covenant has its own logic. Taking Avdimi seriously, the covenant is not a freely chosen pact. It is certainly not a contract among equals. God is transcendent and all-powerful; the Israelites are not. It follows that a divine covenant is inherently a structure shaped by *pre-existing* divine authority. On this view, it makes no sense to say you freely choose to worship the one true God. You have no alternative, not if you want to live and prosper.

As if to underscore this authoritarian perspective, the Talmud offers a statement by yet another, better known rabbi, Rabbi Shimon (Resh) Lakish, that ups the ante of the Israelites' coerced consent. According to Avdimi, if the Israelites had declined the covenant, they would have been destroyed. According to Resh Lakish, if the Israelites had declined the covenant, *the whole universe would have been destroyed*: "The Holy One, Blessed be He, set a condition on Creation and said to [it]: 'If Israel accepts the Law, you shall continue to exist; and if not, I shall return you to chaos and void.'"[13]

The point of Resh Lakish's more extreme scenario is partly to suggest that the universe exists teleologically for the purpose of the Torah. At the same time, Resh Lakish's view also emphasizes the authoritarian structure of the power differential between the parties to the covenant, the omnipotent Creator and the human children of Israel. God's authority over the world inheres in His act of creating it. Within that created world, humans must play their role, or else the world would not exist. The universe would be cast back to the state the second verse of the Bible describes as existing before creation: "when the earth was chaos and void, and the spirit of God hovered over the waters."[14]

To Traditionalists, then, God's authority is primary, primordial, and absolute. The Traditionalist God is the Master of the Universe, the divine King. His realm is not a democracy.[15] To believe in Him is to accept the yoke of His authority. You may plead with Him, pray to Him, reason with Him like Abraham, or even rage at Him in the manner of Job or a Hasidic master questioning divine justice. But you must accept His answer, or His situational silence, as final. That acceptance of God's authority is the condition of believing, and that belief is the condition of belonging.

THE VIEW OF THE TORAH

In Traditionalism, God's authority is not abstract but concrete. The core teaching of rabbinic tradition is that God assigned His authority to human beings: first to prophets and priests and judges, then to the rabbis who succeeded them. The God of the Hebrew Bible directs the children of Israel to act "according to the Torah which they shall instruct you." The same verse concludes, "Do not deviate from the word which they shall tell you right or left."[16]

To Traditionalists, this verse answers the basic theological problem of how Jews today can know what God wants. Their solution is straightforward: the rabbis will tell you. Consequently, *God's will can be known*. It can be known by asking the rabbis what God wills. God may not be in direct communication with the Jews as He was with their biblical forefathers. But that distance does not matter, because the rabbis have the authority to say what God wants.

In this structure of authority, the rabbis in turn must ascertain God's will. Their chief tool to do so is, unsurprisingly, the tradition itself. In the view of Traditionalist rabbis, the written and oral Torah comprise nothing less than a complete system of knowledge—all the knowledge necessary to know what God wants of us. What is required of the rabbis, in this picture, is interpretation and application. Fortunately, that is exactly the stuff the tradition is made of. The tradition is a record of other, previous rabbis interpreting and applying God's laws.

The complicating factor in this structure of concretized divine authority is that rabbis are human beings, hence fallible. In theory, even the greatest rabbis might err in interpreting and applying God's will. To complicate matters further, the rabbinic tradition is a tradition of argument and disagreement. The earliest rabbinic sources already record differing opinions from different rabbis on questions of Jewish law. The activity of Torah study has always consisted of arguing about the true meaning of the Torah.[17]

The way out favored by Traditionalist Jews is to locate final rabbinic authority in an ultimate, quasi-hierarchical institution: the rabbinic court recognized by the Jews of the time. A famous and important Talmudic story exemplifies and explains this solution.[18] It involves a dispute over a matter that no longer troubles Jews, namely the operation of the Hebrew calendar, which was once set not by mathematical calculation but by direct observation of the new moon each month.

In the story, two witnesses came to Rabban Gamliel II, the prince of the rabbinic Jewish community in the aftermath of the destruction of the Temple in Jerusalem in 70 CE. They testified they had seen the new moon at the expected time—the thirtieth day of the month—but had looked the following night and not seen it. Rabban Gamliel, untroubled by the inconsistency, accepted their testimony and, with his rabbinic court in the town of Yavneh, declared the new month, thus setting the dates of the holidays in it, which happened to include Yom Kippur, the Day of Atonement, the holiest day of the Jewish year.

Some other rabbis thought the contradiction between seeing the new moon and then not seeing it the next night rendered the witnesses' testimony invalid. Fatefully, one of these was Rabbi Joshua, an important and widely respected rabbi. In his view, the calendar month did not begin until the next day.

Rabban Gamliel decided to enforce his princely authority. He ordered Rabbi Joshua to appear before him on the day that the latter considered Yom Kippur carrying "your staff and your coins." If that day was actually Yom Kippur, then carrying those objects would be a violation of the strict ordinances that commanded rest on the holy day.[19] The point was to show Rabbi Joshua—and the rest of the world—that Rabban Gamliel's authority about the date of the holiday was final.

In the Talmud's account, Rabbi Joshua was troubled by the order, but he nevertheless obeyed. When he came before Rabban Gamliel with his staff and coin purse on the day Rabbi Joshua had calculated as Yom Kippur, the prince stood up—a mark of respect—and kissed Rabbi Joshua on the head, saying, "Come in peace, my master and my student. My master—in wisdom. My student—in that you accepted my words."[20]

Rabban Gamliel's formulation was, it would seem, intended as a sort of compromise. His decree had been obeyed and his authority definitively established. He could then defer to Rabbi Joshua's greater "wisdom"—provided the hierarchical structure was preserved. The underlying principle of rabbinic authority had been vindicated.

Something like this hierarchical idea, I would argue, undergirds the contemporary Traditionalist solution to the locus of rabbinic authority. To Traditionalists, divine delegated authority today rests with a small number of rabbis known as *gedolim*, great ones. The *gedolim* acquire their status through their reputations for Torah knowledge and personal piety. No single recognized institution has the authority to choose them, although yeshivas and Hasidic dynasties can play a role in shaping their reputations. Nevertheless, there is broad agreement among Traditionalists about who the *gedolim* are.[21]

The *gedolim* are human and so capable of disagreement among themselves. But when the *gedolim* do agree, Traditionalists call their collective opinion *daas Toyre*, a Yiddish phrase that means, literally, "the view of the Torah."[22] To Traditionalists, *daas Toyre*, the consensus of the *gedolim*, has the status of Torah, of Law, and is binding even on matters of policy rather than strict questions of Jewish law. The range of subjects covered can be extremely broad, ranging from a ban on the use of smartphones without software to protect users from worldly influences all the way to instructing adherents on how to vote in Israeli elections.

Because the *gedolim* are not prophets receiving direct revelation from God, *daas Toyre* isn't divine prophecy. That's why it is called "the view of the Torah," not "the view of God." Traditionalists typically believe, however, that *daas Toyre* is formed with a kind of divine guidance or inspiration. By a lifetime of pious worship and study, true *gedolim* gain access to the divine will. *Daas Toyre* is thus similar to Torah study in kind but not in degree. By studying the Torah, any person may ascertain some of God's law. The most learned and most pious scholars are vouchsafed an even deeper understanding of God's will, one appropriate to their station. They intuit God's will out of their knowledge of God's law as revealed to humans in the Torah.

CHALLENGES TO TRADITIONALIST BELIEF

The same structure of authority that organizes Traditionalist belief and maintains the community against the counterforces of the contemporary world is also the wellspring of the most powerful external criticisms of the Traditionalist worldview. Those criticisms may be heard everywhere from popular culture to more serious and sustained intrareligious conversation. They are not the criticisms of Traditionalism leveled by the thinkers of the nineteenth-century Jewish Enlightenment, which mainly had to do with its nonscientific worldview and alleged inability to engage the social and economic realities of modernity. Nor do they resemble the philosophical criticisms of traditional, premodern Jewish beliefs, which tended to focus on deep issues of theology, like whether the world is made of eternally existing matter as opposed to being created out of nothing.[23] In the not-too-distant past, faith was lost and won over such abstractions. Today, while these problems are still of interest to some (especially to those wavering on the edges of belief), the most trenchant criticisms of Traditionalism lie in the realm of human equality, human freedom, and human potential.

Observing Traditionalists' way of life—sometimes after leaving it themselves—contemporary critics level two main charges at Traditionalist Jewish communities. Traditionalism, they point out correctly, enforces rigid, sexist gender hierarchies. What is more, Traditionalism sometimes educates its children from birth, at home and in school, in such a way as to deny them access to the knowledge and skills that would give them the option of leaving the community as adults. Because the community also often cuts off those who leave, the human cost of exit is enormous, potentially resulting in isolation and depression. And the community offers no acceptance or recognition for gay and trans people. When those criticisms are combined, the upshot is that growing up in Traditionalism is especially terrible and cruel for people whose sex, sexuality, or gender identity leave them no way of flourishing within the community but for whom leaving is nevertheless extraordinarily difficult.

These criticisms are not ones that resonate with Traditionalist leaders and probably not with most ordinary Traditionalists either. That is because both criticisms derive from the belief world of contemporary liberal society. The critique of Traditionalism's sexism and nonrecognition of difference is based on the contemporary liberal values of human equality and celebration of difference. The critique of the cost of exiting Traditionalism is based on the liberal belief in voluntary choice and consent with regard to how and where we wish to live.

Traditionalism largely rejects both sets of values. With respect to equality and difference, Traditionalism teaches that God has created all humans as equal in His eyes but has not conferred on them equal rights, responsibilities, or obligations. Jews incur 613 Torah obligations, including both dos and don'ts;[24] non-Jews have seven.[25] Jewish women, unlike Jewish men, are exempt from any dos that must be performed at specified times.[26] The Bible expressly prohibits sex between men, according to the Traditionalist reading of the text,[27] as well as cross-dressing.[28] The canonical rabbinic compendiums of the Oral Law, the Mishnah and the Talmud, are aware of gender nonbinary people and frame them in recognizable legal categories, but do not afford them full and equal status for every legal purpose.[29] And although some Traditionalist rabbinic authorities would offer some sorts of recognition to people who transition from one sex to another, the Traditionalist community does not, at present, offer a clear path to transition and recognition that would afford genuine equality.[30]

None of this much bothers Traditionalists, because they are not committed to liberal ideas of equality, difference, or free choice. Their ideology remains illiberal or even antiliberal, which is not surprising given that it emerged through confrontation with modernity and has sustained itself by continuing to resist developments within liberalism. Here and there, Traditionalists make political arguments that seem to invoke the equality or free choice rights of their own community. Ordered by the city of New York to teach a secular curriculum in the schools, for example, parts of the Hasidic community insist on the liberal right to religious exemption on the basis of the free exercise of religion.[31] These arguments, however, are opportunistic, meant to protect the community against state coercion. They do not reflect internal beliefs about what rights humans ought to have as humans. For Traditionalists, any such beliefs would have to come from the Torah, not from the Constitution.

That is not to say that Traditionalists are completely insulated from the criticisms leveled at their communities, or that their practices are entirely static. The de facto status of women in Traditionalist communities has changed significantly in recent decades as more and more women attain higher education, work outside the home, and even become primary breadwinners. Yet they do so within a religious framework that continues to insist on their second-class legal status. Traditionalist rabbis have quietly grappled with the religious-legal questions around gender dysphoria and transition, and it is just possible that their formal Jewish legal analysis will develop further. Social acceptance for trans people, however, will certainly lag far behind even if that does occur. Recognition for gay people and their unions in the Traditionalist community remains and is likely to remain a bridge too far, precluded by biblical texts and a rigid, heteronormative view of marriage.

Behind these moral criticisms of Traditionalism lies a structural feature: the morality of liberalism requires us to accept and ultimately embrace social changes that are demanded by changing values. We recognize that sexism, homophobia, and transphobia were official features of our societies until very recently. They exist still. At the same time, however, we recognize that the values of equality and liberty require us to update our social practices and beliefs over time. In short, our liberalism is not traditionalist, let alone Traditionalist.

Similarly, our liberalism insists that individuals should be able to change their beliefs and communities. From this it follows, for some liberals, that society may justifiably demand that every child be educated so as to allow for the possibility of change. We're not sure exactly how much children should be taught about how and why they might live differently from their parents and families. But most liberals do want to insist on a bare minimum.

These commitments are so fundamental to contemporary liberal thinking that they make it hard to accept the morality of communities that see things differently. Whatever benefits those communities glean from their illiberalism seem insufficient to justify the burdens that illiberalism imposes. We might look at Traditionalists with occasional nostalgic admiration. We might even admit that if they adapted to contemporary liberalism, they would lose something essential about their Traditionalism. Yet we think they should adapt anyway, because sexism and homophobia and transphobia are morally wrong.

No part of me wants to convince liberals to abandon their own moral beliefs, which as a liberal I share. But some part of me wants liberals to notice that the liberal critiques of Traditionalism, if implemented, would almost certainly lead to the end of Traditionalism itself. If Traditionalists self-consciously updated their practices and beliefs in the light of contemporary liberal morality, they would no longer be Traditionalists, but something else. Their belief patterns would be much closer to the creative-yet-struggling pattern I will discuss in chapter 3.

THE PERSISTENCE OF TRADITIONALISM

Would the loss of Traditionalism be a loss to the world? It would certainly be a gain for liberal values. Liberalism can tolerate a little authoritarianism and illiberalism at its margins. But if illiberal authoritarians become a majority or even a plurality in liberal society—a situation that could conceivably be happening in Israel[32]—liberalism itself will falter and fail. The hard question is whether liberals can, in good conscience, offer not just toleration but acceptance or recognition to illiberal communities that generate certain positive goods, goods like belonging and spiritual fulfillment, alongside their illiberality. In other words, if you are a liberal reading this, can you feel admiration or respect for the Traditionalists, or would that put you in an untenable moral position?

It's so tempting to say to the Traditionalists, "Can't you give just a little? Can't you just be a little more welcoming of difference, a little more open to change? Wear what you want, live as you like, believe as you choose, but for Heaven's sake, stop discriminating and excluding!" The trouble is that the structure of authority that underwrites and sustains Traditionalism is really, truly limited by the tradition, not absolutely but to a greater degree than external critics realize or want to admit. Traditionalism can change. But it can only change slowly, and, more important, it can only change while refusing to admit that it is changing. If Traditionalists could see themselves as one evolutionary strand within the history of Jewish life and experience, they would no longer possess their most valued and most definitional trait, namely their total commitment to the idea that they, and only they, are the true and legitimate carriers of the tradition. To maintain this self-conception, the Traditionalist rabbis must genuinely feel bound by the worldview of the rabbis who came before them. They must imagine themselves in an unbroken, continuous chain. A different form of self-awareness would break the chain as they understand it.

What I'm asking, then, is whether it is valuable that there exists a community of Jews that sincerely believes itself to be the only authentic bearer of Jewish tradition. And here my answer is a qualified yes. Of course Jews may live authentic and legitimate Jewish lives even when they have self-consciousness about the nature of tradition and their relation to it. Of course they may sincerely believe in God or sincerely disbelieve or something else entirely, with self-conscious recognition of how many different Jews have thought about these questions in the past. Indeed, the rest of this part of the book will be exactly about the different ways that can be done, each beautiful and admirable in its own way.

At the same time, it is true, I think, that at every moment in the history of Jewish tradition, there have been some Jews who unselfconsciously saw themselves as bearers of the unbroken tradition. If there were to be none left, that would constitute a fundamental change in Jewish life. It would be a loss to the diversity of Jewish beliefs and modes of living. The loss would be distinctive because, in a basic way, all strands of Jewishness relate *in some important sense* to the idea of tradition. Traditionalism is the most extreme form of connection to the tradition, and

in that respect it stands in a special guardianship relationship to tradition itself. Its presence allows adherents of other forms of Jewish life
and belief to see clearly what the tradition would look like if taken to
extremes. It reveals what God would look like if God assigned His absolute authority in perpetuity to a group of self-defining rabbis committed
to the idea of denying change.

The use value of Traditionalism to other Jews, not as an ideal, but as
an instantiation of the authoritarian power of tradition, lies, I think, behind the nostalgia that many Jews experience in relation to Haredim. It's
a fair observation that, across the generations, for every *Unorthodox* there
is a *Shtisel*. Each generation of Jews for well over a century has produced
an influential work of popular culture that sharply criticized Traditionalism and distanced the viewer from it. And each generation, usually
within the same narrow time frame, has produced an influential work of
popular culture that depicts Traditionalism as beautiful and fulfilling.
The Chosen (novel 1967, film 1981), subtly critical of Traditionalism, was
contemporary with *Fiddler on the Roof* (Broadway 1964, film 1971).*

It would be easy to boil down the nostalgia for Traditionalism to a
yearning for the warmth of one's great-grandparents, real or imagined.
Yet there is more to the nostalgia. Somewhere in every version of Jewish
thought lies the notion that there is a tradition passed down across generations: Moses received the Torah at Sinai and gave it to Joshua, and
Joshua to the elders, and so onward. What to do with that tradition, and
what to do about it, are questions that yield a wide range of answers,
of which Traditionalism is only one. The nostalgia has the function of
reminding those who feel it that the whole enterprise of being a Jew demands some engagement of some kind with the tradition—even if that
engagement is to reshape the tradition radically or even, in important
ways, to reject it.

This engagement also explains why, despite many predictions to the
contrary over the last two hundred years, Traditionalism is not going
to fade away: not now and not ever, so long as there are people who

---

* *Abie's Irish Rose* (Broadway 1922, film 1928) was contemporary with *The Dybbuk*
(stage 1920, film 1937) and *The Jazz Singer* (1927).

self-identify as Jews. The Holocaust failed to destroy it. Contemporary liberal criticism certainly will not.

THE SPIRIT IN THE LAW

Where is God experienced in this renewed and re-created Traditionalist Jewish experience? Here we come at last to a critique that the Traditionalists do take seriously, in no small part because this critique has been with Traditionalist Judaism since the start, and indeed forms part of the fabric of Jewish self-criticism back to the Middle Ages. The critique is that notwithstanding rigorous observance of the law and devotion to Jewish ritual and liturgy, Traditionalists run the risk of acting by rote, without deep spiritual connection to the God they all worship. The shorthand for this critique quotes the last phrase of Isaiah 29:13: "Inasmuch as these people draw near with their mouths / And honor Me with their lips, / But have removed their hearts far from Me, / And their fear toward Me *is taught by the commandment of men.*" In Hebrew, the italicized words are *mitzvat anashim melummadah*, interpreted by Maimonides to mean, roughly, unthinking and unintentional performance of the commandments without consciousness of their divine source. A life of rote performance may satisfy the technical requirements of Traditionalism, but, as Traditionalists acknowledge, it misses the whole point of their way of life, which is, at its core, to live in conjunction with God's will, not merely in automatic obedience to it.

Hasidism was itself partly a response to this danger, coupled with deep concern about the inherent elitism of rabbinic culture that valued intellectual attainment and hence devalued the spiritual capacities of unlearned people. Its earliest masters offered a mystical interpretation of Jewish practice that infused ritual with transcendent meaning and simultaneously made the spiritual domain accessible on the basis of the primary and immediate emotion of worship. Hasidism still holds these aspirations, but over the generations, as charismatic leaders who attracted hundreds of followers by their personal qualities gave way to inherited family-based leadership, the difficulty of sustaining the spirituality recurred.

Today, there is a strand of Traditionalist neo-Hasidism that seeks to make mysticism, music, and dance relevant once again to Jewish spiritual life.[33] Its practitioners are influenced by the thought of Rebbe Nahman of Breslov (1772–1810), a rare example of a Hasidic master who founded a movement but not a rabbinic dynasty. One highly visible group of Traditionalist neo-Hasidim—they're called "Na-Nachs" for reasons I will leave to a footnote[34]—dress differently from other Hasidim. They wear white shirts and black pants but no coats. They look almost like hippies, except for extra-long curled sidelocks and roughly crocheted yarmulkes that cover most of the head in what my brother used to call "basketball warmer" style.

When they dance ecstatically in public, their choreography is totally different from old-school Hasidic circle dancing. It's influenced by rave. You can see them driving through most Israeli cities on Fridays, blasting mystical Jewish lyrics set to their own EDM blend of trance, techno, and sometimes even reggae. Their numbers are small, but their visibility is great. They've made inroads into some of the experimental, vanguard settler communities who live both on and off the grid in the West Bank, communities to which I will return in part II. They need to be taken seriously in any attempt to explore the recurrent need for a renewed spiritual dimension in Jewish Traditionalism. Rebbe Nahman is buried in Uman, in Ukraine. Before the Russian invasion, as many as forty thousand Jews were making their way annually to Uman on a spiritual pilgrimage; in 2022, while the war was in full swing, a reported twenty-three thousand went anyway.[35]

As for Yeshivish Jews, the greatest risk for them is to lose the spiritual dimension of religious experience in the wealth of detail that is the Torah. To an outsider observing Traditionalist ways and words, the most surprising thing is usually how little God is discussed. God's name is invoked thousands of times a day in prayers and even common expressions, but God is not often a direct topic of conversation, not even during Talmud study. Prayer is directed to God, of course. But praying a full liturgy three times a day can actually obscure the human capacity to imagine and experience direct connection to the divine. Rote praying is a bug for Traditionalists, not a feature of their practice. But it is the most common and recurrent bug that could be imagined.

The solutions offered by Traditionalists to the challenge of rote observance can be described as "meta-halakhah" as the term was used by my late teacher, Professor Isadore Twersky, who was both a professor at Harvard University and also, literally wearing a different outfit on the weekends, a Hasidic master of the Talner dynasty.[36] Halakhah means, roughly, Jewish law, the set of obligations and laws that shape the life of Traditionalist Jews. Twersky's version of meta-halakhah refers to the grand purposes that lie above and beyond the practice of the law. Halakhah asks: What is the law? Meta-halakhah asks: For what deeper purpose must we follow the law?

For many centuries, Jewish mysticism has offered one of the most influential meta-halakhic systems to explain what the law is for. Kabbalah, the catchall name for Jewish mysticism, has several subtypes. All of them, however, offer a cosmic perspective on how the observance of Jewish ritual and following of Jewish law shape the nature of the universe, including even the nature of God.* Kabbalah is the meta-halakhah underwriting all forms of Hasidism.

Mysticism does not, however, underlie Yeshivish practice, which is so law-focused that it might be said that its meta-halakhah is halakhah itself, or that it rejects meta-halakhah as an idea. The Yeshivish are relentlessly untheological, even antitheological. The answer to why they study is to study. To the extent there is a meta-halakhic idea behind this approach, it is the value of the study of the Torah "for its own sake," associated with the thinker Rav Hayyim of Volozhin (1749–1821), who in 1803 founded the Yeshiva of Volozhin near Minsk (now in Belarus) and became the progenitor of what would eventually become the Yeshivish movement.[37] One

---

* Another form of meta-halakhah is philosophical rationalism, which seeks the reasons for the law in eternal philosophical truths. Other meta-halakhic approaches include ethical pietism, a focus on the cultivation of individual character; and biblicism, a turn to the narratives and poetry of the Bible to uncover the deeper values of the faith. In II:3 I shall argue that Religious Zionism is the newest and fastest-growing meta-halakhah of the modern era.

might fruitfully compare Rav Hayyim's theory to its rough contemporary, the Romantic, early nineteenth-century notion of *l'art pour l'art*, art for art's sake.[38] The basic idea of both is that the undertaking is inevitably distorted if pursued for some larger instrumental purpose. Torah and art must be pursued in a disinterested fashion, hence for their own sakes.[39]

Rav Hayyim's theory represented a continuation of an old teaching from the *Ethics of the Fathers*: "Be not like servants who minister to their master for the sake of receiving a reward. Rather, be like servants who serve their master not for the sake of receiving a reward."[40] But Rav Hayyim's teaching went even further. Reacting against the Hasidic idea that the purpose of Torah study is to generate *devekus*, cleaving to God, he insisted that Torah must not even be studied "for the sake of Heaven." Study of the law must be utterly and purely an end in itself.[41] It is in this sense that Torah for its own sake comes close to rejecting the notion of meta-halakhah.

In yeshivas influenced by the Volozhin tradition—which includes many yeshivas still in existence—the students can be found reading and discussing and arguing in a characteristic singsong cadence that goes back to the European yeshivas.* Debate is the lifeblood of yeshiva study. The texts record disagreements, and disagreements about the disagreements, and disagreements about those. The students disagree about all of the above. Voices are raised. Decorum takes on its own inner logic: teachers are addressed with respect, but in the war for the truth of the Torah, no punches are pulled and no quarter is given. Outsiders often find the cultural style of the yeshiva to be strangely aggressive. It is. The intensity comes from love of the subject and recognition that studying the Talmud is the fulfillment of the divine guidance, "This book of the Torah shall not depart from thy mouth, and thou shalt meditate on it

---

* The language is unique, too: a combination of the vernacular (English or Israeli Hebrew); Yiddish; Talmudic Aramaic; and rabbinic Hebrew. What emerges is a sociolect (a dialect associated with a particular subgroup) known as "Yeshivish," also called Yeshiva English, *Yeshivishe reid*, or *Yeshivishe shprakh*. See the classic book by Chaim M. Weiser, *Frumspeak: The First Dictionary of Yeshivish* (Lanham, MD: Rowman & Littlefield, 1995). The final line of the translation of the Gettysburg Address into Yeshivish is worth the price of the book.

day and night."[42] But the intense debate normally concerns the technical, halakhic details of the Talmud, not the meta-halakhic question of what it all means at a deeper level. The debate would be about, for example, where one must search for leaven on the eve of Passover and where one may assume leaven has not been left, not about why God would want us to abstain from bread for a week and whether the best answer lies in mysticism, philosophy, or somewhere else.

The absence of a well-articulated meta-halakhah beyond halakhah offers some short-term benefit for contemporary Yeshivism. Unlike Evolutionist and Progressive Jews, who struggle with the moral justifiability of their beliefs and practices in the face of values like equality and freedom, Yeshivish Jews can just do it—where "it" is studying and following the law. This approach helps avoid crises of conscience. It frees energies for study and practice alike. It is probably one of the reasons that the Yeshivish movement is so fast-growing.*

In the longer term, however, the lack of a clear meta-halakhah poses a real risk for Traditionalism. Not for its survival, which seems assured, but for its capacity to sustain itself on its own terms as a manifestation of God's will. When you are a rearguard movement desperately fighting to preserve itself against the onslaught of modernity, as Traditionalism was from its founding in the late 1700s and early 1800s until World War II, you can survive without a grand theory, because your existential fight to preserve your tradition is an all-encompassing motive. When you've been decimated, as Traditionalism has been since the Holocaust, you do not need an explicit theology or philosophy, since your task is the desperate and then joyful one of creating anew a past that was very nearly destroyed in its entirety.

---

* By way of contrast, the motto of Yeshiva University, the flagship Modern Orthodox (not Traditionalist) institution of higher learning, is *Torah u-Mada*, "Torah and science," a phrase that implies both tension and the possibility of resolving that tension. The very name Yeshiva University embodies the same tension: which is it, a yeshiva or a university? The unofficial motto of Lakewood is "Torah, Torah, Torah": no tension, no contradiction, and, when you come right down to it, no official motto. That's because a yeshiva doesn't have a motto, a university does. And Lakewood is not a university, even if it now confers a degree called a Bachelor of Talmudic Laws to enable its students to attend graduate school.

When you are a flourishing community, however, no longer embedded in a defensive war and no longer overwhelmed with the duty to survive and re-create, you eventually need a reason for being. The fulfillment of God's will is as good a reason as it gets. But if you fall away from the immediate, charismatic connection to that will and into rote practice, all the warmth and community in the world will not sustain you. Jewish ritual and Torah study are tried and tested means to make and maintain Jewish life. History teaches that they must be infused with the deeper meaning of meta-halakhah.

In part II, I will explore the possibility that a new meta-halakhah is beginning to make its way into Traditionalist Jewish life, a meta-halakhah associated with the state of Israel. This process is by no means certain to succeed or even to continue. It would have complicated, transformative effects on Traditionalism. And it would not be welcome to many of the rabbis who hold the positions of authority in Traditionalism. Nevertheless, the stage may be set for it. Meta-halakhah abhors a vacuum.

AUTHORITY AND ITS DISCONTENTS

Earlier in the chapter, I used the story of Rabban Gamliel's assertion of authority over Rabbi Joshua to illustrate the role of authority in today's Traditionalism. But I left out the end of the story, which the Talmud tells in another place.[43] The ending shows that the rabbis of the Talmud understood the complexities of asserted authority, even as they accepted its necessity. And it carries a potential lesson about the limits of authority for today's Traditionalist community.

At the end of the dispute over the Day of Atonement, Rabbi Joshua submitted to Rabban Gamliel, despite his disagreement. His submission vindicated rabbinic authority. But the next year, according to the Talmud, another disagreement arose between the two. This time the topic was whether the evening prayer was optional or required. Rabbi Joshua held the former view; Rabban Gamliel held the latter.

In the story the Talmud tells, a student informed Rabban Gamliel that Rabbi Joshua disagreed with him about the evening prayer. Rabban

Gamliel instructed the student to wait until all the rabbis were present and pose the question. (Again Rabban Gamliel's concern for publicly enforcing authority was at work.) When the student asked if the evening prayer was optional or obligatory, Rabban Gamliel publicly answered that it was obligatory. Then he asked the rabbis present if anyone disagreed with him. Rabbi Joshua answered, "No." It would appear from the context that he wanted to avoid a public disagreement with Rabban Gamliel.

But Rabban Gamliel would not leave it at that. He said to Rabbi Joshua, "But they told me in your name that it [the evening prayer] is optional!" Then he told Rabbi Joshua to stand up and be testified against, presumably to the effect that he was hiding his actual view. Rabbi Joshua admitted, using oblique language to avoid conflict, that he indeed had opined that the evening prayer was optional.

The Talmud's story goes on to say that Rabban Gamliel continued to lecture without allowing Rabbi Joshua to sit down, emphasizing his power and his accusation of Rabbi Joshua. The Talmud states that those present were so offended by this humiliating treatment—on top of Rabban Gamliel's similarly humiliating treatment of Rabbi Joshua the year before—that they forthwith removed Rabban Gamliel from his position as head of the rabbinic community.

In the story, Rabban Gamliel, the prince who insisted on authority, is deposed from power for overenforcing his own authority. The Talmud mitigates the disaster slightly by saying that Rabban Gamliel subsequently went and apologized to Rabbi Joshua, who at first refused to forgive him but ultimately did so. Then, at Rabbi Joshua's impetus, Rabban Gamliel was restored to his former princely role. But now he was forced to share it with another rabbi, Elazar ben Azaryah, who had been appointed after his removal.[44]

It would be possible, of course, to interpret the ending of the Rabban Gamliel–Rabbi Joshua story merely as a warning to those in power that they exercise authority collegially, showing respect for other rabbis. It would even be plausible to say that the story shows that rabbinic authority is best exercised by small groups of leading rabbis, rather than by individuals, who might be tempted to overstep, as even the great Rabban Gamliel did.

Yet the story also suggests that the Talmud knows that the exercise of unified, centralized rabbinic authority over the application of the Law runs the risk of alienating the very community subject to rabbinic command. A tradition that is based fundamentally on interpretation and disagreement, as the Jewish tradition is, lends itself to a degree of pluralism, because everyone who engages it knows that multiple perspectives are and can be valid interpretations of God's word and will.

Traditionalism therefore necessarily exists on the knife's edge, between God's authority carried by the rabbis and unending, divinely inspired debate that inherently resists totalizing control. Cleaving to God in Hasidic *devekus* or pursuing Torah for Torah's sake in yeshiva study can yield beauty and meaning. But authority without suppleness will repetitively drive those who think and question out of the bounds of the authoritative system. No group of rabbis within Traditionalism plans to overthrow today's *gedolim* as they did Rabban Gamliel. To maintain their authority, however, the *gedolim* must shape Traditionalism to fit the world of today, while maintaining fidelity to their belief in an unchanging divine Law.

I:2

THE GOD OF SOCIAL
JUSTICE

The faith of the Traditionalists offers community, commitment, and continuity, wrapped in a framework of authority that will challenge anyone whose moral instincts are shaped by those of contemporary society. For two centuries, however, many Jews have yearned instead for a religion expressing moral values that match the liberal worldview in which they are enmeshed. The result is Jewish belief that I will call Progressive: the belief in a divine moral order whose eternal truths of justice and love unfold in progress through history, rather than being fixed in unchanging authority.

Jewish Traditionalism has a brand, its black-and-white outfits. Jewish Progressivism has an iconic photograph that sums up its essence. The photo was taken on March 21, 1965. In it you can see seven people, arms linked, leading the famous civil rights march from Selma to Montgomery. From left to right, they are John Lewis, Sister Mary Leoline,[1] Ralph Abernathy, Martin Luther King Jr., Ralph Bunche, Abraham Joshua Heschel, and Fred Shuttlesworth. They're wearing coats against the cold and leis that had been given to them that day by a minister from Hawaii.

The Black men in the picture, all southern ordained ministers except Bunche, the Nobel Prize–winning diplomat, are giants of the civil rights movement, household names to anyone even slightly familiar with its history. Heschel was born in Warsaw in 1907. He was first ordained as an Orthodox rabbi in Poland, then earned a doctorate and a further, nondenominational rabbinic ordination in Berlin. Deported from Germany back to Poland in 1938, he managed to escape weeks before the German invasion in 1939. In the United States, he became a renowned teacher and scholar of Jewish mysticism affiliated first with Hebrew Union College, the flagship of American Reform Judaism, and then for many years with the Jewish Theological Seminary, which trains Conservative rabbis.

Heschel's participation in the march, and the Progressive beliefs that put him there, stand for a vision of God derived from the ancient Hebrew prophets and the most foundational teachings of the rabbis. For Progressive Jews, these sources can inspire and direct our moral and spiritual lives. Unlike Traditionalists, Progressive Jews are comfortable recognizing the fallibility of the humans who have interpreted and shaped the tradition. Hence Progressive Jews can gently leave aside aspects of the tradition that cannot be reconciled with our deepest moral commitments as we experience them today. As for the halakhah that lies at the heart of Traditionalist thought, Progressive Jews consider it to be a manifestation of Jews' best efforts at making sense of divine moral truths. Seen in this light, the law can sometimes be a guide to conduct. But it need not govern us, especially when it no longer resonates with what we believe to be morally right.

So if you are looking for a strand of Jewish thought that celebrates women rabbis, embraces gay and trans people, and emphasizes civil rights and social values like equality and free choice, Progressive Judaism is it. When a new moral truth becomes prominent in liberal Western belief, Progressive Jews see it as part of the eternal truth that God (however defined) always intended and that has now emerged through the human historical process of experience and reasoning. Traditionalist Jews think of what they call Yiddishkeit as a comprehensive way of life in the path of God. Progressive Jews mostly think of their Judaism as a religion, one that shapes their broader moral beliefs and worldview and is in turn shaped by them. Where Traditionalists see the authority of God's law and the authority of the rabbis who interpret it, Progressives see the moral inspiration of the Bible's teachings and the freedom of humans to make sense of Torah in light of their commitment to human equality and dignity.

The biblical prophets provide Progressive Jews with the strongest textual precedent and basis for their worldview. Take Isaiah 58, a chapter so powerful that the rabbis chose it as the prophetic reading at the morning service on Yom Kippur. For many years when I was a boy, my father received the honor of reading it in synagogue. I can hear his voice in my head, chanting the bracing message in the original Hebrew.

The thrust of Isaiah's transmission to the people of Israel in the chapter is that they cannot achieve the closeness to God that they seek merely by performing religious rituals. They must behave justly and kindly to the weakest among them if they seek connection to the divine. God demands and desires social justice, not empty performance.

In the prophet's presentation, the Israelites, their throats parched from not drinking or eating on a fast day, complain to God that their prayers remain unanswered: "Why have we fasted and you have seen not? Why have we afflicted our throat and you know not?"

Isaiah's God replies contemptuously: "Is a fast I have chosen like this—a day for a man to afflict his throat? Is it to bow down his head like a bulrush, and put on sack-cloth and ash? Is this what you call a fast, a day desirable to the Lord?"

God's own answer to these rhetorical questions is a resounding no.

Is not this a fast I have chosen? Loose the chains of wickedness. Untie the bonds of the yoke. Let free the oppressed and break every yoke. Is it not to distribute your bread to the hungry and bring home the outcast poor? When you see a naked person, cover him, and hide not from your own flesh.

Only then, once justice is established, will prayer lead to salvation and God's presence be felt:

Then shall your light break like the dawn, and your healing shall quickly flourish. Your justice shall walk before you. The glory of the Lord shall follow you. Then shall you call out, and the Lord shall answer; you shall plead, and He shall say "Here am I"—if you put away the yoke from your midst, the pointing of fingers, and the speaking of iniquity. If you pour out your throat for the hungry, and satisfy the afflicted throat, then your light shall shine in the darkness, and your gloaming shall be as the noonday sun . . . You shall be as a watered garden, as a source of water whose waters never fail.[2]

The beauty of Isaiah's language underscores the simple power of the lesson. Connection to God cannot be attained by going through the motions of religious ritual. It requires aligning one's actions—and those of society as a whole—with the divine plan for human justice. That plan means, for Isaiah, feeding the hungry, clothing the naked, and ending oppression. The yoke, Isaiah's preferred metaphor for what must be broken, perfectly exemplifies the hierarchical domination of some humans by others.

For Progressive Jews, the prophetic lesson of love and justice resonates through all of Jewish thought. The paradigmatic Talmudic story that stands for this idea tells of a non-Jew who approached the two leading rabbis of his day, Shammai and Hillel. He made the same request of each: "Make me a Jew on the condition that you teach me all the entire Law while I am standing on one foot."

Shammai, the head of a school remembered for advocating serious study of the Law by serious students, sent away the potential Jew. Shammai was a builder by trade (most of the early rabbis practiced trades like shoemaking or carpentry) and the Talmud says that Shammai "drove him away with the measuring stick that was in his hand." Shammai was understandably put off by the applicant's demand, which reflected either impatience, contempt, or both.

Hillel, whose separate school was open to all comers, reacted differently. According to the Talmud, "He made him a Jew. Then he said to him: 'What is hateful to you, do not do to your friend.' This is all the entire Law. The rest is interpretation. Go study."[3]

This Hillel story is so famous, among Progressive Jews and beyond, that it has become a cliché. As I was writing these words, I found myself worrying that I might lose readers who have heard it since childhood and would then think of this book as too basic to be taken seriously.

But the truth is that the story of Hillel and the applicant, which occupies just a few lines in the Talmud, has the kind of compressed narrative power that the best parables achieve. Like a Zen koan,[4] it is a cliché because it is both profound and profoundly simple.* Hillel does not deny that there is much to learn in the Torah. He ends by telling the new convert to go and study. He simply communicates that only one thing really matters, namely how we treat one another. The rest is secondary. We need Hillel's message too much to dismiss it just because it has been told to children so many times.

With Hillel's worldview to inspire them, Progressive Jews can conclude, justly, that Jewishness is capable of being welcoming and inclusive, not exclusionary or obscure. Far from deflecting or rejecting the potential Jew, Hillel brought him into the fold even before delivering on his implicit promise to teach him the Torah in a nutshell. Thus, *by his actions, Hillel was enacting the same message found in his words.* He was treating the prospective Jew as he would want to be treated, namely with dignity, acceptance, charity of spirit, and perhaps just a touch of humor. And indeed, Progressive Jews have always emphasized the openness that Jewishness can contain once it focuses on respecting each human as an individual.

The first Jews to develop this Progressive vision lived in nineteenth-century Germany, which at the time was undergoing a process of political liberalization that included newfound openness to including Jews within the broader political and cultural community. Those Jews were influenced by the progress that German civilization was (then) mak-

---

* When I told this story to Julia Allison, she said without missing a beat, "Anyone interested in learning a whole religion on one foot should look into Buddhism."

ing, partly as a result of the French Revolution's formal emancipation of the Jews, extended elsewhere by Napoleon Bonaparte. They called their movement Reform Judaism, a name that reflected an idealized picture of the Protestant Reformation as it had come to be understood by liberal Protestant Germans of the time.[5] The concept of reform was meant to capture the effort to go back to the genuine origins of a religious tradition to identify its truest and most fundamental teachings, shorn of superstition, bias, and the self-interested efforts of clergy to maintain their own power. Looking back to the Bible, Reform Jews found a God who loves not only his people but all the peoples of the world; who wants social justice, not ritualized obedience; and who teaches that to be holy is to love your neighbor as yourself.

To emphasize these teachings, Jewish Reformers sought to update and streamline their liturgy and religious practices. In the process, they hoped to save Jews from abandoning their faith altogether in a world where Traditionalism seemed incompatible with modern life. That was not all, however. To Reformers, what needed to be saved was God's universalist message, which Christianity might have co-opted but which, they firmly believed, came originally from the Jewish invention of monotheism.

Reform Jews made their case by interpreting or reinterpreting strands of teaching found in the Bible, the Talmud, and later Jewish authorities. One instructive example is the Jewish abandonment of the ritual animal sacrifices that were at one time central to the ancient Israelite Temple cult. Reformers noticed that even the biblical prophets, who lived in the era of sacrificial practice, sometimes condemned it as a distraction or worse from true divine worship. In the book of Jeremiah, in the course of telling the Israelites not to oppress strangers, orphans, and widows and not to shed innocent blood, God puts it starkly:

> I did not speak to your fathers and I did not command them on the day I took them out of the land of Egypt about matters of burnt offerings or sacrifice. Rather, this is the matter I commanded them, saying, "Listen to my voice and I will be your God and you will be to me a people."[6]

In one of the Psalms, God is presented as going even further, questioning the idea that He is interested in sacrifices at all:

Do I eat the flesh of bulls or drink the blood of goats?
Offer thanks to God; fulfill your vows to the Most High.
Call on me on the day of trouble; I will save you, and you will
 honor me.[7]

After the destruction of the Temple, the rabbis who transformed the Israelite religion into the Jewish one established daily prayers that, they explained, were intended to function in lieu of sacrifices.[8] Although the Talmud devotes whole tractates to studying the laws of sacrifice, the rabbis made no effort to restore the sacrificial cult. To the contrary, they specified that sacrifices should not be reinstituted until the Temple was rebuilt by divine intervention. Study, for the rabbis, substituted for sacrifice, just as prayer did.[9]

Early Reform thinkers understood the rabbinic deferral of sacrifice, following on the prophetic message that God did not need sacrifices, as part of an ethical revolution within Judaism. The medieval authority they invoked for this understanding was none other than Maimonides, himself scrupulously committed to preserving Jewish law in every detail. In the *Guide of the Perplexed*, Maimonides reasoned, radically, that biblical sacrifice was a necessary concession God had made to the cultural milieu of the biblical era, in which the surrounding peoples also sacrificed to their gods and the Israelites could not have accepted a religion based purely on ethical worship. Seen this way, the prophets' skepticism of sacrifice reflected their advanced ethical perspective. The rabbis' eschewal of sacrifice in favor of prayer and study was the next step in making Jewish thought and practice conform to the actual divine ideal. Hence, Maimonides concluded in the *Guide* (although not in his code of Jewish law, intended for a mass audience) that sacrifices would not be restored in the messianic future.[10]

Maimonides's radical philosophical teaching was invoked by Reform Jews as evidence of fundamental, directional, progressive change within Jewish tradition—change driven by ethical objectives. From the Bible through the Middle Ages, reformers observed, Jewish ideas about sacrifice progressed to a higher, more ethical plane. Unlike Maimonides, they concluded that the authority of the tradition is not absolute. Elements, even biblical elements, can and must be reformed and even abandoned in pursuit of moral truth.

In the last half-century, the Progressive teaching of divinely inspired social justice acquired a slogan: *tikkun 'olam*, literally, repairing the world. The phrase originated from the Kabbalistic idea that in creating the finite world, the infinite God contracted, then shattered and broke into a multitude of shards. In the aftermath of that cosmic disaster, it is the ultimate purpose of the Jewish people to perform God's commandments and thereby, act by act, repair the universe and the Godhead itself.[11] Mystically, this is to be accomplished by redeeming these shards, each animated by divine sparks, from amid the *kelippot*, the impure and dark husks or shells that cover the sparks of divine light. As adapted by Progressives, who substituted a social metaphor for the mystical one, *tikkun 'olam* has a this-worldly, more concrete meaning. It calls for human effort, alongside God, to make the world more just and hence more perfect.

PROGRESS

Today, Progressive Jewish thought extends well beyond the Jewish Reform movement, with which 37 percent of American Jews currently identify.[12] What I am calling Progressivism includes much, though not all, of what is confusingly called Conservative Judaism, which with 17 percent is the next largest institutional movement of American Jews. Reconstructionist Judaism, with less than 4 percent, is also Progressive.

As I did with respect to Traditionalism, I am intentionally introducing a new term, Progressivism, that refers to underlying beliefs about the divine. What unites Progressive Jews today is the frank recognition and acknowledgment that to be worth maintaining, Jewish life and thought must cohere with our deepest moral commitments. What God wants (however metaphorically or loosely we understand God) cannot be in contradiction to what is just and right. When we see a new moral truth, we know it must be part of the divine order. Moral truth and divine truth are and must be consonant, perhaps even identical. As a result, Progressive Jewish thought lends itself to social justice activism. Leading Progressive rabbis write or edit books with titles like *There Shall Be No Needy: Pursuing Social Justice Through Jewish Law and Tradition*[13] and *None Shall Make Them Afraid: A Rabbis Against Gun Violence Anthology*.[14]

Perhaps surprisingly, Progressivism has something in common with Traditionalism. Under both worldviews, it is in principle possible to conceptualize the Jewish relationship with the divine as consistent with our moral intuitions. For Progressive Jews, when we achieve what we consider to be moral progress, we can be sure that we are acting as the divine plan would suggest. For Traditionalists, whatever God has commanded—as interpreted by the rabbis—is inherently moral in the deepest sense. In neither system of thought need it be painful to reconcile the divine will with our human efforts to understand the right way to live.

You can see why Progressive Jewish thought has been around for so long—and also why Progressive Jews continue to flourish, notwithstanding the unceasing warnings of Traditionalists for nearly two centuries that Progressivism must inevitably die out. Most human beings look to spirituality to infuse life with meaning and to share community with people they love. Most people aren't looking for constant contradiction and struggle; they are looking for consistency and sustenance. Progressive Jewish thought offers meaning making that aspires to enhance spirituality without contradiction and to create inclusive community without necessary conflict.

Two main challenges nevertheless face the religious-communal side of Progressivism.* One is theological: What makes Jewish belief distinctive when its teachings are interpreted as universal and inclusive? What, if anything, separates Progressive Jewish theology from the theology of Unitarian Universalism, or for that matter from other universalisms like those that can be found in Buddhism or Daoism? Progressive Jews still want to be Jews. Yet the particularist strands of Jewish thought from the Bible to the present can sit uncomfortably with Progressive universalism

---

* I am saving the greatest current challenge to Progressive Jews, that of Israel and Zionism, for part II.

that encompasses the equality, dignity, and freedom of all humans in
their relation to God.

The other challenge is practical: How can Progressivism be institutionalized into a cohesive religious community? If Judaism is conceived
as a religion that teaches high-level moral values, can those values be
connected successfully to the daily life of a religious community, which
for Jews was long shaped by common prayers and ritual practices? Adding to this challenge, for Progressive Jews, God need not be understood
as an omnipotent or omniscient being who answers individual prayers.
God can be a force of moral order, or a cosmic Oneness, or a spark
of divine spirituality in each being, or something else. The Progressive
God is certainly not a Lawgiver whose mandates are concerned with
quotidian details of prayer, food, sex, and Sabbath observance. How can
an abstract Oneness be experienced in an immediate, human way that
unites members of a community?

This difficulty of finding meaning in religious ritual is the problem
faced, for example, by the bar mitzvah boy in the Coen brothers' theodicy film *A Serious Man* (2009). He's going through the motions, reciting
words he doesn't understand in a setting that means little to him except
that it is somehow connected to his ancestors. He's been smoking pot,
the only way to get through the experience and maybe a metaphor for a
nonspecific seeking of spirituality that isn't being remotely satisfied by
the Jewish manhood into which he is supposedly being inducted. If you
haven't seen the movie, you can look up the bar mitzvah scene on You-
Tube, but you almost don't have to. It's meant to be an archetype, one
familiar to every American Jew with any connection to institutionalized
Judaism. The archetype can be summed up in one word: alienation. The
ritual is supposed to be constitutive of being Jewish. But it isn't meaningful. So if that's Judaism, then Judaism itself is not meaningful.

I don't mean to suggest that Progressive Jews can't feel powerful
connection to the temple and the prayers recited there. Historically,
however, throughout the generations, Progressive Jews have tended not
to participate in temple ritual in the way that Traditionalists occupy the
synagogue thrice daily and at length on the Sabbath. The overwhelming
majority of Progressive Jews attend sporadically, finding themselves in

the temple for high holidays a couple of times a year and for life-cycle events like baby namings, bar and bat mitzvahs, and funerals. This pattern of attendance is not so different from the Lutheran Protestantism of Germany and the Nordic countries, where many people mark life events in church but the beautiful edifices remain empty much of the time.

Unlike Traditionalists, who are not terribly concerned by most of the external critiques of their worldview and community, Progressive Jews and their leaders take these challenges seriously. They want to justify, explain, and understand why it is meaningful to be a Jew. And they want to create and sustain strong ties of connection, notwithstanding the recurring worry that most Progressive Jews do not feel fully drawn into the institutional communities to which they may nominally belong.

THE GOD OF THE COVENANT

Progressive Jewish theology in the contemporary era has focused on the covenant between God and the people of Israel as a central organizing theme. When Traditionalists think about the covenant at Sinai, they tend to cite the rabbinic story I mentioned in the last chapter, in which God lifted the mountain above the heads of the Israelites and told them to accept the Law or be buried.[15] In stark contrast, for Progressive Jewish thinkers, the covenant is the archetype of a voluntary act. God and the people choose each other freely.[16] The relationship is therefore mutual at its core, and remains so forever.

Drawing on tradition that imagines all Jews as having been present for the covenant at Sinai, Progressive Jewish thought makes the covenant into an inclusive metaphor for a faith relationship that necessarily recognizes the value and humanity of all Jews. In this picture, *all* Jews are equally Jews by choice.[17] There is therefore no theological difference between someone born a Jew and someone who becomes a Jew at a later time.

What, though, distinguishes the people who choose this covenantal relationship with God from the rest of humanity, who are also God's children? To Traditionalists, the answer is straightforward: God chose the people of Israel, as the Bible recounts, not because the Israelites were more numerous or better than other peoples but simply because God loved their forefathers. The Jews, descendants of the Israelites, are a distinct people and a holy people insofar as they possess God's freely given grace. There is no reason for Jewish chosenness beyond God's will.

To Progressive Jews focused on the reciprocal, voluntary relationship between God and Israel, chosenness must be something different, something grounded in mutuality. Yet it also cannot be exclusive, at least from God's perspective. Progressive Jews are universalists in the sense that they embrace the equality of all humans before God. Their egalitarian God cannot love some people more than others because of who they are. God might choose some people in some way, but then he also must choose all others in some comparable way. If God preferred the Jews or held them to a higher standard or just enjoyed a closer relationship with them, that God would not be a truly universal, egalitarian God.

From this theological perspective, the best solution to the puzzle of chosenness is to say that all humans imagine themselves in some special relationship with a God—and that there is nothing exclusionary about that relationship, because God is, after all, universal and infinite. It is therefore a kind of miraculous feature of the Progressive God to be able to choose everyone and yet have everyone feel specially chosen. The Sinai covenant is just one possible covenant, yet it is meaningful for those who participate in it. All that is required for belonging is to make a voluntary choice to opt in. That is why Reform Judaism makes it easier to become Jewish than do other strands of Judaism. It is why Reform temples are relatively more welcoming of non-Jews as regular participants than congregations of other movements.*

There is something extremely attractive about the idea that anyone may enter the covenant with God and that the barrier to entry

---

* Reform Judaism does draw a communal line. Most Reform temples will not allow a person who has not been born a Jew nor become a Jew to serve as an official of the congregation, to lead services, or to be called alone to the Torah. The justification, to the extent there is one, is that liturgical worship is a communal practice of those who have entered the covenant and that the communal institution of conversion is an outward sign of that commitment. I will discuss these issues of communal belonging in part III.

is nothing more than the desire to seek the connection. This raises, however, an important related question: Does the individual seeking a covenantal relationship with God have to believe in that God's existence?

In mainstream Protestant Christianity, all the believer must do to enter into the kingdom of Heaven is to accept Jesus Christ as savior. But that act of faith cannot be skipped. It is constitutive of being a Christian. No one will object if you participate in Christian worship or study the Gospel, because the faith is available to anyone. And most of the time, no one will check up on you to see if you are faithful, because that is between you and God. Yet as a matter of conscience, which is where true Protestant Christian faith resides, you must believe to be saved.

In believing that the individual may freely choose to enter into covenant with God, Progressive Jewish theology opens the door to a more universal, accessible, inclusive, welcoming form of Jewish life than any other. At the same time, it does seem to suggest that someone who wants to participate in this covenant must believe in God, in some way or form. A covenant must be between multiple parties. It would seem strange for me to enter into a covenant with myself or with my projection of myself onto the divine sphere. How could one seek a covenantal relationship with something imaginary?

THE CIVILIZATION APPROACH IN
CONTEMPORARY PROGRESSIVE JEWISH LIFE

Needless to say, this apparent requirement of belief poses a problem for many would-be Progressive Jews, including for some who would like to be Progressive Jews by choice. Progressivism grew up in tandem with modern beliefs in voluntary choice and equality. Those beliefs have long coexisted with skepticism about whether God exists. What's more, Reform Judaism first arose partly to provide an option for Jews who had rejected the authoritarian God of Traditionalism and did not want to embrace liberal Protestantism.[18] Many people in that situation were not theistic believers but skeptics. In practical terms, Progressivism needs, and has always needed, an option to provide for the skeptical nonbeliever.

An influential solution to this problem was devised by an Orthodox-trained Progressive rabbi named Mordecai Kaplan (1881–1983), who was arguably the most influential American Jewish theologian of the twentieth century. His magnum opus was his 1934 book *Judaism as a Civilization: Toward a Reconstruction of American Jewish Life*. In it, Kaplan proposed that Judaism could be sustained and practiced even if it were separated from its traditional theological underpinnings, including belief in God. The key was to conceptualize Jewish tradition as a civilization into which Jews found themselves thrown by birth and by history. They could choose to draw on that civilization and its traditions, to be its bearers. They could then live and think as Jews without having to insist on a special or unique relationship with an actually existing God who chose them.

From the standpoint of Kaplan's Reconstructionism, the covenant between God and the Jewish people is the historical legacy of a time when Jews did indeed imagine themselves to be uniquely chosen. One need not literally believe the covenant to be real or true to continue engaging in Jewish life. A Jew can just keep on thinking and praying and acting as a Jew without worrying about God's existence. The joke that sums up this point of view is that Reconstructionists direct their prayers "To Whom It May Concern." Or in another version, the Reconstructionist declaration of faith is, "There is no God, and Mordecai Kaplan is His prophet."

Reconstructionism started as distinct from Reform and Conservative Judaism. Over time, however, there has been a gradual convergence between Reform, Conservative, and Reconstructionist communities, that is, between the movements that espouse Progressive Jewish ideals. The movements still maintain formally separate congregations and formally separate rabbinical schools. Nuances of theological difference remain too. But what actually happens in synagogue and home prayer and practice is increasingly similar. Convergence in core beliefs is fueling convergence in ritual.

For example, from the origins of Reform Judaism, one of the key reforms was to reduce the use of Hebrew in prayer (or even eliminate it altogether) in order to make the experience more accessible and meaningful. Today, most Reform temples, under the indirect influence of Kaplan, use significantly more Hebrew in their liturgy than they once did. Where in the past the Reform service was highly formal, with relatively little congregational participation, today most Reform temples encourage singing along and strive for greater informality.

The use of the guitar in worship is a symbol of this convergence. In the early years of the Reform movement, one of the most significant innovations was the introduction of the organ to the temple, an understandable development in the German society that had produced the church music of Bach as an elevated form of divine worship.[19] The organ became part of American Reform Judaism, much as the organ remained an important part of American Christian worship into the twentieth century.[20] In Reform congregations, singing tended to be professionalized rather than participatory, often performed by a trained cantor and choir.

In the late 1960s and early 1970s, a new trend in Jewish worship, known as the Havurah movement, began to use the acoustic guitar in worship. Havurah is a Hebrew word that means, roughly, a group of like-minded people arranged in community for some purpose. The Havurah movement was self-consciously part of the youth culture of the era. Its participants felt uninspired by the large, formal, distant Jewish congregations that predominated at the time. Their prayer circles—for that is what they were—drew organically on the folk music trends that were then popular. (The direct descendant of the Havurah movement today still exists under the name of Jewish Renewal.[21])

The Reform movement did not initially embrace the guitar in temple, although Reform summer camps and youth groups experimented with it. The austere formality of most Reform services persisted through the 1970s and into the early 1980s. In the context of Reconstructionist Judaism, however, the influence of the Havurah movement was felt powerfully and more quickly. The guitar helped create an atmosphere of informality and group participation through song that was highly relevant to the historical moment, and it became a regular presence in

Reconstructionist services. Then, eventually, over a decade or more, the guitar became normalized into Reform worship, no doubt as a result of its use in Reform movement summer camps. In large Reform temples, it became common to see a congregant or even the cantor employed by the temple standing in front of the lectern, playing the guitar and singing. Often the singer would be amplified by a microphone, long present in Reform temples and indeed often necessary as an effect of their size and design.

As singing along to an acoustic guitar gradually became a cultural relic of the 60s and 70s, the use of the guitar in Reform temples nevertheless persisted. Along with it came a Reform rapprochement with collective singing of popular Hebrew liturgical songs as part of the worship service in order to connect worshippers to an accessible, distinctively Jewish spirituality. All this went along with a return to elements of Jewish traditional seasonal liturgy and worship that most Reform temples had abandoned for a century or more. Reform Judaism had treated the prayer shawl, the palm frond on Sukkot, and even the Hebrew language itself as relics of an outdated, superstitious past. Reconstructionism treated these features of traditional Jewish practice as components of the civilization that could be updated but must still be preserved. Today, the vast majority of Reform congregations have taken on the Reconstructionist perspective.

Meanwhile, in Conservative synagogues, historically divided on whether to play instrumental music as part of the Sabbath service, the guitar, formally permitted in 1970, gradually came to be accepted. By 2015, roughly half of Conservative congregations used instrumental music during Shabbat prayer.[22] The change reflected a much deeper shift among Conservative Jews, many of whom, from the 1980s forward, gradually gave up the ideal of adherence to binding Jewish law and began to treat their religious practices as community customs, much like Reconstructionists. While some Conservative rabbis may construe the law differently, most of their congregants are squarely Progressive in their thinking, treating Jewish values as congruent with the ideals of social justice.

THE GOD OF SOCIAL JUSTICE

JUDAISM WITHOUT GOD?
TEMPLES WITHOUT PEOPLE?

Reconstructionist theologians don't object to anyone believing in God. But at the most fundamental level, they treat God as a metaphor—and they treat the Jewish God as a metaphor created by the Jewish people. Can there be Jewish life without God, or at least with a metaphoric God? This theological question is intertwined with an institutional question: Can Progressive Jewish life produce sustaining, spiritually meaningful communities at a large scale?

The reason these questions are connected is that Kaplan's civilizational approach, designed to enable the flourishing of Progressive Jewish life without belief in God, relies essentially on collective community. A civilization is not just a group of people but a group of people united by a comprehensive way of life that includes common geography, practices, cultures, and ideas. That may be a bridge too far for Reconstructionist Judaism in its current institutional format. But a lively synagogue community might conceivably function as a kind of partial substitute. If Reconstructionist Jewish communal life could be sufficiently embracing, then the no-God option might be a viable form of Progressivism.

As we shall see in the next chapter, Judaism as a civilization is alive. There are Jews whose communities are fully civilizational, encompassing intense communal relationships and home-based religious practices that infuse everyday life outside the synagogue. But this cannot be said of most Reconstructionist Jewish congregations, nor of most Reform or Conservative ones. Under the best of circumstances, the no-God option is extremely challenging to maintain at the communal level. When the great bulk of the community believes in God and practices civilizational Judaism accordingly, it's possible, if difficult, to be the skeptic in the corner of the synagogue who thinks God is at most a metaphor but keeps on participating fully in the life of the community. (I've been that person at various stages in my life, so I know both that it can be done and that it can't be done easily.)

What is almost impossible is for the *entire community* to embrace the notion of God as a metaphor while maintaining the communal energy necessary to make a civilization. The recurrent question for any intentional community, including any religious community, is, "Why are we doing this?" A Progressive Jewish community that believes in some sort of God can answer, "We are doing this to become closer to the divine." For believers, nothing could be more transcendently important. A Progressive Jewish community skeptical of God's existence can try to answer by saying, "We are doing this because we believe in sustaining Jewish civilization." But that answer raises the question of why the civilization ought to be sustained.

The best way to make this problem concrete is to imagine a parent telling an eleven-year-old child that the kid will be having a bar or bat mitzvah (or b-mitzvah) in a year or two.* If the family is embedded in a community where the ceremony is the norm, conversation will likely move rapidly to when, where, and who the DJ will be. If the family is less embedded in those norms, the kid may well ask, "Why?" The answer that this will bring you closer to God and our community of believers will work if the kid also believes in God. If not, the answer that Judaism is a civilization or a culture to which the family belongs is possible. Yet it is difficult to give that answer if the family in fact is *not* embedded in a culture where the ceremony is so common as to seem natural and automatic.

Judaism is of course a distinct culture, and all cultures have some inherent value. Yet I don't choose to spend my time sustaining most cultures unless I have a particular affinity for them or love of them. I may have sufficient affinity for Jewish civilization. But to get that affinity, an affinity powerful enough to keep me coming to the synagogue and connected to a close-knit community, it helps for me to have grown up in such a community or to be yearning for a connection to it. That in turn is far more likely to happen when the community offers the comprehensive experience of common ritual observance, support, and connection that

---

* Nonbinary terminology is emerging. *B-mitzvah* seems to be the current leader along with *b'nai mitzvah*, a plural form paralleling they/theirs. See https://www.keshetonline .org/resources/a-guide-for-the-gender-neutral-b-mitzvah/; Alyson Kruger, "Bar or Bat Mitzvah? Hey, What About a Both Mitzvah?" *New York Times*, March 27, 2019.

THE GOD OF SOCIAL JUSTICE

can be found in Traditionalist or (as we will see) what I will call Evolutionist circles. In principle, civilizational community does not require God. But in practice, it almost certainly does require an appeal beyond universal liberal values plus particularized weekly worship.

This is the reason, I think, that Progressive Jewish institutions often struggle to create and shape communities in which most of their nominal members actually want to participate regularly. They don't have difficulty attracting members who share their liberal values, wish to be connected to Jewish life, and are glad to have temples they can attend for life-cycle events and high holidays. God may bring them to the temple. If so, it is a universal God whose worship can be accomplished as well through supporting liberal social causes as through worship; better, even, since the Progressive God cares much more about justice and the repair of the world than about ritual or prayer. Jewish civilization may bring them to the temple. If so, however, that civilization is unlikely to be sufficiently compelling to keep them strongly connected without the more comprehensive set of rituals and practices that come with Traditionalism and are practiced by Evolutionists as well.

PROGRESSIVISM AND SPIRITUALITY

That leaves the option of a Progressive Judaism infused with deep and powerful spirituality, the kind the Havurah movement and its successor, Jewish Renewal, have aimed to create. Jews have long sought after this kind of spiritual experience. Hasidism came into existence precisely to infuse traditional Jewish life with transcendent spiritual experience and meaning. The Havurah movement self-consciously drew on some elements of Hasidism, including its emphasis on melody and song as direct routes to religious experience. Neo-Hasidism does the same, drawing on popular mysticism alongside music.[23] In recent decades, Hasidic mysticism has influenced some Progressive rabbis. I recently heard Menachem Mendel of Kotzk (1787–1859), known as the Kotzker Rebbe, invoked skillfully under a *huppah* in a field in Jackson, Wyoming, to explain the breaking of the glass at a Jewish wedding ("There is nothing so whole as a broken heart").

Today, however, spiritualized Progressive Jewish life outside the temple tends to cluster around thinkers and leaders who openly draw on non-Jewish, Eastern spiritual traditions that are popular in the contemporary West. There is the Jewish Buddhist (lovingly nicknamed the JewBu) and the Jew interested in Hindu yogic and meditative practice (the HinJew). Many of these Jews are also interested in Jewish mysticism, a set of traditions that evolved in complex relation with other mysticisms, including Christian mysticism and Sufi Islam (itself influenced by South Asian mysticisms). Drawing on such parallel traditions as well as on Kabbalah, the scholar-practitioner-mystic Rabbi Jay Michaelson defines what he calls a "nondual" version of Jewish mysticism this way: "The deepest secret is that, despite appearances, all things, and all of us, are like ripples on a single pond, motes of a single sunbeam, the letters of a single word. The true reality of our existence is Ein-Sof, infinite." From this it follows that "ultimately, everything is one—or in theistic language, we are all God."[24] A person who believes in this way may certainly be Progressive, believing in spiritual truths that are divine, eternal, and closely matched with human dignity, equality, and freedom.

One might expect that Kabbalah, in a form like the one Michaelson captures in his beautiful book *Everything Is God* (2009), would become a powerful infusing force in Progressive Jewish thought and life. Americans raised in nearly all religious denominations—or none—increasingly identify as "spiritual" and seek what we ordinarily think of as religious experience through exposure to popular versions of meditative Buddhism, Hinduism, and other New Age spiritualities. Jews are no different. In fact, Jews have been disproportionately influential in bringing Buddhism and Hinduism into American spiritual life. And young Israelis who travel to South Asia in large numbers after their army service have brought Indian meditative practices into Israeli cultural and religious experience.

Somehow, despite the prominence in the 2000s of a popular Hollywood-focused Kabbalah community (some would say a near-cult), distinctively Jewish mystical tradition has not yet become part of mainstream Progressive Jewish institutions. Part of the explanation may be generational: older Jews who dominate Progressive Jewish institutions may not be as drawn to New Age spirituality as younger Jews are. Perhaps the generational dynamic is more subtle: those older Jews who were drawn to Buddhism and Hinduism self-consciously separated themselves from institutional Jewish life, leaving behind (and in charge) those Progressive Jews who were more focused on social justice and less on inward spiritual experience. Or maybe those Jews who favor institutional Progressivism are simply not drawn to mystical experience.[25]

The Jewish Renewal movement, heir to the Havurah movement, has a small number of congregational adherents, such as Romemu and Congregation Beth Elohim in New York. These congregations display undoubted features of Kabbalistic Progressive community. Yet as a sociological matter, mystical Jewish spirituality does not at present play a major role in formal Progressive Jewish life. To see a resurgent Jewish spirituality linked to liberal values, one must look elsewhere: to a conception of Jewishness that seeks to evolve the tradition without turning into pure Progressivism.

I:3

THE GOD WHOSE LAW
EVOLVES

One of the most moving religious moments I have witnessed as an adult took place a few years ago at a conference on "Progressive Hala-khah" that my colleagues and I organized at Harvard Law School. The final panel of the conference, the one everyone was waiting for, was titled, "Who or What Is an Orthodox Rabbi?" The debate was about how and whether women can become rabbis, specifically in the Modern Orthodox world.

The subject holds great significance for understanding the boundar-ies between different Jewish worldviews. Among Traditionalist Jews, the very notion of women serving as rabbis engenders (pun intended) a clear and definitive rejection. The tradition as they understand it did not feature women rabbis, and a transformational change would mark an unacceptable deviation from that tradition. There are no Traditionalist women rabbis acknowledged today. If there ever were to be in the future, that would represent an epochal alteration in Traditionalism.

To Progressive Jews, at the other end of the spectrum, women obvi-ously must be ordained as rabbis. The traditional past needs to be up-dated in the light of egalitarian feminism. Many hundreds of women rabbis have been educated and ordained by Reform, Conservative, Reconstructionist, and nondenominational seminaries since 1972, when Hebrew Union College ordained Rabbi Sally Priesand.[1]

That makes the question of women rabbis a burning one primarily for people whose beliefs lie somewhere between Traditionalism and Progressivism. The four panelists all fell into that category. One was a woman who had passed rigorous examinations in technical questions of Jewish law to become a yo'etzet halakhah, a female Jewish law adviser qualified to render opinions for Orthodox women on what is called "family purity." (That is, the halakhah connected to sex, ritual purification, and menstruation.[2]) A second was a male Modern Orthodox rabbi who is a prominent senior figure at Yeshiva University and had helped write an official policy paper on women rabbis for the Orthodox Union, the official organization of Modern Orthodox congregations. The policy flatly stated that no congregation could retain its affiliation if it appointed a woman as a rabbi or to a position of synagogue leadership equivalent to a rabbinic role.[3]

The other two panelists were Orthodox Jewish women rabbis. Both had passed the full panoply of tests given to Modern Orthodox rabbis. Both had been ordained by other Orthodox-ordained rabbis, thereby becoming links in a chain of ordination that is basic to the logic of Jewish rabbinic authority. Both had chosen to use the title "rabbi" or its Hebrew equivalent, rav, rather than alternative titles used by some other similarly situated women in recent years. The two women were among a tiny number of people occupying a position defined by many Orthodox Jews as impossible.

In the course of the discussion, which you can watch on video if you like,[4] one of these two panelists, Rabbi Rahel Berkovits, found herself telling the Yeshiva University rabbi why she believed that, having studied and received rabbinic ordination, she should be counted as a rabbi. I knew Rahel from when we were schoolmates. I hadn't seen her much since, and I recalled her from our teenage years mostly as the fun-loving, kind, extremely popular cocaptain of the girls' basketball team. In my memory, she was always smiling and laughing. So I was listening especially carefully to what she had to say as Rahel, now Rabbi Berkovits, passionately yet patiently explained the core of her worldview to the rabbi who had written the policy invalidating her:

> For me, as a religious woman, one of the greatest experiences of the divine that I have in this world is the fact I exist. That I'm alive. That I'm created by the divine and in the image of the divine. And so when I see [traditional Jewish texts that treat women as unequal], I have to either annihilate myself [or] annihilate my view of God or I have to say that those texts have been influenced through time by human beings.

This powerful opening presented the core experiential and intellectual argument of Jewish religious feminism: women are equal before God. Consequently, religious sources that present women as unequal must reflect not God's unchanging word but human influence.

Berkovits went on to tell the senior rabbi:

> When you say that [Maimonides] had a specific problem with [appointing women as synagogue officials], that problem stems from a view [of women] which I am 100 percent unwilling to accept is *ratzon Hashem* [God's will]. I am unwilling to accept that.

Rabbi Berkovits was invoking her belief in God and God's will in service of her ultimate argument: the God who created her could not possibly consider women unequal. From this followed her conclusion:

> For me, if halakhah is playing out the divine word of God, I want there to be congruence [with] what I believe to be *ratzon Hashem* [God's will]. You could tell me I'm mistaken. But for me, all I have is myself and my understanding of the divine in this world.[5]

The moment brought tears to my eyes—in fact I'm fighting back tears as I write this—precisely because Berkovits *believes*. She has devoted her life to teaching the Torah for more than two decades at the Pardes Institute of Jewish Studies in Jerusalem. Both she and the senior rabbi she was addressing believe in God. And it was precisely because that believing rabbi could recognize her belief that he had no meaningful answer to make, and wisely did not try to give one. How could he tell Berkovits that her experience of God was any less valid than his own, when her learning and her love of the Torah were so deep and genuine?

The school Rahel and I attended produced a number of rabbis and teachers in my generational cohort, alongside an embarrassment of doctors, lawyers, and PhDs. It was in that moment at the conference that I realized Rahel must be the most profoundly religious of them all. I didn't see it coming when we were kids, likely because I couldn't then break out of sexist convention and imagine an Orthodox woman rabbi. Perhaps by coincidence, but probably not, she is also descended from an important Modern Orthodox theologian, Rabbi Eliezer Berkovits, whom she quoted during the panel. She embodies everything that the Maimonides School was trying to teach us: love of God, adherence to Jewish law, the effort to reconcile tradition and modernity. Whether our Modern Orthodox school would acknowledge it or not, Rahel's place in the vanguard of Orthodox women rabbis is a tribute to her extraordinary education by truly wonderful, religiously sincere teachers.

What Berkovits believes about God, God's will, and their relation to Jewish law differs from the beliefs of either the Traditionalists or the Progressives while having something in common with each. Like the Traditionalists, she accepts that God's will is expressed in laws that are binding on her by virtue of their divine origin. Progressive Jews may find the halakhah inspiring, but they do not feel legally bound by it. Berkovits does. Like the Progressives, Berkovits believes that human beings play a role in interpreting God's will and that halakhah therefore can and should change over time as human interpretation shifts, a view that Traditionalists reject.

Berkovits's beliefs entail a third option, a middle way that lies between the other two. I call Jews who share her belief pattern Evolutionists. They believe that, as Berkovits put it, "halakhah is playing out the divine word of God" through conscious acts of human interpretation. Evolutionists want to acknowledge the ultimate authority of Jewish law while simultaneously seeking to accommodate liberal or at least modern beliefs. They want to create comprehensive, vital Jewish communities that are also in certain respects inclusive. They want to believe in and worship a God who is universal and rational but also chooses and singles out the Jewish people for special privileges and responsibilities.

What makes these people Evolutionists is that while they accept the binding, valid authority of Jewish law as interpreted by the rabbis, they consciously recognize that Jewish law *evolves* and that human choice plays a central role in that evolution. They see Jewish tradition as continuous from the era of the Bible and the earliest rabbis and see themselves as legitimate heirs to that tradition. Yet unlike Traditionalists, they do not believe that today's *gedolim*, or greatest rabbis—or those of any era—enjoy near-prophetic power to channel the divine will. Evolutionists usually seek to accommodate strongly held moral beliefs in equality and freedom with their faith commitments. Yet unlike Progressive Jews, Evolutionists do not assume that any new moral truth settled upon by contemporary liberal thought must be an expression of God's eternal will. Evolutionists recognize the possibility, indeed the inevitability, of tension between what Jewish tradition teaches and what contemporary liberalism maintains.

Like my other categories of Traditionalism and Progressivism, the category of Evolutionism doesn't precisely map onto sociological movements within Jewish life. That's because, like the other categories, it is primarily an interior or internal state of belief, an attitude of the mind and heart. You know Evolutionism is present when someone says he or she accepts the authority of God's Law and also acknowledges that Jews at different historical moments have had very different beliefs about what that Law required or demanded—that normative Jewish belief and practice have changed and are changing still.

Evolutionism can sometimes be ambivalent about articulating the realities of evolutionary change. Evolutionists always want to present their interpretations as authentic readings of the tradition. That makes

Evolutionism the hardest to pin down of the belief patterns I have described. But as we shall see in part II, it is also in a certain sense the most important for our historical moment. That is because Religious Zionism is a type of Evolutionism. It recognizes that Zionism is a modern development influenced by nationalism while simultaneously treating it as a divinely sanctioned expression of God's will, mandated by the Bible and the rabbis.

THE ETERNAL GOD'S EVOLVING LAWS

Like Traditionalist and Progressive Jewish thought, Evolutionism can be captured in an evocative Talmudic passage. It goes under the odd title "the oven of *'akhnai*," a specific type of earthenware oven constructed out of segments, with sand filling in the empty spaces. Imagine a South Asian tandoor (the word has the same etymology as the Hebrew *tannur*) made of layered sections that go around the structure like a coiled snake.

This sort of oven was the subject of a debate between ancient rabbis over whether it ought to be considered a complete, whole vessel, in which case it was capable of becoming ritually impure, or whether it should be conceptualized as incomplete, in which case it could not have the status of ritual impurity attached to it. The majority view among the rabbis was that the oven was functionally complete and therefore capable of impurity. Rabbi Eliezer, a powerful and influential rabbi with a penchant for independent thought, disagreed.

If the disagreement sounds obscure and minor, that is because it is. The Talmud abounds in debates about tiny, technical matters that seem almost unimaginably distant from philosophical or spiritual importance. Yet as the debate over the oven shows, it is the genius of the Talmud to connect these apparently unimportant arguments to matters of the deepest significance.

The Talmud recounts that on the memorable day of the dispute over the oven, Rabbi Eliezer provided "all the answers in the world" to the rabbis' majority view, and nonetheless failed to convince them. Having exhausted rational argument, he sought argumentative support from the supernatural realm. The Talmud depicts Rabbi Eliezer as a powerful wizard. It narrates his efforts, and the rabbis' responses, or rather non-responses, to them:

> He said: "If the law follows me, this carob tree will prove it." The carob was uprooted [and flew] one hundred cubits—some say four hundred cubits. They [the rabbis] said to him: "One does not cite proof from a carob."
>
> He said to them: "If the law follows me, this stream will prove it." The stream flowed backward. They said to him: "One does not cite proof from a stream."
>
> He said to them: "If the law follows me, the walls of the study hall will prove it." The walls of the study hall listed and began to fall. Rabbi Joshua rebuked [the falling walls] and said to them: "If scholars are contending with each other in the Law, what have you to do with it?" The walls did not fall down out of honor for Rabbi Joshua and they did not straighten up out of honor for Rabbi Eliezer; and they are still [to this day] leaning [halfway] while standing.
>
> Once again he said to them: "If the law follows me, it will be proven from heaven." Immediately, a divine voice was heard saying [to the rabbis], "What have you to do with Rabbi Eliezer, for the law follows him in every instance!"
>
> Rabbi Joshua stood on his feet and said: "It is not in heaven."[6] What does "It is not in heaven" mean? Rabbi Jeremiah said, "Once the Torah was given at Mt. Sinai, we pay no heed to a divine voice, because You [God] already wrote in the Torah, 'Incline after the majority.'"
>
> Rabbi Natan came upon Elijah [the prophet]. He said to him, "What did the holy One, Blessed be He, do at that hour?" He answered: "He smiled and said, 'My children have defeated me, my children have defeated me.'"[7]

This absorbing, spectacular passage has achieved iconic status for Evolutionist Jews. It poses the question of who is right, the majority of the rabbis or Rabbi Eliezer. To the extent the passage depicts God or his messengers taking a side, the answer is clearly Rabbi Eliezer. In support of his view, Rabbi Eliezer sends a tree flying through the air, makes water reverse its course, and even threatens to pull down the study house itself. To top it all off, a divine voice actually *declares* that the law ought to follow Rabbi Eliezer, not the other rabbis. There is no hint in the passage that these signs and wonders are dark magic of any kind. They show that on the matter of the oven, Rabbi Eliezer is right and the rabbis are wrong.

And yet, despite divine intervention, the rabbis stand their ground. They establish the law based on a rule they derived from a biblical verse: the majority rules. They will not bend that rule of decision even in the face of Rabbi Eliezer's evident rightness.

The punch line, for Evolutionists, is the verse cited by Rabbi Joshua (the same Rabbi Joshua we saw deferring to Rabban Gamliel in I:1): "It is not in heaven." The "it" in question is nothing less than the Torah, the Law, itself. The Torah *emanated* from heaven. It came from God. But once given to humans, the Torah is no longer *in* heaven. It is in the world. And in the world, the Torah is in the hands, under the control, of the rabbis and their majority.

What does God think of all this? The Talmud answers that question with a report straight from heaven. It is delivered by the prophet Elijah, who in the Talmud can move between the heavenly and mundane worlds because, rather than dying an ordinary death, he ascended into heaven in a whirlwind while still alive.[8] In Elijah's telling, God Himself smiled at the whole exchange. When God said His children had defeated Him, He did so with (rueful?) joy or even pride, as a father who anticipated and welcomed, or at least accepted, His children's victory. The point of Elijah's report is that the rabbis have defeated God *in rabbinic dispute*. They have quoted His own Torah against God to prove they need no longer listen to Him in interpreting His own words.

To Evolutionists, what has happened in the story is that the rabbis have, by acts of interpretation, made interpretation itself the ultimate authority in understanding God's Law as law, over and against God Himself. To be sure, the rabbis are being faithful to God. It is God, after all, who told them to follow the majority in cases of dispute. Evolutionists are committed to God's authority, in principle.

On closer examination, however, it is the *rabbis* who have interpreted the Bible to say they must follow the majority. God's communications in the oven dispute would seem to suggest they should follow Rabbi Eliezer, who is correct about the Law. Yet the rabbis seize for themselves the authority to tell God that He has no place in the study hall, based on His own words. Ultimately, on this view, it is interpretation all the way down. The law to be followed, as opposed to the Law as heaven conceived it, is what the rabbis say it is, no more and no less.

Here is the key takeaway for Evolutionists: The rabbis, not God, are in charge of interpretation. And if the law follows the rabbis, not God's intention, whatever it may have been, *then the law is capable of evolution.* Whatever the Law regarding the oven was before the day of the dispute, the law now follows the rabbis. The rabbis must act in good faith, seeking to understand the Torah. Ultimately, however, they need not be bound by divine intent, even should it somehow become miraculously manifest. In a postprophetic age, human, rabbinic interpretation *is* the Torah.

The consequence of this conclusion is that one may be faithful to the Torah and God and tradition while still acknowledging the capacity of the tradition to change. That in turn enables, in theory, the emergence of communities that are simultaneously traditional and in touch with their historical moment. The members of these communities can be true and faithful and also live contemporary lives in dialogue with the latest ideas of science, morality, and culture.

As a sociological matter, the aspiration to live in this way is shared by Jews who belong to a range of different institutional communities. The greatest number consider themselves Modern Orthodox, affiliating with institutions like Yeshiva University that affirm rabbinic authority while insisting on an interpretation of the Torah that strives to be compatible with living as a modern person in the modern world.* Such otherwise disparate

---

* A different, growing part of the Modern Orthodox community is not committed to Evolutionism but accepts Traditionalism as a matter of theory while belonging to communities that are in practice less insular or restrictive.

figures as Joe Lieberman, Mayim Bialik, Jared Kushner, Ivanka Trump, and Ben Shapiro identify as Modern Orthodox Jews. They wear ordinary clothes and work in mainstream jobs and go to secular colleges and graduate schools, all while professing observance of binding Jewish law.

In Israel, the overwhelming majority of Jews who fall into the Evolutionist category are Religious Zionists (in Hebrew, *dati le'umi*, meaning religious nationalist), who reconcile rabbinic tradition with modern nationalism. Naftali Bennett, who served briefly as prime minister of Israel, is a Religious Zionist (the first to serve in that office, incidentally). Itamar Ben-Gvir, as of this writing Israel's minister of national security and head of the ultranationalist Jewish Power party, is a Religious Zionist. So is Bezalel Smotrich, the right-wing finance minister in Benjamin Netanyahu's government, head of the party known officially as Religious Zionism. I will have much to say about this group and its ideology in part II. For now, what matters is to note that Religious Zionists accept the authority of God's tradition while acknowledging that their Jewishness, infused as it is by practical and theoretical devotion to an actually existing Jewish state, differs from that of their premodern predecessors.

Some American Evolutionists belong to the Conservative movement, so called because its founders wanted to differentiate themselves from Reform Judaism through conservation of the authority of Jewish law and its traditions. A small but growing number of what might be called left-wing Evolutionists associate themselves with cutting-edge startup congregations and schools, mostly in the United States but some in Israel, that can best be described as egalitarian-Evolutionist: men, women, and nonbinary people participate equally in services and study that, apart from the participants and tweaks to the liturgy, resemble Modern Orthodox practices. Their communities, such as Hadar, Yeshivat Maharat, and Yeshivat Chovevei Torah, are small in number but have an outsize indirect influence because of the intellectual-spiritual pressure they place on American Modern Orthodoxy to take a stand on whether to be more inclusive. Among other things, these communities maintain that women may become rabbis, a point that differentiates them from mainstream Modern Orthodoxy.

I am categorizing Evolutionists together, despite knowing that some members of these different subgroups will not want to be included with the others, for the same reason I grouped Traditionalist and Progressive Jews: based on belief pattern, not identity. By grouping today's Jews based on their beliefs about God, I want to help you, the reader, determine what you might believe, not where you feel you might belong. You could, in my analysis, be an Evolutionist Jew who is politically liberal or one who is politically conservative. But you would have to combine belief in God's authority handed down via rabbinic tradition with the belief that God wants us, human beings, to evolve the tradition consciously in the right direction as we see fit. Blu Greenberg (b. 1936), an influential Orthodox feminist thinker, captured this vision in an adage so much quoted by Evolutionists that it could almost be described as their credo: "Where there's a rabbinic will, there's a halakhic way." She meant that when rabbis committed to the tradition choose to evolve the tradition, they can always find the means to do so within the rubric of Jewish legal thought.

The ambitions of Evolutionist Jewish life deserve to be honored. In some of their communities, Evolutionist Jews manage to combine the connection, love, and support of Traditionalist Jewish communities with a degree of inclusion and openness that would be unimaginable in Traditionalist circles. Evolutionist Jews are able to participate fully in mainstream society. Many espouse belief in political freedom and equality even while remaining committed to the authority of God's Law as interpreted by the rabbis. Their most vibrant institutions are innovative and original. Their leaders are learned and intellectually serious. Their community members are actively engaged in the life of the mind and of the soul. Having been raised an Evolutionist, I can testify from direct experience to the remarkable intellectual and spiritual energies these communities generate.

At the same time, Evolutionism faces serious challenges, precisely because of its creative flexibility. While left-leaning Evolutionists make room for inclusion and equality, other, far-right Evolutionists like Ben-Gvir and Smotrich embrace exclusion and inequality. Both claim authority from the tradition as they read it. Neither can appeal to a definitive, final, human decision-maker to say they are right. All Evolutionists must rely on interpretation—their own interpretation of God's words and God's will.

What's more, Evolutionism as a worldview can be extremely difficult to maintain, intellectually, spiritually, and logically. Not by coincidence, the most important characteristic of Evolutionism is internal contradiction. Traditionalists have to struggle against the external forces of postmodernity and against the natural human tendency to lose spiritual focus when fulfilling a multitude of detailed commandments. But they need not struggle much with internal contradiction. When there is an overt contradiction between the tradition and contemporary values, the tradition wins. Traditionalists trust God and the rabbis to have gotten it right. If a Traditionalist Jew loses faith, it creates a struggle between the benefits of staying within the community and the benefits of living sincerely outside it. That struggle, however, is not constitutive of being a Traditionalist Jew. It's a symptom of losing one's faith as a Traditionalist.

Similarly, a Progressive Jew may have to struggle with how best to understand social justice values. But Progressive Jews need not struggle internally with elements of particularist Jewish tradition that directly contradict equality or freedom. Egalitarian values win. Progressive Judaism teaches that unjust elements of the tradition can and should be purified out of Judaism, as a just and loving universal God would wish.

Not so the Evolutionist Jew who is faced with a contradiction between authoritative Jewish tradition and liberal commitments. Such an Evolutionist must seek to reconcile the God of the tradition with the God of universal love and human dignity. This Evolutionist wants the best of both worlds, comprehensive community and genuine inclusion. Yet those worlds can be in blunt contradiction, both as a matter of law and observed reality. To have them both requires tremendous intellectual and spiritual creativity—and an enormous amount of intellectual and spiritual effort. Indeed, being an Evolutionist often seems to require holding two contradictory beliefs at the same time.

MORAL INTUITION AND
THE RELIGION OF REASON

Evolutionism can be glimpsed in contemporary movements that go back well over a century. But by its advocates' account, Evolutionism's origins date back to the earliest rabbis, who themselves evolved the law they found in the Bible. The key tool in this evolutionary process has been the rabbis' willingness to rely on their own inner sense of moral logic and to interpret texts that troubled them in the light of their intuitions.

To see the way the rabbis used moral intuitions to evolve the law—and the ambivalence they retained about that practice—consider a well-known example that appears in the book of Deuteronomy and is discussed in the Talmud: the case of the stubborn and rebellious son. The Bible devotes just four short verses to this subject, but (trigger warning for teenagers) they are shocking. The text reads:

> If a man should have a stubborn and rebellious son who does not listen to the voice of his father or the voice of his mother, and they chasten him, and he does not listen to them; then shall his father and his mother catch him and bring him out to the elders of his city and the gate of his place. And they shall say to the elders of his city: "This our son is stubborn and rebellious (*sorer u-moreh*). He will not listen to our voice. He is a glutton and a drunkard." Then shall all the men of his city stone him until he dies. So shall you eradicate evil from among you; and all Israel shall hear and fear.[9]

The literal import of these verses is that parents who can't manage their children can have them executed. The passage may sound fantastical. After all, what parent would do that? But the verses appear in a legal section of Deuteronomy full of utterly practical laws. The immediately preceding passage, for example, states that a husband who has two wives may not lawfully prefer the chronologically younger son of his favored wife over his firstborn when it comes to inheritance. There is no contextual reason to think the law of the rebellious son is anything other than black letter law to be applied like the law of primogeniture.

The Talmud begins its discussion of the rebellious son the way it often treats biblical laws, namely by filling in details. It states, for example, that such a son may not be executed until he has reached the age of majority, since he cannot be held liable for sinful acts committed as a child.[10] Moving to the ethical plane, the Talmud argues that the rebellious son is to be executed for the sins he would eventually commit if left alive, not for what he has done already. This suggestion seems intended to answer the obvious moral question of how disobedience to parents could merit death.

After a lengthy, associative excursus on the ages of young people having sex and reproducing, and another about what sins of gluttony and drunkenness the rebellious son must have committed (which itself leads to a disquisition on wine), the Talmud eventually gets to the hardest question: Was the law of the rebellious son ever meant to be implemented in practice? The Talmud invokes a rabbinic dictum that asserts, "There never was a stubborn and rebellious son, and there will never be one." Then it asks, "So why was it written" in the Bible? The Talmud answers: "Interpret it and receive a reward."[11]

This perspective, associated with two different rabbis, prefigures Evolutionism because it shows the rabbis actively interpreting the Bible against its apparent meaning to produce a legal outcome that seems to them morally superior. The rabbis reread the biblical text so that it is no longer a practical legal passage but an occasion for rabbinic interpretation. Arguably, the idea is that the passage is there precisely so the rabbis may interpret it as *not being practically applicable at all*. On this reading, the "reward" of interpretation is the reward for understanding the text against its surface meaning.[12]

Notwithstanding the presence of this evolutionary strand in the Talmud, the rabbis also manifested a consistent counterview. In the case of the rebellious son, Rabbi Jonathan pithily rejects the notion that none was ever executed: "I saw him and I sat on his grave." Rabbi Jonathan is asserting that he has direct knowledge of one rebellious son who was executed. By implication, others were too. The Law is the law. It is no mere object of interpretation.

Since the era of the Talmud, another, closely related strand of Jewish interpretive thought has also existed, one that also anticipates Evolutionism: allegory, defined roughly as the interpretation of a text to reveal otherwise hidden meanings beneath its surface. In the Middle Ages, the banner of allegory was taken up by the philosophical rationalist Maimonides. His vision of God and Jewish tradition starts with reason, or rather with Reason. If God is truth, and truth is one, then all truths must be consistent with each other. If the divine revelation contained in the Bible is true, and if logical reason is true, the Bible must be consistent with the truths of reason derived by philosophy.

What challenged medieval rationalists like Maimonides (as well as Muslim and Christian philosophers like al-Farabi, Ibn Rushd, and Thomas Aquinas) was that, read literally, divine Scripture does not always correspond to the philosophical truths of reason. The philosophers' God, for instance, is perfect: omnipotent, omniscient, and without form or body. The Bible describes a God who has hands, throws thunderbolts, flies on a cherub, becomes enraged, feels jealousy, expresses regret, changes his mind, and so on. The key to reconciling these different pictures of God was the idea of allegory. Scripture does not always speak in factual or historical terms. It can be read to include a set of symbolic statements or expressions that, if understood in their truest sense, actually correspond to the truths of reason. God does not have a body or experience emotions. Rather, Scripture speaks in this way to convey symbolic truths to those humans capable of understanding them properly.

For more than a millennium, this approach has enabled Jewish rationalists to accept the rational truths of science, philosophy, and even morality when they appear to differ from the teachings of the tradition. If the Bible can be read allegorically, so can many of the statements of the rabbis, which themselves include stories, allegories, and spiritual as well as philosophical speculation. At an intellectual level, this combination of the commitment to reason and willingness to interpret Jewish tradition allegorically has proven satisfying to many important and influential Jews. It is the cornerstone of contemporary Modern Orthodox thought. It was also the fundamental basis for the worldview of Conservative Judaism as it was originally formulated in the elite circles of its leadership.

The religion of reason is at its best when it is allowing committed religious believers to embrace the latest in scientific developments. Traditionalist Jews cannot easily accept the reality of Darwinian natural selection, or the astrophysicists' account of the Big Bang, because they don't fit the literal meaning of the book of Genesis. Rejecting these fundamental elements of the contemporary scientific worldview leaves Traditionalists in an awkward position with respect to the modern world more generally. Evolutionists have it much easier. They can, following Maimonides, accept the entirety of the scientific picture of the world, knowing that Scripture may be interpreted allegorically to correspond to it. When Genesis says God created the earth in six days, the days may be understood metaphorically or allegorically as eons. Seen from this allegorical perspective, even the Big Bang is potentially consonant with the idea of divine creation ex nihilo, from nothing.

At a practical level, then, Evolutionists are spared having to believe scientifically implausible claims about the world as the price of adherence to their faith tradition. This frees them to enter any intellectual or academic environment. It frees them to enter any profession. It frees them to participate in public life. It frees them, in short, to be fully functioning participants in contemporary society, all the while remaining faithfully, authentically Jewish. The only limiting principle, for Evolutionists, is that they must accept the binding nature of Jewish law and the rabbis' right to interpret it. They cannot jettison a law that is part of the tradition; they can only seek to reinterpret it. And binding reinterpretation requires consensus of the rabbis, taken as a collective.

The result is that Evolutionist Jews can be part of broader liberal society without falling into what they—and the Traditionalists—consider the trap of "assimilation." The term "assimilation" is loaded and means different things to different people. But to the Evolutionists, Jewish assimilation means taking in the essence of contemporary liberal society to the point where one's distinctive Jewishness disappears or evaporates. After assimilation, the Jew may still identify as a Jew but will not be meaningfully distinguishable from non-Jewish neighbors, colleagues, or friends. From the standpoint of both Evolutionists and Traditionalists, the likely result of assimilation is marriage to a non-Jew, followed by the falling away of specifically and distinctly Jewish identity in the next generation.

I will discuss assimilation alongside Jewish concerns with marriage to non-Jews and collective self-reproduction in part III. For now, I am mentioning it to show how the religion of reason enables Evolutionists to avoid what they consider the pitfall of assimilation while still participating in contemporary society. Put simply, their beliefs about the makeup and nature of the world are such as to allow them to join in broader social conversations, whether personal, political, or professional. They can be both in the world and of the world, while simultaneously maintaining fidelity to Jewish tradition. What's more, they can argue, with great plausibility, that Jewish tradition itself contains precedent for their way of thinking and being.

JACOB ALONE

In the relatively recent past, the most serious challenges to the Evolutionist worldview came from Darwinism, cosmology, and perhaps biblical criticism, the field of study that traces the human composition of the Bible to multiple sources and documents edited together. Today, the most pressing challenges come from moral ideas, not from scientific propositions. Homosexuality provides a ready example. To the extent that contemporary science posits that some people are gay and always will be, Evolutionists are able to accept that proposition, albeit not without some initial struggle. But the value proposition that gay people are entitled to equal treatment has been harder for Evolutionists. Not only does traditional Jewish law only recognize marriage between men and women, a verse in Leviticus, read literally, prohibits sex between men as an "abomination." And the rabbis have long interpreted another biblical verse in Leviticus to prohibit sex between women.

Nevertheless, Evolutionists have the resources to allegorize Scripture even in relation to value propositions, and they have begun, gradually, to do so. A central figure in this process has been Rabbi Steven Greenberg, who in 1999 became the first Orthodox rabbi to come out of the closet and self-identify as a gay man. Even before that courageous act, Greenberg prepared the way with a 1993 essay, "Gayness and God," that he published under the nom de plume Yaakov Levado—Hebrew for "Jacob alone."[13]

I remember seeing the essay at the time and being powerfully affected by the name the author had taken, even before I began to read. "Jacob alone" is a reference to Genesis 32:25: "Jacob remained alone. A man wrestled with him until the break of dawn." The sentence begins the famous account of Jacob's struggle with a supernatural being that culminates in Jacob's renaming as Israel, and also in his being injured in "the hollow of his thigh." Greenberg's chosen name invoked, to a close reader of the Bible, not only the notion that the author was alone in his struggles with God but the more radical idea, certainly never stated by Greenberg in the essay, that Jacob's all-night struggle could be understood allegorically as an erotic encounter between men who were strangers yet conferred divinely sanctioned blessings upon each other.

In that first, pseudonymous essay, Greenberg clearly articulated the Evolutionist worldview. He did not call for a halakhic revolution in relation to homosexuality. "As a traditionalist," he wrote, "I hesitate to overturn cultural norms in a flurry of revolutionary zeal . . . Halacha, as an activity . . . is a society-building enterprise that maintains internal balance by reorganizing itself in response to changing social realities. When social conditions shift, we experience the halachic reapplications as the proper commitment to the Torah's original purposes." At the time, he thought, the "shift in social consciousness in regard to homosexuality is a long way off." He called only for "deeper understanding" of gay people:

> In order to know how to shape a halachic response to any living question, what is most demanded of us is a deep understanding of the Torah and an attentive ear to the people who struggle with the living question . . . There is no conclusive psak halacha [halachic ruling] without the hearing of personal testimonies, and so far gay people have not been asked to testify to their experience.[14]

And he predicted that "unimagined halachic strategies, I believe, will appear under different conditions. We cannot know in advance the outcome of such an investigation."

As an Evolutionist, Greenberg set about rereading the tradition—including the Bible—in creative ways to seek the moral objective of equality for gay people. Allegory is the technique that makes this interpretive rereading possible. For example, in a book he wrote in 2004, *Wrestling with God and Men: Homosexuality in the Jewish Tradition*, Greenberg interpreted Leviticus 18:22, which forbids a man to lie with another man "as one lies with a woman," as a moral directive intended to condemn "sexual domination and appropriation."[15] Seen this way, the verse need not be read to condemn gay sex per se, despite its using the word "abomination."

Technically speaking, Greenberg was not, in 2004, saying clearly that the biblical verse actually permitted anal intercourse between men as a matter of Jewish law. Although such an argument could certainly be advanced, using allegory does not necessarily mean eliminating the literal meaning of a legal text. What allegory enabled for Greenberg (at the time, at least) was a shift in perspective. Evolutionists following Greenberg can therefore reread the Bible to downplay or even deny the morally negative assessment of homosexuality that was characteristic of many societies until recently. They may update their moral judgments using the same tools they have long used to update their scientific judgments. To make *legal* change with respect to gay sex, Evolutionists would need some rabbinic consensus about the legal meaning of the biblical text.

Faced with the Evolutionists' strategy of updating by interpretation and allegory, progressive people—whether Jews or non-Jews—may be struck with a kind of repulsion. Wouldn't it be better, they may ask, to jettison ancient texts that seem to be morally or scientifically false rather than allegorically reinterpreting them to fit contemporary beliefs? To full-on Progressives, Evolutionism can seem regressive and apologetic.

The Evolutionists' answer deserves to be taken seriously. They want to believe, truly believe, in the divine origin and nature of Jewish tradition. They fear that Progressivism abandons what they consider the core component of Jewish continuity, namely the ongoing commitment to the validity and authority of the Law. They want to maintain the sense of all-encompassing community that comes with commitment to the Law, a sense of community sometimes lacking in Progressive Jewish communities. Evolutionists can also point to the social reality of their communities as proof that their method works. The vibrancy, connection, and mutually supportive nature of those communities tends to outpace that of most Progressive Jewish communities. If interpretation and allegory are the price of admission to such a rich form of life, they shouldn't be dismissed as backward-looking. They should be embraced as the best way to move the tradition forward. Evolution, after all, can lead to progress.

NATURA NON FACIT SALTUM: EVOLVING THE LAW ONE STEP AT A TIME

As long as the basic challenge of reconciliation is in the realm of ideas, the Maimonidean rationalist approach is highly effective. Where things get complicated is where the reconciliation enters the space of actual Jewish practice—in particular, practice connected to the law. Maimonides himself believed that provisions of the biblical law could be interpreted to find deeper meaning. But he did not believe that interpreting the law meant one could shirk it. To the contrary, Maimonides maintained a laser-like focus on the preservation of Jewish law in its entirety, which he considered fundamental to the whole edifice of creating a functioning Jewish and human society. Maimonides was a giant of Jewish legal study and reasoning alongside his philosophical work and his day job as physician to Saladin, the famous conqueror-sultan whose seat was in Cairo. He served as leader of the Egyptian Jewish community, issuing opinions on matters of Jewish law and writing an enormously influential Jewish law book, the fourteen-volume *Mishneh Torah*. This legal accomplishment is why Maimonides remains a central figure in the Traditionalist canon, despite his radical philosophical beliefs. He is just too towering and influential a figure in the tradition to be sidestepped or marginalized.

That is not to say that Maimonides ignored the reality that Jewish legal tradition evolves. He was among the first to identify that evolution and describe it. Yet Maimonides always insisted that the tradition could not evolve away from observance of the commandments that make up the law. Rabbis could add new restrictions to existing legal practice, provided they did so in order to protect the law itself. Under the right circumstances, properly authorized Jewish leaders could temporarily suspend laws, but they must be clear that any such suspension was tied to the exigencies of the moment and would not survive for future generations. Hence the law could accrete new layers. But it could not slough off layers of practice or obedience.

To see how hard this is in practice, let's return to Rabbi Rahel Berkovits. Evolutionism hasn't yet solved the problem of how to accept her ordination in the framework of tradition. Indeed, viewed through a sociological lens, the ordination of women as rabbis is becoming *the* defining fault line in Evolutionist Jewish life. Conservative Jews and left-wing, egalitarian Evolutionists have accepted the ordination of women. So-called Open Orthodox or Liberal Orthodox Jews—few in number but disproportionately well educated, well connected, and intellectual— are most of the way through a transformational period in which they have gone from seeking a compromise in the form of halfway ordination to fully accepting women's ordination as normative. But they are not (yet?) numerous enough to count as a full institutional movement. They have a handful of small yeshivas and a few scattered congregations, no more.

Modern Orthodox Judaism, however, is overwhelmingly drawing the line at women's ordination, just as it has so far drawn the line at allowing women equal participation in synagogue services. Among other things, crossing the ordination line would create an unbridgeable rift between Modern Orthodoxy and Traditionalism, a rift Modern Orthodoxy is not prepared to create. The way the gender line lends itself to human distinctions makes it particularly difficult to breach for any religious community committed above all to continuity. The Catholic Church, itself a religious body whose mystical character depends on its claims of unbroken continuity, does not seem close to accepting women as priests.

What remains to be seen is whether Modern Orthodoxy can remain Evolutionist at the same time as it continues to reject the ordination of women rabbis. An Evolutionism that stops evolving will look more and more like Traditionalism. A substantial part of what might be described as sociological Modern Orthodoxy has become increasingly Traditionalist in recent decades. Key leaders of the rabbinical seminary at Yeshiva University express themselves in Traditionalist idiom. In dress, manner, religious conservatism, and even higher education, "right-wing" Modern Orthodoxy has become increasingly hard to distinguish from moderate Traditionalism.

The background context here is that when Modern Orthodoxy established itself in American Jewish life in the 1950s and early 1960s, its mores were largely consistent with mainstream American public values. Women were educated equally or semiequally and took lesser leadership positions, much as in American society at the time. Gay people remained closeted, as was the case in mainstream America in the 1950s and 1960s. Religion was treated as an important sphere of private life, much as it was for many non-Jewish Americans in the same period.

In retrospect, the correspondence between Modern Orthodox norms and mainstream American norms in the 1950s and 1960s was more of a coincidence than the Modern Orthodox felt it to be. Equality between the sexes, gay rights, and trans rights left Modern Orthodoxy looking not only socially conservative but actively regressive and discriminatory. Once frozen in place, Modern Orthodoxy can continue to be "modern" in the sense of "1950s modern." But arguably it cannot evolve to become postmodern. True Evolutionism would then become the preserve of a much smaller group of vanguard Jews, at least some of whom embrace what is, in effect if not in name, postmodern orthodoxy.

POSTMODERN ORTHODOXY AND THE QUESTION OF GOD

Does it make sense for a Jew to adhere scrupulously to God's Law if that person does not believe in God? This might sound like a niche problem, but it's one I care about a lot for reasons of personal biography. And as it turns out, it may not even be quite as niche as it sounds. Consider the situation of a Traditionalist who loses faith in God or perhaps never had it in the first place. Without God, there is no theological reason to follow the commandments. Yet there may be strong social and familial reasons to stay within a community that demands strict legal observance as a condition of belonging. Can one live this way in good faith? For how long? A surprising (or maybe unsurprising) number of Traditionalists quietly encounter this challenge at some point in their lives.

Now think about the situation of the Evolutionist without faith. Evolutionists, unlike Traditionalists, acknowledge the primacy of human interpretation in shaping the law. So it might be possible for them, in good conscience, to obey the evolving law on the basis of its own, human power, even if they do not believe that the law may ultimately be traced to God. This is the postmodern version of Mordecai Kaplan's modern idea of Judaism as a civilization. For Kaplan, an encompassing civilization deserved to be sustained and maintained even if God did not will it or bring it into existence. For postmodern Evolutionists, Jewish life and thought are inherently valuable and worthy of adherence because they reflect the ongoing commitments of Jews throughout the ages and simultaneously because they can shape a contemporary life of community, spirituality, and human connection. They can say that they get value and meaning out of *treating* the law as binding, whether God commanded it or not.

This stance should, in theory, make postmodern Evolutionism into the most broadly accepting of all the currently existing versions of Jewish thought and practice. Genuinely Progressive Jews must believe that Traditionalists are getting it wrong in the eyes of God when they treat women or gay people or trans people unequally. Traditionalists necessarily believe that Progressive Jews are getting it wrong in the eyes of God when they deny the binding authority of rabbinic tradition. Postmodern Evolutionists can say that all Jews are trying, by their own lights, to find a rich and meaningful way of engaging with Jewish thought and Jewish life.

I acknowledge that there are not too many self-identified postmodern Evolutionists out there. If you want to create a functioning religious community based on adherence to God's law, you might want to avoid saying publicly that you don't exactly believe in the God whom you worship and obey. Nevertheless, notwithstanding its mildly esoteric character, I find the accepting and affirming aspects of postmodern

Evolutionist thought appealing. Maybe that's because I held it for an important chunk of my life. Maybe it's because a few people I admire very much appear to hold it. The main reason I am discussing it here, however, is that it provides one possible grounding for the perspective I am advancing in this book. I'm trying, in these pages, to show the beauty and nobility of all the currently available modes of Jewish life, even as I point out their limitations and contradictions. This very goal has something in common with postmodern Evolutionism.

Another appeal of postmodern Evolutionism is that it allows you to evolve in your own beliefs over the course of a lifetime. Say you start by believing in God, fall away from your faith, then recover it in some new form. To a postmodern Evolutionist, none of this would require any great change in Jewish practice or attitudes toward other Jews and how they live. The idea is that on the days that you believe in God, you wake up, put on tefillin, and pray. On the days you don't believe in God, you do the exact same thing. As the Talmud puts it in a slightly different context, *mi-tokh she-lo li-shemah ba li-shemah*.[16] From acting not for the sake of the end itself one comes to the end itself.

The challenge for the postmodern Evolutionist, then, is to organize daily routine around the all-encompassing realities of the halakhah during the periods of life when belief is not forthcoming. You can tell yourself that it's beneficial to pray even when you don't believe your prayers are addressed to anyone: prayer is, after all, a form of meditation, and meditation is enriching. You can tell yourself that studying the Law is intellectually stimulating and emotionally regenerative and connects you to your past even if you don't believe the Law ultimately has a divine origin. You can tell yourself that inclusive and encompassing Jewish community provides a sense of connection and collective meaning even if you don't believe the community is constituted by its covenant with God. I promise you, these statements are and can be helpful. I've made them all to myself, like mantras, many times over. They are true, or let us say true in the sense they are intended.

But can you tell yourself all those things every day for your whole life? And even if you could, *should you?* Is living "as if" sufficiently meaningful and consequential to sustain just about all of your most important life choices? The Bible and the tradition enjoin us to love God with all our hearts. Imagine: What if you spent your life with a partner, telling the person "I love you" every day, while not actually loving the person in your heart? Would that be a true life of love, even presuming you always managed to act lovingly on the surface? Is it, in the end, respectful toward God to act as though you believe in the divine when in fact you do not? Or is it a form of disrespect to (a possibly nonexistent) God? To the community of believers? Is it respectful to the idea of sincere belief itself? Is it, can it be, respectful to oneself to live one's whole life "as if" one believed?

Beyond the serious problem of sincerity, or rather insincerity, what happens if your deepest instincts begin to tell you that there are other possible lives available, lives that could not be lived compatibly with totalizing Jewish practice? If you truly believe that God commands you to obey the halakhah, that may be sufficient to keep you in obedience and overcome temptation. If you don't, however—if you are instead resting your lifeways on a postmodern conception of what makes life meaningful—then how can you, in good conscience, refuse to explore those other lives?

The magnitude of this challenge explains, I think, why postmodern Evolutionism remains the publicly stated worldview of only a small number of Jews. Rabbi Rahel Berkovits, for example, is not a postmodernist. She is a believer at the evolutionary forefront of Evolutionism. Some of her colleagues in that vanguard (it's impossible to say exactly how many) are postmodern Evolutionists. They have it harder than Rahel does, to the extent that they cannot address the problem of how far evolution should go by referring to their own inner light of faith. I would venture to suggest that the more Rahels there are in the vanguard, and the fewer postmodern Evolutionists, the better the prospects for the eventual survival and success of Evolutionism. The more God there is in Evolutionism, the better for the movement.

At the same time, the postmodern option is part of what makes Evolutionism appealing. Without it, Evolutionism runs the risk of devolving into merely being in the middle, just a way of living Jewish life that is between Progressivism and Traditionalism. In this picture, all three approaches believe in God; they differ only on what God wants from us: social justice, obedience to the tradition, or interpretive moral updating. If that is right, choosing among these Jewish options would seem to be a matter of faith alone. If you can answer the question "What do you think God wants?" then you know which form of Jewish life to choose. If your answer is "I am not even sure there is a God," then you are out of options. Postmodern Evolutionism gives you a way to be religiously Jewish based on something other than faith. It subtly strengthens Evolutionism even as it subtly undermines it.

This account reveals, I think, the grave difficulties Evolutionism faces as a functioning system for Jewish communities. And once again, the Talmud can be read to have anticipated part of the challenge. As it turns out, the story of the oven and the rabbis' interpretive victory over God has a dark postscript, one normally neglected by Evolutionists when they tell it.

On the day of the oven, the Talmud recounts, they brought all the vessels that Rabbi Eliezer had declared pure according to his legal view and burned them in the fire. This authoritative act of burning presaged an even more definitive rejection of Rabbi Eliezer himself. The rabbis consulted with each other, the Talmud says, and chose to excommunicate Rabbi Eliezer, placing him under a ban of total social ostracism. The rabbi whose views God had just endorsed was being excluded from the rabbinic community.

Rabbi Akiva, one of Rabbi Eliezer's students, worried that an alienated Rabbi Eliezer might use his wizardry to "destroy the entire world." Rabbi Akiva wrapped himself in black cloth, went to Rabbi Eliezer, and delivered the news as gently as he could. Rabbi Eliezer "ripped his garments, took off his shoes, dropped, and sat on the earth. His eyes dropped tears."[17] According to the Talmud, "the world was afflicted." A third of the olive trees, the wheat, and the barley in the fields was destroyed by plague. Anyplace Rabbi Eliezer cast his eyes was consumed by fire.

Meanwhile, Rabban Gamliel, the prince who had presided over the excommunication, was at sea. His ship was suddenly engulfed. The prince uttered a spontaneous prayer to God, who calmed the sea and spared him. But the respite was temporary. Rabbi Eliezer's wife, Imma

Shalom, who was also Rabban Gamliel's sister, feared that if her husband were to recite the daily *tahanun* prayer, a form of especially humble supplication, it would unleash divine punishment on her brother.

She was right. One day she found Rabbi Eliezer reciting the supplication prayer. "Arise," she told him. "You have killed my brother." As she spoke, a ram's horn sounded from Rabban Gamliel's house signaling that the prince had died. Rabbi Eliezer asked Imma Shalom how she knew that her brother had died. She replied, "Thus have I received the tradition from the house of my father's father: All the gates of prayer may be locked except for [the prayer of those subject to] verbal humiliation."[18]

Notice that Imma Shalom did not say that the rabbis' excommunication of Rabbi Eliezer had led to the death of the prince. The true cause was the verbal humiliation Rabbi Eliezer had suffered at the hands of the rabbis on the day of the oven dispute when they rejected his views so starkly.

According to this reading of the entire story, the day the rabbis defeated God and took over interpretive authority, they *disrupted the order of the natural world*. Rabbi Eliezer was humiliated *because God was displaced from his authoritative position*. On this understanding, the Talmud acknowledges that when the rabbis take conscious control of the Torah, the risks to the overall religious order are substantial. If God is not enthroned and acknowledged, the rabbis' very prince may be killed by God.

The allegorical lesson for the Evolutionist worldview is that consciously evolving the tradition carries foundational risks to the stability of the system. If God's will is not fully respected, if God-consciousness is lost, then evolution will look and feel like a rebellion against God. God may let his children defeat him for a time. But his justice will only be deferred, not avoided. The oven, in this reading, symbolizes both the opportunities and the dangers of rabbinic interpretation. The Talmud sees both in total clarity.

Faced with this challenge, some Jews have always wanted to embrace a more radical solution: to dethrone God altogether. They have wanted to be Jews without God, or not to be Jewish believers at all. It is to these ways of imagining Jewishness, and non-Jewishness, that we now must turn.

I:4

JEWS WITHOUT GOD

Can you be a Jew if you don't especially believe in God or practice Jewish rituals? The answer is indisputably yes. But what kind of a Jew can you be? What beliefs or practices or ways of being in the world would make you Jewish? These are much more interesting questions. In previous chapters I mentioned the option of living exactly the same Jewish life without believing in God as one would if one believed, what I've called "as if" Judaism, theorized by the theologian (or antitheologian) Mordecai Kaplan. In this chapter, I want to explore something very different. I want to explore ways of thinking and being Jewish that *don't* consist of praying in synagogues with other Jews or studying specifically Jewish texts or following the halakhah, but are somehow still identifiably and distinctively Jewish. If you wanted to be flippant, you could say that this chapter is in defense of the bagels-and-lox Jew. If you wanted to be serious, you could say that this chapter affirms the legitimacy of a Jewishness that rejects not only God but certain aspects of Jewishness itself, especially its particularism.

This argument might frustrate some readers. But it's important because, too often, discussions of contemporary Judaism lay out the primary denominational options and then just end. It's as if they assume that a Jew who doesn't associate with any of the existing denominations or engage in some sort of classically Jewish practices isn't much of a Jew at all. That Jew might be described as "assimilated," a term that mistakenly implies both that the Jew has swallowed general civilization whole, or alternatively that general civilization has swallowed the Jew. (Such Jews rarely if ever exist, and in any case, general civilization in the West today has many Jewish elements in it.)

The thinker Isaac Deutscher (1907–1967), who was raised as an observant Jew in prewar Poland and became a Marxist and later a critic of communist regimes, spoke of what he called the "non-Jewish Jew," a "Jewish heretic who transcends Jewry" and whom he characterized as belonging "to the Jewish tradition."[1] In his category Deutscher included Benedict de Spinoza, Heinrich Heine, Karl Marx, Rosa Luxemburg, Leon Trotsky, and Sigmund Freud. That same sort of Jew might even be called by some a "bad Jew," a category that, I've suggested, is not meaningfully grounded in Jewish sources. Or if it is a meaningful category, then many of the most interesting and important Jews to have lived in the past four hundred years were bad Jews—and the label should be embraced as a badge of honor.

I don't think any of Deutscher's listed Jews were non-Jewish at all, even if they might sometimes have wanted to be. I prefer to call Jews like this Godless, Godless in the sense that most would deny the existence of God or at the very least would consider God irrelevant to being Jewish.* Jewish Godlessness, however, is not a state of ignoring God. It is, I want to propose, a state of struggling to deny God, and in the course of that struggle, displacing God into channels of thought that are nevertheless recognizably Jewish.

Even the tradition recognizes the possibility of a Godless Jew who nevertheless somehow lives Jewishly. It does so through the figure of

---

* Spinoza, condemned by many as a heretic, is a complicated and complicating case. He did not precisely deny God, whom he considered immanent in nature. He may indeed have been "God intoxicated," as the poet-philosopher Novalis put it, or a pantheist, or something else. See Steven Nadler, *Spinoza's Heresy: Immortality and the Jewish Mind* (New York: Oxford University Press, 2001).

Elisha ben Abuyah, an early rabbi who "went sour." The Talmud offers three different accounts of what caused Elisha to break God's law and to keep on breaking it. In one, Elisha underwent a mystical experience in the course of which he mistook the angel Metatron for God's equal and ended up punished by permanent exclusion from Heaven.[2] In a second, Elisha could not reconcile why good people who follow God's laws nevertheless suffer in this world.[3] In the third, Elisha was influenced to break the law by the general Hellenistic culture of his time,[4] or perhaps by early Christianity.[5] On the basis of the report of Elisha's connection to Greek thought, modern writers set him up as the archetype of the Jew who tries to reconcile secular, Western knowledge with traditional Jewish thought. Elisha, whom Deutscher cited as a role model, has been the subject of plays and novels exploring this idea throughout the past century.[6]

According to all the Talmud's versions of Elisha's story, Elisha broke God's law. In all of them, Elisha was in some sense Godless, whether because of a philosophical or cultural objection to God or because mystical experience led him astray. The rabbis were so troubled by his conduct that the Talmud refuses to use his given name, instead referring to him euphemistically as *Aher*, meaning "Another."* Yet in the Talmud's stories, Elisha remains unquestionably a Jew. The Talmud records that Elisha never ceased to teach the Law, even though he refused to follow it. His most devoted student, Rabbi Meir, one of the greatest sages in the Talmud, continued to learn from him. And the Talmud itself preserves the record of Elisha's legal opinions notwithstanding his deviation.

---

* The Talmud explains the name as follows: Elisha, in a spiritual crisis after his mystical experience, "went and found a harlot" and proposed sex with her. Recognizing him, and knowing him as a prominent rabbi, she exclaimed, whether in reproach or astonishment or both, "Are you not Elisha ben Abuyah?" In response, Elisha uprooted a radish from a nearby patch and gave it to her. This was a radical act for a rabbi because it was the Sabbath, when the act of uprooting violated the biblical injunction to do no work. The woman concluded, "He is another" (BT Hagigah 15a). Often *Aher* is translated as "Other" or "the Other." But in ordinary English, the singular form of "other" is "another." That is both what the woman said of Elisha and also the natural translation of the word *Aher* when it is used to name him.

THE CULTURAL JEW AND
THE JEWISH QUESTION

If the Jew who has "transcended" Judaism into universalism is one sort of Godless Jew, another is the Godless Jew who identifies with the Jewish collective through culture and belonging but not religious belief. Classical secular Zionism, which I will discuss at length in part II, offered a nationalist version of this kind of Jewishness, in which Jewish faith had outlived its usefulness and the nation-state would offer a substitute. Some American Jews follow a modified version of this approach, expressing their Jewishness primarily or solely through support of Israel, especially but not only when it is embattled. In Israel today, Jewish religion flourishes, but there are also many self-described secular Israelis who embody some version of Jewishness-as-nationalism. For them, being Israeli, speaking Hebrew, and bearing Israeli culture is the way they manifest a Godless Jewishness, more or less as classical Zionism intended.

A different variant is cultural Jewishness without (Zionist) nationalism. In prewar Europe, before the Holocaust and the state of Israel, this notion often corresponded to an embrace of the Yiddish language as the unifying, quasi-secular connective tissue among European Jews. The General Jewish Labor Federation, or Bund (1897–1920), was a European socialist organization that wanted to unite Jews within a framework comparable to other ethnic or nationalist socialisms.[7] YIVO, the Yiddish Scientific Institute, founded in Vilna (Vilnius) in 1925, amassed a vast archive of pre-Holocaust Jewish life, using Yiddish as its organizing cultural principle. Much of the archive miraculously survived World War II, courtesy in part of Nazi plans to create a museum of the Jewish world they were destroying. The archive now exists in New York, where YIVO acts as its steward, and in a few eastern European libraries.

Today's Diaspora version of cultural Jewishness does not focus on language, but on a general identification with Jews and Jewish ways of being. The religious studies scholar Michael Alexander lightheartedly compares it to affiliating with and rooting for a sports team. The fan-Jew wants the best for other Jews, takes pride in their accomplishments, and suffers in their misfortunes. He cares, but, following the sports metaphor, his care may not be existential. He offers his children the opportunity to become fans too. But he isn't crushed if they become only fair-weather fans, or even if they don't end up with a strong team affiliation at all.

How distinctive is the idea of the Godless Jew? If I were writing a book about contemporary Christianity or contemporary Islam, it's unlikely that I would devote a whole chapter to whether these religious traditions could be sustained by self-conscious atheists. It's not that the question makes no sense at all. Christian and Islamic ideas can be secularized, the same way the ideas of just about any religious tradition can be translated into a secular idiom. In this way, it's possible to identify Christian and Islamic strands of thought among nonbelievers who are nonetheless influenced by these traditions. Similarly, Christianity and Islam are each embedded in culture, or rather many cultures. So we could identify a practice or a custom or a way of being as in some sense Christian or Islamic even when it manifests itself without professing the faith.

What makes Godless Jewishness special is the seriousness and resilience with which it has been pursued by so many Jews in the modern era. The historical cause is subtle, but I think it can be stated with just the right amount of oversimplification for our purposes.

Until the nineteenth century, very few Jews in the world enjoyed rights to civil and social equality with the Christian or Muslim majorities under whom they lived. Consequently, Jewishness evolved not only as a set of identifiable ritual practices and beliefs about God but also as a communal identity, one with concrete legal meaning attached. Before the emancipation of the Jews—a technical term meaning, roughly, the acquisition of civil rights—Jews' only realistic options were to remain within the Jewish community or to convert to Christianity or Islam, taking on board the costs of exclusion from families and the always uncertain reception of converts by the majority.[8]

After emancipation, however, Jews had more possibilities available to them, including the possibility of living outside the official Jewish community without embracing a different faith. Jews who chose this option often did not believe in God. Often they felt critical of the

Jewishness from which they emerged. Yet they did not feel entirely like comfortable members of the majority, because of their distinctive background, because of their unwillingness to embrace the majority faith, and because they often sought something more than the then-existing majority culture offered. That something could be a fully open and egalitarian society, or full political membership, or a richer inner life within the framework of secularism, or all of the above.

The predicament of the Jews after their emancipation came to be called "the Jewish question," in German, *Die Judenfrage*. It encompassed both the internal question of how Jews should live and the external, political question of how Jews should relate to and be treated by the nation-states in which they resided and of which they were now becoming citizens. If the Jews were no longer defined as a legal community, should they become public citizens who retained a private Jewish religion? Should they give up Yiddish, their distinctive internal language? Was there a way to maintain cultural difference while still participating as citizens? Should Jews cease to be unique in any way at all, and disappear into the general culture of their countries? Would they truly be accepted as citizens of European nation-states, even if they did? Should they embrace a transnational, cosmopolitan identity? Both internally and externally, these questions added up to a perceived crisis, one that demanded answers from Jews and non-Jews alike.*

THE GOAT JEWISH ATHEIST

The most obvious form of Godless Jewishness to emerge from nineteenth-century Europe was Zionism. (Don't worry, you're almost there.) Zionism presented itself as a definitive answer to the Jewish question. It posited that without God, the Jews should not define themselves as a religious community. They should instead define themselves as a nation, a term that had a specific meaning at that time and place. A nation was a group of people who were racially related (the term "race" was widely

---

* The most horrifying answer was, of course, the Nazis': the murder of the Jews as the "final solution to the Jewish question," *die Endlösung der Judenfrage*.

used to describe Jews at the time, including by Jews); shared a language, a culture, and a history; and who, ordinarily, lived in some proximity to each other in a historically defined homeland. From this definition it followed that the Jews must have their own political independence in their own geographical space, whether in the historical land of Israel or somewhere else. The Zionists' efforts to prove the Jews were in fact a nation and to find and win them a homeland were, in the deepest sense, a self-conscious manifestation of being Jewish without God.

Zionism, however, was only one kind of Godless Jewishness, and not even the most consequential in world-historical terms. That distinction goes to Marxism, a grand theory and even grander political movement imagined by a Godless Jew who wanted to supplant and replace Jewishness itself and who would have flatly rejected the notion that his worldview was a manifestation of being Jewish. Other influential modes of Godless Jewishness include Freudian psychology, the forerunner of most of our contemporary ideas about trauma, sex, and the unconscious; Franz Boas's cultural relativism; Ayn Rand's libertarian perfectionism; and, arguably, liberal humanist secularism, which can't be identified with any single figure but represents a commonly held worldview in the United States that is inflected by Godless Jewish beliefs, values, and cultural ideas.

Before discussing some of these different ways of being Jewish without God, I want to be clear about what I'm *not* doing. This isn't an effort to claim that Marxism or Freudianism or secular humanism are "really" Jewish in some essential way, either as a good thing, the way proud Jews have sometimes claimed, or as a bad thing, the way antisemites have. They aren't. For one thing, none of these ideologies thinks of itself as particularly Jewish. To the contrary, all would deny the characterization.* Scientific movements want to be scientific, not Jewish. Political move-

---

* Consider this passage, in which the historian Yosef Hayim Yerushalmi imagines saying to Freud, "I think you believed that just as you are a godless Jew, psychoanalysis is a godless Judaism. But I don't think you intended us to know this." Yerushalmi, *Freud's Moses: Judaism Terminable and Interminable* (New Haven: Yale University Press, 1991), 99. Cf. Gila Ashtor, *Exigent Psychoanalysis: The Interventions of Jean Laplanche* (New York: Routledge, 2022), 23–29. Special thanks to Farrah Khaleghi Aizenman for sending me Ashtor's book.

ments that consider all humans to be the same want to avoid or overcome specificity, not reinscribe it. And in characterizing a movement or set of ideas, it's important to take seriously what it thinks of itself.

For another thing, the notion that some movement or idea is "essentially" or "really" Jewish is so difficult to define it might as well be meaningless. At the very least, an argument about whether something is or isn't Jewish would need to proceed on the grounds of some working definition of what counts as meeting the category. And we manifestly don't have a good working definition of what makes something Jewish, which is part of the reason I'm writing this chapter.

So what I'm setting out to do is not to reduce these ideas and movements to Godless Jewishness. Rather, I want to argue that for many Jews, past and present, the development and exploration of Marxism, Freudianism, secular humanism, and so forth *constitutes the full manifestation* of their Godless Jewishness. They became and remained Marxists, for example, *as Jews*. And they lived and played out their Jewishness through Marxism. The intellectual and emotional and personal energies they put into their movements came from the place of their Jewishness, and fulfilled it. Put another way, they in particular would not have believed and acted and lived as they did unless they were Jews—Godless Jews. Their struggle to make sense of being a Godless Jew led them to their self-expression.

Crucially, I am also arguing that for these Godless Jews, their expression of their situation through their ideas and actions was itself meaningfully and distinctively Jewish. In other words, I need to be able to point to specifically Jewish or Jewish-seeming features of what they thought and what they did. It's not enough just to say that they were Jews and that, as a result, everything in their lives was Jewishly inflected. At the 1972 Munich Olympics, the swimmer Mark Spitz won seven gold medals. Before Michael Phelps, he was generally thought to be the greatest American swimmer of all time. Spitz is Jewish. He figured in the (slim) volumes about the exploits of great Jewish athletes that I eagerly consumed as a child.* But so far as I can tell, his athletic success

---

* Their names—Hank Greenberg, Sandy Koufax, Sid Luckman, Dolph Schayes, even Daniel Mendoza—flood me with nostalgia for a youth spent playing ball and reading

was not a manifestation of his Jewishness, Godless or otherwise. If a biographer were to argue that Spitz was motivated to succeed because he was trying to overcome the burden of being Jewish, or if he was motivated to make Jews proud of him, that wouldn't count. Swimming faster than anyone else on earth is an extraordinary accomplishment, but there is nothing distinctly or meaningfully Jewish about it.

I would say the same thing about Albert Einstein. Einstein was a Jew, and antisemites around Hitler would go on to claim that the theory of relativity was somehow Jewish. (Exactly how is a bit difficult to explain. But thank God for the idiocy of the critique, which arguably contributed to the Nazi regime's failure to develop a nuclear weapon.) Yet a mathematically consistent, empirically verifiable set of scientific claims about the nature of the universe is not and cannot be described as identifiably Jewish. Certainly Maimonides taught that knowledge of nature was part of the divine command to know God. And a disproportionate number of important scientists were of European Jewish origin in the extraordinary period that lasted from Jewish emancipation almost to the present. No doubt their Jewish backgrounds helped encourage them to study the sciences and theorize about nature. But neither the scientific method nor the content of scientific discoveries can plausibly be characterized as Jewish.

In contrast, consider Karl Marx, his ideas, and the world-historical communist movements those ideas spawned. Marx was descended from rabbis on both sides of his family. His parents had been baptized as Christians before his birth, and he was baptized a Lutheran at age six. In his work, he certainly did not set out to self-express Godless Jewishness. He set out to develop a scientific theory of history, one that would account for the known past and also specify universal historical laws, like the laws of physics.

Unfortunately for Marx and Marxists, it turns out that history is not like physics (or even like biology). Because of the variability of human

---

books. The collections can tell us much about American Jewish cultural identity and attempts to construct masculinity within it, but next to nothing about meaningful Jewishness or, for that matter, sports.

affairs, strict scientific laws cannot be derived to describe and predict historical events. Yet it is precisely the fact that scientific Marxism does not correspond to scientific fact that enables us to identify how Marxism came to manifest Godless Jewishness for some of its practitioners, Marx included.

What Marx accomplished, at least for himself, was a form of what I would call *faith by negation*. Marx was, famously, an atheist. He described religion as the opiate of the masses. He was committed to a view known as historical materialism. According to this view, the laws of history may be deduced and discovered not in relation to the spirit or ideals of the times, as Hegel had argued, but in the concrete, material substances of history: technologies, means of production, and the social classes of people who are acted upon by these forces. Historical materialism can be understood as part of a conscious effort to take God out of the equation of the Marxist worldview. Yet at the same time, historical materialism intentionally substituted something for Hegel's spiritual force, namely the material force of class. Instead of a God or gods or ideals shaping the course of history, the historical laws of class do so. For Marx, God is negated and replaced by historical materialism. The Law of God is replaced by the Law of History.

The law of history for Marx is a law of class conflict: dialectical materialism, which means the constant, repeated struggle of different classes against one another to produce new historical outcomes. And, crucially, the law of history has a direction. It points to an end stage, the stage of history in which the rule of the proletariat will be accomplished, the state will wither away, and humankind will achieve a final, secular salvation. That salvation consists in a utopian society in which all people contribute work according to their abilities while still enjoying the leisure to think, paint, write, sing, dance, or engage in whatever productive pursuits make their lives meaningful. This ultimate stage of history corresponds to what most forms of Jewish thought consider the messianic age.

Seen in these terms, Marxism negates Jewish faith by reiterating it. The God who makes himself known through the Law is denied but replaced by historical laws that are equally universal and, in a sense, even more deterministic.* The cycles of reward and punishment, exile and redemption reflecting the divine will are negated and replaced by historical processes determined and described by dialectical materialism. The messianic end stage is negated and replaced by the communist ideal.

The extraordinary neatness of the correspondence is enough to depict Marxism as a form of Jewish faith by negation in which the divine is displaced by the revolution of the proletariat. But that is not all. For Marx and for many Jewish Marxists, Marxism also answered the Jewish question. In fact, Marx wrote a notorious essay, "On the Jewish Question," which explained what should happen to the Jews who were being emancipated and becoming citizens. Marx first defined Jews not in terms of their spiritual beliefs (as what Marx called "Sabbath Jews") but instead in material terms. Seen materially, he argued, the "secular basis" of Judaism was "practical need, self-interest." By this analysis, Marx defined the Jew as "the man of money"—effectively, the bourgeois merchant whose existence was based upon economic exchange. Marx noted that once Jewishness was defined in this way, it was no longer limited to Jews. Every Christian engaged in bourgeois economic exchange had become a Jew. European bourgeois society was therefore, in a deep sense, Jewish.

To Marx, the bourgeoisie was the social class that must be displaced by revolution of the proletariat. By defeating the bourgeoisie, the revolution would solve the Jewish question: there would be no more Jews, to the extent that Jewishness was defined materially. Marxism therefore addressed the question of what should happen to the Jews as a people by concluding that the Jews, understood materially, represented a stage in the material dialectic that would be transcended, or, in Marx's terrifying formulation, "euthanized."

You can see why critics have often depicted Marx as a Jewish anti-

---

* There is a large scholarly literature about how Jews think about history, much of it in conversation with the scholar Yosef Hayim Yerushalmi's important book *Zakhor: Jewish History and Jewish Memory* (Seattle: University of Washington Press, 1982), which argued for an ahistorical or even antihistorical consciousness in traditional Jewish writing and thought. I am not, in this book, directly addressing this important topic, except to note that I am trying to provide historical context and trace possible future historical directions in order to illuminate the possible paths available to Jews today.

semite. Both the identification of Jews with money and the prediction that in a postrevolutionary, quasi-messianic end stage there would be no Jews resonated with strands of classic Christian antisemitism. At the same time, Marx's theory of the Jews reveals that, as a Jew, Marx was seeking to work out his role in history and the role of others like him. By becoming the prophet of a communist revolution, Marx was identifying for himself a role that enabled him to step outside the particular Jewishness of his class position.*

Many Jews followed Marx. From the start, Jewish intellectuals were overrepresented in the leadership of European communist revolutionary circles. Those who took Marx most seriously rejected Jewish religion as a delusion and also rejected Zionism as a bourgeois nationalism. A substantial number of Zionists managed to remain socialists, using the same tools that many other socialists used to reconcile their socialism with the nation-state. That is why the early state of Israel had so many socialist features. A small number of Zionists were simultaneously committed Marxist communists, a self-contradictory enterprise that demanded an impressive degree of Talmudic reconciliation of opposites. The kibbutz movement, which founded collective agricultural settlements in Palestine, had socialist origins, and some of its settlements were overtly Marxist-communist. The kibbutz is the most striking example of the interplay between the Marxist way of working out Jewishness and the Zionist way: its members aspired to de-Judaize money and demonetize Jewishness by returning to the land and by returning to the Land.[9]

When the Bolshevik revolution took place in Russia, Jews were again heavily overrepresented within its leadership. It took a generation for Stalin to purge the communist leadership of its Jewish overrepresentation. Yet even as that occurred, many Jews elsewhere in the world continued to adhere to Marxism. (Others, of course, became anti-Marxist critics.)

This matters because, for perhaps a century, Marxism was a powerful

---

* Maybe, on a Marxian analysis, it was precisely Marx's Jewish origins as a product of the bourgeois, money-obsessed class that enabled him to discover the theory of history that identified the material as the true motivating force of history.

set of beliefs and practices that could fairly be considered a central mode of Godless Jewishness. Not all Marxists were expressing Jewishness, of course. There were plenty of non-Jewish Marxists, and perhaps some Jews for whom Jewishness played no role, conscious or unconscious, in their espousal of Marxism. But for many Jews, Marxism marked their way of being Jewish. Today, the mode of Godless Jewishness that is most prevalent is not Marxism but a type of liberalism: secular humanism, which can come alongside patriotism, as it does for many Jews in the United States, or take a more cosmopolitan, antinationalist form, mostly found among Jewish intellectuals in the academy.

BAGELS, LOX, AND SECULAR HUMANISM

Secular humanism today functions more as a tacit worldview than as a formal system.* Nevertheless, it has substantive content. The secular part of secular humanism refers to a this-worldly orientation, one that either rejects religion or, more gently, assigns religion to the private sphere rather than the public sphere. The humanist part of secular humanism is meant to be universalizing, applying to all humans, not just some.

The claim that secular humanism is in some way distinctively Jewish is usually made by its critics, not by sympathizers like me. The criticism makes sense, because secular humanism is designed, broadly speaking, to enable its adherents to be free of religious particularism. To tell secular humanists that there is something Jewish about their point of view is, in a sense, to deny their very objectives.

The point I'm making, however, is similar to the one I just made about Marxism and Jewishness: secular humanism need not be Jewish in any inherent sense, but it can represent a way for Jews to express their own Jewishness. It functions as a worldview that can replace or supplant religious Jewish particularism. And it offers an answer to the old Jewish

---

* Felix Adler (1851–1933), the founder of the Ethical Culture movement, was the son of the German-trained rabbi of the flagship New York Reform Jewish congregation, Temple Emanu-El of Fifth Avenue. His clear objective was to (further) universalize and transcend Reform Judaism. The Ethical Culture Fieldston School still bears the name of the movement and there still exists a New York Society for Ethical Culture.

question, even though the question has been updated to contemporary circumstances in liberal democracies.

The way secular humanism can stand in for Jewishness is by offering a stance on morality, community, and politics. This is a stance particularly fitted to the self-perception of Jews who want to be full members of the broader political community and who want to be free of the insistence, Jewish and otherwise, that they are somehow different or other. It is particularly fitted for a paradoxical reason: it claims universality while, in practice, reflecting particularity.

Here's what I mean. According to most forms of secular humanism, religious beliefs and affiliations are or should be irrelevant to membership in the political community. It follows that people who were born Jewish are not merely entitled to be full members but actually *are* full and equal members. They can, according to this logic, leave their Jewishness behind them. Yet in practice, the only time anyone needs to insist on this secular humanist point of view is when it is being questioned by others who want to define political membership by religious belief or identity. Often the secular humanists are in a minority. Often they are embattled. As a result, people who define themselves as secular humanists turn out, despite themselves, to be members of a distinctive community—a community of secular humanists.

In this way, the secular humanists can end up re-creating some of the communal, identitarian features of Jewishness, even while denying that they are doing so. They may be seen as—and may actually be—a group of Jews insisting that their stance has nothing to do with being Jewish precisely because religion and communal identity shouldn't matter for the task at hand. Meanwhile, it could be argued that in some unacknowledged way, they are living out their Jewishness precisely through denying its relevance.

This phenomenon can be observed practically when secular humanists organize themselves for action, or sometimes when they are just speaking among themselves. You might glimpse it in the American Civil Liberties Union or the boards of trustees of major American museums and symphony orchestras and ballets and (some) universities. Jews who participate in these institutions are often aspiring to universality, but implicitly or unconsciously, they may *also* be having an experience of particularity. An old Jewish joke captures something of this experience. The setting is an international conference of people who speak Esperanto, the internationalist language dreamed up in 1887 by a Polish-Jewish ophthalmologist named L. L. Zamenhof. The signs announcing the talks are in Esperanto. The lunch menu is in Esperanto. All the lectures are given in Esperanto, as are the formal responses and the panels. But the moment the participants leave the conference room and go out into the hall, they greet each other with, "Nu? Vos macht du, Yid?" the universal Yiddish version of, "Hey dude, how've you been?"

The joke is funny—or rather was funny once, to those who understood it—on multiple levels. The first, of course, is that so many advocates of Esperanto were Jews. Their drive for a universal, cosmopolitan language was therefore inspired by their dream of universal belonging. If nationalism posited that each nation had its own language, Esperanto responded by proposing the value of getting beyond linguistic particularity. For these Jews, by implication, embracing Esperanto was both a way of denying their Jewishness and a way of working it out. A further level of humor is that although Esperanto was designed to be an international language to be spoken by everybody, it amounted in practice to a replacement of Yiddish, which was already an international language, albeit spoken only by Jews. The joke here is that Zamenhof just reinvented Yiddish. The participants at the Esperanto conference are therefore every bit as Jewish as they ever were.

Jewish secular humanists have been more successful in advocating for their point of view than were the Esperantists. At the same time, the United States has never embraced secular humanism as its formal or informal norm, despite efforts by secular humanists to convince the Supreme Court to interpret the establishment clause of the U.S. Constitution to mandate that any law without a secular purpose or secular effects be held unconstitutional.[10]

The upshot is that a distinctively American Jewish secular humanism has remained salient. Often it takes the form of deep patriotism. Justice Felix Frankfurter, who immigrated to the United States from Austria as a boy and gave up Jewish orthodoxy in college, liked to say that for him, Americanism had replaced Judaism. The Constitution was his holy scripture. In one of his most famous Supreme Court opinions—a dissent—he wrote, "As judges we are neither Jew nor Gentile, neither Catholic nor agnostic. We owe equal attachment to the Constitution and are equally bound by our judicial obligations whether we derive our citizenship from the earliest or the latest immigrants to these shores." This formulation captured the intensity of Frankfurter's Americanism. At the same time, however, Frankfurter was speaking as a Jew even while he insisted that as an American judge he must not speak as a Jew. He began the very same opinion by writing: "One who belongs to the most vilified and persecuted minority in history is not likely to be insensible to the freedoms guaranteed by our Constitution."[11] Today, Jewish neoconservatives, neoliberals, and even (as in the case of Bernie Sanders) democratic socialists all provide examples of secular humanist American patriotism.

Another variant on American Jewish secular humanism can be so cosmopolitan as to be, arguably, antipatriotic. The central idea here is that true humanists ought to be so devoid of particularist attachments that they consider themselves citizens of the world, not committed to the goal of advancing the interests of a particular country like the United States ahead of others. This cosmopolitanism can be understood as a logical extension of a humanism designed to render Jews the same as all other people, regardless of group origin. If Jews are the same as other Americans because all are human, why should not Americans be the same as people from everywhere else on earth?

Indeed, this logic can be extended beyond humans to all sentient beings. The philosopher Peter Singer was born in Australia to Jewish parents. Three of his grandparents died in the Holocaust. In his now-classic book *Animal Liberation* (1975), Singer argued that the distinction between human and nonhuman animals is morally arbitrary and that the suffering of nonhuman animals should be weighed heavily in our moral calculus. Singer is an example of a super-cosmopolitan. His philosophy seeks to transcend the very notion of "humanism" as insufficiently universal, indeed as species-ist. He is also one of the world's most practically influential living philosophers, credited with inspiring the animal rights movement and effective altruism.

Secular humanism and cosmopolitanism address the contemporary version of the Jewish question by making it clear that Jewishness, whatever it is and however it may be defined, should be irrelevant to public affairs. In their hardest forms, secular humanism and cosmopolitanism would go so far as to say that Jewishness is an active impediment to full moral human expression. Softer forms—such as what is sometimes called "rooted cosmopolitanism"—would find it perfectly acceptable for individual Jews to hold religious beliefs in their private capacity or affiliate privately with Jewish communal organizations so long as these beliefs and affiliations did not interfere with their full public embrace of human values. These forms, too, offer a solution to a contemporary version of the Jewish question, one appropriate to the liberal state. Jews may be full, loyal citizens of their countries. They may at the same time experience a sense of connection and loyalty to the Jewish community, however they define it, including to Israel. These commitments are mutually compatible. Anyone who criticizes them as incompatible is wrong—and maybe antisemitic, whether the criticism comes from the left or the right.

The phrase "bagels-and-lox Jews" is often used critically to describe Jews who have little or no connection to specifically Jewish belief or practice or community but who maintain a vestigial cultural connection to Jewish ethnicity, in this case via foodways. Strictly speaking, this identity, if it were real, would belong to our upcoming conversation about Jewish peoplehood. In practice, I want to suggest here, bagels-and-lox Jews are mostly secular humanists in belief and affiliation. Instead of an absence of Jewishness in their moral, political, and communal commitments, there is a *displaced* Jewishness that is itself powerfully, distinctively Jewish.

THE LIMITS OF REASON

The obvious benefit of Godless Jewishness is to provide space for Jews to engage the universe as Jews even when they find they cannot embrace any conception of God. The drawback is that Godlessness can harden into a dogma of its own, a dogma of atheism that, unchecked, can approach the fundamentalism of theistic belief. This dogma, taken to its logical extreme, may cause Godless Jews to refuse the content of their own distinctively Jewish experience.

Maimonides anticipated a version of this dogmatic risk, and he did so, intriguingly, through the figure of Elisha ben Abuyah, the Talmud's Godless Jew. In his *Guide*, Maimonides invoked Elisha to warn the reader not to make the philosophical errors of believing that there exists demonstrative proof for that which cannot be proven, or thinking that something that cannot be proven therefore is necessarily untrue. If you can avoid attempting to conceptualize things that are beyond your conception, Maimonides says, then you will have achieved the highest available degree of human perfection. You will be like Rabbi Akiba, who shared Elisha's mystical experience with him but, unlike Elisha, emerged from it unscathed.

If, however, you exceed the bounds of your cognitive capacities and deny the truth of things that are unprovable or unlikely, says Maimonides, "you will come to be Elisha/Another":

> Not only will you not be perfect. You will be more lacking than the most lacking. You will come under the domination of the imaginary and you will tend toward imperfections and repugnant and bad traits that impede the intellect and dim its light.[12]

Maimonides is saying that Elisha was an intellectual Icarus. Entranced by the exercise of his intellect, he made the mistake of believing that what could not be proven must therefore not be true. There is nothing wrong with attempting to understand the world through reason, according to Maimonides. The trouble arises when you get things wrong because you do not recognize the limits of your human cognition. Some things cannot be proven by logic or understood fully by humans. Or as Hamlet puts it, there are more things in heaven and earth than are dreamed of in our philosophy.

There are, then, limits to what we know and what we can know. Accepting those limits is the key to avoiding fateful error. We must learn to be satisfied with what we are able to achieve. A Godless Jew who does not believe in God need not deny God in any possible form. Put a little differently, as Jews—as humans—we must learn to live with the impossibility of certainty. We strive to know and to understand. We should not, necessarily, expect to arrive at the desired destination.

Let me conclude by emphasizing once again that by identifying secular humanism, cosmopolitanism, and atheism as ways for Jews to live Jewishly without God, I am not setting out to discredit or disqualify these approaches. To the contrary. In keeping with my suggestion that we avoid labeling others as bad Jews, I am arguing that even those Jews who shape their Jewish identities around denial of the relevance of Jewishness are living meaningful Jewish lives. For me, Maimonides's Elisha errs only in his certainty, not in his Godlessness. I am not arguing, either, that you can't escape Jewishness. You can, at least sometimes, as I will suggest in part III.

What I'm saying is that our conception of what counts as a meaningfully Jewish life needs to be broadened and strengthened. We need to see the beauty in the many forms of Jewish thinking and believing, including Jewish displacement and disbelief. Even conscious rejection of Jewishness may be meaningfully Jewish. The test is whether, in shaping your worldview, you are struggling with God, the God of Israel. In the next chapter, the last of this part of the book, I will try to explain what I mean.

I:5

THE STRUGGLE

Is there a unifying Jewish theological worldview, one broad enough to include God as understood by Jewish Traditionalists, Progressives, and Evolutionists, and also the possibility that there is no God? I think the answer is yes. I want to suggest it is possible to characterize Jewishness in the way the Bible explains the meaning of the name *Israel*: to strive, struggle, and contend with God. The nature of the striving-struggling-contending differs for each form of Jewishness, as it does for each Jew. But anyone who embraces the self-definition of belonging to the people of Israel, in whatever way, will find something powerful and familiar and meaning-making in the process.

This Jewishness may have much in common with other faith traditions, but it is nevertheless distinct from them and wholly (holy) its own. It can involve accepting divine authority, but it is not the submission of Islam. It can involve acts of perfect faith, but it is not the same as the Christian acceptance of God and the divinity of Christ. It can involve mystical union with the divine, but it is not the same as the transcendence of Buddhism. It can involve radical skepticism or denial of God, but it is not the same as the familiar forms of agnosticism or atheism.*

---

* I am acutely aware here of the influence of my close and deeply missed friend Shahab Ahmed (1966–2015). His masterwork, *What Is Islam: The Importance of Being Islamic*

Here I want to sketch this inclusive vision of Jewish experience briefly and suggestively. To do so, I will draw on that most distinctive of Jewish interpretive methodologies: *midrash*, a creative and open-ended way of giving meaning to the Bible—and the world.

To elucidate what unites very different Jewish ways of encountering God and the world, consider the enigmatic and beautiful story of Jacob's nighttime struggle with a being who might be a man, an angel, a god, and/or God. This is the passage in the Bible where the word "Israel" is first introduced and its meaning explained. (It is also the same story that Rabbi Steven Greenberg used to express his own struggles with God and sexuality.)

The explanation, as we shall see, uses a Hebrew verb, *sarah*, which only occurs in the Bible in the context of Jacob's encounter story.

Here is Genesis 32:25–31:

> Jacob remained alone. A man wrestled with him until the
>   break of dawn.
> He saw he could not prevail against him. He touched the
>   hollow of his thigh. The hollow of Jacob's thigh was injured
>   in his wrestling with him.
> He said, "Let me go, for the dawn has broken." He said, "I
>   shall not let you go unless you have blessed me."
> He said, "What is your name?"
> He said, "Jacob."
> He said, "Jacob shall no longer be said to be your name, rather
>   Yisra'el, for you have striven with Elohim and with men
>   and have prevailed."
> Jacob said, "Tell me your name."

(Princeton, NJ: Princeton University Press, 2016), is a 609-page exploration of what makes Islam *Islam*. Ultimately, Shahab answered his grand question with a capacious hermeneutical engagement around what he called the Pre-Text, Text, and Con-Text of the Qur'an (301–404). To Shahab, this engagement made Islam unique and distinctive, much more than just a religion or a culture or a civilization or even a discursive tradition. My (much shorter) attempt to make sense of Jewishness does not make the same claim to uniqueness. It does borrow in some ways from Shahab's idea of hermeneutic engagement, but it is more an account of *experience* than of interpretation.

He said, "Why do you ask for my name?" He blessed him there.
Jacob called the name of the place Peni'el, "Because I saw God
face to face and my soul was delivered."

Before offering an explanation and explication, let me add one more
text, from the book of Hosea, 12:4–5. This is the only other instance in
the Hebrew Bible where this episode is mentioned and the only other
place where the Bible uses the verb to strive, *sarah*. Speaking of Jacob,
the prophet says, in poetic form:

In the womb he grabbed his brother's heel;
By his strength he strove with Elohim.
He strove with an angel and prevailed;
He wept and begged him.
He found him in Bethel;
There he speaks to us.

Nearly everything about the material in these two crucial passages
is puzzling. With whom did Jacob wrestle? The Genesis passage calls
Jacob's antagonist "a man." But he has no name himself, and he has the
power to confer a name on Jacob. That makes him sound like an angel.
And indeed, Hosea says that Jacob strove with an angel.

Yet when the time comes to give Jacob his blessing, the "man" tells
him that he, Jacob, has striven with Elohim as well as with men. Hosea echoes this formulation. Elohim is itself an extraordinarily tricky
biblical word. It is one of several proper names of God. Sometimes it
means "gods," plural (as in, "on all of the gods of Egypt I shall perform
wonders").* Does the biblical text mean that Jacob has striven with gods,
plural, as he has with men, plural? Does it mean that he has striven with
a god named Elohim? In the Hebrew Bible, El and Elohim can both be
names of God. The name Israel means, according to the text, "he strives
with El." Jacob gives the place the name Peni'el, roughly, "the face of El."
Does this mean that Jacob has striven with the one true God, Elohim?

---

* *Elohim* has other biblical meanings too. Sometimes it means "human judges."

Has he seen God face-to-face, as only Moses is otherwise said to have done in the Bible?

I don't propose to answer any of these challenging questions adequately. I want to focus, instead, on what it might mean to strive with God. It is from there that I seek to derive a picture of Jewish experience that might account for its extraordinary multiplicity while providing some degree of unification.

What does the verb *sarah* mean? Because it occurs in the Bible only in the two places I've mentioned, we might want to look at related terms. In biblical Hebrew, *sar* means an officer or someone who rules. The name Sarah is the feminine form of that same word. Ordinarily, then, we might think that to engage in the act captured by the verb *sarah* would mean to achieve mastery or rulership. The King James Version of the Bible translates our verse: "He said, Thy name shall be called no more Jacob, but Israel: for as a prince hast thou power with God and with men, and hast prevailed." Taken a bit more literally, the meaning would be that Jacob rules over gods (or God) and men.

To deepen this possible interpretation, consider the Hebrew names that have the form of an imperfect verb followed by El. These ordinarily mean that El does or has done something. Yishma'el (Ishmael), for example, means "God hears." Were it not for the story, we would therefore think that the name Yisra'el meant something like "El rules," or "El rules as prince." The narrative, however, wants Jacob to be the subject of the verb. So it might well follow that according to the narrative, the verse means to tell Jacob that he rules over El. He has after all, "prevailed" in the conflict.

The difficulty with this interpretation arises because to us, it seems like an anomaly or an impossibility for Jacob, a man, to rule over God. This leads us to interpret Yisra'el as striving or struggling or contending *with* God, not, as if it were possible, ruling *over* God. Even Hosea seems to share this concern. He says that Jacob "strove" with Elohim, but he restricts the conclusion that Jacob "prevailed" to the line where he says that Jacob strove with an angel. Even if Genesis says that Jacob strove with Elohim and prevailed, Hosea apparently cannot bring himself to say precisely that.

This impulse tells you a lot about Jewish perspectives on God. Whatever the ancient meaning of the biblical verse, for later Jews at least, it is unthinkable that a human could prevail over God. God is far too great for that to be contemplated. Yet God *is* a being with whom it is possible nevertheless to strive, to struggle, to contend.

For Traditionalists, God is all-powerful, all-knowing, and all-authoritative. For the people of Israel to strive with God, then, cannot mean, or must not mean, struggle with God's power or authority. Instead, for Traditionalists, striving with God takes two other forms.

The first is the human struggle to accept the yoke of God's authority in the face of our limitations and our incomprehension of God's thoughts and ways. To struggle with God in this Traditionalist sense is to force oneself willfully to accept the judgment of Heaven, notwithstanding the impulse to question it. Almost no one in the entirety of the classical rabbinic tradition has suggested that it is easy—or even easeful—to accept divine authority, perform God's commandments, and come to terms with the way God's world appears to us to operate.

The most familiar Traditionalist manifestation of this struggle is associated with the Hasidic masters, who, in the tradition of Abraham demanding that God not destroy the cities of Sodom and Gomorrah, challenge God's justice. There is no doubt that ultimately they will acknowledge the finality and justice of the divine decree. The struggle comes from their effort to demand that God manifest mercy alongside judgment.

The second way in which Traditionalists can be said to strive with God is in the contentious effort to understand God's Law. This is not so much struggling against God as it is struggling *alongside* God, striving and contending to comprehend the Law. From the Talmud until today, the main mode of studying and learning the Law is through argument and debate. To call the debate contentious is to understate the case considerably. The study of Torah can be likened to a war—a war of ideas, but a war nonetheless. "The zealotry of scribes" (*kin'at soferim*) is a rabbinic trope that describes the intense and intensely felt stance of oppositionality that Torah scholars constantly occupy. Even the most irenic great scholar of the Talmud lives and breathes disagreement, dissension, and dissensus. The words of God, says Jeremiah, are "as a hammer that fragments a rock."[1] The fragments, say the rabbis, are the multiplicity of Torah opinions: "Just as this hammer produces several sparks, a Bible verse may have several meanings."[2]

Much of the contentious nature of Jewish collective life—among, it seems, all Jews, regardless of whether they study the Talmud directly or not—is influenced by the multiplicity of sparks produced by the tradition of Talmudic debate. Contending alongside God, Jews contend with one another. To outsiders, this contentiousness can look fearsome (which it is) and off-putting (which, to be honest, it sometimes is too). Yet in its essence, the unceasing argument among Jews is a reflection of divine worship, channeled through the human activity and obligation of studying God's word to ascertain its best meaning, or meanings. If Jewishness is creative and productive, its creativity and productivity can be traced to this contentious mode of being-by-interpreting. Hence the paradox that Traditionalists, who so value authority and communal cohesion, communicate invariably in terms of (holy) conflict.

For Jewish Progressives, striving or struggling or contending with God partly takes the form of actively reviewing and revisiting God's laws and God's words with an eye to extracting moral truth from them. If Traditionalist Jews make the tradition alongside God by reasoning their way through the logic of the Law, Progressive Jews make their Judaism alongside God by determining which of its teachings to keep as essential and eternal and which to reject as the product of past human limitations. To Progressives, the word of God as passed to Moses and the elders and the rabbis is in need of editing and renewal in the light of morality as we are given to realize and apprehend it over time.

There is another sense in which Progressive Judaism counts as a struggle alongside God. There need be no struggle, for Progressives, about God's goodness or morality, or even about God's core message. God embodies love and social justice, as we understand those evolving concepts. The struggle alongside the God of justice comes in applying unfolding moral truths to the world. God too is struggling, say some Progressive theologians, to effectuate justice in the world. The original Kabbalistic conception of *tikkun 'olam*, repair of the world, depended on the human duty to repair the fabric of the Godhead by fulfilling the commandments with proper mystical intentions. Progressive *tikkun 'olam* calls for human struggle to restore the world to justice through good deeds.

The Evolutionist struggle with God is perhaps even more dramatic than the struggle of Traditionalists or Progressives, incorporating as it does aspects of both approaches. Evolutionist Jews in principle accept God's authority and joyfully embrace the contention of Talmudic reasoning. But they are committed to doing so at the same time as they seek to understand what morality requires, so as to evolve the law in that direction. Consequently, Evolutionists find themselves struggling in both directions. They struggle to ascertain what morality demands, influenced as they are by the weight of the tradition. And they struggle to interpret the Law in good faith, even as they know what they want the Law to mean. No wonder their experience feels so much like a constant struggle to make meaning out of lived tradition that accords with contemporary moral intuition.

The extremity of the struggle is, however, also what makes Jewish Evolutionists so nobly archetypal as struggling Jews. The Talmudic imperative to second-guess every known truth, to ask "why" in the face of every jot and tittle of the Law, is made manifest in their daily efforts. Meanwhile, the Jewish need to do more than simply obey—to understand why one is obeying and what applied version of the law deserves obedience—is itself a recipe for near-permanent internal struggle.

For Jewish mystics, of whatever Jewish stripe, striving with God means striving for union with the divine order, and hence with both God and the universe. In wrestling with God, Jacob simultaneously embraces God. (I will return to this loving embrace at the end of part III.) The physical-metaphysical joining of bodies stands for the possibility of *unio mystica*, the conjunction of the human soul with the divine Soul that is sought by mystics of many traditions. This union would be a union beyond contention.

Achieving it, however, is not without effort. To the contrary. Kabbalah teaches spiritual exercises associated with knowing God, with shaping God, and with developing the practical mystical skills to attain union with God. Mystical union is figured, in much Kabbalah, as the joinder of the "feminine" and "masculine" elements of the Godhead into a transcendent union that is far beyond and above sex or gender. Jacob and the man and the angel and the gods and God become, and are, one. Jacob says that he has seen Elohim face-to-face. For the Kabbalists, that is the highest possible expression of mystical union. And it is achieved through the mystical mechanism of striving.

Godless Jews and cultural Jews and secular Zionists, in all their multifarious manifestations, are struggling with God too, whether they like it or not. To deny God is to wrestle with him, always. To deny God while still belonging to a Jewish people that classically self-defined in relation to God is a struggle of a still taller order.

The effort of Godless Jews to remain Jews is perhaps the most Jewish struggle of all. What greater mark of respect for God could there be than continuing to struggle with that God once one is utterly convinced of God's nonexistence? What covenant could be more honored than one that continues to carry weight for people who are certain that, on the other side of that covenant, there is no divine partner? To secularize a nonexistent God and a self-fashioned covenant is to take on a struggle so hard and so basic that the effort can only be marveled at in wonderment, if not always in admiration. If, in certain moments, some Godless Jews have imagined they have prevailed over the deity, the challenges they face in explaining what Jewishness still means to them can reveal that the nonexistent God they refuse to worship is looming close, undefeated.

In biblical narrative and poetry, Jacob "prevails." But does he? The Hebrew word here is *yakhol*, which can mean "to prevail" but ordinarily means to be able to do something. In the theological picture I am painting, it is not that Jacob prevails in his struggle. Jews can never prevail in their struggle alongside the divine, or against God—not while remaining Jews. In place of "prevail," read, rather, "to be able." Israel is the people who strive with the divine—*and are able.*

The capacity *to strive with God and be able* is neither more nor less than the ability to ask again and afresh the questions that have animated Jewish life for millennia, as well as new ones that are being added every day. So long as Jewish people undertake their efforts to make meaning through the rubrics of Jewish thought and life and practice, that striving will never be done. However Jewish beliefs about God continue to develop, however the actually existing state of Israel continues or does not continue to shape the major trends in Jewish belief, however Jewish peoplehood evolves, striving with God will remain the defining and unifying marker of Jewish living and thinking and breathing. The Jew who strives with God cannot be a bad Jew. And every Jew strives with God—because that is what it means to be a Jew.

PART II

OF ISRAEL

II:1

THE IDEA OF ISRAEL*

There is no time in my conscious, remembered life when I was unaware of Israel. My parents, moderate in all things, were moderate Zionists, like many American Jews of their generation. In 1971, when I was one, they spent a year in Israel; my father had a fellowship to support his research while he was an assistant professor, and my mother was working on her PhD. From their account, it seems like they might have been vaguely considering a permanent move to Israel. In any case, when the year was up, they came back home to Cambridge, Massachusetts. One of my brothers was born while we were in Israel, and my parents always spoke warmly of their experiences there.

Shortly afterward, my father joined an organization called Professors for Peace in the Middle East. The organization hoped to "elicit new ideas and approaches for the solution of the Israeli-Arab conflict, and to work for a just and lasting peace in the region." The mission sounds just about right as a description of my parents' Israel-related

---

* I have in mind the example of Sunil Khilnani, *The Idea of India* (New York: Farrar, Straus and Giroux, 1997), which influenced me heavily when it came out and in the years since, not Ilan Pappé, *The Idea of Israel: A History of Power and Knowledge* (New York: Verso, 2014), which I read only in researching this book.

politics when I was growing up. They cared about Israel, they had Is-raeli friends, and they hoped for a two-state solution that would enable Israelis and Arabs (they did not then say "Palestinians") to live along-side each other. The 1978 Camp David Accords, in which Menachem Begin and Anwar Sadat laid the groundwork for an Israel-Egypt peace treaty, were treated as a world-historical event in our household, by which I mean that the eight-year-old me was given his own subscrip-tion to *Time* magazine.

My parents didn't speak much modern Hebrew, but they sent me and my brothers to a Modern Orthodox day school that made Israeli Hebrew language an important part of the curriculum alongside tradi-tional Jewish study. To be a bit more precise, the school didn't formally distinguish the modern Israeli language from the ancient Hebrew of the Bible or the rabbinic Hebrew of the Talmud and its later commenta-tors. Hebrew was just Hebrew. The technical name for the technique of making us translate ancient Hebrew, which we kids didn't speak, into modern Israeli Hebrew, which we also didn't speak, is *'Ivrit be-'Ivrit*, literally, "Hebrew in Hebrew." The description, like the curriculum, had an ideological point: The modern Hebrew language spoken in Israel wasn't a newly invented language, an Esperanto for Israel. It was the *same* language as the ancient Hebrew of the Jewish past, self-consciously revived and updated for the purposes of modern use.[1]

The analogy to Israel itself was so obvious that no one needed to explain it to us. The modern country of Israel was the *same* land as the ancient Land of Israel described in the Bible. The state of Israel was self-consciously revived and updated, but it was still, spiritually, the same state. In my school, in the dozen years I attended, we had no separate course in the history of modern Israel. The word "Zionism" was rarely used, even by the excellent Israeli teachers who taught us to love the Hebrew language and the land of Israel. But there was no doubt that the creation of the modern state of Israel was a signal moment in Jewish history. On Israel's Independence Day, we sang the Hallel prayer, a specific set of Psalms designated for festivals, albeit without the formal blessing that ordinarily accompanies the prayer.

As an adolescent, I followed the lead of my school and my parents in thinking about Israel—at first. We took a family trip to Israel when I was eleven, and it made a big impression on me, stronger even than the impression made by occasional family trips to Europe. (We were, somehow, extremely culturally privileged but not rich.) Soon after, I asked my parents if I could use my bar mitzvah money to spend the summer in Israel. They agreed, only to discover that there was no organized program taking thirteen-year-old children halfway across the world for a summer abroad experience. I convinced them to let me buy a plane ticket and go on my own. By then I could speak modern Israeli Hebrew fairly well. I would stay with three or four sets of family friends who would in principle keep an eye on me. I would set my own tourist itinerary and travel across the country by public bus and by hitchhiking.

That my parents agreed to this scheme says a lot about their implicit idealization of Israel circa 1983. There's no conceivable way they would have allowed me to take a Greyhound bus across the United States at thirteen, much less hitch. They weren't naïve, at least not about America. But in Israel, they must have imagined, there were no people who might have designs on a kid traveling around on his own. Or maybe they figured I was clever enough to stay out of trouble.

Anyway, they seem to have been right. I had a great time. The adults didn't always know exactly where I was, but I checked in weekly by phone. I was lonely, which I somehow hadn't imagined in advance. Maybe I thought just being in Israel would be socially fulfilling. But I learned more in that concentrated six-week period than almost any other time in my life, except perhaps freshman year of college. By the end of the summer, I could speak Hebrew fluently and I had amassed what you might call a professional tour guide's knowledge of Israel. It was broad, it was detailed, it was superficial, and it reflected the official histories that I found in Israeli books and guides to archaeological sites, which I found particularly fascinating.[2]

I knew no Palestinians. I spent a lot of time in the market of the Old City of Jerusalem, and I was intrigued by the Middle Eastern qualities of the primarily Arab space. I formed a plan to start studying Arabic, because I believed it was one of the national languages of Israel and because I now knew Hebrew, the other one. I had a vague notion that achieving "peace in the Middle East" would require bringing together Hebrew and Arabic speakers. But I don't think it really occurred to me, at the age of thirteen, that Palestinians might have a sharply different perspective on the Israeli culture I was trying to absorb. Back at home, in school, I grew to love the music of the early Zionist pioneer-settlers, taught by Israelis who loved it too. I can still sing the Hebrew songs of Palestine in the 1920s and of Israel in the 1950s and 1960s. I know most of the lyrics by heart.

Learning Arabic as a teenager expanded my perspective. I began to realize that there were actual Palestinian people who understood the creation of Israel in 1948 not as a miracle but as a nightmare. But it was the first intifada, which began in December 1987 and lasted until 1991, that really awakened me to the complexities of the Israel-Palestine situation.

The intifada was a transformative moment in Palestinian history, a spontaneous uprising led mostly by young people who were protesting the very fact of the Israeli occupation of the West Bank and Gaza. Like most American Jews at the time, I had been brought up on the narrative that embattled Israel had won a great victory in the Six-Day War of 1967, had ended up governing several million Palestinians, and had been unable (not unwilling) to reach an agreement with the governments of Jordan and Egypt to return those territories in exchange for peace. The Palestine Liberation Organization featured in the story as a terrorist organization committed to destroying Israel and spoiling the prospect of coexistence.

The moment of the intifada that shocked me most came in January 1988. I was seventeen. *The New York Times* reported that in response to stone throwing by Palestinian teenagers—people my age—the Israel Defense Forces had adopted a policy of having its own soldiers—also roughly my age—intentionally beat the protesters with clubs to the point of breaking their bones.[3]

If something was reported in *The New York Times*, I had no doubt it was true. That was why the story gave me cognitive dissonance. Breaking bones felt like such an obvious and outrageous human rights violation, so crude in its brutality. It was at odds with my received image of the IDF as a disciplined, modern fighting force that strove to reduce civilian

casualties and maintain what it called "the purity of arms." I was aware
of the 1982 massacres of Palestinian refugees that had taken place in the
Sabra neighborhood and the Shatila camp in Lebanon. But those massacres had been carried out by Lebanese Christian Maronite militias allied
with the IDF, not by the IDF itself. Perhaps Israeli generals, particularly
Ariel Sharon, had let the massacres happen and so bore moral responsibility. That was, it seemed to me at the time, a far cry from a "liberal"
general like Yitzhak Rabin, then Israel's defense minister, directly order-
ing his teenaged soldiers to break teenagers' bones.

I vividly remember calling one of my closest friends on the phone to
discuss the *Times* article. We couldn't really get our heads around it. In
retrospect, I think we understood that we shouldn't or maybe couldn't
discuss it at school. She was weeping. Of course it was partly our age,
which was a good one for discovering that not everything you've been
taught your whole life is, strictly speaking, true. But it was also the loss
of the innocence that characterized our idealized picture of Israel. Or at
least it was innocence when seen from our point of view. From a more
critical standpoint, whether left or right wing, it was a kind of privileged
self-delusion: the self-delusion of imagining that a nation-state could be
rebuilt after two thousand years of exile without sometimes breaking the
bones of the people who happened to be living there already.

THE ZION OPTION

In this part of the book, I am going to argue that the idea of Israel has
become something the state's founders did not precisely intend it to be:
a transformative, defining factor within Jewishness, both in and outside
the actual country. To make this case, I need to begin with Zionism, the
idea that lies behind the contemporary idea of Israel.

Classical Zionism* began as a response to the Jewish question, men-

---

* Throughout the book, I use the term "classical Zionism" in a broad way, to refer to a
line of strongly secularist, nationalist Zionist thought that can be traced back through
Theodor Herzl to figures like Moses Hess, Leo Pinsker, Moshe Lilienblum, and Peretz Smolenskin, and forward at least through David Ben-Gurion. I am aware of and
appreciate the sophisticated historiography of Zionism that points out nuance, variety,

tioned in the last chapter: What should become of the Jews of Europe once they were formally emancipated and allowed to become citizens of European nation-states? The question itself was a product of the climactic era of European nationalism, when it seemed natural that to be a citizen of a European state was to be a member of the nation that went with that state. Seen in nationalist terms, the Zionist answer seems inevitable. If the Jews were not part of the German nation or the Italian nation or the French nation, as many (though by no means all) Germans and Italians and French people seemed to believe, then Jews must be a nation of their own.

Being a nation required having a state. A state needed a location. And although a few Zionists were open to accepting land wherever it could be gotten, such as Uganda in east Africa (proposed at the World Zionist Congress in 1903), most concluded that the Jewish nation should have its Jewish state in its ancestral homeland, known since late antiquity as Palestine.

If the Zionists' classical answer to the Jewish question emerged from nationalism, the particular qualities of Zionism reflected secularism, another major social force of the nineteenth century. Secular modernity was emerging as a response to disillusionment with religious faith and religious institutions. Many classical Zionists held genuinely radical views about the Jewish religious tradition.

In its most stylized, extreme form, secular Zionism maintained that Jewish religion had reached a dead end, historically speaking. Religious belief had played a key role in keeping Jewish national consciousness alive for two millennia, but it had no inherent worth beyond that. The path to national self-expression therefore lay in rejecting the religious aspects of Jewishness altogether. For Zion to live, Judaism had to die.

The paradoxical logic of the secular Zionist rejection of religion can be understood through a Zionist slogan: "the negation of the Di-

---

tension, and contradiction within the category "Zionism." For every generalization I make about classical Zionism, it would be possible to show exceptions. Nevertheless, some generalization is necessary in a work like this that is directed to the general reader, not only to specialists.

aspora." The word "Diaspora" refers to the dispersion of Jews throughout the world. To nationalists, the background assumption is typically that people of a given nation live in a fixed place, from which they originated. In the nationalist-Zionist narrative, the Jews began as a nation, with a national home and a national language and a national culture, then lost those things when they entered the Diaspora. So Diaspora, from the nationalist point of view, reflected an unnatural state, one of exile and loss of state power. Never mind whether the narrative was historically exact.* What mattered to Zionists was that the status of nationhood must be restored. Negation of the Diaspora meant eliminating the distinctive features of Diasporic Jewish life and replacing them with a renewed language and culture that would match the status of modern nationhood.

For classical secular Zionists, the religious and spiritual practices of Jews that had existed for two thousand years of Diaspora thus came to be associated with oppressed, exilic status. They had to be negated. Secular Zionists depicted Jewish religious beliefs and practices as intertwined with Jewish weakness. Belief in God, they maintained, had held Jews back from asserting sovereignty and nationhood. In a sense, the secular Zionists argued, Jews had come to focus on God rather than the nation. Now they must reverse course and focus on the nation instead of God.

In retrospect, the secularism of much Zionist nationalism looks like a manifestation of the generally antireligious sentiment of disillusioned modernity. To modern thinkers, religion was a kind of enchantment, and a modern attitude required rational disenchantment.[4] The difficulty for Jewish nationalism was that religious practice and sentiment had to be recognized as having kept the Jewish nation in existence during the lengthy historical era in which Jews had no state, no language, and no

---

* In some ways, it was not. For example, the Jews of Judea in the Hellenistic period spoke Greek and Aramaic, not Hebrew, which seems already to have been reserved primarily for scholarly and liturgical use. As a matter of historical reality, some people who identified as Israelites or Judaeans—and later as Jews—lived outside the historic land of Israel from early in recorded history. The Jewish community in Egypt had a temple of its own (mentioned in the Talmud) and a population of tens of thousands even while the Second Temple in Jerusalem was standing. In nationalist thinking, however, the idea of the Diaspora came to be associated specifically with the loss of Jewish sovereignty after the destruction of the Temple in Jerusalem in the year 70 CE.

national culture. To negate Jewish religious experience as Diasporic was to negate the very thing that had constituted Jewishness.

The Zionist solution to this puzzle was, first, to turn God into the nation. Israel's Declaration of Independence referred to God as "the Rock of Israel." That was a rare biblical name for God, sometimes used in later Jewish liturgy. Israel's founders used it because they didn't want to employ one of God's more familiar names, which would have sounded too religious,* and because that name defined God precisely as the sustainer of Israel. To secular Zionists, God did not exist. Yet God was a projective name that could be used to remind Jews of what did exist—or could be made to exist—in the real world, namely the Jewish nation.

Second, Zionism proposed to take the most usable elements of Jewish religious-spiritual tradition and repurpose them for the project of nationalism. The most important of these was the traditional Jewish yearning for the coming of the messiah and the return to the land of Israel—to Zion. In fact, the main reason that Jewish nationalism came to be called Zionism (rather than, say, "Israelism") was that in the Bible and in subsequent Jewish liturgy, the idea of "return" was closely associated with "Zion," a poetic name for the city of Jerusalem. To yearn for Zion was to yearn for messianic return. Secular Zionism was therefore a dream of return that built itself on the idea of messianic redemption.

To secular Zionists, the messiah was not a man, much less a divinely appointed messenger. The messiah was a metaphor for the nation acting collectively to restore itself to full national status and sovereignty. The metaphor of messianic return was what could be salvaged from Diasporic Jewish religious belief. The rest of the belief structure could and must be negated, denied, erased.

The result would be a healthy, normal modern nation, one in which religion would play no role except as a national symbol. Judaism and Jewishness, conceived in religious terms, would be replaced by Zionism and Israeliness, conceived in national terms. Jewishness had outlived its historical usefulness. The solution to the Jewish question was that Jews

---

* Compare Jefferson's "the Laws of Nature and of Nature's God" in the first sentence of the U.S. Declaration of Independence.

would no longer be Jews. They would be Israelis, members of a Jewish nation.

The comparison to Marx's solution for the Jewish question is worth noting. To Marx, Jewishness was essentially the status of being bourgeois. The solution was to wipe away the bourgeoisie, thereby solving the Jewish question. To secular Zionists, Jewishness was the status of being Diasporic and disempowered. The solution was to wipe away the Diaspora and its disempowerment, thereby solving the Jewish question. In both solutions, Jewishness was treated as an anomaly. In the normal or proper state of affairs, Jews would be people like anyone else, either members of a newly constituted, postclass communist society or citizens of a nation-state like other ordinary Europeans. For both Marxists and Zionists, the ideal end-state was a secular utopia that displaced and replaced messianism.[5]

The key point is that from the standpoint of classical, secular Zionism, the Jewish state was meant to transcend and replace Jewishness. Israel was not supposed to be an event *in* Jewish history. It was supposed to be the *end* of Jewish history and the re-creation of a new national era, the era of Israel. The secularization of the idea of the messiah would then be exact. The coming of the messiah was not understood in (most of) the Jewish messianic tradition as an event in history but as an event that would represent the end of history. The utopian messianic age would put an end to the vicissitudes of Jewish survival and suffering that marked God's intermittent reward and punishment of the Jewish people.

I am emphasizing the Zionist plan that Israel should not be just another event in Jewish history because of what eventually happened when the Jewish state did come into existence. For some decades, the creation of Israel was certainly an important event *in* Jewish history. It was a significant event, no doubt, but not immediately the transformative event that was hoped for by those who conceived and accomplished it.

Israel did not put an end to the Diaspora. (Even the Holocaust did not do that.) The Diaspora continued to exist alongside the state of Israel. Most Jews who lived outside Israel did not flock to the country, at least not willingly. In fact, notwithstanding its nuclear weapons, Israel did not fully achieve the nationalists' maximal aspiration of being independently capable of protecting the Jews who lived there, much less all Jews everywhere. Israel remained (and, as the two U.S. carrier groups that were moved to the eastern Mediterranean in October 2023 show, still remains) partly dependent for its security on a close relationship with the United States, a relationship that itself relies in no small part on the support of the American Jewish community. This outcome was not unique to Israel. The early twentieth-century nationalist fantasy that small countries could be self-sustaining without the protection of large neo-imperial powers turned out to be just that, a fantasy.

Over time, however, the relationship between Israel and Jewishness changed. Now, three-quarters of a century after the state's creation, Israel *has become a defining component of Jewishness itself,* or so I am about to argue. Israel did not end Jewish history. But it is, today, essential to Jewishness itself. In the process, Israel has transformed Jewishness into something significantly new and different. The Jewish question of the nineteenth and early twentieth centuries has become the Israel question in the twenty-first.*

IDENTITY, SELF-DEFINITION, AND ANTI-ZIONISM

If Israel were simply a country like any other, the way many classical Zionists hoped it would be, it would not exercise anything like the transformational power that it currently has on the Jewish experience of people who live outside the country—or in it. If Israel were an ordinary country, Jews who chose not to live there would not have to spend all that much time thinking about it.

I do not want to suggest that Israel's effects on Jewishness worldwide are utterly unique. They are, rather, distinctive and noteworthy.

---

* The Israel question—what to believe about Israel and how to act in relation to Israel—is intimately intertwined with the Israel-Palestine question, which includes also the question of how Israelis and Palestinians can live alongside each other, if that is indeed possible. They overlap but are not identical. In this book, I do not purport to answer or even properly address the Israel-Palestine question. It is pressing and crucial nevertheless, and its gravitational pull can be felt.

THE IDEA OF ISRAEL

Compare Irish Americans or Korean Americans or Indian Americans, who today often feel pride and connection to the country where they or their ancestors originated. They visit, especially if they still have relatives in the old country. They might lobby their elected officials in the United States to support their country of origin in its regional political struggles. In some cases, their religious and spiritual worldviews will be shaped and framed *primarily* in relation to where they or their parents or grandparents or great-grandparents once lived. In general, however, there will be substantial attenuation of the religious centrality of the country from which they derive ethnic identity relative to their distance from immigration. As a general rule, the more generations you are from the old country, the less it defines your inner spiritual life.

Similarly, people who live in Ireland or South Korea or India certainly think about and reflect on their own national identities. They argue with each other about what it means to be Irish or Korean or Indian. In some cases, their debates are intense, even existential. Ireland has traditionally had to define itself in relation to Great Britain, its longtime colonial occupier. The Catholic-Protestant divide in Northern Ireland still shapes politics in that part of the island. The Korean Peninsula remains split between North and South, two countries implacably opposed but whose populations are ethnically identical and linguistically extremely close despite more than seventy years of enforced separation. India must grapple with philosophical differences between the inclusive idea of India developed and promulgated by Gandhi and Nehru and the type of Hindu nationalism propagated by Prime Minister Narendra Modi and his party, the BJP. And to be sure, Modi's version of Hindu nationalism has complex religious dimensions. Yet these complicated, difficult, engrossing intranational questions do not today *inevitably* permeate the inner spiritual (as opposed to political) lives of the citizens of these countries, whatever may have been the case in earlier generations. To put it another way, nationalism today does not usually exercise definitive power over religious belief and experience.

Zionism is a bit different, or seems to be. True, in Israel's first decades of existence, many Jews who lived outside the country did not define or experience their Jewishness in relation to Israel. Indeed, a large number of Jews outside Israel were not then Zionists at all. To be a Zionist in eastern Europe before World War II typically meant aspiring to move to Palestine. Many classical Zionists believed that all Jews should move to the land of Israel. So at the time, Jews who remained in Europe or who emigrated to the United States (or South America or wherever) rather than Israel were, by some strict definition, not full Zionists. Sympathy to the existence of a Jewish homeland was understood as different from dedicating oneself to participating actively in the creation of the Jewish national home.

Now, however, Jews outside Israel, wherever they live, find themselves necessarily self-defining in relation to Israel—religiously, spiritually, and politically—whether by support or criticism or some complicated combination of the two. If they attend a synagogue or temple, Israel finds its way there, as I will discuss in the next couple of chapters. If they are unaffiliated with Jewish religious institutions, they still find themselves working to figure out what they think about Israel in relation to their own sense of Jewishness. The Hamas-Israel war brought home the inevitability of this process at this moment in historical time.

For some Jews who feel little connection to the religious aspects of Judaism, whether because they don't believe in God or for other reasons, Israel can function as the chosen focal point of their Jewish identity and connection. Caring about and supporting Israel can be constitutive of what makes them actively Jewish. Feeling commonality with others who support Israel can be their Jewish communal identity. There are a range of nonreligious pro-Israel organizations they can join, corresponding to different political orientations. Reading about Israel in the media can be their Jewish study and reflection, and there is a steady stream of material about Israel they can consume, again ranging across a continuum of different pro-Israel positions. For pro-Israel, religiously unaffiliated Jews like these, support for Israel comes close to being what classical Zionists hoped their movement would be for everyone: a replacement of religious Jewishness with nationalist affiliation and fellow feeling.

I have noticed—you may have too—that a number of American

Jews seem to adopt this kind of pro-Israel focus as they begin to get older, even when Israel is not under attack and at war.* It's not that they didn't support Israel earlier in their lives so much as that they often did not previously make pro-Israel sentiment so central to their identities. Perhaps the explanation is that older Jews have stronger memories of the aftermath of the Holocaust or Israel's past wars. But another factor could be that as people age, their religious-spiritual inclinations emerge. (Impending mortality will do that to you.) Because they think of themselves as secular rationalists and have never felt all that positively about Jewish religion, these aging Jews cannot comfortably turn to Jewish spirituality or faith to address their existential concerns. So they focus instead on the aspect of Jewishness that seems most compatible with their rationalist-agnostic worldview: Israel. On this interpretation, older Jews who become especially impassioned about supporting Israel are transmuting their religious longings into Zionism, unconsciously repeating the Zionists' conscious, intentional plan for all modern Jews.

More surprising is the situation of those Jews who do not embrace the support of Israel as their sole or primary Jewish expression, yet still find, whether they like it or not, that Israel lies at the core of their Jewish identity, because they are enmeshed in a struggle about what to think of Israel and what to do about what they think. This kind of internal struggle happens especially on college campuses, where so much of the work of politics and self-definition happens in the United States. It can also happen to postcollege Jews who want to think about U.S. national politics from a Jewish perspective. Some Jews may even find themselves disinclined to affiliate with organized Jewish communal institutions precisely because they feel uncomfortable with the way Israel is discussed or engaged in those spaces. In that case, their Jewishness is still being shaped by Israel, albeit negatively.

Within Israel, too, the meaning of Zionism and the character of the

* This phenomenon feels especially common among successful, intelligent, older Jewish men; but maybe that is just the group that is most comfortable and effective being highly vocal about it.

state permeates Jewish life and thought. It does so for secular Israelis who derive meaning from their Zionist or post-Zionist beliefs. It does so for Religious Zionists, whose whole Jewish self-conception is inextricably bound up in the Zionist project. And it has turned out to do so even for nominally non-Zionist Traditionalists. Once, Traditionalists espoused a policy of formal indifference toward the state of Israel. Increasingly, however, Traditionalists find themselves identifying with the state and driving its politics, as I will discuss later in this part of the book. Some are actually prepared to conceptualize their Torah study in relation to the spiritual sustenance of the state.

The upshot is that most Jews today find they have little choice but to self-define in *some* relation to Israel whether they want to or not. This is what I mean when I say that Israel has become a defining part of Jewishness. Some Jews, perhaps a growing number, may find this reality undesirable. They might prefer to go back to a time where many Jews outside Israel, from secular to Reform to Traditionalist, chose not to define their Jewishness in *any* relation to Israel. Turning back the clock, however, is not so easy. The reason is that Jewishness is a collective identity or identities, defined and shaped by what groups of people think. So if most groups of Jews self-define in relation to Israel, it is challenging for any Jews to choose not to do so.

This reality in turn raises complicated questions about antisemitism. Consider the reaction Donald Trump encountered in October 2022 when he said that "U.S. Jews have to get their act together and appreciate what they have in Israel—Before it is too late!" Trump was saying that because, in his opinion, "No President has done more for Israel than I have," American Jews should support him. Jonathan Greenblatt of the Anti-Defamation League, the closest thing to an institutional arbiter of antisemitism in the United States, responded on Twitter that "when the President says 'before it's too late,' it sounds like a threat in an environment where Jews already feel threatened." Greenblatt went on:

We don't need the former president, who curries favor with extremists and antisemites, to lecture us about the US-Israel relationship. It is not about a quid pro quo; it rests on shared values and security interests. This "Jewsplaining" is insulting and disgusting.

If Trump's argument that American Jews should appreciate Israel was antisemitic, as Joe Biden's White House was quick to assert, it would have to be because Trump was telling Jews how they should support Israel. That is, Trump was assuming or arguing that American Jews should affirmatively self-define in relation to the Jewish state. By implication, if a non-Jew tells that to Jews, he is being antisemitic by virtue of not allowing Jews to decide for themselves what their relationship to Israel, if any, should be.

But of course (some) Jews say this sort of thing to other Jews all the time without being called antisemites. Jews tell other Jews they ought to support Israel or criticize it or whatever they happen to believe is right. That fact might lead you to conclude that Trump was in fact not being antisemitic. But what feels potentially antisemitic about Trump's argument is that he was presuming to define good Jewishness in a particular way—*namely as Zionist commitment.*

Now consider a different but related charge: the argument that anti-Zionism either is itself antisemitism or is tantamount to it. Of course, anti-Zionists themselves almost invariably insist they are not antisemites. They say they have nothing against Jews, but rather oppose Israel and its policies and sometimes even its existence. Jewishness and Zionism have no necessary connection, they claim. And some of these anti-Zionists are themselves Jews.

Why does anti-Zionism nevertheless seem like antisemitism to many Jews? The answer is not only that Jews should have the same right to self-determination as other peoples. Nor is it only that some anti-Zionists knowingly or unknowingly draw on antisemitic tropes. The deeper explanation is that for many Jews, Israel is central and essential to Jewishness. If you feel that Jewishness is or should be fundamentally linked to Israel, then when someone says Israel should not exist, the criticism impugns the core of your Jewish identity and belief. It rejects who *you* are *as a Jew.* It rejects both the content of your Jewish commitment and the identity you have based on it.

In essence, Jews who say that anti-Zionism is antisemitism are

objecting to other people telling them that they as Jews are wrong to treat
Israel as fundamental to Jewish life and experience. The anti-Zionists are
saying the opposite of what Trump said. Yet they have in common with
Trump that they are implicitly telling Jews how to self-define in relation
to Israel. Trump told Jews they should support and identify with Israel.
Anti-Zionists tell Jews they should not support and identify with Israel.
Either way, some Jews experience the argument as negating their own
capacity for self-definition.

Who is right? Your answer must depend on your answer to the question of what it means (to you) to be a Jew and who has the right to suggest answers. Regardless, the debates about Zionism and antisemitism
become much clearer when you see them in the light of who gets to
define Jewishness in relation to Israel.

ISRAEL AS NARRATIVE

Why is Israel so omnipresent in the thought-world of Jews (and others), outside Israel and inside? The answer is that Israel is not only a place but a narrative: a rich, complex set of different stories that we tell ourselves and that
are meant to instruct us about what Israel means and why it is good or bad.

The reason Israel has such power as a narrative is that Jewishness itself has long possessed extraordinary story-making power, and
Zionism has assumed, incorporated, and transformed key aspects of
the Jewish story. The narrative of Jewishness has not only dominated
the consciousness of Jews for two thousand years. It is interwoven with
the basic stories and structures of Christianity, and has been since the
lifetime of Jesus himself. The Jewish story is also intertwined with
the story of Islam, and has been since the life of the Prophet Muhammad,
who received a Qur'an that retold biblical stories and himself interacted
extensively with Arabian Jews. A version of the Jewish story, in a displaced form, is baked into modernity through Marx and Freud. And a
part of the Jewish story is also, in a different way, enmeshed in today's
consciousness through the phenomenon of modern antisemitism, exemplified by Nazism and Adolf Hitler, who figure centrally in the stories
we tell ourselves about war, peace, and human rights.

The narrative of Israel derives its special power from its capacity to take on board all the power of the Jewish story while constantly adding to it a range of other, contemporary sets of stories and ideas that matter globally. Those include the narratives of nationalism, national self-determination, constitutional democracy, modernization, secularization, religious fundamentalism, economic development, European colonialism, European imperialism, racism, sex, sexual orientation, gender equality, the clash of civilizations, technological utopianism, and many more. In an astonishing, protean way, the narrative of Israel manages to intersect and be intersected by many of the most contentious and generative ideas that permeate contemporary political and spiritual consciousness. The narrative of Israel is a can't stop/won't stop maelstrom of stories, beliefs, arguments, and claims on our thought and attention. In this sense, the narrative of Israel is utterly religious and spiritual and political and moral, all at the same time.

What's more, this nexus of stories is, to a degree that is rare in most other domains of human discussion, constantly oppositional, binary, argumentative, dialectic, and psycho-emotionally generative. For everything you can say about Israel, you can say the opposite. For every argument that Israel is good, there is an opposite argument that Israel is bad. For every argument that Israel is bad, there is a corresponding argument that it is good. None of these arguments has any ending place. The result is that the very idea of Israel conjures up a field of ongoing argument that extends in all directions, as far as the eye can see. The word "Israel" conjures *energy*—mostly the energy to argue. You can get exhausted by talking about Israel, but that somehow doesn't seem to make the conversation stop. It keeps going. Not everyone wants or needs to be in the conversation all the time. But the people who keep talking about it seem to care infinitely, whether they are for Israel or against it, whether violent conflict is active or not.

All this is what makes Israel, or rather the narrative of Israel, distinct from most other nation-states' narratives. In terms of practical reality, Israel is just another country. The people who live there are just people, like people anywhere else. But the *idea* of Israel, its narratives and its counternarratives, stands apart from normality. Israel's narrative stands apart from normal national narratives as much as (maybe more than) the narrative of the Jews stood apart from other religious-spiritual-communal narratives before the state of Israel came into existence. The Israel narrative is the Jewish narrative, plus many other ideas of modernity and postmodernity that never made their way into the old Jewish narrative. And it is sustained by people, supporters and critics, Jews and non-Jews alike, who are transmuting and transforming the ancient narrative of the Jews' uniqueness into the idea of Israel.

ONE LAND, TWO PEOPLES

The narrative of Israel has a crux in it that cannot be ignored. It derives from a reality that Zionism has struggled with since its inception: the reality that the land to which the Zionists sought return was peopled. The people who lived in the Ottoman imperial provinces that became British mandatory Palestine after World War I were mostly Muslims and Christians, with some Jews and some members of other miscellaneous religious groups, such as the syncretistic Druze. Their ethnicities were mixed and complicated, as were ethnicities throughout the cultural area covering Palestine and what would become the countries of Lebanon, Syria, Jordan, and parts of Turkey. Their lingua franca was Arabic. They belonged to several social classes, ranging from aristocratic landholders to urban merchants to religious scholars and peasants and seminomadic herders. Some of the people who lived in what would become mandatory Palestine began to think of themselves as Palestinians at just about the same time that they began to encounter Jews who thought of themselves as members of a Jewish nation, which was also around the same time that Turkish nationalism, Arab nationalism, and Armenian nationalism began to enter consciousness in the crumbling Ottoman Empire.[6]

From early in the history of Zionism, aspirants to a Jewish national homeland had to consider how to encounter this population. One approach was to deny that the people who lived in Palestine constituted a distinct group capable of making claims of national self-determination. The most famous slogan capturing this viewpoint is that Palestine was "a land without a people for a people without a land," namely, the Jews. The phrase, or something like it, first appeared in Christian Restorationist publications in the 1840s.* Some Jewish Zionists adopted the idea thereafter. Israeli Prime Minister Golda Meir (1898–1978), who was born in Kyiv, raised in Milwaukee, and moved to Palestine in 1921, famously expressed a version of it in an interview with the London *Sunday Times* in 1969.[7] Her statement that "there was no such thing as Palestinians" was intended to deny that a Palestinian national identity had existed before the creation of Israel.

Many Zionists realized from an early period that Palestine was a land that had people in it, whether they should be defined as "a people" or not. The most famous example is the Zionist writer Ahad Ha'am (the pen name of Asher Tzvi Hirsch Ginsberg, 1856–1927), who in 1891 wrote a series of articles that appeared as a pamphlet titled "Truth from the Land of Israel." Speaking to a European Jewish audience, Ahad Ha'am (the name means, literally, "one of the people") asserted, "We who live abroad are accustomed to believe that almost all the land of Israel is now uninhabited desert and whoever wishes can buy land there as he pleases. But this is not true. It is very difficult to find in the land cultivated fields that are not used for planting."[8] The writer was not addressing the question of Palestinian national identity. He was acknowledging the reality that Palestine was densely populated by actual residents.

As Zionists began to buy land and settle in Palestine, the reality of the Palestinian population became their most significant obstacle. In 1929, riots broke out in which more than a hundred Jews and roughly as many Palestinian Arabs died. The nominal flashpoint was access to the Western Wall in Jerusalem, but the deeper cause was growing Palestinian concern about the rising number of Jewish immigrants and the emerging realization that those Jews were serious about constructing a state of their own.[9] From 1936 to 1939, Palestinians rose in open revolt against the British government. They expressly demanded a stop to

---

* Christian Restorationism was the precursor to Christian Zionism, an important phenomenon in its own right. Briefly, Christian Restorationists believed and believe that Jews must resettle the ancient land of Israel as part of the divine plan that will lead to the Second Coming.

Jewish immigration and settlement. Although Palestine was technically not a British imperial possession but a mandate to govern temporarily conferred by the League of Nations, the British responded the way they were accustomed to doing in their colonies: they suppressed the uprising violently.[10] Somewhere between two thousand and five thousand Palestinians died and perhaps three times as many were wounded. More than 300 Jews were killed, as well as some 260 British soldiers.

In May 1939, having tried and failed to facilitate negotiations between Palestinian Arabs and Jews, the British government adopted a "White Paper" intended as a blueprint for governing Palestine. It recommended that an independent binational state for Arabs and Jews eventually be established. The White Paper also sharply limited Jewish immigration. As it would turn out, 1939 was a disastrous moment for Jews' opportunities to leave Europe to be so restricted. Germany invaded Poland in September of that year, and the destruction of European Jewry began its awful, tragic trajectory.

After World War II, as the British Empire crumbled, the newly formed United Nations proposed the creation of two countries in historic Palestine, one Jewish and one Arab. Fatefully, the Zionist leadership accepted the proposal and in May 1948 declared the establishment of the state of Israel. Equally fatefully, the Palestinian leadership took the opposite path. The Arab League, purporting to speak on behalf of Palestinians, rejected partition as inconsistent with the rights of Palestinian Arabs to national self-determination. Beginning in late 1947, Palestinian Arabs and the almost-Israelis began what was effectively a civil war. Once Israel declared independence, Arab states formally joined the fight, with significant numbers of troops from Jordan, Syria, and Egypt entering the war.

The 1948 war had multiple phases, and a detailed analysis is so far beyond the purposes of this chapter that I wish I could avoid the subject altogether. (Indeed, this truncated, incomplete history of the Israel-Palestine conflict is pretty much guaranteed to satisfy nobody.) What matters for our purposes is that Israel survived—and Palestinian Arabs suffered a catastrophe (in Arabic, the *nakba*). Hundreds of thousands of

Palestinians fled or were forced from their homes and became permanent refugees. Most of the territory that the United Nations had proposed as a Palestinian Arab state instead was seized by Jordan and Egypt.

The events of 1947–1948 are the subject of the kind of unending, ideologically driven historical debate that leaves committed advocates on both sides certain they are correct. Roughly speaking, supporters of Israel maintain that the Jewish state faced the possibility of destruction, as directly threatened by the Arab League and its members. They depict the losses suffered by Palestinians as the consequence of their failure to accept partition and their fantasy of destroying Zionism and driving the Jews into the sea. Supporters of the Palestinian cause argue that the nascent Israeli military, following Zionist leadership, knowingly and intentionally planned to create majority-Jewish territory by forcing Palestinian civilians out of their homes. They view the outcome as fundamentally unjust, especially insofar as it left Palestinians as a stateless people, without the opportunity for the self-determination achieved by Zionists on land that was historically Palestinian.

When people ask me what to read to get an objective view of the history, I first tell them that historical objectivity is a moving target. Then I tell them the story of the Israeli historian Benny Morris. In 1987, Morris published a book called *The Birth of the Palestinian Refugee Problem, 1947–1949*. He used Israeli archives to trace what was known as "Plan D," a military plan for (in its own words) "operations against enemy settlements which are in the rear of, within or near our defence lines, with the aim of preventing their use as bases for an active armed force." This plan, according to Morris, "provided for the conquest and permanent occupation, or levelling, of Arab villages and towns."[11]

Morris's book established him as one of a group known then in Israel as the "new historians," associated with a left-wing critique of how Israeli military conduct in 1947–1948 had shaped the Palestinian experience. In 1988, Morris refused to report for reserve duty in the IDF because he did not want to participate in suppressing the first intifada and because he favored withdrawal from the West Bank; the refusal earned him three weeks in a military prison.[12] Other new historians, like Avi

Shlaim (who wrote about Israel's "collusion" with the Hashemite King-dom of Jordan) and Ilan Pappé (who went on to write a book called *The Ethnic Cleansing of Palestine*), have remained staunch critics of Israel.[13]

Morris, however, underwent a political transformation in reaction to the second intifada that began in 2000. In 2004, as he was publishing a revised and updated version of his book, he told a newspaper interviewer that without the "transfer" of Palestinians out of what would become Israel, "a state would not have come into being. That has to be clear. It is impossible to evade it. Without the uprooting of the Palestinians, a Jewish state would not have arisen here." David Ben-Gurion, the leader of the Zionist establishment, shaped the undertaking of transfer, accord-ing to Morris. But he did not go far enough. "The non-completion of transfer was a mistake," Morris said:

> I know that this stuns the Arabs and the liberals and the politi-cally correct types. But my feeling is that this place would be quieter and know less suffering if the matter had been resolved once and for all. If Ben-Gurion had carried out a large expul-sion and cleansed the whole country—the whole Land of Israel, as far as the Jordan River. It may yet turn out that this was his fatal mistake. If he had carried out a full expulsion—rather than a partial one—he would have stabilized the State of Israel for generations.[14]

What is fascinating about Morris is that despite flipping his political perspective on its head, he did not change his view of the facts. In the revised edition of his book on the birth of the refugee crisis, he noted new evidence that Israeli forces had massacred roughly eight hundred Palestinians and committed a dozen rapes. He told the interviewer that in April and May 1948, units of the Israeli military "were given opera-tional orders that stated explicitly that they were to uproot the villagers, expel them and destroy the villages themselves." But Morris also noted that "at the same time, it turns out that there was a series of orders issued by the Arab Higher Committee and by the Palestinian intermediate levels to remove children, women and the elderly from the villages." He concluded: "On the one hand, the book reinforces the accusation against the Zionist side, but on the other hand it also proves that many of those who left the villages did so with the encouragement of the Palestinian leadership itself."[15]

The fact that Morris drew two radically different political lessons from his research at two different points in his life (and in Israeli history) does not prove he is objective, of course. He could have been biased at every moment. Critics of Morris have complained, for example, that he relied on Israeli sources, not Palestinian ones. All historians carry biases. That's because all humans do. Even historical sources are biased, because they are limited, human-made, and human-interpreted. Yet Morris's arc does say something about how we should read the history of the Israel-Palestine conflict: we should try to glean the facts as best we can, recognizing that even the same facts can be understood radically differently depending on context.

Historians with no stake in the politics of Israel-Palestine—not that anyone can really be described that way in the real world—might notice that the whole conflict bore more than a passing resemblance to the conflict between Indian Hindus and Muslims that emerged after Britain partitioned India and Pakistan in 1947. What had been ruled as a single British Raj became two countries with newly created borders. In that process, mass violence broke out, more than 14 million people ended up crossing the borders, and somewhere between a few hundred thousand and two million people died in the process. The India-Pakistan conflict that emerged has never been resolved. The status of Indian Kashmir (population 12.5 million) remains disputed by the two sides, eliciting ongoing ideological disagreement alongside geopolitical confrontation. In Israel-Palestine, as in India-Pakistan, the British Empire has a lot to answer for. In both contexts, too, the actors on the ground all sought military and ideological victory. No one came away satisfied.[16]

There are, I'm sorry to say, more chapters in the historical story. It will have to suffice, however, to remind the reader that in 1967, Israel defeated Syria, Jordan, and Egypt in a brief war that left the Golan Heights, the West Bank of the Jordan River including all of Jerusalem, and the Gaza Strip and Sinai under its control. More Palestinians went into exile, and others found themselves living under Israeli military occupation. Since then, Israel formally annexed East Jerusalem and the Golan Heights. It returned the Sinai to Egypt as part of the Anwar Sadat–Menachem Begin peace deal that cost Sadat his life. Gaza remained under direct Israeli military control until 2005, when Israel "disengaged," leaving approximately two million Palestinians to self-govern. Hamas came to control Gaza, at least until the Hamas-Israel 2023 war. The West Bank of the Jordan, which the government of Israel calls Judea and Samaria, remains occupied according to both Israeli and international law. Under the Oslo Accords signed in 1995, the territory is divided into three areas, known as A, B, and C. A is officially administered by the Palestinian Authority; B is administered jointly by the authority and the Israeli military; and C is controlled solely by Israel and contains Israeli settlements that international law considers illegal but Israeli courts consider lawful.

THE MEANING OF CONFLICT IS CONFLICT

I have tried here to describe the emergence of the Israel-Palestine conflict as neutrally as possible. Yet I know perfectly well that every word I've written could be hotly contested by people on both sides. That's the last thing I want, not because I don't care—I care a lot—but because, in this book, I am not trying to address the question of what is fair or just in the context of this conflict. The reason I needed to lay out the history, however minimally, is to begin to explain to readers today and in the future why and how Israel has become such a contentious part of the contemporary thought world, Jewish and otherwise.

To put it in the simplest way possible: Israel exists. But the nature of Israel's existence is mired—inextricably mired—in its conflict with the Palestinian national cause and in the particular way that conflict has developed.

Today, some critics of Israel maintain that the state's whole existence is illegitimate and would like to see a Palestinian state in all of historic Palestine. Others question the legitimacy of Israel as a specifically Jewish state, preferring to imagine a "one-state solution" in which all the people living between the Jordan River and the Mediterranean Sea are citizens of a single democratic entity. Still other critics concede (at least rhetorically) the legitimacy of Israel's existence as a Jewish state, then go on to criticize what they see as the injustice of the situation in which Palestinians do not have a state of their own while Israeli Jews do. That version of the critique typically leaves supporters of Israel exasperatedly trying to point out that the reason Palestinians do not have a state is surely in part that they did not want the Zionists to have one. Having tried and failed to eliminate Israel militarily, Palestinians turned to the argument that their rights to self-determination and their basic human rights to live as equal citizens are being denied by Israel.

You can see why there's an impasse. You can see why it's not going away.

Now recall, if you would, my main hypothesis in this part of the book: that the idea of Israel has become central to Jewish life and thought. That idea also finds itself in constant, dynamic, global conflict. To say that Israel is a central preoccupation for Jews is to say that conflict and conflicting ideas about Israel have become foundational to Jewish life and thought. For Jews today, whether they like it or not, Israel is often at the center. That means conflict over Israel is at the center of Jewish spiritual life and identity. That central conflict has consequences.

II:2

ISRAEL IN THE JEWISH
SPIRIT

How is Israel manifest in Jewish religious and spiritual thought today? The answer varies across the different Jewish belief patterns. But in every case, Israel has become far more important in defining Jewishness than it was even in the recent past. And in every case, changes in how the idea of Israel functions are having epochal consequences for the future of Jewish experience, thought, and self-conception.

I began part I with Jewish Traditionalism, because Traditionalists explicitly claim to constitute the true, authentic Jewish way of life and because the conflict between their worldview and liberal values is so clear. I'm going to begin my analysis of Israel's place in contemporary Jewish thought with Jewish Progressivism, because it is experiencing the most easily visible internal conflict over Israel. That conflict calls out for a framework to make sense of it and illuminate its trajectory.

So far, I will argue, there have been three phases in the history of Progressive American Jewish engagement with the idea of Israel. The first phase was identity-based skepticism. The second was total theological embrace. The third phase is internal contradiction, characterized by the conflict between the holdover of the second phase and the challenge that Israel now poses to Progressive Jewish values. We are in the middle of the third stage now, and a potential fourth stage is dimly discernible. That stage, which would certainly not come until some time after the dust of battle has settled, would constitute a substantial realignment of Progressive Jewish belief about Israel, back to something resembling stage one. But it would require a major theological revolution, one that many Progressive Jews are loath to undertake, and that might not occur at all so long as Israel is embattled and the trauma of Hamas killing women and children and taking hostages remains fresh.

The earliest Reform Jews, the founders of Progressive Jewish thought, were decidedly not Zionists. Classical Zionists insisted that the Jews were a nation and that Jewishness was not a religion, or rather should not remain one. Jewish Reformers insisted that the Jews were not a distinct nation and that Judaism precisely was and must be a religion, not a communal or ethnic or other group. Zionists held that Jews would never be accepted as full citizens of European nations. Reform Jews believed that only by making Judaism into a private religion, parallel to Protestantism, could Jews be accepted as full public citizens of the European nations to which they rightly belonged.

That is why the early Reform point of view on Zionism was the epitome of skepticism: Zionism posited a Jewish national identity that conflicted directly with the Jewish religious identity that early Progressive Jews were seeking. That skepticism lasted longer than most Progressive Jews today realize, or in some cases would care to admit. The Pittsburgh Platform, the ideological blueprint adopted by American Reform Jewish leaders in 1885, specifically rejected Zionism. "We consider ourselves," it read, "no longer a nation, but a religious community, and therefore expect neither a return to Palestine, nor a sacrificial worship under the sons of Aaron, nor the restoration of any of the laws concerning the Jewish state." In 1898, the Union of American Hebrew Congregations, the main Reform association, declared that "America is our Zion." Even in 1950, two years after the establishment of Israel, the UAHC offered a mixed message about the new government: "Although mindful that it is the primary privilege and obligation of this Union of American Hebrew Congregations generously and wholeheartedly to further and support

Judaism in America, we do now endorse moral and material support for Israel and recommend to our constituency wholehearted assistance to the United Jewish Appeal and Bond drive for Israel."[1]

The second stage of the Progressive Jewish attitude to Israel began in the early 1960s, as American Jews gradually became more confident in their status as full American citizens who could support Israel without compromising their loyalty to the United States. Its primary inflection point was the Six-Day War of 1967, which had massive effects on all American Jews' feelings for Israel. Trepidation in the run-up to the war was followed by pride in Israel's military success. I recall my father describing older academic colleagues of his suddenly "coming out" as Jews after the war. The 1967 victory consolidated and enshrined the state of Israel in the minds of American Jews. Israel no longer appeared to be a beleaguered, semisocialist experiment. It was a proud model of victory, at a time when the United States itself was losing the war in Vietnam.

But pride in Israel's military accomplishments was only part of the picture of how Progressive Jews began to embrace Israel in this second stage. The other, crucial element of the embrace was belated recognition of the tremendous losses of the Holocaust and the attempt to make theological sense of their enormity. This process was complex, and the argument I'm going to make about it treads on sensitive ground. So let me proceed carefully, and please judge my argument charitably as I lay it out.

The story of how the Holocaust became part of the national consciousness of American Jews turns not on the immediate aftermath of World War II but on a specific event that occurred in 1973: the Yom Kippur War, referred to in the Arab world as the October War. If that sounds strange, it should. Not only did the Yom Kippur War take place almost thirty years after the Holocaust ended, it had little if anything to do with the Nazis, Germany, or Europe.[2]

To see how the 1973 war triggered modern American Jewish Holocaust memory, you have to begin by realizing that until that time, most American Jews, including the organized American Jewish community, did not spend much time speaking publicly about the Holocaust or focusing on it. There were no Holocaust museums or memorials in American cities. The technical term "survivor" was not in use. Elie Wiesel was an unknown, struggling writer. His first draft of the book that would become *Night* was an 862-page memoir—in Yiddish. Wiesel managed to get a much-shortened version published in French in 1958. The first English edition, published in 1960, took three years to sell three thousand copies, its initial print run.[3] Anne Frank's *Diary* received significant attention when it came out in English (in 1952) and subsequently became a play (1955) and a movie (1959). But the diary, written by a young girl in hiding from the German occupation in Amsterdam, had nothing direct to say about the camps or the destruction of the Jews. And its well-known message that "In spite of everything I still believe that people are really good at heart" could be read as avoiding the problem of evil posed by the Holocaust.

You don't have to be a Freudian to conclude that American Jews were, in that postwar period, unconsciously suppressing the trauma of the Holocaust, which was literally too much to bear. Even today, it is hard for any Jew, myself included, to contemplate the enormity of the death of six million of one's people, among them a million and a half children. American Jews, the great majority of whom had (themselves or their parents and grandparents) immigrated to the United States in the period from 1880 to 1925, felt unspoken guilt about their own survival. They also no doubt felt unconscious guilt about their collective inability to do anything meaningful to stop the Holocaust other than supporting the U.S. effort to win the war. It was not that American Jews stood idly by while their literal cousins were killed, but that they were impotent to affect U.S. or Allied policy.

Nor was downplaying the Holocaust uniquely Jewish. At the Nuremberg trials, Justice Robert Jackson, who was the chief prosecutor, did not charge the Nazi defendants with a separate crime of genocide for perpetrating the Holocaust. Rather, the Nazis were charged with crimes against peace, war crimes, and crimes against humanity. The Holocaust was presented as only a subpart of the Nazis' wrongdoing. Jackson's reasoning, shared by the U.S. establishment, not to mention the Soviet, British, and French governments who participated in the trials, was that it would not serve anyone's interests to depict the Nazis' crimes as primarily targeting

Jews. The war had been fought on behalf of humanity, they posited. The Nazis' crimes were against all humanity, not a specific, targeted subgroup.[4]

If the 1967 war inspired Jewish pride, the 1973 war inspired Jewish fear. In 1967, Israel achieved victory via a lightning surprise attack on Egypt and Syria. In 1973, the Egyptians and Syrians reciprocated, surprising Israel on Yom Kippur. For several weeks, as Israel struggled to win the elaborate tank battle that took place in the Sinai Peninsula, world Jewry had occasion to fear what would happen if the Egyptians broke through. Independent of the actual military risks, American Jews found themselves contemplating the theoretical possibility of a Jewish bloodbath.

That contemplation, followed by Israel's eventual, costly victory in the 1973 war, seems to have awakened in American Jews a willingness to revisit the Holocaust. It also awakened an emotional and intellectual association between the Holocaust and the state of Israel. Israel's victory had averted an imagined possible massacre of Jews. That conjured up the powerful idea that Israel itself was a response to the Holocaust.[5]

The notion that Israel should be understood in relation to the Holocaust was not completely new. The international debate that led to the United Nations' 1947 partition plan rested implicitly on the idea that after the Holocaust, most European Jews could not or would not return to their prewar homes—and that there was some moral justice in affording them a homeland. In 1958, the Jewish American author Leon Uris had published a bestselling novel, *Exodus*, which was made into a successful 1960 film starring Paul Newman and Eva Marie Saint. The novel and film focused on the efforts of displaced Jews to reach Palestine from Cyprus after World War II, toward the end of the British mandate, when Jewish immigration was still banned. *Exodus* implied clearly that Israel was necessary for Jews to defend themselves and so avoid another Holocaust, this time, by implication, at the hands of hostile Arabs.

Yet it is also important to recognize that Zionism predated the Holocaust by more than half a century. The Zionist institutions in mandate-era Palestine that were transformed into the government of Israel in 1948 long preceded the Holocaust. Zionists had certainly pointed to antisemitism and pogroms to argue that Jews should leave the European countries where they would never be truly safe or accepted. But even the most doomsaying Zionists did not predict the full scope of the Holocaust, any more than other analysts of the Jewish question did before the rise of Nazism. In historical terms, the Holocaust contributed to the United Nations' willingness to recommend partition and so played an oblique, tragic role in fulfilling the dreams of Zionism. In ideological terms, however, the Zionist vision of Israel was complete and instantiated before the Holocaust even occurred.

The bringing together of Israel and the Holocaust was therefore itself an important historical development. The relationship between these two epochal events in Jewish history was not obvious, however. Multiple models of the connection could be imagined, and multiple models were advanced.

In Israel, the model of the relationship took a specifically Zionist form. Many Israelis viewed the deaths of six million Jews, most of whom offered little in the way of violent resistance, as to a degree shameful—shameful because they had not resisted. Those Jews had gone "like sheep to the slaughter," the poet and anti-Nazi partisan fighter Abba Kovner (1918–1987) put it. Kovner, who emigrated to Israel in 1947, was using a metaphor that could be traced to the Bible and had been used by earlier Zionists to argue in favor of resisting antisemitic attacks. The Zionist way was to fight, not to be passive.[6]

Consequently, when Israel's parliament, the Knesset, considered when to commemorate the Holocaust in the early years of the state, it settled on the date that the Warsaw Ghetto uprising had begun. The holiday established on that day was not named Holocaust Remembrance Day but "Remembrance Day for Holocaust and Heroism." The heroism, exemplified by the brief and doomed uprising, got equal billing with the Holocaust. Conveniently, on the Jewish calendar, the date of the Warsaw Ghetto uprising fell eight days before Israel Independence Day. The Holocaust and the heroic resistance could be assimilated into the narrative that the establishment of the state of Israel repaired the tragedy of the destruction of European Jews.

In the United States, the model evolved differently. Some American Jews certainly believed that the main purpose of Israel was to protect against another Holocaust. But many American Jews instead viewed the United States as the better guarantor of the safety and security of Jews around the world. In the struggle of the 1970s to obtain freedom for Soviet Jews who wanted to express their Jewish identities, American Jews took the lead. They sought to influence and work alongside the U.S. government, not Israel, which had no leverage over the Soviet Union during the Cold War.

What was more, for American Jews in that era, Progressive Jews especially, it would have felt strangely self-denying to view Israel as the only place of true safety for Jews, as many Zionists continued to insist through the 1990s. After all, American Jews had achieved full citizenship as well as sociocultural and economic influence in the United States. For American Jews, the United States really had become their Zion. Jews were safer, better off, and more secure in the United States than they had been in any other country at any moment in world history, including Israel, where Jews remained subject to the threat of Arab invasion.

For Progressive Jews comfortable in their American identity, the ideas of the Holocaust and Israel slowly began to take on a different relationship. Increasingly, the two ideas became twin polestars of the expression of American Jewish thought and practice. To put it in the simplest possible way, American Jews recognized the importance of the Holocaust as a moral-historical event, and they supported the existence of Israel.

As I explained in part I, for Progressive American Jews, God is best served, honored, and worshipped by acts of social justice. As I also explained, this formulation does not fully answer the question of what makes Jewish religious or spiritual experience unique, even when it is married to the idea of a covenant between God and the Jewish people. Jewish thought and spirituality, however, call out for some version of Jewish specialness or chosenness, which is so enmeshed in the Jewish tradition.

As consciousness of the Holocaust began to grow among American Jews in the 1970s, 1980s, and 1990s, the experience of the Holocaust itself began to function as a solution to the question of what made the Jews special. Most Progressive Jews would be uncomfortable saying out loud that the Jews are the chosen people, an idea arguably inconsistent with the basic moral proposition that all people are equal and therefore must be equally loved and chosen by God. In this era, however, most Progressive Jews were comfortable saying that the Holocaust was a unique event in world history, unique in its intent and unique in its effect. The Jewish people might not be God's chosen people, but they were subjects of a unique historical event. They were in that sense distinct and special.

The slogan "Never again," intended as a moral exhortation, gave social justice content to the intuition that the Holocaust determined Jewish uniqueness. In old-fashioned, pre-Holocaust, Progressive Jewish theology, Jewish chosenness mandated that Jews play a special role as "a light unto the nations," spreading the message of monotheistic ethics. Jewish suffering played a role in that Progressive theology. As the Bible had put it, "You shall love the stranger, for you were strangers in the land of Egypt." The Holocaust could now be interpreted to provide a similar moral guidance. "You must never again allow a Holocaust to occur, for you yourselves suffered a Holocaust in the old country of Europe."*

At the level of theodicy, this theory also hinted at a response to the nearly overwhelming challenge that must plague any believer after the Holocaust: How could a just God allow the Holocaust to happen? Progressive Jewish theology offered no single, overt solution.† But it did offer an authentically Progressive Jewish reaction: from the fact of suffering, one could infer a duty to prevent the suffering of others.

Through this Progressive moralization of the Holocaust, the historical event gradually assumed a central position in Progressive Jewish religious thought. The theologian most closely associated with this process is the philosopher and Reform rabbi Emil Fackenheim (1916–2003), who

---

* This social justice formulation could be interpreted as imposing a special duty on Jews to prevent genocide worldwide. What remains ambiguous—and therefore contested to this day—is whether Jews must do so by bearing witness to the Holocaust, by drawing attention to other genocides when they are happening or about to happen, or by favoring military intervention to prevent or end genocide.

† Interestingly, what must be the most widely read book of Progressive Jewish theology—a *New York Times* bestseller read by Jews and non-Jews alike—did obliquely address this question. Rabbi Harold Kushner's *When Bad Things Happen to Good People* (New York: Schocken Books, 1981) argued that God was not all-powerful, and himself suffered in the suffering of the just. Although the book was framed as a response to individual human suffering, in particular the death of Kushner's son at the age of fourteen from a degenerative disease, it also deserves to be read as an important work of post-Holocaust theology.

himself escaped Hitler. Fackenheim framed the Holocaust as creating what he called a 614th commandment in addition to the 613 commandments commanded by God in the Bible: "Thou shalt not give Hitler a posthumous victory." As Fackenheim explained this proposition, it entailed a range of duties:

> We are, first, commanded to survive as Jews, lest the Jewish people perish. We are commanded, secondly, to remember in our very guts and bones the martyrs of the Holocaust, lest their memory perish. We are forbidden, thirdly, to deny or despair of God, however much we may have to contend with him or with belief in him, lest Judaism perish. We are forbidden, finally, to despair of the world as the place which is to become the kingdom of God, lest we help make it a meaningless place in which God is dead or irrelevant and everything is permitted. To abandon any of these imperatives, in response to Hitler's victory at Auschwitz, would be to hand him yet other, posthumous victories.[7]

Much can be said about this formulation, beginning with the extraordinary notion that a human act—the Holocaust—could be described, even metaphorically, as creating a divine commandment. What matters for our purposes is that the theology of the 614th commandment makes the Holocaust into *the* normative ground for affirmative Jewish life and faith: for belief, for practice, and for the Progressive objective of seeking social justice.

I could give many concrete examples of the penetration of the theological idea of the Holocaust into Progressive Jewish thought, but one proof-text should suffice. It appears in the liturgy for Yom Kippur found in the official prayer book of the Conservative movement. Designed for dramatic recitation, it consists of the ancient text of the mourner's Kaddish prayer, in which each Aramaic word is followed by the name of a Nazi death camp or the site of a Nazi massacre of Jews: Auschwitz, Buchenwald, Treblinka, and so forth.

This version of the Kaddish makes the Holocaust into a theological event: a martyrology intimately connected to the sanctification of the divine name for which the prayer stands. One who recites this new prayer literally sanctifies the Holocaust, through commemoration of the holy martyrdom of the Jews who died in the camps.

The Jewish tradition has long recognized the sanctification of martyrdom. The section of the Yom Kippur liturgy in which this new form of the Kaddish appears includes poetic laments over ancient as well as medieval Jewish martyrs. "The death of the righteous atones," according to a rabbinic statement that appears in the Talmud and elsewhere.[8] Of course, the sanctification of martyrdom as an expression of divine presence also resonates with Christian ideas about martyrdom. There is a healthy scholarly debate about whether and how medieval Jewish conceptions of martyrdom were affected by Christian context.

Like historical Jewish martyrology, the development of the Holocaust into a liturgically recognized theological component of Progressive Jewish thought is *not* reducible to Christian influence. Nevertheless, like older Jewish martyrology, the Christian context deserves to be noticed. Progressive Jewish thought does not exist in a vacuum, nor has it ever. Early Reform Judaism grew up in close theological proximity to Protestant Reform theology, in both Germany and the United States. Today's Progressive Judaism is, in a different way, part and parcel of broader American Progressive religious thought.

The centrality of the Holocaust to Progressive American Jewish belief can be summed up in a thought experiment. Imagine the rabbi of a large Progressive temple getting up in front of the congregation and beginning a Yom Kippur sermon with the words, "Some days I find I do not believe that God actually exists." The congregation might be mildly surprised, but it would not be scandalized, particularly if the rabbi went on to say that she does believe in God on other days. Indeed, in 2001, Rabbi David Wolpe, one of the most prominent Conservative congregational rabbis in the United States, made headlines with a Passover sermon questioning the historicity of the exodus from Egypt.[9] His career continued to thrive.

Now imagine the same hypothetical rabbi in the same temple on the same day. This time the sermon begins, "Some days I think that we should just get over the Holocaust and move on." The rabbi would be fired by the board of directors—at a special meeting that would be convened as soon as the services were over, if not before. It would not matter if the rabbi's sermon went on to say that, on the whole, she was convinced of the historical importance of the Holocaust. Questioning the central religious place of the Holocaust would be a firing offense.

A good test of orthodoxy in any religious context, including one that claims to deny that it has any orthodoxy, is to ask what words would get a member of the clergy fired from her job. By that measure, the deep religious significance of the Holocaust is today a central, orthodox component of Progressive American Jewish belief. For now, for a long time to come, and perhaps for all time, it cannot be questioned.

THE ORTHODOXY OF ISRAEL

At roughly the same time that the Holocaust came to function as one theological pillar of Progressive Jewish thought, Israel came to function as a similarly fundamental pillar. The process was complicated, perhaps more so than the theologizing of the Holocaust. Taking place from the 1970s through the 1990s, it was bound up in a transformation of classical Zionism into a form much more palatable to Progressive American Jews. And in comparison to the Holocaust, the idea of Israel occasioned a greater degree of ambivalence among Progressive Jews, an ambivalence that has returned with a vengeance in the current, third era of Progressive Jewish thought on Israel.

For Progressive Jews to embrace the idea of Israel, the first necessary step was for Israel to be reimagined not as the single national home for the whole Jewish people but as one place of refuge in which Jewish life could flourish. In its original, nationalist form, Zionism contradicted the Reform embrace of full national citizenship, first in Germany and then in the United States. Genuinely nationalist Zionism denied that Jews could be full citizens of any but a Jewish nation. That rendered the Reform vision of equal citizenship through privatized religion a vain hope. Equally important, classical secular Zionism rejected the very notion that Judaism should continue as a religion, picturing instead the transmutation of Jewish religion into a secular Israeli national identity. That would have heralded a historical situation in which Reform Judaism would be unnecessary and, indeed, barely imaginable. This is why Progressive Judaism is, statistically, almost nonexistent in Israel, and was indeed barely visible in Israel until very recently.

Put simply, in the era after the 1973 war, Zionism in Israel shifted its attitude toward Jews living outside the land of Israel. Much of the unconscious motivation for this change was political-pragmatic. Like other nationalisms, Zionism long held the aspirational idea (some would say fantasy) that political sovereignty equated to genuine national autonomy, understood as the military capacity to deter all enemies and provide for the country's own security.[10] The ideology of autonomy followed Zionism in Israel from 1948 up until 1973, as Israelis imagined their country being self-sufficient and capable of protecting itself and therefore, by extension, all Jews who might immigrate there. The fact that Israel became a nuclear power in 1966 or 1967 contributed to this ideological aspiration. Nuclear weapons were, then and now, understood as crucial tools of the sovereign capacity to self-defend. The apparent ease of the lopsided 1967 victory underscored the ideal of autonomy; if Israel could easily defeat her neighbors in a war fought alone, Israel must be truly autonomous.

The Yom Kippur War sent a sobering message to Zionists with respect to autonomy. A nuclear threat was of limited use, even in the face of an Egyptian attack that threatened briefly to reach Israeli population centers. Israel could have launched missiles to kill many Egyptians, but at what cost? And with what gain? Nuclear deterrence, it turned out, did not fully guarantee safety from invasion.

What was more, in October 1973, Israel badly needed U.S. supplies and support to win the war. Henry Kissinger, then U.S. secretary of state, was perceived in some quarters as having delayed that support so as to push Israel to learn the lessons of its dependence and act in a correspondingly more accommodating manner when pressed by the United States to negotiate peace with Egypt. Whether that was accurate or not (Kissinger was still denying it in an interview to mark his one hundredth birthday in 2023), the reality was that Israelis had to acknowledge that in a world of great power competition, Israel needed the United States to act as guarantor of its national security.[11]

Without American Jewish support, Israel could not then rely on the American alliance, because it was not at all certain that Israel was objectively the best regional ally for the United States to choose. The energy crisis of the 1970s showed the vast importance of Saudi and other Arab oil supplies to the U.S. economy. It followed that Israel needed to engage American Jews more fully, as a practical matter, and treat them as partners in protecting Israel's national security. That was a far cry from the view that many Israeli Zionists took of Diaspora Jews before 1973, roughly that they were weak, second-class Jews who should send donations but should remain silent if they disagreed with Israel's policies. For their part, American Jews also observed after 1973 that Israel needed them, at least insofar as it needed the United States.

The result was an Israeli Zionism that increasingly treated Israel as a Jewish national homeland for those who sought refuge there, not as the historically necessary culmination of two thousand years of Jewish history or the negation of the Diaspora in its entirety. This chastened, modified version of Zionism welcomed American Jews to see themselves as, in a sense, partners in the Zionist national project even without moving to Israel. To be sure, to Israeli Zionists, the partnership was not equal. The government of Israel was to take the lead and specify both strategy and tactics. American Jews were to follow that lead. But American Jews were nevertheless to be treated as part of the overall effort to maintain and enhance Israel's national interests.*

This form of Zionism-as-partnership suited both Israelis and Progressive American Jews. On the Israeli side, it cost relatively little in

---

* Not by coincidence, at this time a coalition of Israelis and American Jewish Zionists began a historic process of outreach to American Christian evangelicals, who would eventually come to be important supporters of Israel on the U.S. political scene. Zionism had a long history of support from British Christian evangelicals. But those mainly liberal nineteenth- and early twentieth-century British evangelical Christian Restorationists and proto-Zionists had a very different cast from the politically conservative American evangelicals whom Zionism successfully recruited between 1980 and the present.

practical terms. Ideologically, the newer version of Israeli Zionism lacked some of the absolutist insistence on a single homeland associated with the older form. But that seemed like a small price to pay for greater American Jewish support. And as a matter of practical reality, it had already become evident that American Jews had no intention of emigrating en masse to Israel. So Zionism without its aim of negating the Diaspora had the advantage of being a bit closer to reality than a more totalizing Zionism.

On the Progressive Jewish side, the benefit of the more inclusive (to American Jews) version of Israeli Zionism was ideologically and theologically substantial. Israel existed, and by its persistent existence implied that American Jews needed to take it seriously. Progressive American Jews were proud of Israel after 1967. It was no longer viable for Progressive rabbis or lay leaders to assert that the main responsibility of American Jews must be to support the American Jewish community, not Israel.

At the level of Progressive Jewish religious belief, the idea of Israel also offered a solution to a problem created by a forthright acknowledgment of the Holocaust. Without a forward-looking narrative of redemption, an American Judaism focused on the Holocaust would have become a backward-looking religion of mourning. Before fully confronting the immensity of the Holocaust, Progressive Jewish thought had tried to redeem the historical legacy of Jewish suffering through equal citizenship and social justice work. Abraham Joshua Heschel's embrace of the civil rights movement fit this model well: African Americans could, like Jews, be redeemed from their subordination through equal citizenship, and Jews would redeem themselves by supporting this struggle.[12]

But once American Jews began to confront the reality of the Holocaust, it became harder to rely on this traditional, citizenship-and-social-justice solution to the theological question of redemption. The devastation of the Holocaust showed, among other things, that equal citizenship, as Jews had formally achieved in Germany, France, and even Poland before World War II, had not sufficed to protect or save Jews from genocidal murder. Jewish survival through equal citizenship in the United States looked like an almost accidental feature of the superiority of American liberal constitutionalism, not a success of the Progressive

Jewish strategy of relying on liberalism. To a significant degree, omitting the United States, the classical prewar Zionist critique of Progressive Jewish political liberalism had been correct. Equal citizenship, privatized religion, and the struggle for social justice had not saved Europe's Jews, much less redeemed them.

American Progressive Jews could not and did not want to abandon their commitment to America or to liberalism. They were not prepared to redefine Jewish redemption entirely in classically Zionist terms as the achievement of a unitary nation-state. But they were willing and even eager to work to protect Israel. And they could now admit that in the light of the Holocaust, Zionist nationalism might have a role to play in Jewish historical redemptive experience. Redemption could not plausibly be restricted to social justice activism insofar as that narrative of redemptive activism sat poorly with the narrative of the destruction of European Jewry.

After 1973, then, Zionism came to offer an alternative, supplemental account of post-Holocaust Jewish redemption for Progressive American Jews. The Holocaust had martyred European Jewry. But the modern state of Israel had been born from the ashes. Israel did not redeem American Jews, who were in no need of a separate redemption. It did, however, redeem the suffering of the martyrs of the Holocaust. Their deaths had not been entirely in vain. From destruction came rebuilding. And Israel's existence would prevent another Holocaust from occurring by providing Diaspora Jews with an escape hatch should antisemitic pressures make life untenable.[13]

This shift in the American Jewish Progressive view of Israel in the post-1973 period may seem incremental, but it was also transformative. For the first time, Progressive American Jews could integrate Israel into their theological picture of the relationship between God and the Jewish people. The liberal social justice ideals that were essential to Jewish Progressivism could remain, because they were still relevant to the religious-spiritual lives of Jews in the United States. Yet simultaneously, the suffering of the Holocaust could be paired with the redemptive power of the idea of Israel. Instead of Progressive American Judaism devolving into a cult of Holocaust memorialization, it could pair the martyrdom of European Jewry with the redemptive possibilities of Zionism.

As a result, support for Israel became a theological orthodoxy for Progressive American Jews. Return to the thought experiment of the rogue rabbi. Imagine she told her congregation, "Some days I find I do not believe that the state of Israel should exist." She would be fired as quickly as if she had questioned the Holocaust. Progressive rabbis have maintained the capacity to criticize Israel's formal refusal to acknowledge them legally as rabbis. But that is about as far as foundational criticism of Israel has been allowed to go in most Progressive American Jewish temples and synagogues, at least until very, very recently.*

SYNTHESIS: MARTYRDOM AND REDEMPTION

What emerged in the 1980s and 1990s was a new, distinctively Progressive American Jewish synthesis of the centrality of the Holocaust and the redemptive narrative of the creation of Israel. This synthesis constituted the core of Progressive Jewish post-Holocaust theology. At the level of theological narrative, it made some partial sense out of the deaths of the six million by depicting Israel as the redemptive solution to the problem of genocidal antisemitism. At the level of practice, it enabled Progressive American Jews to organize for two supplementary purposes: memorializing the Holocaust and supporting the state of Israel.

The Holocaust memorialization project became a staple of American Jewish local activism after the Jewish-Black alliance of the 1960s splintered, making it harder for Progressive Jewish communities to coordinate local social justice activism with national liberal Democratic politics. Beginning in the 1980s, local American Jewish communities built hundreds of public Holocaust memorials. Today sixteen Holocaust *museums* exist in the United States, with more planned to open soon.[14] I will use the largest and most important, the United States Holocaust Memorial Museum, to explore the project of Holocaust memorialization, its religious-theological character, and its complex relationship to the idea of Israel.

---

* This has been changing, as I will shortly explain, although the Hamas-Israel war may curtail the change.

The origins of the museum lie with a President's Commission on the Holocaust, created by Jimmy Carter's administration in 1978, precisely when Holocaust consciousness was rising among American Jews. The commission was the brainchild of Elie Wiesel, not yet a household name, who became its chair. The stated goal was to explore the creation of a national memorial to the Holocaust. The commission duly recommended exactly that. The funds to build and endow it, some $200 million, would be raised privately. But the location, on almost two acres of land adjacent to the Washington Monument, just off the National Mall in Washington, DC, belonged to the federal government. In 1980, Congress voted to dedicate the land to the museum/memorial. The building opened in 1993 and as of 2023 had hosted 47 million visitors.

That the government of the United States should take an interest in the creation of a Holocaust memorial or museum was itself remarkable. The Holocaust did not happen in the United States. Its perpetrators and victims were not Americans. That the institution should be established in such close proximity to the National Mall, where the Smithsonian and its family of museums resides, was more remarkable still. The Smithsonian museums collectively represent an effort to document and represent American national experience, past, present, and future. At the time the Holocaust Museum was conceived, the National Museum of the American Indian had not yet been created, nor had the National Museum of African American History and Culture.

The presence of the Holocaust Museum so close to the symbolic epicenter of American culture represented, in no small part, an expression of identity for American Jews. The political power to acquire the site and the economic clout to build and create the museum were clear markers of American Jewish capacity. Visitors to Washington, DC, would encounter the museum and with it the implicit presence of American Jews.

The choice of the Holocaust as the identity marker for American Jews was particularly significant. Historically, Jews of all persuasions have always memorialized Jewish suffering in prayer and fasting, but put their financial and cultural resources into building institutions of Jewish learning and prayer—of Jewish life, not Jewish death. They built synagogues, schools, and yeshivas, not memorials or museums. The Holocaust Museum made the commemoration of trauma into the leading concrete, public manifestation of Jewishness in the American capital, and beyond.

The Jewish community could conceivably have sought congressional approval for a museum of American Jewish history. But such a possibility, which so far as I know was never even considered, would have lacked the distinctive moral-theological quality of the Holocaust. It would have established the Jewish community as just another ethnic American immigrant community, no different from Italian Americans, Irish Americans, and so forth, none of whom have or had museums or memorials on the Mall. In contrast, the Holocaust could be interpreted to assert a claim of universal significance for the particular Jewish experience of suffering. To build a museum, and build it in that location, was to treat the Holocaust as an event of national, indeed global consequence, one in which the Jews played a central and identifiable role, even if it was the role of victims.

Seen from the standpoint of Progressive Jewish theology, the Holocaust Museum embodied and literalized the centrality of the Holocaust as a defining event that conferred or reconferred uniqueness on the Jewish people, and that carried a lesson for all humanity. The lesson was "Never Again," a moral-ethical takeaway from the horrific facts of the destruction of the Jews of Europe. The museum was intended to turn the Holocaust into a moral lesson of universal significance.

As ultimately built, the Holocaust Museum thus came to function as a pilgrimage site for American Jews that would also hold meaning for all Americans, or rather all people. Not unlike a medieval cathedral, it simultaneously depicted and embodied a narrative of martyrdom. It was dedicated to symbolizing the transcendent meaning of a particular religious event. And it reflected the piety, wealth, and political power of its builders.

So perhaps it is not a coincidence that in the building of the Holocaust Museum, the most noteworthy policy debate centered on whether relics of the Holocaust—the eyeglasses, human hair, gold fillings, and other physical and cultural remains found at Auschwitz-Birkenau—should be literally brought to the museum or should be represented by replicas.[15] A medieval cathedral ordinarily houses the relics of a saint that are, to use the technical term, "translated" there from wherever they may have been found. The debate over the Holocaust relics was settled in favor of the translation of actual relics from actual death camps.

The narrative presented at the U.S. Holocaust Museum does not directly culminate in the creation of the state of Israel. Within the permanent exhibitions, the section named "The Last Chapter" scrupulously shows Jewish Holocaust survivors settling in "Europe, Israel, and the United States."[16] This is in contrast to Yad Vashem, "The World Holocaust Remembrance Center," first established in Jerusalem in 1957 and entirely rebuilt in 2005. The Israeli Holocaust memorialization more closely links the Holocaust to the deep history of European antisemitism. It depicts the state of Israel as the historic solution to that problem. And it treats post–World War II Middle Eastern and Islamic antisemitism as continuous with the antisemitism that led to the Holocaust.[17]

It would therefore be crude, and I think inaccurate, to argue that the role of the Holocaust in Progressive American Jewish thought is to drive support for Israel. The lessons of the U.S. Holocaust Museum are meant to be universal, in keeping with the intellectual and spiritual legacy of Progressive Jewish universalism. The Holocaust Museum is not, in its design or its narrative, a pro-Israel entity.

Yet the idea of Israel does come into complex interplay with the idea of the Holocaust in Progressive American Jewish thought through the pairing of Holocaust martyrdom with the redemptive story of Zionism. If one were to see it through the lens of Protestant theology, translated into the American Jewish context, the Holocaust would stand in for the passion, and the state of Israel for the resurrection. The social gospel of *tikkun 'olam* can sit comfortably alongside this implicit theology.

It is certain that no Progressive American Jewish thinker ever consciously intended to re-create the theological structure of American Protestantism in translation, any more than medieval European Jews trying to make sense of Jewish martyrdom at the hands of Christians were conscious of being influenced by Christian ideas of martyrdom. Heaven forfend. The very thought is anathema. What I am suggesting is that the enormous theological challenge posed by the tragedy of the Holocaust (once acknowledged) called out for a response. In the context of American religious thought more generally, the attraction of Israel as a paired, redemptive, resurrectionary supplement to the Holocaust was and is overwhelming.

For purposes of comparison, consider the Israeli secular Zionist reception of the Holocaust. It treats the state of Israel as a nationalist solution to the problem of the Holocaust, itself understood as a problem of what happens to a people when they are stateless. In so doing, the Israeli view, unlike the Progressive American Jewish view, does not have to make the Holocaust into an event that proves Jewish uniqueness or that has a universal moral message for all humanity. That is because the Israeli secular Zionist view of the Holocaust doesn't have to embody a theology of Jewishness or Jewish chosenness. The American Jewish Progressive view of the Holocaust does. In that theology, the Holocaust becomes a transformative and transcendent world-historical event that establishes Jewish uniqueness. And the idea of Israel comes to soften the depressive qualities of unique martyrdom by giving meaning to the martyrdom of the six million, whose deaths were redeemed by the creation of the state.

The result is, or rather was, a coherent Progressive Jewish theology of the Holocaust and Israel. Together they formed the twin orthodoxies of a Progressivism that preferred to think it had no religious orthodoxies at all.

LOOMING CONTRADICTION: JEWISH AND DEMOCRATIC

The third phase of Progressive American Jewish theology is the one we are living through now. Its beginning point cannot be specified precisely, but it is simplest to date it to the period immediately after the second intifada. Unlike the first intifada (1987–1991), which was characterized by stone throwing, the second intifada (2000–2005) was characterized by suicide bombing aimed at civilians. In response to the bombings, Israel gradually erected a barrier or wall along much of the border between the occupied West Bank and Israel. (The wall also protects Israeli settlements and infrastructure in the West Bank and does not follow the border exactly.)

The combination of the bombings and the barrier precipitated a crisis of confidence among left-leaning Israelis and Progressive American Jews who had hoped for the fulfillment of a two-state solution in the aftermath of the Oslo peace accords. As late as the summer of 2000, on the eve of the second intifada, it was still possible to imagine a functioning Palestinian state emerging in ever-increasing swaths of the West Bank. I brought a group of international CEOs to visit the West Bank at the time, and I can vividly recall the hopefulness of the scene as they were welcomed at a new Palestinian stock exchange and a new Palestinian telecommunications company and were fêted at a brand-new casino reached by cable car on a cliff outside Jericho. The bombings within Israel that followed convinced many (loosely pro-Israel) observers that peace was not a realistic possibility from the Palestinian side. The barrier in turn convinced many (loosely anti-Israel) observers that Israel intended to make its occupation of the West Bank permanent and avoid any serious efforts to reach a two-state solution.

The consequences of these shifts in perception have been felt intensely—and generationally—by Progressive American Jews. The structural challenge derives from applying the progressive, liberal values those Jews hold in respect of U.S. politics to the situation of Israel, in particular in relation to the rights of Palestinians living as noncitizens under Israeli rule.

For Progressive Jews who embraced Israel in the 1980s and 1990s, it was important that Israel self-define as a "Jewish and democratic" state, a formulation that appears in Israel's declaration of independence. To classical Zionists, the "Jewish" in "Jewish and democratic state" did not mean the state would be *religiously* Jewish or fulfill God's prophetic plan. They meant the state would be *nationally* Jewish: it would possess a Jewish majority, be controlled by the Jewish nation, and express Jewish cultural-national values. It was in this sense that Theodor Herzl had titled his secular Zionist classic *Der Judenstaat*, The State of the Jews. Under the version of nationalism they espoused, a state with all its modern institutions—law, language, a parliament, an army, and so forth—was the sine qua non of national self-expression. With a state, a people could play out the state's identity and defend its physical as well as spiritual well-being. Stateless, a people would be lost to history, culturally and maybe literally. Stateless people, as the philosopher Hannah Arendt noted, were people without rights.

Notwithstanding its original meaning in context, for Progressive Jews living fifty years after the establishment of the state, the dual formulation "Jewish and democratic" could be read in a different way: as an assertion of the compatibility of Jewish values and democratic values. That promise of compatibility appealed uniquely to Progressive Jews, who believed (unlike secular Zionists!) that the Jewish religion in fact entailed a commitment to liberal democratic values.

Making the ideal of the Jewish state as a liberal democratic state even more attractive, Israel's High Court of Justice in exactly this same historical period undertook what is sometimes called a "rights revolution," creating and announcing fundamental liberal rights even though Israel has no single, written constitution. The court, led then by its president, Aharon Barak, singlehandedly gave legal effect to an ideology of a Jewish and democratic state. In one of the iconic decisions of the rights revolution, the 2000 Ka'adan case (also called the Katzir case), the court held that it was unlawful for the state to allocate land to the Jewish Agency, a quasi-governmental institution created before the state of Israel, if the agency refused to sell or lease land to Palestinians. As an assertion of formal legal equality, the decision had echoes of *Brown v. Board of Education*.[18]

In the process of expanding liberal rights, Israel's high court encountered some criticism from other Israelis who denounced the court's judicial activism. In the United States, however, among those aware of the court's activity, the rights revolution contributed to the perception that one could support Israel while simultaneously and consistently espousing liberal beliefs. Even when it came to Israel's use of force in this period—whether in Gaza or the West Bank—the high court attempted to play a supervisory role, applying international humanitarian law to require the IDF to respect human rights as the court interpreted them.

Seen from an external perspective, the challenge to the narrative of Israel as a Jewish and liberal democratic state came, first and foremost, from the legal and political status of Palestinians who were not citizens of Israel and lived in the West Bank or Gaza. Those Palestinians were, according to Israeli judicial rulings, entitled to the protections conferred by international law on people living under military occupation. But they were not citizens of any liberal democratic state and did not enjoy the equal civil or political rights of Israeli citizens. That they lived under Israeli authority but without political or legal equality called into question Israel's claim to be a liberal democratic state.*

For effectively the entire second phase of Progressive Jewish Holocaust-Israel theology, Progressive American Jews who worried about the rights of Palestinians had an answer to this problem. They were able to tell themselves that Israel was in the process of negotiating a lasting peace that would lead to the creation of an independent Palestinian state. In such a Palestinian state, liberal rights would be respected, and if they were not, blame would lie with the Palestinian government, not with Israel.

The possibility of such a Palestinian state did not seem especially remote. The 1978 Camp David Accords were a hopeful start, and the peace between Israel and Egypt, however cold, created optimism about a potential future solution. Although the first intifada worried many American Jewish Progressives, it was followed almost immediately by the Oslo Accords, the first directly negotiated deal between Israelis and Palestinians. The Oslo Accords suggested the possibility of resolving the question of Palestinian rights in the foreseeable future. They allowed Progressives to believe that Israel was a liberal democracy for its citizens, Jewish and Arab, and that the anomalous status of noncitizen Palestinians was an unfortunate artifact of the history of the Israel-Palestine conflict that ultimately would be fixed.

The second intifada and the wall broke that complex of beliefs—not

---

* The situation of the 1.6 million Palestinian Arab citizens of Israel is more complicated. They have civil and political rights but also face systematic discrimination not entirely dissimilar to the systemic racism that faces African Americans. Their status is increasingly an important concern for critics inside and outside Israel. And since the 1990s, some of their politicians have, as non-Jewish citizens of Israel, challenged the Jewish character of Israel, pointing out the difficulty of Israel being a democracy if it self-defines as Jewish in a way that necessarily excludes Palestinian citizens.

all at once, but gradually and thoroughly. Today, Progressive American Jews increasingly find it difficult to see Israel as a genuine liberal democracy, mostly because some three million Palestinians in the West Bank live under Israeli authority with no citizenship rights. Two million-plus more Palestinians live in Gaza, which was self-governing under extreme constraints until Hamas attacked Israel and Israel responded, leaving the political fate of its population uncertain. The idea that Israel is a democratic state has become possible to sustain only by excluding those Palestinians from the calculus.

Many Progressive American Jews would still point out that the reason for this situation is complex and related to the history of failed peace negotiations and Hamas's refusal to accept Israel's existence. Yet it is also true that those same American Jews recognize and privately acknowledge that the occupation of the West Bank has become effectively permanent. Israel has existed since 1948. During its nearly seventy-five years, it has ruled the West Bank for all but nineteen.

To compound the problem, Progressive American Jews fully understand that mainstream Israeli politics have moved far to the right since the early 2000s and are today by far the most right-wing they have ever been. When he was prime minister from 2009 to 2021, the second of his three times holding that office, Benjamin Netanyahu openly allied himself not only with the Republican Party but with Donald Trump. That left little doubt about Netanyahu's orientation from an American perspective. But the government Netanyahu formed on returning to power in 2022 went considerably further right.

In a column titled "The Israel We Knew Is Gone," the *New York Times* columnist Thomas L. Friedman described Netanyahu's coalition as an "alliance of ultra-Orthodox leaders and ultranationalist politicians, including some outright racist, anti-Arab Jewish extremists once deemed completely outside the norms and boundaries of Israeli politics."[19] The government depended on a number of far-right parties, at least until some centrists joined a temporary wartime coalition government in October 2023. One of these is called Jewish Power (*'Otzmah Yehudit*). It is a lineal descendant of the old Kach ("Thus") Party, founded by the ultranationalist Rabbi Meir Kahane; its name echoes (maybe unwittingly) the Black Power movement that influenced Kahane in the late 1960s.[20] Kahane's original party was outlawed by the government of Israel for its incitement of racism against Arabs and advocacy of domestic terrorism. Itamar Ben-Gvir, the leader of Jewish Power and a disciple of Kahane, is so extreme that when he was eighteen, the IDF refused to conscript him because of his racist anti-Arab beliefs. Weeks before the assassination of Israeli prime minister Yitzhak Rabin in 1995, Ben-Gvir appeared on Israeli television showing off a hood ornament stolen from Rabin's official car and saying, "We got to his car, and we'll get to him, too."[21] In 2007, he was convicted of inciting racism and supporting a (Jewish) terrorist organization. In short, Ben-Gvir's views contradict every principle of democracy and civil rights that Progressive Jews hold dear.

Another party in Netanyahu's coalition is the Religious Zionism party, led by the outspoken ultranationalist Bezalel Smotrich, who has made opposition to gay rights one of his signature issues. The Religious Zionism party combined with Jewish Power and another ultranationalist, religious party called Noam to form an electoral bloc that emerged from the 2022 election as the third-largest party in the Knesset. Ben-Gvir and Smotrich are both senior members of Netanyahu's cabinet.

Meanwhile, in the same 2022 election, left-of-center liberal democratic parties crashed and burned. The Meretz party, founded in 1992 to advance civil rights and civil liberties, failed to win even a single seat in the Knesset. The old Labor Party, the party of Yitzhak Rabin and Ehud Barak, which pursued and favored peace with the Palestinians, won a total of four seats out of 120.

In the aftermath of Netanyahu's victory, the ongoing internal debate over Israel's status as a liberal democracy turned into a major societal conflict. Netanyahu, already under criminal indictment, initiated legislation changing the way Israel's high court justices are selected so as to give his coalition government a decisive voice. This was considered a prelude to other proposed laws that would allow the Knesset to overrule the high court with a simple majority vote, crushing judicial review. In response, hundreds of thousands of Israelis, including a large number from the country's high-tech sector, took to the streets in protest, warning that passing the laws would destroy Israeli democracy and send the country down the road of Hungary and Poland. When Netanyahu's coalition actually passed legislation that denied the court the power to overturn governmental acts as unreasonable, the protests increased further. Israelis on both sides of the issue feared the possibility of a constitutional crisis should the high court strike down laws that interfered with its powers and the government in turn refuse to acknowledge or implement the judicial decision.

On the one hand, the protests could be read as strong evidence that many Israelis care deeply about the country's liberal democratic character, so much so that they were prepared to fight for the high court's capacity to check the majority. On the other hand, the legislation reflects a willingness by many other Israelis to favor majoritarian electoral democracy over liberal democracy based on judicial review. As of this writing, it is impossible to know which side will prevail or what eventual compromise might mean for the country's liberal democratic future, especially in light of the Hamas-Israel war that broke out while the two Israeli sides were locked in political conflict with each other. In any case, Israel's high court had already ceased to issue stirring proequality decisions after being chastened by the argument that the justices were usurping the role of the democratically elected Knesset. The court is unlikely to be highly activist in the wake of the curtailment of its judicial review powers and the threat to change its membership.

None of the challenges to Israel's liberal democratic bona fides came as a surprise to Israel's critics on American university campuses, among the first places where Progressive American Jews began to attack Israel openly. Writing in 2010, the journalist Peter Beinart alerted mainstream American Jews to an emerging generational rift over Israel, which he attributed roughly to college-aged Progressives' liberal sympathies for the plight of the Palestinians.[22] The organized American Jewish community responded by trying to kill the messenger, stunning Beinart, who at the time identified as a centrist Democrat, a liberal internationalist, and a Zionist. Beinart's prediction was, however, accurate; since 2010, the views of Progressive Jews on college campuses have become in many cases decidedly anti-Israel, not merely questioning or skeptical, as responses to the Hamas attacks on Israel have demonstrated.

Some of the older generation of Progressive American Jewish Zionists continue to defend the views of previous decades and lament young people's turn to the left. Israeli Zionists observe acidly that as the left wing of the Democratic Party becomes more openly critical of Israel, American Jewish Democrats are pulled alongside it. Both analyses are accurate yet superficial. Both fail to confront the actual problem faced by Progressive American Jews in relation to Israel. It is not primarily a problem of identity politics. It is a problem of morality, theology, and belief.

THE PROGRESSIVE GOD AND THE EXISTING
STATE OF ISRAEL

As you read these words, the community of Progressive Jews is going through a painful generational conflict. On one side are the people roughly my age: the Gen X leaders of the movement, rabbis and lay-people alike. They are Progressive Jews in my terminology. They are also, for the most part, progressive Democrats in the current political meaning of the term in the United States. When it comes to domestic policy, they lean left of center, identifying more with Elizabeth Warren and Bernie Sanders than, say, Hillary Clinton.

The Gen X Progressive Jewish leaders are (still) liberal Zionists. They love Israel. They also criticize it. They wish Israel would recognize Reform and Conservative rabbis. They wish Israel would be more just to Palestinians. They wish there were some solution to the Israel-Palestine conflict. They often don't identify with AIPAC, the powerful American Israel Public Affairs Committee, which coordinates much pro-Israel lobbying by American Jews and that historically has allied itself closely with whatever government is in power in Israel, no matter how right-wing. Instead, they have their own liberal Zionist organizations that they favor and fund, like J Street, a lobbying body that calls itself "the political home of pro-Israel, pro-peace Americans," and the New Israel Fund, which says its "aim is to advance liberal democracy, including freedom of speech and minority rights, and to fight the inequality, injustice and extremism that diminish Israel." They publish anguished books justifying their positions with titles like *Fault Lines: Exploring the Complicated Place of Progressive American Jewish Zionism.*[23] When Israel is attacked, however, they respond instinctively with solidarity and support. Their commitment to the Jewish state, and to fellow Jews, is unquestioned.

On the other side of the conflict are the kids, whose views on Israel are very different.* Some Gen Z Progressive Jews participate in campus organizations like Students for Justice in Palestine, a "collective of organizers that supports over 200 Palestine solidarity organizations on college campuses across occupied Turtle Island (U.S. and Canada)." On October 12, 2023, as Israel began its response to Hamas's attack on Israeli civilians, SJP's national office posted on social media "condemning the Zionist project and their latest genocidal attack on the Palestinian people." Closely associated is the campaign for Boycott, Divestment, and Sanctions, which self-describes as "a Palestinian-led movement for freedom, justice and equality." Its view is that "Israel maintains a regime of settler colonialism, apartheid and occupation over the Palestinian people." BDS, "inspired by the South African anti-apartheid movement," encourages boycotting Israeli cultural institutions and businesses and anyone associated with them.

Jewish Voice for Peace is a specifically Jewish group that supports the BDS movement and works alongside SJP. Its website boasts of sixty chapters, two hundred thousand supporters, and ten thousand donors. The organization says it "is guided by a vision of justice, equality and freedom for all people." It follows, for JVP, that "we unequivocally oppose Zionism because it is counter to those ideals." On October 14, 2023, the organization posted: "As U.S. Jews [we] believe that never again means never again for anyone, and that includes Palestinians. Never again is now."

It seems probable that a relatively small proportion of Gen Z Progressive Jews has been radicalized to the point of embracing formal

---

* Not all are kids. Consider Judith Butler (b. 1956), who in 2012 published *Parting Ways: Jewishness and the Critique of Zionism* (New York: Columbia University Press, 2012). In the book, Butler draws on "certain religious concepts" of Jewishness to mount a critique of Zionism and a defense of Diasporism. The chapter titled "Is Judaism Zionism?" is particularly suggestive.

anti-Zionism outright. Many are conflicted themselves about what they should think about Israel. Others would prefer not to focus on Israel at all. Yet it is fair to generalize by saying that many have been moved by the analogy, widespread on college campuses, between Israel and apartheid-era South Africa. In 2021, Human Rights Watch issued a long report finding that Israel's treatment of Palestinians satisfied the definition of apartheid under international law.[24] So did the Israeli human rights group B'Tselem.[25] In 2022, Amnesty International did the same.[26] Progressive American Jews are accustomed to treating these human rights groups as mainstream exponents of liberal values. A students'-eye version of the issue was expressed by the *Harvard Crimson*, an undergraduate newspaper, in an April 2022 editorial endorsing BDS. "The arguments made against BDS could have been and indeed were once made against South Africa," the editorial board wrote. BDS tactics "helped win the liberation of Black South Africans from Apartheid, and have the potential to do the same for Palestinians today."[27]

The upshot is that Gen X and Gen Z Progressive Jewish leaders and activists often find themselves seriously at odds with each other about Israel. The disagreement is painful for both sides, the way generational arguments often are. The middle-aged Progressives think the kids have failed to learn how important Israel should be for them as Jews. The kids think the old folks are mired in a discredited ideology they can't escape.*

I want to suggest that the generational rift reflects not two different conceptions of Progressive Jewishness but something else: two different

---

* The Millennials, between Gen X and Gen Z, are a more complicated matter. Their conflict is often internal. Consider the magazine *Jewish Currents*, originally a communist-affiliated publication founded in 1946. It was refounded in 2018 by a self-described "team of millennials" and is now "committed to the rich tradition of thought, activism, and culture of the Jewish left, and the left more broadly." The magazine publishes fascinating articles like one on the crisis of the organization IfNotNow, founded by millennials in 2014, a crisis driven, the article proposes, by the organization's attempt to be a big tent to include liberal Zionists and anti-Zionists. (The article also notes that "many IfNotNow founders were heavily involved in Conservative, Reform, and Reconstructionist Jewish organizations.") See Aaron Freedman, "What Happened to IfNotNow?: The Close of the Trump Era Finds the Millennial Anti-Occupation Group at a Crossroads," *Jewish Currents*, April 26, 2021, https://jewishcurrents.org/what-happened-to-ifnotnow.

visions of Israel, refracted through a common commitment to social justice. As I argued in part I, Progressive Judaism gives expression to what it considers the biblical values of justice, equality, freedom, and the like. When the Holocaust and Israel became part of this social justice theology, both had to accord with it. The Holocaust became a moral lesson of Never Again on par with the Hebrews' slavery in Egypt. Israel became a model of aspirational redemption, a role it could play only because it was possible to imagine the Jewish state as liberal and democratic.

If Israel does not embody the values of liberal democracy, however, it cannot serve as a moral ideal for Progressive Jews whose beliefs mandate universal human dignity and equality. In the starkest possible terms, a God of love and justice cannot bless or desire a state that does not seek to provide equality, dignity, or civil and political rights to many of the people living under its authority. Progressive Jewish belief can be reconciled with a Jewish and democratic state, provided the state aims to treat Jews and non-Jews equally. But to Progressive Jews, a state that denies equal treatment to its subjects is neither democratic nor properly Jewish.

Put another way, the "Jewish" part of Jewish and democratic means two different things for Zionists and American Jewish Progressives. To Zionism, the Jewish part of Jewish and democratic originally meant *nationally* Jewish, not religiously so. That much followed from the Zionist belief that Jewishness itself must be understood as a national quality, not a set of religious beliefs or practices. To American Jewish Progressives, however, inheritors of the Reform movement, "Jewish" means "religiously Jewish" in the Progressive sense. A Jewish state must be a state committed to Jewish values, and those values are the values associated with the Progressives' faith. The Jewish and democratic state was, Progressives believed, possible because Judaism's values matched those of democracy. If Israel abandons the ideals of equality, freedom, and dignity for all, it can no longer be genuinely Jewish in the Jewish Progressive religious sense. Nor is it democratic in the American progressive political sense.

From this it follows that for sincere, committed Progressive Jews, it would be a self-contradictory betrayal of their Jewish commitments to remain Zionists if Israel does not match the ideals of liberal democracy.

Israeli Zionists who are shocked by this development have forgotten that Progressive Judaism was long skeptical of Zionism because Progressives saw Jewishness as a set of moral teachings, not as a national identity. Israeli Zionists often assume that Progressives are irreligious (in Hebrew, *hiloni*), as secular Israelis typically describe themselves to be. That is a mistaken projection, one encouraged by the outdated Zionist belief that Jewish religion could not survive in the Diaspora. Today's Israeli Zionists sometimes think and act as though American Jewish Progressives owe Israel a duty of loyalty. For Jewish Progressives, however, the higher duty of loyalty lies to divine principles of love and justice, not to the state of Israel.

For the middle-aged and older generations of American Jewish Progressives, the painful difficulty of the current situation is that they find themselves trapped in the mire of intergenerational apologetics. They believe as Jews in a divine order of love and social justice. Indeed, it is they who (successfully) taught the younger generation of Jewish Progressives to believe in that vision. They want to believe in the possibility of Israel as a genuinely Jewish and democratic state. But they find they must spend their energies excusing Israel's treatment of Palestinians in order to reconcile their competing beliefs. That sort of apologetics is agonizing, painstaking work. No one enjoys it. And like most religious apologetics, it rarely convinces anyone who doesn't already have the relevant set of commitments.

One can feel sympathy for the Boomer Progressives who made Israel central to their contribution to Jewish theology. The Holocaust-Israel juxtaposition, their distinctive generational contribution to Progressive theology, is now foundering because of the politics of the actually existing state of Israel. On the one hand, the association is as powerful as ever: images of Israelis murdered and taken hostage recall the horrors of the Holocaust. On the other hand, Israel is a real-world nation-state, populated by living Israelis whose beliefs and views differ from those of American Jewish Progressives. That actually existing Israel, with its geopolitical and domestic political struggles, has put the older generation of Progressives into a condition of internal turmoil that can be resolved only by holding fast to an interpretation of Israel's form of political governance that may not compel or even convince their own grandchildren.

As for the most thoughtful of the young Progressives, they, too, face a deep challenge. On the one hand, they believe in the prophetic teachings of social justice that compel them to social action. On the other hand, they find that they cannot avoid the broken reality of Israel, a reality that, they believe, Jewish tradition commands them to repair.

Their great-grandparents, if they were Reform Jews, had the option of de-emphasizing Israel, almost to the point of ignoring Zionism. Before the state of Israel existed, they did not need to reconcile their beliefs about Judaism as a private, Diasporic religion with the aspirations of Zionist Jews. Even after the state arose, it was possible, for a time, to treat it as separate from Jewish thought, practice, and identity.

The young Progressives do not have that luxury. They inherited a form of Judaism that already incorporated Israel into its theology. They do not know how to be Jews without engaging Israel. Yet the content of their broader theology—their beliefs about Jewish morality and *tikkun 'olam*—make support of Israel difficult or even repugnant to them.

Their solution—their Jewish, Progressive, sincerely felt solution—is *to express their Jewish belief in social justice by criticizing or condemning Israel for its failures of equality, liberty, dignity, and human rights.* If Israel were a liberal democracy, they could conceivably support it. If it isn't, and has no realistic prospect of becoming one, it must be subject to the critique that could produce social change.

It emerges that young Progressive Jewish critics of Israel feel an unstated connection to Israel even as they resist and reject it. They do not feel committed to the actually existing state nor connected to the secular nationalist Zionism on which it was built. But while they feel no special duty or obligation to criticize most other illiberal states around the world, they do feel a particular need to criticize Israel, because it matters centrally to their worldview as Jews. They cannot easily ignore Israel, like early Reform Jews ignored Zionism. (Although some Jewish students on American college campuses certainly do try to avoid involvement with Israel in any way, positive or negative.) So they engage Israel—through the vehicle of Progressive critique. The phrase "Not in

Our Name," sometimes used as a slogan of this critique, captures the sense of personal implication in Israel's conduct that both marks and challenges their sense of connection.

This is why many young Progressive Jews are at the forefront of the pro-Palestinian movement on college campuses. Difficult as it is for older generations to accept, the cause is not self-hatred, a tendency characteristic of an isolated and scorned minority, not a successful and powerful one. It is, rather, that criticism of Israel and support for the Palestinian cause is the very essence of their Progressive Jewish self-expression.

In some fascinating cases, the nature of this religious Jewishness as critique becomes overt. For a handful of Jewish congregations, the spiritual and even liturgical glue of the community comes from critical activism. In an absorbing work of participant ethnography titled *Days of Awe: Reimagining Jewishness in Solidarity with Palestinians* (2019), Atalia Omer, a professor at Notre Dame, describes one such community, called Tzedek Chicago.[28] In that community, a Yom Kippur sermon might be about Israel, as it could be in many other American congregations. But it would take the form of multiracial, multiethnic intersectional critique of Israel, not support. Seen in the light of current trends in Progressive American Judaism, this sort of critique demonstrates a mode of Jewish self-expression that criticizes and even condemns Israel because it feels connection to Israel. That connection is a result of the promotion of Israel to a central place in Progressive Jewish thought in the 1980s and 1990s.

It is unlikely that the Tzedek Chicago mode will take over American Jewish Progressivism. As today's college students become adults and gradually assume leadership of their movements, however, Progressivism will have to work out its attitude toward Israel—both the idea of Israel and the actually existing state. Whatever solutions it reaches will have to be innovative. Going back to the old Progressive model of ignoring Zionism would be hard to do, at least for now. But so is embracing simultaneously a God of loving social justice and a state that rejects the path of liberal democracy. Israel will not change just because Progressive American Jews want it to. They will have to find their own answers to the looming crisis facing them, and soon, before a new generation finds itself alienated from a Jewishness whose inner contradictions it cannot reconcile.

II:3

ISRAEL AT THE CENTER

And now, halfway through the book, we come at last to the messiah. Not the messiah as a man or a king: he will have to wait for the next chapter. (Or we will have to wait for him, every day, for so long as he takes to arrive.) The messiah in this chapter is, instead, the messiah of Religious Zionism. This messiah is not a specific, single person, or not necessarily one. This messiah has undergone a process of allegorical interpretation at the hands of Evolutionist Religious Zionists.

The messiah depicted in the Bible is a literal, anointed king of the House of David, selected by God to rule the Jewish people. Evolutionists of a Religious Zionist persuasion made the coming of this messiah into a collective, depersonalized event, expressed in the achievement of total Jewish sovereignty over the entire historical Land of Israel. They did so, as we shall see, by rejecting the Traditionalist view that God had forbidden the Jews from establishing a Jewish state without miraculous messianic intervention and by consciously evolving classical Jewish beliefs about the messiah in the light of modern, nationalist, Zionist ideals. The messianic age as ultimately conceived by Religious Zionism is one in which the Jewish people are safe and free and rule their own land, inspired by God and his Torah. To simplify a bit: for Religious Zionism, the messiah is the state of Israel itself.

The origins of Religious Zionism can arguably be traced back to the middle of the nineteenth century, when a Prussian-born rabbi named Tzvi Hirsch Kalischer (1795–1874), seen now as a kind of proto-Zionist, began arguing that messianic salvation and the return to Zion must occur through human effort. In midcareer, Kalischer shifted from the writing of scholarly Talmudic commentaries to raising money for Jewish agricultural settlements to be built in Palestine. His efforts led to the establishment in 1870 of a single settlement, Mikveh Yisra'el, which still exists. He is counted as a forerunner to Theodor Herzl, the secular journalist usually considered the founder of modern (secular) Zionism.

Kalischer is mostly ignored or forgotten by Religious Zionists today. Instead, the intellectual origin story of Religious Zionism as told by Religious Zionists often starts with Rabbi Abraham Isaac Kook (1865–1935).[1] Kook, to whom I am about to turn, had few followers in his lifetime. Yet through the legacy of his son, himself a key Religious Zionist thinker, and the posthumous influence of his writings on contemporary Religious Zionism, Kook has become one of the most important thinkers in modern Jewish history.

This chapter tells the story of what Religious Zionism is and what it has become. That story matters centrally for this part of the book's account of Israel in Jewish thought and life, for two different, interrelated reasons.

First, over the past twenty-five years, something remarkable has occurred. The Religious Zionist idea of Israel has so infused the mainstream of Evolutionist Jewish thought, in Israel and the United States, that it has come to dominate it almost completely. In the process, this version of the idea of Israel is becoming the meta-halakhah of Evolutionism: the deeper reason for obeying the Law that infuses all Evolutionist Jewish life and thought.

Second, as secular Zionism has faded as an ideological force within Israel, Religious Zionism has gradually replaced it as the most energized, active type of Zionism, even though it was secular Zionism, not Religious Zionism, that actually built the state of Israel. Religious Zionists influence Israeli politics and public life far more than they ever have before in the country's history. In Israel's 2022 election, Religious Zionist parties far outperformed their historical numbers, winning, as we've seen, fourteen seats in the Knesset, the third-highest total of any bloc, and gaining prominent cabinet posts. After years of dedicated, self-conscious planning and preparation, Religious Zionists now also and increasingly serve in important roles in the IDF.

The transformed Religious Zionism that has become so important in Israel today is pervasively messianic. It operates by interpreting contemporary events as evidence of God's hand in history and forming policy on that basis. As a result, messianism, in its Evolutionist, Religious Zionist form, itself influenced by secular Zionism, has come to pervade Zionist ideology and belief. The God whom secular Zionists eschewed has found His way back into Zionism, and He is transforming Israel itself in His image.

THE MESSIAH AND THE TWO KOOKS

The first Rav Kook, as he is today reverently called by Religious Zionists, was born in Russia and was an heir to the great Lithuanian Talmudic tradition. Recognized as a boy genius, he was educated among other places in the yeshiva of Volozhin, the near-mythical origin point of today's great yeshivas. Alongside his elite Talmudic training, Kook also assimilated the mystical teachings of Hasidism. On his mother's side, Kook was descended from a Hasidic master, the rebbe of Kopust, who traced his spiritual lineage to the founder of Chabad Lubavitch Hasidism. Kook's intellectual formation was thus a hybrid of the two leading strands of Traditionalism, namely rationalist Lithuanian Talmudism and mystical Hasidism.

At the turn of the twentieth century, Kook began to develop a rich, idiosyncratic set of theories about the relation between Zionism and Jewish traditional belief. He moved to Palestine in 1904, spent World War I in Switzerland and in the United Kingdom, and returned to Palestine in 1919, where he was appointed the Ashkenazic (European-origin) chief rabbi of Jerusalem and then of Palestine. In this role he further developed his worldview, which is recorded in a series of dense, personal manuscripts, most of them edited and published by his son, Rabbi Tzvi Yehudah Kook (1891–1982).

Kook's most profound and important teaching was that the secular Zionists then settling Palestine were unwitting instruments of God's will. Most Traditionalists of his era condemned the classical Zionists' radical secularism and rejected Zionism outright. A few sought various forms of arm's-length détente with the movement. Kook, in contrast, believed that secular Zionists must be treated with respect and love. Their secularism was certainly misguided, he thought, and he hoped gently to reframe it. But he sacralized the fundamental undertaking of secular Zionism as well as the secular Zionists who were carrying it out. His brand of mysticism differed markedly from other kinds of Hasidic mysticism because, as Kook put it, "I am building the nation."[2]

In his lifetime, Kook's then-outlying worldview gained few adherents. All his life he retained warm personal relations with the European Traditionalist giants of the Torah who were his colleagues and contemporaries. And he interacted on friendly terms with secular Zionist leaders. Yet he was far too Zionist to influence Traditionalists, and far too religious for secular Zionists. He never had a large following of Evolutionist support in his lifetime, in Israel or elsewhere. His influence turned out to be generation-skipping, in a way that is unusual but not unheard of in religious history. It began to reach fruition starting in the 1970s, through the activism of the students of his son, Tzvi Yehudah, students who became the ideological progenitors of today's Religious Zionism.

The context for Tzvi Yehudah's transmission of his father's teaching was very different from the one in which the elder Rav Kook had initially written. In Rav Kook's lifetime, secular Zionism was a movement that had not yet created a state. In Tzvi Yehudah's lifetime, secular Zionism succeeded in creating a state. A movement devoted to national self-determination typically loses steam when that self-determination has been accomplished. As a result, by the late 1970s, secular Zionism had begun to seem like a spent ideological force. Once Israel existed, and once its continued existence seemed relatively secure, the psycho-emotional intensity associated with pioneering, settling land, and giving material existence to the abstract reality of the nation inevitably declined for its most active practitioners, namely secular Israelis. (In the United States, by contrast, Zionism was gaining ground at the time.)

The terrible losses of the 1973 war also contributed to a decline in Israelis' public faith in the institutions of secular Zionism that had, up to that point, managed to deliver almost unimaginable levels of success in creating the state. When Menachem Begin and his right-of-center Likud coalition came to power in 1977, the event was broadly interpreted as a rebuke to the socialist, secularist labor Zionism that had governed the country since its inception.* Begin belonged to a branch of Zionism known as "Revisionist" Zionism, defined by its maximalist claims to Jewish sovereignty over the entire historical land of Israel. Revisionist Zionists were not themselves religiously observant. They were hard-core nationalists who believed it was naïve folly to think that any accommodation was possible with Palestinians given that settlement of the land was a zero-sum game.[3] But they ordinarily did not express the classically antireligious views of the secular socialist Zionists. If Israel's earliest prime ministers liked to talk about "Israelis," Begin made a point to speak often of "Jews." The ground was ready for the surprising emergence of Religious Zionism as a force within Zionism.

Until then, Religious Zionists had been perceived by mainstream secular Zionists as relatively minor actors in the Zionist drama. There were a handful of well-known Religious Zionist politicians associated with the small National Religious Party, founded in 1956. There were a handful of Religious Zionist kibbutzim at the edge of the larger, highly secular kibbutz movement. The chief rabbis of Israel were sometimes Religious Zionists, most prominent among them Rabbi Shlomo Goren (1917–1994), famous for blowing a ram's horn at the Western Wall in June 1967 while in military uniform as chief rabbi of the IDF. Religious

---

* The election also represented the rise to political power of Mizrahi Israeli Jews: roughly, Jews from majority Muslim countries, most of whom had come to Israel in 1948–1949 after the establishment of the state. Mizrahi Jews have long faced discrimination and cultural and economic marginalization in Israel despite their large numbers. (The word *Mizrahi* in this context is the Hebrew translation of the word "Oriental," meaning from the countries of the Near and Middle East.)

Zionists were perceived in Israel as betwixt and between, people who did not fit into the secular or Haredi categories and were largely harmless and even irrelevant to political life.

At exactly the mid-1970s moment when secular Zionism had begun to fade as a self-consciously effective ideological motivating force for secular Israelis, Tzvi Yehudah's students took Religious Zionism as it then existed and effected a startling transformation of its role and character. From being perceived as a peripheral ideology, at the margins of the larger Zionist project, Religious Zionism became a vanguard movement. In its vanguard form, Kookian Religious Zionism exemplifies the living possibilities of Zionism and seeks to define its future, all the while claiming to embody the true heritage of Zionism as a whole.

This self-transformation, encouraged by Tzvi Yehudah, amounted to a kind of leveraged buyout of mainstream, secular Israeli Zionism by Religious Zionism. It had, and still has, two parts: the direct, unapologetic claim that settling the whole land of Israel is the ineradicable essence of Zionism, commanded by God; and the declaration that the Jews' return to Zion is the divinely sanctioned fulfillment of the messianic vision of the prophets.

The reason it was so transformative for Religious Zionists to insist that the real goal of Zionism is to settle the whole historical land of Israel according to God's command is that classical, secular Zionism never said as much. As secular nationalists, classical Zionists didn't want to talk about God having given the land of Israel to the Jewish people. Their argument for why their state should be in Palestine was that the Jews had a long-standing historical connection to the land and that as a nation, the Jews deserved their own state. They preferred to define the goal of Zionism in nonreligious terms as the creation of a Jewish state, not the fulfillment of God's will.

Without a doubt, mainstream classical Zionists hoped to create their state in as much of the historical land of Israel as they could get, ideally the whole of it. But mainstream Zionist leaders were always prepared to compromise as necessary on the extent of Jewish territory in order to secure a state, as evidenced by their acquiescence to the United Nations partition plan. The Camp David Accords also underscored this pragmatic willingness to compromise, as Israel returned the Sinai Peninsula to Egypt in exchange for a peace treaty.

In the years between 1973 and Camp David, the prospect of eventual Palestinian sovereignty over the West Bank became for the first time politically conceivable. To Religious Zionists, such an outcome would betray the core objective of divinely sanctioned Zionism. They began to assert openly that the God who commanded settlement of the land had also prohibited retraction from that settlement. In this religious conception, no pragmatic accommodation, however necessary it might appear, could ever justify giving up Jewish sovereignty over any part of the biblical land of Israel.

In effect, the Religious Zionists turned the secular, Zionist, nationalist logic of settlement upside down. The purpose of settling the land was not to deliver the Jews a national state. To the contrary, the ultimate purpose of the national state was to facilitate Jewish settlement of the land. The God of the Bible did not, in the first instance, command the people of Israel to create a sovereign entity. He commanded the Israelites to enter, conquer, and settle the land, and to eliminate or subjugate its inhabitants. Ancient Israelite sovereignty was (in the biblical account) a side effect of fulfilling this divine command, not the aim of it. Secular Zionism made settlement of the land subordinate to the state. Religious Zionism made the state subordinate to settlement of the land.

In practical terms, this meant that Religious Zionists must undertake their own settlement project. This they began to do in 1974, when some of Tzvi Yehudah's students formed an organization known as Gush Emunim, the Bloc of the Faithful. Its members, believers in the divine command to settle the land of Israel, established the strategy that would become the cornerstone of Religious Zionism for the next fifty years and counting. Not only did they seek to establish new settlements with the sanction of the government, but without permission from the state or its institutions, they started to set up small communities in the West Bank, then sought to regularize those settlements and make them permanent by staying put.

The Israeli name for this practice is establishing "facts on the ground." The basic political logic is that once Jewish families have put down roots, the cost to an Israeli government of removing those Jews from their homes becomes high enough to deter the elimination of the settlement. That logic depends on the Religious Zionists' premise that the mainstream secular Israeli public still maintains a deep if residual belief in the Zionist project of settlement, and that they, the vanguard, are effectuating that Zionist objective.[4]

Tzvi Yehudah typically presented himself as a humble and loyal perpetuator of his father's teachings, not as an original thinker in his own right. Yet his reception and interpretation of his father's complex body of thought, perhaps more than the thought itself, became the basis for today's Religious Zionist ideology. Tzvi Yehudah took the view that the state of Israel, which his father did not live to see, was the real-world manifestation of the divine processes that had acted through secular Zionism. The state of Israel therefore itself had a sacred, religious character insofar as it continued to serve the objectives of God's will.

Consequently, Tzvi Yehudah's students were of two minds about the actually existing state of Israel. On the one hand, that state had functioned as the engine of God's will. It was therefore religiously appropriate to devote oneself to it, serving in the IDF, participating in Israeli politics, and praying not only for the state's well-being but for its role in the messianic redemption (about which more in a moment). At the same time, when and if the state faltered in supporting the divine objective of settling the land, Tzvi Yehudah's students were willing to disregard its authority. Gush Emunim felt little compunction about disobeying the IDF or the Israeli government to create new settlements. An offshoot of Gush Emunim, known as the Jewish Underground, reacted to the Camp David Accords by becoming full-on terrorists. The Underground exploded bombs that maimed the mayors of two Palestinian cities. They attacked an Islamic college in Hebron, killing three students and injuring thirty-three. The same group plotted to blow up the Dome of the Rock on the Temple Mount, hoping to precipitate a crisis that, they anticipated, might lead to regional or even global war and hasten the apocalypse.

This turn to violating the laws of the state of Israel in order to advance the objective of settling the land of Israel points to the other aspect of the elder Kook's mystical theology of Zionism. That aspect was messianism. Specifically, Rav Kook held the belief that the settlement of the land of Israel constitutes a crucial step in the unfolding of the historical process of the coming of the Jewish messiah and the redemption of the Jewish people. That all-important belief came to motivate the students of the second Kook and their students, who are today the leaders of Religious Zionism.

THE EVOLVED MESSIAH

The history of Jewish thinking about the messiah is complicated, the subject of a whole body of scholarly literature.[5] Probably the most important thing to know about it is that for most of recorded Jewish history, the messiah has not been of day-to-day practical interest to most Jews most of the time.

Of course, the eventual coming of a messiah descended from David is indicated in the Bible, discussed by the rabbis, and invoked daily in Jewish liturgy. The rabbis associated the messianic age with the ingathering of the exiled and the return to Zion. Mystical Jewish thinkers paid somewhat sporadic attention to the messiah. Systematic Jewish theology spent relatively less time exploring the timing, nature, and qualities of the future messiah, except to specify that the messiah would be a successful redeemer, a king who actually ruled the Jewish people under conditions of sovereign independence.[6] One reason for the neglect of the subject may have been a long-standing need to distinguish Jewishness from Christianity, the offshoot of Judaism whose self-definition begins with the idea that the messiah (*Christ* is Greek for messiah, meaning the anointed one) has already come and will return. Another is the rabbis' this-worldly, pragmatic bent, which sits uneasily with imagining an idealized future when everything will be the way it should be.

The rabbis had also been burned by messianism. According to the Talmud, during Bar Kokhba's ultimately unsuccessful revolt against Roman rule (132–136 CE), Rabbi Akiba, one of the greatest of the early rabbis, proclaimed the rebel leader to be the messiah. To the rabbis, the failure of the rebellion and Bar Kokhba's death showed that he was not in fact the messiah. The Talmud warned against messianic speculation of the sort that involves figuring out when the end of days is coming.

Notwithstanding the warning, Jews have, at various moments in their history, been tempted by Rabbi Akiba's path and have entered into intense periods of messianic speculation. A series of shadowy figures in Jewish history declared themselves to be messiahs. Some of the best known, such as Sabbatai Zevi (1626–1676) and Jacob Frank (1726–1791), briefly gained thousands of followers over a wide geographical expanse before they disappointed them by not actually becoming kings of a Jewish commonwealth. Others had more limited reach, like the would-be messiah (whose name we do not know) who inspired Yemen's Jews in the twelfth century. We know of this messiah mostly because he was the subject of an important letter by Maimonides warning the Yemenite Jewish community not to validate a false messiah or be seduced by his ideas.

Classical Zionism took the history of Jewish messianism and secularized it, recasting the religious ideals of messianism as manifestations of a political, nationalist aspiration to sovereignty in the land of Israel. This metaphoric, nationalist rereading of messianism fit perfectly with secular Zionism's aim of reimagining the Jews as a nation, not a religious group. Zionism took its very name from the act of secularizing the traditional Jewish, messianic yearning for return to Zion. In the secular Zionist reinterpretation, the Jewish nation would not be redeemed miraculously by a messiah sent from God. The nation would redeem itself.

Inevitably, the successes of the secular Zionist enterprise—the immigration of many Jews to Palestine, the establishment of the state, the conquest of the Old City of Jerusalem—raised messianic questions for religious Jews. Religious Zionism used the tools of Evolutionism to reconcile modern, secular nationalism with biblical and rabbinic messianism. It assimilated the Zionists' secular nationalism while retaining and developing a spiritual-religious vision of messianic redemption. Religious Zionism followed secular Zionism and deviated from Traditionalist Jewish messianism in embracing the idea that the Jews as a people could take political action that would encourage or hasten the messianic redemption, rather than waiting for God to choose the timing. At the same time, Religious Zionism parted ways with secular Zionism in believing that God was necessarily immanent in the redemptive process. Following the path of Rav Kook, Religious Zionists hold that the settlement of the historic land of Israel and the creation of a nation-state there is part of the divine plan to redeem the Jewish people in a messianic age.*

The key Evolutionist element in the Religious Zionist reconception of the messiah was the interpretation of the messiah not as a single man but as a collective. Some hints that aspects of the messianic narrative might not be literal could arguably be gleaned from older Jewish sources.[7] The major development toward a collective messiah for Religious Zionists seems to have occurred when Rav Kook associated secular Zionists as a group with a figure the Talmud calls Messiah son of Joseph, a precursor to Messiah son of David who fights the wars of the Jewish people and prevails over evil.[8] This suggestion, made in a eulogy for Theodor Herzl, collectivized the pre-messiah. Kook was not saying that a particular secular Zionist person, even Herzl himself, was Messiah son of Joseph, but that *the whole secular Zionist movement* fit into the mystical-messianic paradigm that corresponded to this figure. By implication—although Rav Kook said so only obliquely—the ultimate messiah, the Messiah son of David, could also be a collective entity: presumably, the community of Jews who would govern in the land of Israel in the light of God's Law.

Collectivizing the messiah changed the game for Religious Zionist messianism. It meant that the Jews need not wait for an identifiable individual who would reveal himself as the king-messiah. By their own efforts they could produce a collective state, ruled by Jews as collective

---

* One could, in principle, be a religiously committed Evolutionist or Traditionalist Jew and also, separately, a secular Zionist who understands the settlement of Israel and the creation of the state in wholly mechanistic-secular terms, not in spiritual terms. This was, roughly, the view of the complex thinker Yeshayahu Leibowitz, reflected in English translation in Leibowitz, *Judaism, Human Values, and the Jewish State*, ed. Eliezer Goldman (Cambridge, MA: Harvard University Press, 1992). I know (and revere) a few Jewish intellectuals who, I believe, still hold something like this view, and they will recognize themselves in these words. But this view, possible in theory, is vanishingly rare in real-life practice. And those who hold it are not practitioners of Religious Zionism. They are religious Jews who are also Zionists.

TO BE A JEW TODAY

sovereigns under God. That state's flourishing existence would constitute the messianic age. The messiah, correctly understood, would be revealed through the process of such a state emerging. The students of Tzvi Yehudah identified that process as occurring in real time. They did not say it had been completed, to be sure. Tzvi Yehudah and his students taught that the messianic age was presently underway.

What does it mean, practically, for Religious Zionists to say that they (and the world) are living through the unfolding of the messianic age? The short answer is that it's complicated and varies for different people within the movement. It's common ground for Religious Zionists that the return of Jews to the land of Israel marked the beginnings of a new moment in history, one foretold by the prophets. It's common ground that the full utopian accomplishment of the messianic ideal hasn't yet occurred but is ongoing. And it's common ground that current events in Israel should be understood in terms of how to guide the messianic process toward its ultimate goals.

Religious Zionists do not all agree, however, on *where* we are in messianic history. Some think the ultimate revelation of the messiah is imminent or even has already occurred, and that the Temple will soon be rebuilt. They are preparing to sacrifice animals and craft golden vessels for cultic use. Others think that the climactic event of restoration lies some time off. Religious Zionists do not all agree on how to acknowledge the messianic redemption in their religious practices, liturgical and otherwise.[9] Most striking, Religious Zionists do not even all agree about whether the Jewish messiah will be an actual human king or whether the biblical messiah is best understood allegorically, following Rav Kook, as the whole people of Israel ruling itself collectively as an independent sovereign.

This messy messianism expresses itself most powerfully in the inward religious experiences of Religious Zionists. Their daily experience is transfused, transfixed, and transported by their messianic experience of the vicissitudes of the state of Israel in the land of Israel. The condition of living in a messianic age heightens the significance of each and every action a person takes. It can encourage or require doing things that would be strange or wrong in ordinary circumstances, including lawbreaking and sacred violence. Living in a semipermanent condition of heightened messianic awareness and sensitivity is by turns exhilarating, motivating, reassuring, risky, and crazy-making. The constant prospect of transcendent fulfillment must coexist with the ever-present fear of bitter disappointment and disillusion.

To understand daily life this way, through the prism of messianism unfolding in real time, is to transform Jewishness itself. Historically, Jews have almost always talked about the messiah as *potentially coming*, not already arrived. My teacher, the late great philosopher Robert Nozick, once remarked lightheartedly to me that maybe Jews could be defined as people who are always skeptical of messianic claims. After all, they rejected the idea that Jesus was the messiah. As the Sabbatean movement shows, some Jews have sometimes embraced here-and-now messianism. But, to Nozick's point, they have done so briefly, in punctuated moments. Communities who persisted in believing in a messiah after those moments were over have typically come to be seen no longer as Jews, but as members of new religions.

Religious Zionist messianism breaks that mold. It is a living, enduring Jewish messianism. It has been around for some half a century, longer if you date it back to Rav Kook himself. Its followers have created durable, unquestionably Jewish communities and institutions, all the while negotiating their relationship to the state of Israel. Measured by their numbers and influence, they are growing, and growing fast. Their worldview requires that messianic meaning be made of Jewish life at all moments, and that is what they are doing.

RELIGIOUS ZIONISM TODAY

What does Religious Zionism look like in Israel today? If you were to observe it from the perspective of an anthropologist from, say, China, with no prior knowledge of Judaism or Jewish practices, you would immediately notice the ways that its practitioners and proponents engage with the idea and reality of Israel in their religious lives. Religious Zionist schools in Israel teach Jewish law and Jewish history through the framework of Israel. Religious Zionist young men serve in the IDF, increasingly in elite units and the senior officer corps. Before their service, many spend a year in special preparatory programs that teach the ideology of Religious Zionism even as they ready their students for the physical and intellectual challenges of military life. Some continue to study in yeshiva even as they serve in the military, through a special program called *Hesder* that lets them alternate Torah learning and active duty. Young Religious Zionist women either serve in the army or, much more frequently, perform alternative national service within a Religious Zionist institutional framework.

Religious Zionist yeshivas and seminaries train and produce religious intellectual leadership that directly engages the subject of the state of Israel. Many Religious Zionists vote as a bloc, supporting Religious Zionist politicians. Religious Zionists acknowledge the state of Israel in their prayers and their songs and their sermons. Official Israeli state holidays, such as Independence Day and Jerusalem Day, assume religious forms alongside traditional Jewish holidays, and so on and so forth. In short, Religious Zionists' observed and observable Jewishness is pervasively shaped by the idea of Israel.

Settlement of land is a crucial aspect of daily life for the Religious Zionist movement. To Religious Zionists, the act of settlement is first and foremost a religious duty necessary to effectuating the fulfillment of the messianic ideal. Religious Zionists fulfill the obligation to settle the land of Israel by living in the country, and often by populating West Bank settlements.

The centrality of West Bank settlement to the movement is captured by the special position in the Ministry of Defense demanded and received by Bezalel Smotrich, the head of the Religious Zionism Party, after his party's unprecedented success in the 2022 Israeli elections. Smotrich, who separately became the country's finance minister, was also given authority within the Defense Ministry over Israeli civilian settlement in the West Bank. That includes not only planning new settlements and blocking Palestinian development but power over military enforcement of settlement activity that Israel would historically have considered illegal.[10] In other words, as long as he holds the post, Smotrich has the authority to determine whether to remove Religious Zionist settlements created without permission. He can be expected to exercise that power to allow such settlements to persist, and to approve new ones. No other power could be more important to the Religious Zionist settlement project.

For today's Religious Zionists, settlement has a further symbolic component: it is a way to claim the legacy of secular Zionism and present their movement as the true manifestation of Zionism itself. The Religious Zionist practice of creating facts on the ground resonates with the old secular Zionist settlement project dating to the decades before the creation of the state and indeed the early years of the state of Israel itself. Secular Zionists also established what they, too, called facts on the ground, first with the objective of guaranteeing the state, then with the objective of expanding it, and finally with the objective of Judaizing as much as possible of the state of Israel after 1948. As much or even more than the Religious Zionists, secular Zionists acquired land by any means necessary, whether purchase from absentee landlords or pressure or conquest. As much as or more than the Religious Zionists, secular Zionists built Jewish settlements in place of Palestinian villages, near them or on their ruins. Secular Zionists, not Religious Zionists, invented the custom of naming their settlements after biblical place names that were theorized to be the original sources of the Arabic names of Palestinian hamlets, hills, towns, and cities.[11] Religious Zionists acknowledge all this, and with pleasure. It fits into their narrative of being the true inheritors of the secular Zionist project.

Today's remaining Israeli secular Zionists, especially those on the center or the center-left of the political spectrum, are often uncomfortable with Religious Zionists' claim that their Zionism is the true heir to classical Zionism. In opposition to the Religious Zionists' attempt to take over Zionism itself, these secular Zionists insist that their kind of Zionism was always pragmatic. They maintain that the settlement imperative of Religious Zionism runs counter to Israel's pragmatic interests and endangers Israel as a state. They believe that secular Zionism achieved its fundamental objectives and that the task of modern Israelis is to protect those objectives from being eroded or destroyed.

This criticism of Religious Zionism is less convincing to contemporary secular inheritors of Revisionist Zionism, like Benjamin Netanyahu.

Maximalists themselves with regard to settling the land, they tend to value the Religious Zionists' maximalism even if they themselves still hold a secular nationalist conception of the Jewish state, rather than a religious one. And crucially, the pragmatic-secular argument against Religious Zionist settlement has little weight for anyone who believes, consciously or unconsciously, that the Jewish claim to the land of Israel is based on a divine right of ownership. For the vast majority of believers, to accept the divine right to the land of Israel is to concede that the God who gave the land to the people of Israel has commanded them to settle it.*

TWO EVOLUTIONISMS OR ONE? RELIGIOUS ZIONISM OUTSIDE ISRAEL

From my account of Israeli Religious Zionism, it should be clear how the idea of Israel has transformed this strand of Evolutionist Jewish thought and how, in turn, Religious Zionism is transforming Israel. What remains in this chapter is to show the transformative effect that Religious Zionism has had on Evolutionist Jewish thought outside Israel, in particular on Modern Orthodoxy in the United States.

For most of the twentieth century, Israeli Religious Zionism and American Modern Orthodoxy were two separate movements, sociologically and spiritually. Both were examples of Evolutionism. But Israeli Religious Zionism set out to evolve Jewish tradition to reconcile it with Zionist nationalism. American Modern Orthodoxy aimed to evolve the tradition to reconcile it with science and 1950s-era American cultural values. The primary objectives were different even as the Evolutionist method was common to both. Two different slogans capture the similar

---

* The great Sephardi chief rabbi Ovadiah Yosef (1920–2013), the spiritual leader of the Shas Party, took the view that while God had given the land of Israel to the Jewish people, God also authorized the people's leaders to engage in pragmatic determinations of what would keep Jews alive, including the pragmatic determination of exchanging land for peace. The view is certainly logically coherent and finds support in Jewish sources. It has not, however, garnered substantial public support, notwithstanding its association with the revered figure of the rabbi known to this day as *Maran* (Our Master).

method and the contrasting emphasis. The youth movement of Religious Zionism, called Bnei Akiva (the children of Akiba, the rabbi who thought Bar Kokhba was the messiah), uses the slogan "Torah and Labor," the Zionist labor of building a nation. Yeshiva University, the flagship Modern Orthodox institution, uses the slogan "Torah and Knowledge," the general scientific and scholarly knowledge of modernity.

Today Israeli Religious Zionism and American Modern Orthodoxy are converging, a development with major consequences for how Israel is transforming Jewish life and thought. Really, convergence is too mild a word. The ideology of Religious Zionism is gradually coming to dominate American Modern Orthodox Judaism. In the process, Zionism, in its religious form, is becoming the meta-halakhah of Modern Orthodoxy: the deeper idea or belief that underwrites halakhic observance. I am about to try to demonstrate how this is happening. To do so, I need to tell you a bit more about American Modern Orthodoxy's historical attitude toward Israel.

Officially, Modern Orthodoxy in the United States always espoused a form of what might be called sympathetic theoretical Zionism. The most important spiritual exponent of Modern Orthodox Zionism was Rabbi Joseph B. Soloveitchik (1903–1993), who was also the intellectual father of American Modern Orthodoxy as a whole. Soloveitchik, known in American Modern Orthodox circles simply as "the Rav," was a scion of the Brisker dynasty, a unique Traditionalist line of brilliant Talmudic scholars. The Brisker scholars, originally from the city of Brest-Litovsk,* gave their name to an especially creative form of conceptual Talmudic analysis; to a number of important yeshivas all called "Brisk"; and to a highly conservative worldview that included confirmed non-Zionism.

Soloveitchik, the Rav, maintained the Briskers' rigorous Talmudism but otherwise parted from his family's tradition in a number of crucial ways. He earned a PhD in philosophy from Friedrich Wilhelm University in Berlin in 1932 (now Humboldt University), writing a thesis

---

* The city is now in Belarus. It was at various times part of Russia, Poland, and the Polish-Lithuanian commonwealth. Jews from Brisk defined themselves as "Litvak" or "Litvish," meaning Jewish-Lithuanian. Much of my own family comes from not far away.

about neo-Kantian epistemology and metaphysics. He endorsed the Evolutionist, Modern Orthodox undertaking of reconciling Torah and modern thought and became the head of the rabbinical school of Yeshiva University in 1941. And he deviated from Brisker non-Zionism by embracing a moderate Zionism. His classic essay, *Kol Dodi Dofek*, "Hark! My Beloved Knocks," was first given as a lecture in 1956 as part of an Israel Independence Day celebration at Yeshiva University. It depicted the state of Israel as a divine proffer to the Jewish people to embrace God's offered salvation.[12] Yet Soloveitchik himself never moved to Israel and never even visited after 1935, when he had campaigned for the position of chief rabbi of Tel Aviv but had not been chosen.[13]

At the level of theory, following Soloveitchik, Modern Orthodoxy welcomed the establishment of a Jewish state as an indication of the ongoing divine presence in the world. The Modern Orthodox school I attended was also founded by Soloveitchik. There we recited the Hallel prayer without its formal blessing on Israel's Independence Day, as I mentioned earlier. But under our Brisker-conceptual form of moderate Zionism, we recited the Hallel prayer *with* the blessing on Jerusalem Day, which celebrated Israel's conquest of the Old City of Jerusalem in 1967. The Talmudic distinction had to do with the legal categorization of what sort of miracle had occurred on each of these days. The conquest of Jerusalem counted as an overt miracle, meriting the recitation of the blessing; Israel's independence was in contrast at most an implicit miracle, which might not count.

This hair-splitting legal ambivalence about the divine nature of current events can stand in for the disconnected, largely theoretical nature of most Modern Orthodox Zionism before the 1990s. The Zionism of Modern Orthodoxy in the United States was part of what made it different from non-Zionist Traditionalism. Nevertheless, in practice, Modern Orthodox American Jews before the 1990s rarely had close personal or familial ties to Israel. We visited Israel as tourists, like other American Jews. But our political and personal identities were bound up in being "modern" Americans, not in spiritual Zionism. The movement aspired to produce a Joe Lieberman—a homegrown American U.S. senator who observed Jewish law and was the Democratic candidate for vice president in 2000—not a Naftali Bennett, the son of Modern Orthodox American immigrants to Israel who went on to become prime minister of the country.

Thus, despite certain parallels, American Modern Orthodoxy and Israeli Religious Zionism remained fairly uncoordinated with each other until the 1990s. American Modern Orthodox schools taught modern Hebrew, a function of their theoretical commitment to Zionism. To do so, they employed young Israelis who had come to the United States on teaching missions, sent by specific Israeli Religious Zionist institutions like the Bnei Akiva youth movement. In my experience, these Israeli teachers—many of whom I loved—conveyed a sense of Religious Zionist culture. They were not, however, in any way central to the ideological self-definition of American Modern Orthodoxy. Their prestige was lower than that of our American rabbis. They were visitors, welcomed and respected but understood to be fundamentally different.

The respectful but somewhat distant relationship between Modern Orthodoxy and Religious Zionism began to change markedly in the 1990s. The change was, in retrospect, driven by two factors, one sociological, the other ideological. We did not recognize it at the time, but the change would become foundational for Modern Orthodoxy.

The sociological driver was the rapid uptick in the number of young Modern Orthodox American Jews, male and female, who began to study in Israeli Religious Zionist institutions for a year after high school, beginning in the middle of the 1980s. This development reflected the increased economic success of Modern Orthodox American Jews, who could afford to pay for what was essentially another year of college. In response to growing American demand, Religious Zionist yeshivas (for boys) and seminaries (for girls) in Israel began to create year-abroad programs specifically for graduates of Modern Orthodox day schools in the United States. This change was crucial, because only a small number of elite day school graduates could speak modern Hebrew well enough to immerse themselves in a full year of study at an Israeli institution where the language of instruction was Hebrew. The year-abroad programs broadened access.

The American day schools that sent their graduates to Israel were not, at first, doing so with consciously Zionist motivations. Rather, the primary goal was to deepen their graduates' Jewish knowledge in anticipation of their arrival on secular American college campuses, where they would have to confront the temptations of giving up religious orthodoxy. Had study-abroad been marketed to parents as a mechanism to drive eventual immigration to Israel, that would have been poor salesmanship—at the time. Modern Orthodox American Jews until the 1990s theoretically considered emigration to Israel (*'aliyah*, "going up," to use the Hebrew term favored by the Modern Orthodox) religiously desirable. But precious few Modern Orthodox Jews actually did emigrate in that era. The professional skills they were obtaining at American universities were not particularly valuable in Israel before the technology startup era of the Israeli economy. Unlike in the United States, doctors in Israel were poorly paid participants in a system of socialized medicine. U.S.-trained lawyers were not able to find jobs in Israeli law firms, where in any event their pay and status would have been considerably lower than in the United States. During my twelve years in a Modern Orthodox day school, 1976–1988, a handful of families from the school moved to Israel, and several moved back home after realizing the difficulty of the transition.

Although mostly unintended, at least on the American side, the systematic exposure of eighteen-year-old Americans to a year of intense study and spiritual-emotional growth in Israel had a transformative effect on relations between Modern Orthodoxy and Religious Zionism. When it came to studying Traditional Jewish texts, the year typically functioned as an advanced opportunity to enhance students' skills and knowledge, substantially improving but not necessarily transforming their abilities. Not so with regard to the spiritual project of Religious Zionism, conceived as fulfilling the messianic, Torah ideal of settling the land of Israel.

Here the ideological aspect of the transformation of Modern Orthodoxy enters the picture. In the Religious Zionist institutions they attended in Israel, Modern Orthodox American Jews encountered—and still encounter—Israeli rabbi-teachers motivated by deep and sincere religious commitment, married to an intense and spiritually infused political ideology. Nothing remotely of the kind existed in the day schools from whence they came. In the United States, the project of Modern Orthodoxy was conceived as coolly rational and intermingled with typical upper-middle-class American high school objectives, from sports to music lessons to competitive college admissions.

In the Israeli Religious Zionist institutions attended by Americans, Israeli students were either preparing for or already participating in national service, usually in the IDF. The Israelis were shaped by an ascendant, charismatic, increasingly triumphant Religious Zionist theology, the worldview on the basis of which they were preparing to live their lives, a worldview that was coming into its own for the first time in the history of Israel. At a historical moment when Modern Orthodoxy was ideologically moribund (Soloveitchik died in 1993 after a long, impairing illness), its future leaders were exposed to a Religious Zionist movement approaching its historical apogee.

The ideological problem for Modern Orthodoxy, beginning in the 1990s and continuing today, was that the movement's successes have rendered its central spiritual project of reconciling modernity and orthodoxy insufficiently challenging to motivate its members at the level of meta-halakhah. From being a tiny movement in the post–World War II era, when all Jewish orthodoxy seemed to be on the brink of collapse, Modern Orthodoxy has gone on to become institutionally rich, successful, and self-confident. Its schools are flourishing. Its synagogues are full, much fuller than its American Jewish Conservative and Reform competitors when measured by how much of the membership actually turns up on a weekly basis.

Ideologically, Modern Orthodoxy appears to have solved the theological challenges it initially set out to address, which were the challenges of modernity. Today most people in the Jewish world (except some Traditionalists) accept that one can be an observant Jew and also acknowledge Darwinian evolution and the multibillion-year antiquity of the earth. Modern Orthodox Jews attend university and work as professionals and participate fully in American society without in any meaningful way compromising their religious beliefs or observance. They are fully accepted by modern American society and are treated as completely typical upper-middle-class citizens.

All this success tends to make the underlying motivation of Modern Orthodoxy seem too weak to generate a deep answer to the question, "Why follow the Law in this way?" If everyone takes it for granted that your undertaking is possible and can be easily achieved, then there is nothing especially extraordinary about undertaking it. Of course, believing Modern Orthodox Jews could still be motivated by the spiritual objective of fulfilling God's will and following his Law. But that objective today appears insufficient to motivate the entire community. This might be because the faith of Modern Orthodoxy is to a significant degree attenuated relative to the literal, authoritarian beliefs of the Traditionalists. More likely it is because, like Jews from time immemorial, Modern Orthodox Jews need a meta-halakhah, a spiritual framework of motivation that justifies and transcends following the Law. Regardless, Modern Orthodoxy, at the height of its institutional success, experienced a subjective need for some new spiritual motivation, and found the idea of Israel to provide it.

In the past decade, a further ideological factor has pushed Modern Orthodoxy toward the idea of Israel: the looming danger of a renewed theological crisis with regard to reconciling Jewish law with contemporary life. Modern Orthodoxy solved the theological problems it set out to confront in the twentieth century. But it has fewer or weaker answers to the theological problems of the twenty-first century, which are focused on the compatibility of Jewish tradition with liberal values, not its compatibility with modern science or the social mores of the Baby Boomer generation. When it comes to those challenges, Modern Orthodoxy finds itself caught between vanguard Evolutionists like Rabbis Rahel Berkovits and Steven Greenberg on the left and Traditionalism on the right, unable to pick a side without losing its own reason for being. Modern Orthodoxy gave Jews a way to be modern and Orthodox. It does not seem poised to give them a way to be postmodern progressive and still Orthodox.

Faced with this potential for ideological failure, Modern Orthodoxy again needs a spiritual focal point that can keep its adherents motivated and committed. In Religious Zionism, its cousin, Modern Orthodoxy saw and sees a movement that is utterly committed and existentially motivated. So it borrowed the core of Religious Zionism as its own motivator, out of fellow feeling, influence, and admiration. Of course, it only borrowed the essence of Religious Zionism to the extent it was able to do so in its own national context. But that borrowing is nonetheless foundational and transformative.

This set of ideological challenges helps explain why today, the idea of Israel functions as the primary spiritual underpinning of Modern Orthodoxy in the United States. As the astute legal scholar and cultural critic Chaim Saiman puts it, *"Israel has come to define Judaism . . .* for [Modern] Orthodoxy, which increasingly views the State of Israel as its spiritual center and normative core."[14] Fostering identification with the state of Israel is now treated as an important, formal component of the mission of Modern Orthodox American educational institutions.* Instead of preparing students to remain Orthodox while at university—once a preoccupation of Modern Orthodoxy—yeshiva day schools consciously prepare their students to engage in Israel advocacy on their future college campuses. In Modern Orthodox synagogues, liturgical tunes, always an important part of Jewish religious self-expression, often derive from Israeli Religious Zionist sources, far more so than they did thirty years ago.

Politically, Modern Orthodox Jews have become overwhelmingly, almost monolithically Republican. Progressive or Godless American Jews remain as Democratic as nearly all Jewish voters were half a century ago. The reason is Israel, which has played a crucial role in the Republicanization of the Modern Orthodox Jewish community. The perception that the Republican Party is more pro-Israel has made affiliation with the Democratic Party almost unthinkable for prominent Modern

---

* From the website of the school I attended:

> Maimonides School's mission is to produce religiously observant, educated Jews who will remain faithful to religious beliefs, values, and practices as they take their place as contributing members of general society. Maimonides provides students with both an outstanding religious education and an excellent college preparatory general education in an atmosphere that reinforces their commitment to the values of Torah and to the observance of mitzvot, and that fosters a strong sense of identification with Medinat Yisrael [the State of Israel; note Hebrew transliteration without English translation, itself a Zionist assertion].

Orthodox leaders. Even Donald Trump did not displace Modern Orthodox support for the Republican Party. He may actually have intensified it: Jared and Ivanka Kushner remain among the most prominent Modern Orthodox Jews in the United States.

When it comes to supporting Religious Zionism, Modern Orthodox American Jews are, on the whole, fully committed to the settlements of Israeli Religious Zionists. It is often Modern Orthodox American Jews who fund those projects. Some of the Religious Zionist vanguard in Israel are themselves American-born.

To take a spiritual example from the synagogue service, consider the prayer for the Israel Defense Forces, composed by Rabbi Shlomo Goren.* This prayer began to be recited in a growing number of Modern Orthodox American synagogues in the middle of the first decade of the 2000s. Although I am not aware of a study documenting the process, I believe that the relevant context was the one in which special prayers were instituted in some of the same synagogues for the safe return of some six IDF soldiers who had gone missing in action and were thought to be held by Hamas or Lebanese Hezbollah.[15] Praying for the return of those soldiers in turn created the impetus to institute a special prayer for all IDF soldiers.

Once the IDF prayer was added to the Modern Orthodox American Jewish liturgy, it took on a remarkable and distinctive pride of place. In the large Modern Orthodox synagogue where my parents pray, congregants rise for the IDF prayer and recite it aloud, alongside the prayer leader, with great fervor and intention. No other prayer in the Saturday morning liturgy in this urbane Upper East Side syna-

---

* Goren composed the prayer using a liturgical formula that would naturally place it in the context of the Torah-reading service on Sabbath mornings. In Israel, it was used in that way among Religious Zionists from the time of its drafting. In the United States, however, the adoption of the prayer was slower and more sporadic. Most American Modern Orthodox synagogues already recited a separate prayer for the state of Israel at a different point in the Sabbath morning liturgy, adjoining the prayer for the government of the United States, which was itself the lineal descendant of prayers for the monarchies of the states in which Jews lived that can be traced back to the early modern period. The prayer for the state of Israel included a specific prayer for the "defenders" of the land of Israel, rendering the extra prayer for the IDF arguably unnecessary.

gogue setting gets similar affective treatment. The IDF prayer matters spiritually to the congregants because it is a manifestation of support for the state of Israel, specifically for the state of Israel in its military aspect.

In Religious Zionism, Israel is the concrete and ever-present messianic redemptive reality, the beating center of the whole enterprise, without which the undertaking would be incoherent. For Modern Orthodoxy, Israel has moved to the religious center (under the influence of Religious Zionism). The idea of Israel is functioning as the solution to a question of practical religious life, namely, what motivates our faith? At one time, in the not-too-distant past, the answer for Modern Orthodoxy was that its faith was motivated by the imperative to be both modern and also fully committed to the Law. Now that objective, while still present, has far less motivating power than it once did. Today Israel fills Modern Orthodoxy's need for deep spiritual motivation.

EVOLUTIONISM AND ZIONISM: THE FUTURE

Is there a necessary connection between Evolutionism and Zionism? As a historical matter, the answer might well appear to be yes. The earliest Jewish Evolutionists were always interested in Zionism, and for good reason. Evolutionism in Judaism begins with the authority of the tradition, then self-consciously interprets the tradition to match the felt necessities of the moment, moral or spiritual or otherwise. Zionism was a product of modern nationalism, itself the very archetype of a modern moral, spiritual, and political phenomenon. Naturally, Evolutionists would want to see if Jewish tradition could be interpreted to match nationalism.

In the case of Religious Zionism, the match could be made with relative ease. The return to Zion did, after all, exist in the tradition. All that was needed was for Evolutionists to explain away the idea that the Jewish people must wait for divine redemption and interpret the tradition to permit their active participation. Evolutionists also needed to allegorize the biblical messiah into collective national self-redemption. Secular Zionism had already done part of that work, so all Evolutionism had to do was insist that a similar move could be performed within the framework of authoritative tradition.

Today, it remains the case that nearly all Jewish Evolutionists are Zionists. This includes not only Modern Orthodox Jews but essentially all the left-Evolutionists who seek to achieve full gender egalitarianism within the bounds of Jewish law. Some important Evolutionist institutions, like Pardes (where Rabbi Rahel Berkovits teaches), are in Israel. In the American partnership minyanim where men and women worship on equal terms with equal participation in a mostly traditional version of the liturgy, the tunes show the marked influence of Religious Zionist yeshivot. The prayer leaders in the partnership minyanim mostly minimize the musical influence of mainstream American Conservative Judaism.

At the left edge of Evolutionism, however, conflict with Religious Zionism is brewing. Left-Evolutionists have lots of social and intellectual contact with other progressives, Jewish and otherwise. Those progressives have in recent years come to be troubled by the Religious Zionist program of settlement. Left-Evolutionists are worried about the rightward turn in Israeli politics and the high degree of difficulty in believing that Israel will remain a Jewish and democratic state. They recognize that Evolutionism itself can't resolve the underlying political realities of where Religious Zionism has led and where it is likely to go.

One possible outcome of this emerging conflict is that some Evolutionists may increasingly begin to turn away from Israel altogether in their spiritual lives. Although this would not be easy for them, practically or religiously, it is conceivable, precisely because Evolutionists are willing to identify their liberal values and then consciously evolve their interpretation of the tradition to correspond to those values. If putting Israel close to the center of their religious and spiritual lives would lead Evolutionists into a conflict with their liberalism, then they can choose to interpret the tradition as requiring less engagement with the actually existing state of Israel and even the idea of Israel than they currently have.

Such an interpretive move within Evolutionist Jewish thought would involve self-consciously turning away from the Religious Zionism that predominates in Israel and has so influenced Modern Orthodoxy.

It might lead to the interpretation of the tradition with respect to Israel that once prevailed among Traditionalists. That version of the tradition began as frankly anti-Zionist, reacting to the secularism that was characteristic of classical Zionism. It could conceivably be adopted by Progressive Evolutionists. Indeed, a few intellectuals who exercise an oblique influence on Progressive Evolutionism have already shown significant interest in the work of a prolific and influential anti-Zionist Traditionalist, the late Satmar Rebbe, Yoel Teitelbaum, whom I will discuss in the next chapter. Daniel Boyarin, the most creative and controversial academic scholar of Talmud in his generation and a self-described anti-Zionist, is the most prominent example.[16]

Explicit anti-Zionism on the Boyarin model would be an extremely difficult position for the great majority of Evolutionists to maintain, not least for sociological reasons. Today almost no part of the organized Jewish world calls itself anti-Zionist. The central argument of this part of the book is that Israel has become utterly central to contemporary Jewish thought and spirituality. Left-leaning Evolutionism wants to be at the heart of Jewish life, not on the outskirts. The cost of anti-Zionism would, for now, be too great.

I feel the emerging conflict within left-Evolutionism particularly strongly, probably because I was raised both as an Evolutionist and as a liberal. As a young person, I was taught that Evolutionism offered the best way forward for Jewish life. Of all the belief patterns I knew, only it, I believed, could combine authentic Jewish tradition with the capacity to meet new moral, ethical, and intellectual challenges. Left-Evolutionists hold that view and are striving mightily to evolve Jewish law toward genuine equality for all Jews, regardless of sex or gender identity or sexual orientation.

Yet as I grew older, I came to understand how protean Evolutionism is, how capable it is of adapting to any modern idea, not just the liberal ideas I liked. Evolutionism had the capacity to evolve into the moderate-seeming Religious Zionism espoused by thinkers I admired and admire still. But it also had the capacity to evolve into extreme messianism. Extreme Religious Zionist messianism has given us Itamar Ben-Gvir and Bezalel Smotrich and has contributed to the ideas of some even more frightening figures whom I will discuss in the next chapter. And that Religious Zionism hasn't restricted itself to Israel. It has come to infuse American Jewish Evolutionism. The upshot is that Evolutionism need not lead to a form of Jewishness compatible with liberal democratic moral values. American Jewish Evolutionists, whether right-wing or left-wing, need to understand that Religious Zionism as it is presently developing in Israel is increasingly diverging from contemporary American ideals about how all people should be treated and what rights all people deserve.

Some American Evolutionists may find themselves perfectly willing to accept Religious Zionist politics, even if those politics become undemocratic. Israel is not the United States, they may feel, and the democratic principles they favor in their own country may not have to apply in the Jewish state. Some right-wing American Evolutionists may actually think the United States could do with being less liberal and egalitarian in its own government. That is their prerogative, and in my view it is perfectly legitimate for their Jewish beliefs to influence their beliefs about U.S. politics and about democracy more generally. To the extent they find their Jewishness pulling them away from democratic beliefs, they will be privileging their religious faith above their inherited political norms.

For left-leaning Evolutionists, the challenge is to acknowledge and admit that not all evolution of the Jewish tradition counts as progress toward the ideas they hold dear. Jewish tradition is capacious. Much—most—of Jewish tradition isn't especially liberal or democratic. Ultranationalism and extremist messianism can be derived from the tradition, just as liberalism and democracy can be derived from it by the process of conscious evolution. The crisis facing Evolutionist Jews is how to balance those different possible interpretations of the evolving tradition.

For its part, Traditionalism over the past thirty years has come to offer a different model of engagement with the idea and reality of Israel than has old-school religious anti-Zionism. Traditionalist thinking about Israel has itself evolved, from rejection to accommodation to a distinctive mode of identification. The Traditionalists don't acknowledge evolution, of course. They cannot call themselves Zionists and so cannot easily embrace the official positions of Religious Zionism. Nevertheless, their thinking about Israel is undergoing a sub rosa transformation. It is to that process of development—denied by Traditionalists—to which we must now turn.

II:4

ISRAEL WITHOUT ZIONISM

From the time Zionism was born in the nineteenth century, nearly all Traditionalist Jews rejected it as a secular heresy. Yet today, Haredi Traditionalists make up 12.6 percent of Israel's population. The political parties that represent them play an outsize role in determining the direction of Israeli domestic politics. During the early days of the Covid-19 crisis, when Israel for the most part found itself at the global cutting edge of mandatory imposed restrictions and contact tracing, a Traditionalist named Ya'akov Litzman, a follower of the Ger Hasidic sect, was the country's minister of health. Asked in March 2020 about the possibility of a national shutdown in the run-up to the spring festival of Passover, he replied, "We pray and hope that the messiah will come before Passover; I am certain he will come and save us as Moses brought us out of Egypt and we will be freed."[1]

With Litzman's tacit or express approval, the Traditionalist community refused to subject itself to the Covid prevention standards that applied to the rest of Israel's population. Yeshivas stayed open. Funerals of rabbis, with thousands of Traditionalists in attendance, took place as though there was no pandemic. Religious services continued to be held in many Traditionalist synagogues without legally mandated social distancing. The simple explanation for this permissive Covid exceptionalism was that the coalition government led by Benjamin Netanyahu depended on the active support of Traditionalist political parties. That is, the Traditionalists held power by virtue of their participation in the apparatus of the state of Israel.

To hear this description, you might think that Traditionalist Jews had become belated Zionists. If Zionism were defined in totally nonideological terms and restricted to participation in the life of the state of Israel, then that would be at least partially accurate. Zionism, however, cannot really be defined in nonideological terms, because Zionism in its essence is an ideology, defined as a set of beliefs and ideals that undergird a specific social or political system.

Traditionalist Israeli Jews who participate in the political, economic, and social life of the state are therefore not Zionists in any ordinary sense of the term. But neither are they anti-Zionists, as many Traditionalists were from the nineteenth century until late in the twentieth. Today, a handful of Traditionalists still recite from the script of the anti-Zionist past. But the overwhelming number of Traditionalist Jews today are *non-*Zionists of a new type: they are self-proclaimed non-Zionists who nevertheless identify in some ways with the actually existing state of Israel.

In this chapter, I am going to explain how even Traditionalists, the community of Jews historically most skeptical of Zionism, have had their worldview transformed by Israel over the last thirty-plus years. The core of my argument is that Traditionalists in Israel and the Diaspora have come to identify with the state of Israel in two ways: by identifying with Israel's military might, and by pushing the state to implement Jewish law and the viewpoint of the Torah (*daas Toyre*).

I will argue, too, that both aspects of this identification pose tricky problems for Traditionalism. The vast majority of Haredim refuse to serve in the IDF, so identification with the state's military prowess calls for a lot of creativity.* As for lobbying the Israeli government to apply Traditionalist values and Jewish law, it places Traditionalism in the posi-

---

* Although Traditionalists don't serve in the IDF, neither do Palestinian Arabs, with a few exceptions. A number of Bedouin who hold Israeli citizenship serve voluntarily in special units of the Israeli military. They are ethnic Arabs, speak Arabic, and have

tion of advocating for a specific Jewish vision of the Jewish state, which sits uncomfortably with its official pose of non-Zionism, and it goes even further than the position of most Religious Zionists. Simultaneously, that effort puts Traditionalists into direct conflict with secular Israelis, not to mention Progressive Jews abroad, who want Israel to be inclusive and liberal.

Demonstrating this new Traditionalist identification with Israel is a subtle business, because Traditionalists don't like to talk about it directly. Their broader worldview, after all, depends on never admitting that anything in their practice and belief has ever changed. Consequently, Traditionalists in Israel have shifted their beliefs about their relation to Israel *without developing an explicitly stated theory* for why their deepening participation in the life and politics of the Zionist state is religiously permissible, much less desirable.

The essence of their identification can be glimpsed in the public answer made by contemporary Traditionalists when secular Israelis complain about their ongoing refusal to serve in the military. In the past, the main Traditionalist explanation for the refusal was that military service constituted *bittul Torah*, a prohibited waste of time that ought to be spent studying the Law. Traditionalists sometimes added that the IDF was by design a secularizing social force and that it would threaten the religious fervor and commitment of young men if they were obligated to serve alongside secular Jews.

Today, in contrast, Traditionalists are much more likely to assert that by studying Torah in yeshivas, Traditionalist young men *are* defending the state of Israel. By the merit of their learning, they are earning the divine protection without which the Israeli military would fail. This idea is encapsulated in a proposal to the Knesset, advanced by the Traditionalist United Torah Judaism party, to adopt a new Basic Law (Israel's closest thing to a constitutional amendment) titled "Basic Law: Torah Study." The proposed law formally declares that "Torah study is a basic value in the heritage of the Jewish people" and that those studying Torah

---

every right to be called Palestinian if they wish. Men of the Israeli Druze community, an Arabic-speaking religious minority, also serve in the IDF and are subject to conscription, as are members of the tiny Circassian community in Israel.

full-time must be seen "as performing meaningful service to the state of Israel and the Jewish people."

What makes this idea a form of identification with the state of Israel is that it directly allies the interests and actions of Traditionalists with the interests of the state. An anti-Zionist who believed that the state of Israel was itself an illegitimate effort to break Jewish law and tradition would not be likely to depict yeshiva students as spiritual fighters in the service of that state. A Traditionalist anti-Zionist would answer the charge of dereliction of duty by explaining that there was in fact no duty for a Jew living in Israel to defend a state whose very existence flouts God's will. To say that the yeshiva student is fulfilling a duty to protect the state is to acknowledge not only that the state exists but that there exists a moral duty to defend it, or at least the people in it. One must identify with the state to some limited degree in order to express pride in defending its borders, spiritually or otherwise.

Although today's Traditionalists wouldn't like to admit it, this perspective can actually be traced back to Rav Kook, the spiritual father of today's Religious Zionism. In a 1917 letter to the then-chief rabbi of the United Kingdom, Rav Kook urged his colleague in London to use his influence to get yeshiva students exempted from being drafted into the British army during World War I. In an addendum to the letter, he wrote, "The success of the country in its war depends upon scholars toiling in Torah. By their merit, the war will be won. They help the country more than combat troops."[2]

Kook was not speaking of the state of Israel, which would not exist for another thirty years. He was arguing that Torah study would help the British Empire win the war. But understood along this spiritual dimension, Traditionalist study in Israel today *is a form of service to the state*. Its value is not merely the good of fulfilling the divine command to study Torah day and night. Its value lies, too, in its contribution to the safety of Israel. Traditionalists, in this analysis, are not shirking their duty as soldiers. They are performing the duty of being spiritual soldiers.

Meanwhile, in the United States, Traditionalist Jews, beginning in the 1990s, have increasingly developed much closer ties than before to Israel. Nearly all Yeshivish young men who can find the means study

Talmud in Israel for a year or two after the age of eighteen before returning to the United States to continue their advanced Talmud studies.
Many of them learn (that is the preferred verb) at the nine-thousand-
student Mir Yeshiva in Jerusalem. A more select group learns at the
Brisk Yeshiva in Jerusalem, an institution where admission is so selective
that attendance is treated as a marker of real intellectual distinction in
Traditionalist circles.*

As a result of this time studying abroad, a fair number of American
Traditionalists now speak excellent modern Israeli Hebrew and are con-
versant with the realities of contemporary Israeli life. They are far more
inclined to travel to Israel regularly and to buy property there than were
their grandparents. Lest there be any confusion, these Yeshivish Jews
could not be mistaken for Modern Orthodox. They are black-and-white
Traditionalists through and through. They dress and speak and act differently from Modern Orthodox Jews. If asked, they would say that they
are not Zionists, whereas Modern Orthodox Jews would say they were.

American Jewish Traditionalists also hold views about Israeli
politics—and domestic American politics with respect to Israel—that
reflect their identification with the state. They tend to support the policies of Benjamin Netanyahu. They reject the idea of land for peace. They
vote Republican in U.S. elections and supported Donald Trump partly
because of his pro-Israel stance. What is noteworthy about these political positions is that they make sense only in the context of identification
with a particular type of American Jewish support for right-wing Israeli
governments. Where prior generations of American Jewish Traditionalists might have thought of secular Israeli politicians as irrelevant or
orthogonal to their concerns, today's American Jewish Traditionalists
are knowledgeable about Israeli politics and feel solidarity with right-
wing Israeli secular politicians. American Jewish Traditionalists have,

---

* The institutional prestige of Brisk is captured in this humorous, American-inflected
anecdote from an English-language Israeli newspaper: "On Mea She'arim Street in
Jerusalem you can buy a baseball cap with an inscription that is meant as a subversive
comment on the current yeshiva reality. 'I got accepted to Brisk' the cap announces,
'but I learn in the Mir.'" See Micha Odenheimer, "'Harvard' of the Haredim," *Haaretz*,
January 28, 2005, https://www.haaretz.com/1.4716757.

in short, taken on some of the aspects of right-wing American Jewish Zionist support for Israel, all without committing themselves to Zionist ideology.

In previous decades, the Traditionalist non-Zionist theory was that they ought to treat the state of Israel the same way that their Diasporic ancestors once treated the European states in which they lived. This point of view, however, has been superseded as Traditionalists gain greater political power in Israel and set their sights on more ambitious religious-political objectives like enforcing some provisions of Jewish law on the entire population. At the same time, Traditionalists do not embrace the Religious Zionist project of treating the state as a stage in the process of messianic redemption. Traditionalists do not say that the Jewish people must be a nation in the full modern sense or that Israel is a legitimate manifestation of a justified nationalist project. It is not that they have consciously replaced their historical anti-Zionism with a new ideology of non-Zionist identification with Israel. Rather, their attitude toward the state of Israel is mostly unstated and implicit. Within their community, no one much seems to mind.

FROM ANTI-ZIONISM TO ACCOMMODATION

How did this transformation happen? Like so much about Traditionalism, the backstory lies in nineteenth-century Europe. From the dawn of classical Zionism, Traditionalists recognized the antireligious, atheistic, radically secular aspects of the movement and were horrified by its whole enterprise. They (correctly) saw Zionism as a modernist project bound up in modern ideology. The Traditionalists of the time were antimodern, or at least against the modernization of Jewish life.[3]

One strand of Traditionalist anti-Zionism went further, condemning Zionism as a violation of a teaching known as the "three oaths." The three oaths are, in their origin, three parallel verses from the Song of Songs. In each, the speaker tells the "daughters of Jerusalem," in poetic language, "I have adjured you: do not awaken or arouse love until it please." The Talmud offers an allegorical reading of the three adjurations:

Whence these three oaths? First, that Israel should not go up [to the Land of Israel] in a wall [or, shall not scale the wall]. Second, the Holy One adjured Israel not to rebel against the nations of the world. Third, the Holy One adjured the nations that they not oppress Israel over-much.[4]

The key oath is the first one, the one about the wall. It is also the most obscure. For the most part, medieval and early modern authorities interpreted the oath to mean that Jews must not go to the land of Israel en masse (as it were, in a wall of people) or by force (more or less: over the wall). This interpretation did not necessarily contradict medieval authorities who believed the Law commanded that every Jew try to settle in the land of Israel. That command could be interpreted as an *individual* duty, whereas the oath was a ban on collective action. This distinction between individual and collective immigration explains why it was considered appropriate for Traditionalists, both before Zionism and after, to move to the land of Israel. They understood themselves to be permitted or even obliged to do so individually, but not as part of a self-conscious effort at the movement of all Jews to the homeland.

The theology of the three oaths translated into a definitive rejection of the Zionist project, not a mere objection to its secularism. If authoritative rabbinic teaching prohibited the Jews as a people from attempting to settle the land of Israel, then (in theory) nothing, not even the desecularization of Zionism, could cure the Zionist project of its heretical qualities. The very objective of returning the Jewish people to their homeland without miraculous divine intervention was itself a violation of Tradition.

The three oaths loomed large in Traditionalist writing about Zionism until some fifty years ago.[5] The most important anti-Zionist Traditionalist of the twentieth century was the Transylvanian-born Satmar Rebbe, Yoel Teitelbaum (1887–1979), who established his Hasidic community in Williamsburg, Brooklyn. He made the oaths the centerpiece of his magnum opus, a collection of his writings that, among other things, treated Zionism as the sin for which the Holocaust was divine punishment.[6] The small number of Traditionalist leaders who were open to

Zionism had to address the oaths to explain their apparent deviation from them.* Sometimes they offered clever explanations for why Zionism had not in fact violated the oaths. Other times they urged Zionists not to violate the oaths as they interpreted them.

Today, in Traditionalist circles, the three oaths are rarely discussed. The main reason is surely that the state of Israel is now an accomplished fact. Any prohibition that might have existed on settling the land en masse and trying to create a state there has now been violated. The practical question facing Traditionalists is therefore not whether to move to Israel or support Zionism but rather *how to interact with the existing state.* A tiny fraction of Teitelbaum's Satmar followers and fellow travelers refuse to interact with the state at all because they deny its divine legitimacy. But this sort of after-the-fact intransigence is not characteristic of Traditionalists, who as a historical matter have largely taken political affairs as they find them rather than demanding revolutionary change. Indeed, the second of the two oaths—adjuring Jews not to rebel against the nations of the world—amounts to a kind of basic theology of political quietism, one that would reject revolutionary action against even a Jewish state.

Traditionalist skeptical accommodation of the state of Israel was set in place first by Rabbi Avrohom Yeshaya Karelitz (1878–1953), known as the Hazon Ish, the first of the giants of Traditionalist Torah to bring eastern European Traditionalism to the Holy Land. The Hazon Ish was born in the town of Kosava, then part of the Russian Empire and now part of Belarus, territory that for the Jews of the time was characterized culturally as "Lithuania." A gentle man of extraordinary piety and genius, he appears under a different name as a main character in Chaim Grade's masterpiece *The Yeshiva,* the greatest Yiddish novel ever written, one of the few that can stand alongside the masterworks of Russian literature. (The novel's English translation is now inexplicably, outrageously, out of print.) While living in Vilna (modern Vilnius), the Hazon

---

* These existed, although to avoid confusion I have not discussed them. Some of them founded the Mizrachi movement in Vilna in 1902. They could be characterized as early Religious Zionists.

Ish became close to the other leading *gedolim* of Eastern European traditionalism, who recognized his greatness. But his personal modesty precluded him from taking a public position while still in Europe. He moved to Palestine in 1933 and emerged as the major public leader of Traditionalist Jews only after the Holocaust destroyed the world of the Lithuanian yeshivas from which he had emerged.[7]

The Hazon Ish moved to Israel for reasons of individual faith, not as a Zionist. Once in Palestine, he self-consciously avoided giving direct political advice to the Agudat Yisrael party, the political party that had represented Traditionalist Jews already in Europe and continued to do so in Palestine. He preferred to express his reservations about the possibility of a Jewish state obliquely. Once the state of Israel emerged, however, the Hazon Ish did engage in an intense political fight over the military conscription of women, a crucial piece of Zionist-socialist modernism that he rejected.

In a famous meeting with David Ben-Gurion, Israel's first prime minister, the Hazon Ish was asked how religious and secular Jews should live together. In response, he referred to a Talmudic passage in praise of the value of compromise (in Hebrew, *pesharah*). As a model of compromise, the Talmud gives the example of two camels simultaneously approaching a narrow path up the hill at a place called Beit Horon, where there was no room for both camels to walk side-by-side. If one camel is bearing a load and the other is not, the Talmud says, the load-bearing camel should go first. The Hazon Ish told Ben-Gurion that observant Jews were burdened by the load of Torah and the commandments and that secular Jews should therefore "clear the way" for them.[8]

Ben-Gurion may have been a secularist, but he replied, in true Talmudic form, with a question: "And non-religious Jews are not carrying a load? And the settlement of the land is not a heavy burden?" In the ensuing debate between the two men, Ben-Gurion asserted that even the radically socialist, antireligious youth of the *Shomer ha-Tza'ir* (Young Guard) movement were "protecting you." The Hazon Ish replied, "They are sustained because we learn Torah."

The exchange reflected two disparate worldviews: "If those young men weren't protecting you, the enemies would have destroyed you," Ben-

Gurion rejoined. The Hazon Ish answered, "On the contrary, because of our Torah learning, they can live and work and guard." Ben-Gurion tried again: "I do not discount the Torah, but if there are no living humans, who will study Torah?" The Hazon Ish answered, "The Torah is the tree of life, the elixir of life."

It has sometimes been thought that the Hazon Ish was advancing a theological view of the superiority of Traditionalism to secularism. Ben-Gurion may have believed something of the sort, given his testy response. A better interpretation of the Hazon Ish's invocation of the Talmudic passage about the two camels is that he was suggesting the value of compromise between the state of Israel and its Traditionalist population, which was then extremely small. Compromise was the point of the Talmudic passage about the two camels. The Hazon Ish was proposing compromise as a mode of coexistence.

Implicit in this proposed compromise was mutual accommodation. If the state of Israel were to accommodate Traditionalist Jews, then those Jews would impliedly not impair the state. The Hazon Ish was not offering any formal recognition to the state of Israel or its prime minister. But he was acknowledging that the state was an entity with which compromise could legitimately be effectuated.

As for his suggestion that because of Torah learning, secular Zionists were able to "live and work and guard," the Hazon Ish was articulating a point of view importantly different from Rav Kook's view that scholars studying Torah win wars. He was expressing (in response to Ben-Gurion's insistence on the primacy of human agency) the view that the Torah, as the tree of life, provides a reason for humans' being. God's protection of all the Jews of Israel was meant to protect the continuity of Torah. In the Hazon Ish's formulation, the point of Torah study was not to protect the state. Rather, Torah study was the basic element of human value and worth. This was the Traditionalist belief in a nutshell.

The compromise the Hazon Ish was proposing subsequently came into being, notwithstanding Ben-Gurion's instinctual skepticism of it, as a result of Israel's form of parliamentary government. Israelis elect the Knesset by proportional representation, voting for parties rather than individual candidates. Then the parties form coalition governments. As a result, even when there were few Traditionalist voters and the Haredi parties held only a handful of seats in parliament, those parties were able to achieve an outsize influence by joining whatever coalition government needed them—at a price. Israeli Traditionalists started by demanding exemption from military service. Ben-Gurion and his allies grudgingly agreed, both because the Haredi community was so small and because, as secularist-nationalists, they could not imagine that Traditionalism would grow so much so fast.

Over time, as the numbers of Haredi voters increased, Traditionalist parties multiplied and their influence expanded. These parties gained state subsidies for housing, welfare, child care, and religious education. These all matter vastly for a community that has many children and nearly half of whose adult male members study Torah rather than working full-time. By serving in ministerial posts, Haredi politicians get access to patronage jobs and the power to target government aid to their neighborhoods and institutions.

By the 1990s, Haredi engagement with the state of Israel through political participation and patronage had drastically reduced the number of anti-Zionists among them. Traditionalist politicians initially avoided serving as government ministers, which was a mild symbolic sign of refusal to legitimate the state. But that taboo was broken because the power associated with controlling ministries was too valuable to be passed up. As Traditionalists gradually became full participants in Israeli political life, they began to use political rhetoric that sounded more like mainstream Israeli democratic discourse, asserting their own rights as equal citizens and occasionally even calling for national unity.[9]

Yet political participation in government and identification with the state are not the same, particularly for non-Zionist Traditionalists who had tried to think of the state of Israel as a nonsacred entity akin to the government of a Diaspora state. Identification came later than participation, not alongside it. Its unlikely originator was a Russian-born Hasidic master who came into his full flourishing in the United States and never visited Israel in the entirety of his long, productive life.

THE REBBE, THE STATE, THE MESSIAH

Traditionalist identification with the state of Israel is entirely distinct from Religious Zionism. Its origins lie with the most fascinating, important, and controversial figure in post–World War II Traditionalism: Rabbi Menachem Mendel Schneerson (1902–1994), the seventh successor to the leadership of the Chabad-Lubavitch movement, known in his lifetime and beyond as the Lubavitcher Rebbe, or, for short, "the Rebbe."

Schneerson inherited the Chabad dynasty after marrying the middle daughter of the sixth Lubavitcher Rebbe. Steeped in Talmud and Hasidic thought from his Russian childhood, Schneerson deviated from the usual path of a Hasidic master by attending lectures at the University of Berlin between 1928 and 1933 and by earning an engineering degree in Paris while living there with his wife before 1940. His erudition, piety, and charisma, combined with his descent from an earlier Lubavitcher Rebbe, led to his installation at the head of Chabad in 1950 after the death of his father-in-law, who had no son.

In a public career that spanned the time of his installation to his passing on the third day of the Jewish month of Tammuz in 1994, Schneerson made three transformational contributions to Traditionalist Judaism in general and Chabad in particular. First, he established what might be called "outreach Traditionalism": an institutionalized practice of sending emissaries (in Hebrew or Yiddish, *shluhim*) to locations throughout the world. Once in post, they would buy a house, form a small congregation to pray in it, and attempt to draw local nonobservant Jews into a rudimentary religious community by the force of kindness, charisma, and convenience. The outreach movement further included public performances of the commandments such as lighting large Hanukkah menorahs in public places, waylaying passing pedestrians and inviting them, if Jewish, to don tefillin, or urging them to wave the palm frond on the festival of Sukkot. After the fall of the Soviet Union, Chabad emissaries also took up official rabbinical positions in various eastern European countries, enmeshing them in complex governmental and intergovernmental politics, including, in one case, a close

connection to Vladimir Putin, and in another, a strong public advocacy
of Ukrainian resistance to Russia. Chabad schools, established wherever
sufficient demand could be identified or created, were another important
aspect of the outreach.

All this outreach represented a radically new direction for Traditionalist Jews. Since the nineteenth century, Traditionalists had occupied a
position of conservative defensiveness relative to nonobservant Judaism.
The Rebbe's emissaries, in contrast, were undertaking an enthusiastic,
optimistic, and as it were "offensive" mission to bring Jews back to the
fold of faith. The Merkos Shlichus campaign that sent young rabbis to
far-flung places began as early as 1942. Gradually it extended to countries around the world, so many that a pair of scholars has associated
Chabad outreach with the Peace Corps created under John F. Kennedy's
presidency.[10] Whatever Schneerson's influences, the conceptual foundations of Chabad's global strategy are wholly original. Although today
some other Traditionalist groups, in particular Yeshivish Traditionalists,
have begun to emulate the Chabad outreach model in part, Schneerson
deserves credit for its invention.

The second transformation associated with the Rebbe was his unbri-
dled messianism. Throughout his career, Schneerson developed a complex religious-philosophical theory of a potential messiah who existed in
all generations and would become manifest in the era that merited his
unveiling. This theory, on which volumes have been written, drew on
earlier trends in Jewish messianic thought. And as we shall see, it joined
the profound mysticism of earlier Hasidic masters, including those of
the Lubavitch dynasty, to Maimonides's essentially political, rational
account of the messianic age.

For now, the crucial point about the Rebbe's messianism is that at
its core lay the idea of the potential king-messiah and the possibility of
his actualization. That actualization was in turn captured in a Hebrew-
Yiddish word, *mamash*. The word can mean "actually" or "literally" or
"definitively" or "really." And it is spelled with the three Hebrew letters
that made up the Rebbe's monogram, MMSh.

Following the Rebbe's teachings, his followers began, quietly in the
1970s and then with growing fervor through the 1980s and early 1990s,

to believe and assert openly that Schneerson himself was the potential messiah of his generation. Through pursuit of his spiritual program, they could bring about his unveiling and actualization. The public appearance of the immanent messiah was imminent.

The resulting wave of overt Chabad messianism crested after the Rebbe's death. Many followers insisted that the revealed messiah had not died but had only gone into occultation in anticipation of an eventual spiritual return. Nearly the entirety of the Traditionalist world outside Chabad rejected Schneerson's messianic status, both before and after his death. His most important "Lithuanian" (i.e., non-Hasidic) Traditionalist contemporary, Rav Elazar Man Shach (1899–2001), went so far as to warn that Chabad messianism might cross over into idolatry. Yet the pervasive and continuing influence of Chabad messianism represented the introduction of immediate messianic speculation and discussion into Traditionalist Jewish life and thought for the first time since Traditionalism itself began to coalesce almost two hundred years ago.

The third, related transformative aspect of Schneerson's worldview was a radically different Traditionalist attitude toward Israel. The Rebbe's teachings repositioned the state of Israel in Jewish life. The state was not a human-driven step in messianic redemption, as the Religious Zionists would have it, nor a wholly profane nationalist project, as most Traditionalists had long believed. Under the influence of Schneerson's thought and actions, it became possible for Traditionalists to view the existing state of Israel as a *partial blueprint for a potential messianic actualization.* That messianic actualization would take place through the miraculous emergence of a king-messiah who would rule Israel as a religious state, marking the ultimate manifestation of the messianic promise.

Although to a casual observer this vision might not sound so different from Religious Zionist messianism, in fact it differed substantially. Unlike Religious Zionism, Schneerson did not collectivize the messiah. He did not treat Zionism as legitimate. The fifth Lubavitcher Rebbe (Sholom Dovber Schneerson, the Rebbe Rashab) had openly opposed secular Zionism. His dynastic successor, the seventh in the line, could not have explicitly disagreed. He did not hold that the state of

Israel was a necessary stage in the fulfillment of the messianic process. In his view, the state did not have any inherently sacred qualities.
Rather, for Schneerson, the state of Israel was an unmentioned—almost
unmentionable—occasion for the gathering of Jews in the land of Israel
in readiness for a miraculous messianic intervention.

The jumping-off point for this remarkable idea was Maimonides's
rationalist interpretation of a Talmudic dictum, "There is no difference
between our days and the days of the messiah other than the [salvation
of Israel from] subordination to the kingdoms [of the world]."[11] For Maimonides, the messiah was not a wonder worker or a resurrector of the
dead but rather a kingly political leader capable of enforcing the laws of
the Torah and defending Israelite sovereignty. By embracing this vision,
laid out in Maimonides's code of Jewish law, Schneerson connected the
messianic age with the reign of Torah law in an independent Jewish
state. From this perspective, the state of Israel could be understood as a
kind of messianic entity *in potentia*, having achieved a measure of independence and sovereignty while still lacking a legal system based upon
the true Law and a messiah-king to enforce it.

Schneerson's attitude toward Israel could not be called a full-blown
theory of the Jewish state or its role in history, because Schneerson assiduously avoided articulating such a theory. For a highly systematic
creative genius who spoke and wrote prolifically for some fifty years,
this absence cannot have been accidental. Schneerson did not articulate
a grand theory of Israel because he did not want to. Nevertheless, it is
possible to reconstruct the steps that led through his well-articulated
theory of outreach and his even better-expressed theory of potential
messianism to his distinctive views about Israel. From there, it is possible
to glimpse the ways that Schneerson's beliefs about Israel have come to
influence the rest of Traditionalist Jewish thought, even as non-Chabad
Traditionalist Jews reject the Rebbe's messianic theology and much of
his approach to outreach.

Chabad outreach as conceived by the Rebbe interacts in a complex
way with the establishment of the state of Israel and the three-oaths
idea that preoccupied Traditionalist anti-Zionists like Schneerson's Hasidic nemesis, the Satmar Rebbe, Yoel Teitelbaum.[12] Sending emissaries

ISRAEL WITHOUT ZIONISM 227

wherever Jews might be found throughout the world implied that the
Jews had not all collectively chosen to immigrate to Israel, and so were
not violating the oath against scaling the wall. If Jews still existed in the
many places where Chabad emissaries went, that was, in a certain sense,
evidence that the ingathering of exiles had not yet occurred.

Crucially, the Chabad emissaries were not setting up shop at the four
corners of the earth to convince Jews to move to Israel. To the contrary,
by their presence, Chabad Houses (as they are called) are designed to
enable Jews to live anywhere while still performing the commandments.
While this goal of facilitating Jewish existence everywhere on earth was
not inherently anti-Zionist, it certainly undercut the Zionist aspiration to
universal voluntary immigration. Even as Zionism was declaring that all
Jews all over the world had only a single homeland, namely Israel, Chabad
emissaries were suggesting that Jews belonged wherever they wanted to
live and could prosper in those places, with the emissaries functioning as
the glue that would hold local Jewish communities together. In a remarkable development that demonstrates how the Chabad emissaries sustain
the Diaspora, today at Passover or Yom Kippur one can find Israelis on
their postmilitary service *wanderjahr* congregating at Chabad Houses
in places like Kathmandu, Mumbai, and Shanghai.*

Chabad's emissaries all over the world paralleled the state of Israel's
own diplomatic outreach through its official diplomatic corps. In a real
sense, the emissaries even competed with Israeli diplomacy. Where the
government of Israel might have expected that its diplomatic representative was the only representative of the Jews in a given far-flung place,
in fact the Chabad emissaries, with their distinctive Traditionalist garb
and their own diplomatic pretensions, might well be seen by locals as
more emblematic representatives of world Jewry. The network of Chabad
emissaries functioned as a competing alternative to or refutation of the
Zionist claim to be *the* Jewish state speaking on behalf of Jews. While

---

* Actually, there are at last count three different Chabad Houses in Shanghai alone:
Chabad of Pudong, the Shanghai Jewish Center, and the Intown Jewish Center. When
I last prayed in the synagogues of two of them, brought by host-extraordinaire David
Orenstein, they were flourishing.

the Rebbe lived, he—not the president or prime minister of Israel—was arguably the Jewish leader with the greatest global visibility, especially in places where the Chabad House was the only Jewish institution to be found.

Once this outreach is taken into account, Chabad messianism emerges as a *competitive* messianism—competitive, that is, with the secularized nationalist messianism of the Zionist state. The classical, secular Zionist state sought to embody the ingathering of exiles and the expression of Jewish sovereignty. Religious Zionism desecularized that self-consciously secular version of Jewish messianism and hence ascribed redemptive, messianic religious meaning to the state as national collective. Chabad messianism showed Israel *not* to be the messianic state, while hinting at the possibility of integrating the Jewish state into an eventual, actual messianic age with the Rebbe as messiah-king.

Here lies the core of Schneerson's unique attitude to Israel: the presently existing state can be construed as a potential *precursor* of the genuine messianic state to come. To create it would take a miracle, the miracle of universal Jewish embrace of Jewish Law, and hence of the messiah-king. That miracle, however, might occur by what would outwardly appear to be natural means. Chabad never ruled out the possibility of more obvious miracles, like the magical translocation to Jerusalem of the Rebbe's home at 770 Eastern Parkway in Crown Heights, Brooklyn. But in case the miracle should not take that form, Chabad built an exact replica of 770 (as the home is called) in the Israeli village of Kfar Chabad, close to Tel Aviv.[13]

Thus, as the Rebbe's followers speculated, not about when the messiah would come, but about when the messiah *who had already arrived* would reveal himself, they were picturing their messiah-king, the Rebbe, taking the reins of the existing Israeli state as its king. They expected him to replace Israel's governing structure with divinely validated kingship and its laws with the Torah as interpreted by the rabbis. The state of Israel was, in other words, part of their messianic imagination, even though they did not attribute sacral or redemptive character to the existing state, as Religious Zionism does.

In congruence with this vision, Schneerson's attitude toward the state of Israel amounted to identification, even as he never said anything formally Zionist. Instead, the Rebbe expressed support for the state's military undertakings by praying openly for the success and the safety of IDF troops who were sacrificing on behalf of the Jewish people.[14] He argued that Jews had a Torah obligation to defend themselves from external physical threat, wherever they might be. This obligation extended to Jews living in Israel, who must defend themselves collectively against their foreign enemies. The IDF was the entity fulfilling this obligation.

In this way, Schneerson created a mechanism for identification with the state of Israel through its military character. This was a doubly radical innovation for Traditionalism. Traditionalists like the Hazon Ish had rejected the IDF root and branch as the secularizing force of a secular Zionist state. The exemption from mandatory conscription was constitutive of Israeli Traditionalism. The Rebbe not only reversed this view. He used his praise of the IDF as a point of identification with the state—a state very much self-identified with its own citizen-conscript military. Subtle though it might seem, the transformation aligned and identified Chabad Hasidim with the state of Israel, all without a stated theory about Zionism or the character of the Israeli state.

Equally important, as Israel-Palestine negotiations progressed, the Rebbe publicly opposed the exchange of land for peace and insisted on God's grant of the whole land of Israel to the Jewish people.[15] This development mattered because by taking a stand on the single most important issue in Israeli politics, Schneerson was further identifying with the state of Israel. He was offering his opinion about the course the ship of state should steer. Crucially, he was doing so not as an outsider but as a self-identified participant in a global Jewish conversation about the future path of the Zionist state.

To this extent, if to no other, the Rebbe was implicitly accepting the Zionist claim to act on behalf of the Jewish people as a whole, and even to rule legitimately in the land of Israel. He cared what the state would do because the state was, at a minimum, the entity assuring the safety of the Jewish people in the land of Israel. Moreover, by objecting to the cession of Jewish sovereignty over any part of the divinely gifted land, the Rebbe was acknowledging that the state of Israel *was already* exercising Jewish sovereignty over the land of Israel. By implication, that sovereignty was in some sense legitimate. If and when the king-messiah-Rebbe would assume his throne, the sovereignty would be his—and God's.

What the Rebbe left unanswered was what to make of the state of Israel if it turned out that he did not actualize his potential as the king-messiah by assuming rule over it. When the Rebbe died, his followers were left without guidance on how to proceed. The third of Tammuz, his death day, became a central event in their spiritual lives. It is the newest recognizable date to be added to the Jewish calendar, commemorated only by Chabad Hasidim but familiar to all Traditionalist Jews, regardless of their opinion of the Rebbe.

Following the Rebbe's death, a divisive messianist crisis gripped Chabad. But both factions, those who accepted the Rebbe's death (in some sense) and those who supported the theory of the Rebbe's occultation, retained his identification with the state of Israel. A growing percentage of male Chabad Hasidim in Israel accept conscription in the IDF rather than obtaining exemptions. Those who do can plausibly be termed Zionists, even if they are Zionists without a theory of Zionism.

IDENTIFICATION WITH ISRAEL WITHOUT THE MESSIAH

In contrast to Schneerson's identification with the state of Israel, Traditionalist anti-Zionism long held that if the secular Zionist state is wholly illegitimate, then there is no reason for the state to wield sovereignty. Today a tiny number of Traditionalists, some followers of the Satmar Rebbe and some members of a group called Neturei Karta (Aramaic for "Defenders of the City"), embody that anti-Zionist position by expressing symbolic sympathies with entities like the government of Iran or even Hamas. Neturei Karta in particular looks for public opportunities to appear in anti-Israel political postures. Thus one of its spokesmen, Rabbi Dovid Feldman, addressed a rally in Montreal in the aftermath of the 2023 Hamas attacks on Israel, wearing Traditionalist black and white with a green and red Palestine scarf over his shoulders. He told the crowd that the very existence of the state of Israel was "criminal" and "forbidden" according to Jewish law. A TikTok video of his remarks had more than half a million likes as of this writing, surely the most viewed Neturei Karta speech of all time.

The numbers of such radical anti-Zionist Traditionalists are minuscule. Their importance lies in their isolation, even from other Traditionalists. By their radical anti-Zionism, they unintentionally hold out to mainstream Traditionalists the possibility of identifying with Israel. Mainstream Traditionalists have thus been able to refine their relationship to Israel as against various options without defining it. Unlike the Satmar/Neturei Karta version of anti-Zionism, they do not consider the state of Israel an enemy. That leaves them with the question of what their relationship to the state in fact should be.

Increasingly, for Traditionalists in and out of Israel, the answer corresponds to the answer developed by the Rebbe, without his explicit messianism. Increasingly, Traditionalists identify with the IDF's military successes. Unlike some Chabad Hasidim, most have no desire to serve in the IDF. But they do not see the IDF as necessarily sacrilegious. (The increasing prominence of Religious Zionists in senior officer ranks makes this perspective more plausible than it was when the IDF really was dominated by secular, antireligious officers.) These Traditionalists do not pray in synagogue for the safety of the IDF's soldiers. But their children might dress up as IDF soldiers on Purim, the Jewish Halloween/Carnival. This is a sign of identification, however mediated by the topsy-turvy theme of the holiday. The Traditionalists' children are not dressing up as U.S. Marines or as professional athletes.

Beyond identification, Traditionalists, especially in Israel, increasingly think about how the state of Israel may be governed by Jewish law. They don't discuss this future in specifically messianic terms. They prefer not to speculate too concretely about the coming of the messiah, lest they fall into the Chabad trap. But in the current Knesset alone they have proposed and advocated for laws that enforce observance of the Sabbath, that prohibit the consumption of bread and other leavened products in public hospitals on Passover, and that would enforce sex-segregated bathing at public pools and in national parks.

The proposed quasi-constitutional Basic Law: Torah Study, mentioned above, further demonstrates the Traditionalists' interest in the legal order of the state. The practical effect would be, at a minimum, to make the exemption from conscription for Torah study permanent. More fundamentally, such a Basic Law would mark the embedding of Haredi ideology into the state of Israel's formal constitutional structure. This constitutionalization of Haredi belief would exemplify the gradual process whereby Rav Kook's idea that Torah study protects the state has worked its way into Traditionalist discourse. It is almost impossible to imagine the Hazon Ish seeking such a law, despite his opposition to conscription. To seek constitutional status for Torah study would have been—and would be—to acknowledge the state of Israel and its laws as fit and proper vehicles for enshrining Torah values.

Another example: on the assumption that pedagogy is a guide to cultural self-conception, consider *Just Imagine! COVID-19*, a 2021 graphic novel produced in Israel in Hebrew and English. Printed in a large-format hardback suitable for kids, the comic explores the counterfactual of how the Covid crisis would have been handled by a government in Israel guided entirely by Jewish Law.[16] In the book, policy decisions are made by a government that takes its lead from the authoritative Torah giants, the *gedolim*. They in turn address the most difficult questions using *daas Toyre*, the view of the Torah, the practical wisdom inspired by and embodied in the leaders' Torah knowledge. How the imagined Torah state came to be is not discussed, nor are the halakhic underpinnings of such a state theorized. The scenario of Traditionalist rabbinic control is, rather, taken for granted. There is no mention of elections, but also no mention of a messianic king or prince.

The purpose of the graphic novel is, on one level, to offer an account of desirable Covid policy from the perspective of Jewish law. The book's approach is informed by the primacy of Torah study and prayer and faith in God. Simultaneously, it also recognizes the value of medical science and the halakhic duty to preserve life by relying on the best medical advice.

At a deeper level, the book aims to present the worldview and framework of Traditionalism as adequate and appropriate to the government of a functioning modern state in Israel. Its message is that if the Traditionalists were in charge, the Covid crisis would have been handled smoothly, not only by the grace of God but by a well-run, God-fearing state. (Recall that a Traditionalist was the minister of health when the Covid crisis began, but he was not the final authority, as the *gedolim* would be in the book's utopia.) That was definitely not the approach taken by earlier non-Zionist or anti-Zionist Traditionalists. They saw Jewish law today as restricted to the limited spheres of ritual law and the law of private property. They did not anticipate expanding it into areas of regulatory policy such as those implicated by public health measures taken during a global pandemic. The Traditionalist authors of the book may not at present have a comprehensive program they would like to see implemented by legislation in the Knesset. But they can picture the circumstances in which the existing influence of Haredi politics on Israeli law would expand into total legislative control.

Without the influence of Schneerson's speculation about a state governed by a messiah-king under the Law of the Torah, it is unlikely that Traditionalists would be writing about a Torah state with this much descriptive detail. To be sure, the rest of Traditionalism rejected and rejects the Rebbe's form of messianism. And there can be no doubt that rising Traditionalist political power contributes to the imaginative possibility of Traditionalist rule under Jewish law. Yet the imaginative leap from today's state of Israel to a state governed by Jewish law need not require supernatural divine intervention. All it takes is to imagine a Traditionalist majority assuming power and enacting its own constitutional revolution in the existing state of Israel. What is historically significant about this picture is that Traditionalists are increasingly picturing how they would govern Israel if they came to power. And this is happening in a world where Traditionalist parties made up the second-largest bloc in Netanyahu's 2022 government, larger even than the bloc of Religious Zionist parties.

Seen against the backdrop of the old Traditionalist anti-Zionism or non-Zionist quietism, this development marks a victory achieved by Zionism in relation to Traditionalism. Traditionalists who once rejected the state are now aiming to insert their values into it and govern under it. Yet secular Zionists, past and present, must surely see this victory as Pyrrhic, or rather as a defeat. To secular Zionism, Traditionalism was a dead end of Diasporic history, to be supplanted by nationalism. Instead, Traditionalism—if it continues on this course—proposes to supplant the very nationalism that created the state of Israel. In terms that would have made some sense to Rav Kook, the ideologue of Religious Zionism, secular Zionism would then turn out to have been an unwitting vehicle for the ultimate victory of the Jewish spirit contained in the Law itself. God would remain enthroned and would be recognized as the ultimate authority, having acted through apparently secular historic forces. The result would be, let us say, non-Zionist Zionism: a nonmessianic Traditionalist state governed by Jewish law.

THE DEVIATIONISTS—AND THE FUTURE OF
POST-ZIONIST ZIONISM

I have been arguing in this chapter that mainstream Traditionalist Jews, both inside and outside Israel, have significantly shifted their attitudes to Israel in recent decades. Notwithstanding their official non-Zionism, Traditionalists identify with Israel, especially its military undertakings. Traditionalists increasingly imagine the possibility of Israel transformed into a state governed by Jewish law. To underscore this mainstream transformation, I would like to end the chapter by considering a marginal, fascinating, and terrifying deviation from Traditionalism and Religious Zionism. The people I am about to describe are extremists even to other extremists. Repudiated (or at least criticized) by mainstream Traditionalists and Religious Zionists alike, they nevertheless reveal what can happen when different messianisms converge and recombine in new and frightening ways.

Their movement represents a fusion of two mystical messianisms, that of the Lubavitcher Rebbe and that of Religious Zionism, into a single radicalism that has already occasioned acts of terrorism and murder. This movement as yet has no conventional name. But it does have a recognized spiritual leader: Rabbi Yitzchak Ginsburgh, born in St. Louis in 1944. He is revered by an inchoate group of young Israelis referred to as "hilltop youth," named after the relatively isolated West Bank hilltop settlements where they grew up or went to live.

Ginsburgh was raised in the United States by Zionist but not particularly religious parents and showed an early affinity for mathematics and music. At fifteen, after spending a year with his parents in Israel, where he studied at a well-established secular high school in Jerusalem, the Rehavia Gymnasium, Ginsburgh declared his intention to become an observant Jew. He went to college at the University of Chicago, where he studied mathematics and philosophy, then earned a master's degree in math from the graduate school of Yeshiva University. He moved to Israel in 1965 at the age of twenty-one, and from that time on immersed himself in Traditionalist Torah study, with a special emphasis on mysticism. He enrolled in the leading Chabad yeshiva in Jerusalem in 1967, after the Six-Day War, and came to see the Rebbe as his leading spiritual influence.

I have provided this background because it shows how, in many respects, Ginsburgh was typical of his generation of American *ba'alei teshuvah*—second- or third-generation American Jews whose parents had moved away from Traditionalism and who themselves discovered and embraced either Modern Orthodoxy or Haredi orthodoxy as a conscious choice. Many of these "returnees" to Traditionalism were intellectuals of one sort or another, and, like Ginsburgh, they sought after different paths until they crafted a spiritual-intellectual direction of their own. Ginsburgh himself appears to have considered himself a fully committed adherent of Chabad Hasidism from 1967 until 1987, when he became head of a five-year-old yeshiva founded near a pilgrimage site traditionally identified as Joseph's Tomb. The yeshiva, Od Yosef Chai, "Joseph Still Lives,"[17] was then on the outskirts of the Palestinian city of Nablus in the northern part of the West Bank that Israel refers to as Samaria.[18]

Under Ginsburgh's leadership, Od Yosef Chai became a center for the development of a new fusion of Chabad messianism and Religious Zionist messianism, alongside a powerful turn away from the familiar forms of both. It was not a Chabad yeshiva. Although Ginsburgh himself continued to dress in the distinctive Chabad style (wearing the oversized fedora that is Chabad's answer to the sable or mink Hasidic shtreimel), the students in the yeshiva mostly did not dress that way, nor did they identify as hasidim of the Lubavitcher Rebbe. Rather, most of the students were (and are) hilltop youth, born into the Religious Zionist–settler milieu that inherited the legacy of Gush Emunim, the Bloc of the Faithful, the students of Rabbi Tzvi Yehudah Kook. Today, the yeshiva's website describes it as a "Hasidic" yeshiva, and it would be fair to characterize it as neo-Hasidic, with Ginsburgh himself, styled the "prince of the yeshiva" as its spiritual leader, the closest thing to a Hasidic master or rebbe for its students.[19]

The original location of the yeshiva, in the shadow of a Palestinian city known for its anti-Zionist resistance going back a century, essentially guaranteed that the only students who would attend were those with a special interest in settling every inch of the historic land of Israel. The possibility, or rather the probability, of conflict between yeshiva students and the local Palestinian community was ever-present, particularly during the first intifada. And indeed, students associated with the yeshiva were alleged to have rampaged in the nearby Palestinian town of Kifl Haris in 1989, causing an incident in which a Palestinian boy was killed and two others were injured.[20]

Ginsburgh served as day-to-day head of the yeshiva until 2001, when the IDF withdrew its protection from Israeli settlers at the Joseph's Tomb site and the yeshiva moved to the settlement town of Yitzhar. (The yeshiva building in Yitzhar was taken over by the IDF for a time in 2014, after students were involved in violent attacks on Palestinians as well as on IDF soldiers.[21]) He was succeeded by one of his leading students, Rabbi Yitzhak Shapira, who would become a public exponent of some of Ginsburgh's most radical teachings. While at the yeshiva, Ginsburgh continued to compose mystical, philosophical, and psychological works. He has published over a hundred books, with more than twenty translated into English. Consistent with his mathematical background, many address topics in gematria, the Jewish tradition of mystical numerology.

As a student of the Rebbe, Ginsburgh necessarily participated in the speculation surrounding Schneerson's potential messianic unveiling. After the Rebbe's death in 1994, however, Ginsburgh did not associate himself with the Chabad faction who believed Schneerson had gone into occultation. Instead, slowly but perceptibly, his followers began to interpret his teachings as indicating a different possibility, namely that Ginsburgh himself was now the potential messiah of his generation, as Schneerson had once been.

Ginsburgh has never, to my knowledge, expressly described himself as the potential king-messiah. But then, neither did Schneerson. The Rebbe's followers assiduously interpreted their teacher's words as leading to the inevitable conclusion of his messiahship. The Rebbe never openly assented. The closest indications of his possible acquiescence came when young Chabad Hasidim would sing their favorite song in Schneerson's presence: "Long live our master, our teacher, our rabbi, the king-messiah, forever more." As Schneerson aged, his students reported seeing him acknowledge their fealty by waving his hands in time to the music. Conservatives within Chabad quietly suggested that the aging Schneerson may not have understood what his gestures meant to his followers. But that objection carried no weight for the energized and motivated messianists. In any case, they had an entire body of Schneerson's thought and work to support their speculation. What was more, the Rebbe never denied his status as a potential messiah.

Although not themselves veterans of this era of Chabad messianism, Ginsburgh's students have followed a similar path. They have reportedly sung the "Long live" song in his presence, apparently without being discouraged from doing so. Like Schneerson, Ginsburgh has not, it would seem, rejected the suggestion that he is a potential messiah awaiting unveiling.[22]

Schneerson's vision of Jewish law governing the land of Israel was abstract, rather than concrete. It depended on a messianic advent to trigger it. Ginsburgh and his students have gone further, articulating a blueprint for governance under Jewish law in the immediate future. In Ginsburgh's view, Israel should be ruled by a monarch or prince who would govern according to Jewish law. His followers created an organization called Derech Chaim, "The Way of Life," which on its website (now defunct) laid out their constitutional program in detail, leaving little doubt that Ginsburgh was their candidate for prince.

Where Ginsburgh's messianic vision converges with that of Religious Zionism is his apparent belief that there is no need to wait for any miraculous events to bring about such a state of affairs. Simply by creating a monarchic Jewish state in the land of Israel, the messianic situation will have arrived. The administration of Jewish law will be both a feature of that situation and a proof of genuine messiahship. The state in question would undoubtedly operate in continuity to the existing state of Israel. It would be Israel under new leadership, with a new, monarchic constitution derived from Jewish Law.

Where Ginsburgh differs from Religious Zionism is in his critical view of the actually existing state of Israel. For most Traditionalists, what is wrong with Israel is its secularism, a critique derived from the early Traditionalist critique of classical Zionism. For Ginsburgh and his followers, the problem with the state of Israel is that it has failed to remain true to the settlement project with which it began. Most Religious Zionists believe that by taking up the settlement project themselves in the aftermath of the 1967 war, they became the vanguard of Zionism. Ginsburgh's followers believe that by signing the Oslo Accords with the Palestinian Authority, the state of Israel lost its legitimacy as the entity chosen by God to implement the settlement project.

The hilltop youth, from whose ranks Ginsburgh's followers mainly come, exist in a state of conflict not only with the Palestinians around them but also with the IDF, as the anthropologist Assaf Harel has shown.[23] As the Israeli military seeks to shut down their illegal settlements and prevent their violence against Palestinians, the hilltop youth have become increasingly alienated from the state of Israel. Ginsburgh and the leading exponents of his ideas provide them with a mystical-messianic worldview that places them still at the vanguard of redemption. But they are no longer the vanguard of *Zionism*, which as a movement has now been discredited by the actions of the state and overtaken by the potentiality of a messianic state ruled according to Jewish law.

The culmination of this ideology—and the occasion for the state of Israel's (partial) turn against Ginsburgh and the hilltop youth—took place in July 2015 in the Palestinian village of Duma. Masked men, one later identified as Amiram Ben-Uliel (then twenty years old), and the other a teenager unnamed in the press, firebombed two houses. One was empty. The other held the Dawabsheh family. Ali Dawabsheh, eighteen months old, was killed at once. His parents later died of their wounds. Around the burnt-out houses, the attackers spray-painted graffiti associated with Ginsburgh's worldview. It included the words "Long live the king messiah," from the song originally composed in honor of the Lubavitcher Rebbe but in this instance evidently devoted to Ginsburgh. The graffiti also featured the Hebrew words for "revenge" and "price tag."[24]

The attacks focused public attention on a work of legal theory and mysticism composed by two of Ginsburgh's followers, *Torat ha-Melekh: Dinei Nefashot bein Yisra'el la-'Ammim*, roughly: The Torah of the King: Laws of Life and Death Between Israel and the Nations.[25] The main body of the work is a legal treatise offering new interpretations and applications of traditional Jewish legal sources regarding rules of engagement and the use of force against civilians. Interspersed in six "appendices" throughout the book is a distinct work of mystical philosophy devoted to explaining the differences between Jewish and non-Jewish souls. Its views are mostly drawn from the teachings of Ginsburgh.

The most widely discussed, horrifying passage in the book, and the one with chilling connections to Duma, concerns the killing of children: "There is an argument for killing them because of the future danger that will be caused if they grow up to be evil like their parents." In a more expanded discussion of "revenge"—one of the words written in graffiti at the site of the Duma attack—the writers explain that "according to this calculus, children aren't killed because of their [inherent] evil, but rather because there is a general need for revenge against evildoers, and the children are those whose death will satisfy that need."[26]

In response to the attacks and their association with Ginsburgh's teachings, the Israeli government shuttered the Od Yosef Chai yeshiva for a time. After Israeli prosecutors declined to charge the authors of the book with incitement to violence or incitement to racism, both of which are crimes under Israeli law, moderate Religious Zionists asked Israel's high court to compel the prosecution. The court declined, in a 2-1 judgment that emphasized the importance of free speech even as it repudiated the teachings of the book as "anti-Jewish." In dissent, Israel's lone Arab justice argued that the book was intended to set rules of engagement for settlers killing Palestinians and called for the prosecutors to reopen the case. The official state of Israel had, after a fashion, expressed its condemnation of Ginsburgh's beliefs, even if he remained free to express them.[27]

From the standpoint of his followers, the Ginsburgh worldview remains in place. The state of Israel is, for them, the entity that once fulfilled the divine command to settle the land. But now it must be transformed into the true container for messianic rule via the adoption of a Jewish constitutional monarchy. It is this combination that leads some analysts to call Ginsburgh's followers post-Zionists, "post" in the sense that their perspective would not be possible without Zionism as a precursor, yet no longer adheres to the existing state of Israel.* To his followers, Ginsburgh is still a potential messiah. When he dies, unrevealed, they may find another candidate—or perhaps it will suffice for them to pursue the goals of settlement and Jewish constitutional monarchy without a specific prince in mind.

Ginsburgh and his followers matter. Itamar Ben-Gvir, the ultranationalist who is now Israel's minister of national security, shares a good deal of Ginsburgh's worldview. Each month on the eve of the new moon, thousands of hilltop youth gather in the Old City of Jerusalem and circumambulate the city's gates, singing songs and asserting Jewish sovereignty.[28] Each year at Passover, a few Jews are arrested for trying to sacrifice a lamb somewhere near the Temple Mount. Though not all followers of Ginsburgh, the people participating in these activities belong to a milieu in which Religious Zionist messianism and settlement are closely aligned to the aspiration for a state ruled by Jewish law—and not democratically. The hilltop youth are less on the periphery of both Religious Zionist and Traditionalist Jewish life in Israel than they have ever been.

---

* This is a secondary use of the term "post-Zionism," which primarily stands for the liberal, secularist view that Zionist ideology exhausted its usefulness after the establishment of the state of Israel in 1948 and need not be perpetuated.

What matters about Ginsburgh's ideas is that they refract trends of Zionism and mystical messianism that have also affected much of the rest of Traditionalist and Evolutionist Jewish thought. The state of Israel, coming into existence in the wake of the Holocaust, has precipitated deep transformations in Jewish ways of seeing the world. Zionism did not supplant or replace Jewishness, as it aspired to do. But it has changed Jewishness by pervading the Jewish religious beliefs that it expected to render obsolete. Thankfully, the overwhelming number of Jews in the world reject and repudiate the violence embraced by Ginsburgh's followers. Yet they, too, must reckon with the meaning of Israel for their Jewish theology and for their beliefs in redemption, in whatever form it may take.

II:5

ISRAEL AS STRUGGLE AND
THE QUESTION OF SIN

The book of Deuteronomy is set in the desert. Before bringing the
children of Israel into the promised land, God instructs Moses to deliver
a warning to the chosen people:

> Beware . . . lest you eat and become satisfied, and build good
> houses and dwell in them . . . and your heart become high and
> you forget the Lord your God who brought you out of the land of
> Egypt . . . and you say in your heart, "My strength and the power
> of my hand has made me this wealth."

If this should occur, Moses concludes, "I testify of you this day that
you shall surely perish, like the nations whom God now destroys before
you."[1]

This passage captures the essence of the Bible's theology of the Israelites' presence in the land of Israel, from start to finish. It is God who
gives them "the power to make wealth, in order to fulfill the covenant
that he swore to your fathers." That covenant demands that the people
of Israel obey God's word and not sin. If they do sin, "following other

gods," they will be punished. That punishment will be at once simple and awful: the children of Israel will lose the land.

This theology of covenant, collective sin, and collective punishment pervades the Hebrew Bible. It structures the Bible's narratives of good and bad kings. It haunts and underscores the ethical exhortations of the prophets. Jeremiah, one of its greatest exponents, daily warns the Israelites that they are sinning, that they must repent, and that if they do not, they will be punished with expulsion. His message was so defining that it gave the name "jeremiad" to any comparable sermon that warns of a coming crisis.

The rabbis of the Talmud and the middle ages accepted this biblical theology without serious question: it matched their reality. In the wake of exile and the passing of Israelite or Judahite sovereignty, they used it to make sense of their predicament. The poetic liturgy for holiday prayer includes a formula, just four words long in the original Hebrew, that sums up the rabbis' version of the biblical idea: "Because of our sins, we were exiled from our land" (*mipnei hata'einu galinu me-'artzenu*).

The rabbis did not restrict the Jewish theology of sin and punishment to God's expulsion of the people from the land of Israel. They extended it to each and every one of the many disasters that befell the Jewish people in exile. When the Jews suffered, the rabbis asked why. Their invariable answer, until recent times, was that the Jews had done wrong in the eyes of God. The nations that harmed the Jews were blameworthy, but they were also instruments for working out the divine will. The proper Jewish response to disaster, according to the rabbis, was to search their own deeds for how they had sinned and to return to the Lord in repentance— with humble heart, not the high heart that Deuteronomy depicted as the source of sin.

To the classical, secular Zionists, this Jewish theology of sin was worse than foolishness. It was a kind of self-defeating psychosis. Like the rabbis, the classical Zionists engaged in soul-searching to explain Jewish suffering. But they reached the opposite conclusion. No God was punishing the Jews and keeping them in exile. No God was running the affairs of the world in the Old Testament way. By blaming themselves for sin and ascribing their oppressed condition to divine justice, the Jews were keeping themselves in a state of exilic subordination. If the Jews had a collective sin, it was imagining falsely that they had sinned.

The classical, secular Zionist solution was to abandon the old theological picture of sin and embrace the modern conception of agency. To be agents of their own destiny, not victims, the Jewish people must redefine themselves as a nation. As a nation, they could and should take up shovels, plows, and, when necessary, arms. They would go to Israel as a people, scale the wall, and settle the land. Their collective strength would bring them out of exile.

I have been arguing that making sense of the Zionist enterprise has become the central theological question for almost all Jews today, whether they know it or not and whether they believe in God or not. Those of us who bother to think about Jewish theology have been so accustomed to treating the Holocaust as the dominant theological problem of our era that we have not fully noticed that the idea of Israel has displaced the Holocaust in that particular role. On careful consideration, however, the development should not surprise us. The scale of the Holocaust was unprecedented and its consequences are still unfolding. But the *structure* of the Holocaust as a Jewish tragedy was not unparalleled when seen from the standpoint of traditional Jewish theology. Israel, in contrast, is something structurally new in Jewish history, if you assume that Jewish history begins with the destruction of the Temple in the year 70 CE. In all that time, the Jews never immigrated en masse to the land of Israel, settled it, and created a state, with all the consequences and complexity that entails.

In pursuit of understanding contemporary Jewish theology of Israel, I've considered the Progressive embrace of Israel alongside the Holocaust, and the growing crisis engendered by the conflict between social justice Judaism and the actually existing state of Israel. I've offered an account of how Evolutionism has consciously developed the ancient Jewish idea of the messiah into the worldview of Religious Zionism. I've offered an interpretation of how Traditionalist Jews have adopted an incompletely theorized theology of Israel, increasingly identifying with the state's military might and simultaneously reimagining the Jewish state as a state of (non-Zionist) Jewish law.

What I have not done so far is to speak explicitly of how the idea of Israel might be understood in the light of the Jewish theology of struggle that I outlined at the end of part I. That is the burden of this chapter, coming at the end of part II.

My contribution, such as it is, begins with the simple fact that Israel exists, is real, and is home to half the world's Jews. It is not going away anytime soon. If it did, that would represent a crisis in Jewish life greater than the Jewish expulsion from Spain in 1492 or, arguably, the Holocaust. It therefore is not theologically useful, in my view, to argue about whether Israel should ever have come into existence. Even if the anti-Zionist Satmar Rebbe were correct that Israel's existence violates God's will as expressed in the three-oath theology, the state now exists. Similarly, even if left-wing critics of Israel's existence were correct that the creation of Israel morally harms the Palestinian people in a permanent way, the seven million Jews who today live in Israel consider it their home, much as Americans today live in places that once belonged to the Native peoples the United States displaced, dispossessed, killed, and put on reservations.

Turning one's back on Israel in favor of a Jewish life focused exclusively on the Diaspora is also not theologically viable, much as some might wish it. I remember encountering this idea first in Philip Roth's novel *Operation Shylock: A Confession* (1993). In the book, a character named Moishe Pipik, posing as another character named Philip Roth, advances an ideology that he calls "Diasporism: The Only Solution to the Jewish Problem." Pipik's grand idea is that Israel was a mistake. Jews of European origin, he urges, should leave Israel and go back to Europe.

Although *Operation Shylock* may be understood as satirizing the mad idea of Diasporism, it may also be read as subversively advocating something much like it. In the book, a Palestinian character named George Ziad offers this devastating assessment of the realization of the secular Zionists' ideal:

> This is their great Jewish achievement—to make Jews into jailers and jet-bomber pilots! And just suppose they were to succeed, suppose they were to win and have their way and every Arab in

Nablus and every Arab in Hebron and every Arab in the Galilee and in Gaza, suppose every Arab in the world, were to disappear courtesy of the Jewish nuclear bomb, what would they have here fifty years from now? A noisy little state of no importance whatsoever. That's what the persecution and the destruction of the Palestinians will have been for—the creation of a Jewish Belgium, without even a Brussels to show for it.[2]

Sure enough, because life is stranger than fiction (even Philip Roth's fiction), there has subsequently emerged a Jewish ideology that actually calls itself Diasporism. Its different advocates have in common the idea that the Jewish condition of Diaspora offers a distinct, attractive way of thinking about the ethical relationship between people and places. For its adherents,[3] Diasporism teaches, roughly, that no one should believe that being a majority at home in a certain place confers special rights superior to those of other people who live in the same place, regardless of their geographic origin.[4] No one "belongs" anywhere. The eminent critical theorist Judith Butler offers this account of how to make Diaspora inherent to Jewishness:

I'm trying to understand how the exilic—or more emphatically the diasporic—is built into the idea of the Jewish . . . In this sense, to "be" a Jew is to be departing from oneself, cast out into a world of the non-Jew, bound to make one's way ethically and politically precisely there within a world of irreversible heterogeneity.[5]

The idea that the Jewish experience of Diaspora over two thousand years has something to teach Jews, Israelis, and maybe even the rest of the world is appealing. Surely there is something distinctively Jewish about the experience of being outsiders, strangers in a strange land. And surely there is an important ethical takeaway along the lines of "You shall love the stranger, for you were strangers in the land of Egypt." But how viable is Diasporism when considered as a theory about how Jews should experience, understand, and encounter the existing state of Israel?

At one time, non-Zionist Traditionalists thought it was appropriate to treat the state of Israel the same way they would have treated any other place they lived as Jews. Arguably, that was a form of Diasporism. By treating Israel as just another state, they were treating their own lives lived under the state as no different, metaphysically speaking, from the lives they would be living in Vilna or Brooklyn. If we thought of Israel as just another place where Jews lived, that might Diasporize even the state of Israel by denying that it is the Jews' unique national homeland. Put another way, to Diasporize Israel would be to treat it exactly the same way you would treat a Jewish state established in Uganda, or in Sitka, Alaska, as Michael Chabon imagines in his novel *The Yiddish Policemen's Union* (2007). The trouble with this form of what you might call soft theological Diasporism is that Israel today isn't just another place Jews live, even for non-Zionist Traditionalists. The idea of Israel has become infused with special theological meaning for them, as for all Jews, even those who oppose Israel's existence.

A harder form of theological Diasporism might mandate that the creation of Israel be reversed and all the Jews living there go live somewhere else. But even the architects of the three-oaths theology stopped short of advocating Jewish abandonment of the land of Israel, despite condemning the state as illegitimate. After all, even when it prohibited moving to Israel en masse, Jewish tradition never *valorized* Diaspora. The three-oaths theology, like the rabbinic theology of exile, and like the biblical theology it was based on, *invariably treated exile as a punishment for sin*. The classical Zionists were correct that Jews always lived with some religious hope or fantasy of a return to their imagined Israel. That return, accomplished at scale, necessarily must have some significance for a Jewish theology other than pure repudiation.

Of course, many secular Israelis may eventually leave a state of Israel that is dominated by Religious Zionist messianists and Traditionalists. When Israelis leave Israel, that is arguably a form of Diasporization, a negation of the Zionist expectation that all Jews would move to Israel, not leave their homeland voluntarily. But even if all secular Israelis were to move to Los Angeles, Israel would still exist as a theologically distinctive Jewish state. Maybe especially then, given how many secular

Israelis are now post-Zionists who would like to believe that Israel is not theologically special but simply a state like any other. Without them, the state would likely become more theologically Jewish than ever.

If Diasporism cannot offer a comprehensive theology of Israel, where should we look? My answer refers back to the biblical and rabbinic sources of Jewish theology that predate Zionism and the state of Israel itself. In particular, I want to propose that we take seriously the idea of sin and punishment in relation to the land of Israel. We can do that as literalist believers or as allegorical readers of the tradition. What we cannot and must not do is to make the devastating mistake of imagining a theology of Israel that has no room for the concept of sin.

Consider that from Deuteronomy onward, Israelites and later Jews were told that entering and settling the land of Israel carried with it the ever-present threat of sinning against God by breaking the covenant. The Israelites who entered the land were not, according to the Bible, a chosen people beyond sin. To the contrary, they were a chosen people prone to sinning from the get-go. To paraphrase Genesis, sin was crouching at their door. Their characteristic sin, the one prophesied already by Moses, was the sin of pride: the sin of believing they were perfect, that their strength and the power of their hands had given them homes and prosperity.

The risk of that sin looms larger today than ever in Jewish history, because never before in Jewish history have Jews achieved such strength and prosperity in a land they called their own. Consider the name of the single most extreme ultranationalist party in Israel today: Jewish Power. The word "power," *'otzmah*, in the name of the party is the feminine form of the very same word, *'otzem*, used by Deuteronomy to warn against the prideful sin of ascribing success to "my strength and the *power* of my hand." The name Jewish Power is hence a sacrilege in the most literal sense: a violation of a sacred, divine command. God warned the Israelites not to become high-hearted and declare that their power gave them a land. The Jewish Power party precisely insists that it is *their* power, the power of the Jews, on which they rely and that they celebrate.

The source of this sin of pride can partly be attributed to secular

Zionism, with its rejection of God and the associated idea of sin. The Hebrew word for independence is *'atzma'ut*, a modern Hebrew coinage based on the same three-letter root as the word for power. To achieve independence, on this reading of the word, was to achieve power on one's own, autonomously, without external help, divine or otherwise. Perhaps, then, once Zionism successfully created a Jewish state, it was inevitable that its citizens, dwelling in good houses, would ascribe that status to their own power, not to God.

Yet Jewish Power is also in an important sense a religious party, religious in its derivation from the thought and politics of Rabbi Meir Kahane and religious in its current leadership. That religious quality means its ideology, like its name, cannot be blamed solely or even squarely on secular Zionism. And that same religious quality of the party's ultranationalism makes its name especially inexcusable, even sinful. Jews who read the Bible to prove that God gave them the land of Israel must be held accountable for ignoring the verses of that same Bible that tell them not to boast of their own power.

Let me say a bit more about the Jewish notion of collective sin that derives from collective pride. In its most unrestrained form, the sin of pride is what allows, enables, and encourages us to forget about the interests and needs of other people, in violation of the biblical command to love the stranger, who is the Other. When the sin of pride is allowed to spread, it takes the particular form of insisting that one's own nation—in this case, Israel—is always in the right and that its enemies are always in the wrong.

The great American theologian Reinhold Niebuhr (1892–1971) identified and categorized this sin. Writing about the United States during the Korean War, he observed that "nations, as individuals, who are completely innocent in their own esteem, are insufferable in their human contacts."[6] His point was that, if you as a nation believe you are always free of sin, you will impose your will on others and harm them grievously in the process. Niebuhr was a profound (and profoundly) Christian thinker, whose emphasis on sin pushed against the spirit of his times. His effort to deploy the Christian idea of sin to address American collective action, still relevant to U.S. foreign policy, holds a powerful lesson for Jewish theology today. To use a Jewish formulation from the *Ethics of the Fathers*, sin begets sin. A Jewish people unable to imagine the possibility of its own even occasional sinfulness will go forth and sin more.

It is understandable that Jews, in Israel or outside, would resist the idea that Israel is ever in the wrong. Overcoming global, regional, and local resistance to create the state of Israel required overwhelming single-mindedness. Israel's legitimacy is still not accepted by its enemies, as the Hamas attacks on Israel, supported by the government of Iran among others, so vividly showed. In the realm of states and wars, criticism is a tool of conflict. Supporters of Israel became accustomed to rejecting every criticism of the state, however valid, because doing so felt necessary for survival, and often was. What is more, some criticism of Israel doubtless reflects antisemitism, a further reason to reject it.

From an internal Jewish perspective, however, refusing to see that Israel can *ever* do wrong amounts to the indefensible theological assertion that Jews acting in defense of Israel cannot sin. The messianism of Religious Zionism holds particular dangers in this regard. Believers in the grip of messianic or apocalyptic or revolutionary fervor can find themselves doing things they would condemn as morally unacceptable under normal circumstances. That can include killing the innocent to achieve historic-transcendent objectives. It is not only that one cannot make an omelet without breaking some eggs. It is that to someone who interprets contemporary events as occurring in messianic time, death may actually be sacralized as necessary to the emergent process of divine self-revealing.[7]

What I am saying is that a theology of Israel must take on board the traditional Jewish theological idea that settling the land of Israel opens the door to sin, sin that can and will be punished by God. The Bible and the rabbis are clear on how to relate to that possibility: Jews must scrutinize themselves and their conduct. They must search out and identify their sins. They must repent from them. And they must strive to stop sinning. To ignore the possibility of sin is to ignore sin. To ignore or excuse sin is to court more of it. And in the realm of a just God, the kind depicted by the Bible and the rabbis, to commit sin is to invite divine punishment.

For those who prefer allegory to literalism, or doubt that God punishes sin by direct intervention, here is a Maimonidean-rationalist account of how this kind of sin and its punitive consequences operate. Faced with the challenge of explaining how it is possible to believe in free will and also to accept the biblical statement that God hardened Pharaoh's heart, Maimonides explains that God created human nature such that when men exercise their faculties, they accustom themselves to patterns of learned behavior. Seen in these terms, God hardened Pharaoh's heart in the sense that God gave him the free will to become an open-minded, generous king or alternatively to develop the habit of closed-minded refusal. Pharaoh chose the latter.[8]

Applied to sin more broadly, this naturalist type of allegory teaches that when men become prideful, they train themselves so that they fail to notice what is wrong with their conduct, morally and practically. A person—or a nation—who systematically exercises the human capacity for pride will systematically fail to notice wrongdoing. Allegorically, sin begets sin, and sin opens the door to its own punishment. The punishment comes, naturally, from the massive dangers of failing to address one's own wrongdoing. Collective sin means collective ignorance of consequences. It erodes morals and it erodes the capacity to think morally. It erodes the rational evaluation of the effect of one's actions, and it erodes the capacity to think consequentially.

You will notice that I am not trying here to specify exactly what sins may be committed by a state that forgets it can ever be in the wrong. Even so powerful a thinker as Niebuhr trod lightly on that kind of specificity. What I am noticing is that in many of the contemporary Jewish theological responses to Israel I have described, the classically Jewish move of self-questioning in search of sin has taken a back seat to self-confident assertions of correctness. I am urging Jews to be more Jewish in their thinking about Israel: to explore the dynamic of sin, of pride, and of punishment, no matter where it originates and with whom. To repeat, there is nothing un-Jewish about looking for collective sin and trying to do better. What is un-Jewish, in theological terms, is to imagine we as Jews are beyond sin.

This brings me back to the theology of struggle, sketched earlier in the book. In that picture, the Jewish way of experiencing the world entails struggling with God: with who God is, with what God wants, with whether God exists. Self-evaluation in search of sin and repair is a manifestation of exactly this Jewish struggle. As embodied in the self-examination and repentance of Yom Kippur, it is a struggle with our own intuitions about what is right, and where we have fallen short. As a struggle, it may be directed inward, toward the conscience. But it also must be directed outward, toward our collective reckoning with our collective actions. A Jeremiah who spoke only to his own soul and did not preach the sins of Jerusalem to the people of Jerusalem would be no prophet.

In offering this theology of struggle with sin, I am *not* claiming that there is a single right answer to how to think about Israel in theological terms. The whole thrust of my struggle theology is to validate a range of divergent Jewish beliefs about how the world should be in relation to the divine, real or imagined. I am, rather, harking back to a central Jewish teaching about what can happen to Jews in the land of Israel. In its essence, that teaching was not especially messianic. When the Israelites entered the land the first time, it was in fulfillment of a divine promise. That promise, however, contained within it the seeds of their exile. When some Israelites returned to the land with Ezra and Nehemiah to rebuild the second Temple, they again came with the confidence that their arrival was blessed by God. They were correct, according to the Bible. Yet their descendants, too, ended up exiled into Diaspora. According to the rabbis, this exile was also a consequence of their sins, or rather "our sins," to use the inclusive, collective language favored by Jewish prayer.

It follows, I think, that from the standpoint of Jewish theology, the current return to Zion must not, cannot be understood as permanent or irreversible or outside of time, much less outside the framework of adherence to the covenant. If the Jewish people sin, they (we!) will be punished again with exile, whether the terms sin, punishment, and exile are taken literally or figuratively.

This knowledge, this consciousness of the possibility of sin, is ineluctably Jewish. Christ liberated his followers from the Law and promised them forgiveness from sin. The Jews did not partake of that theological turn. For them there is, instead, the struggle to determine what is right and eschew what is wrong. That struggle has consequences. The consequences are what make the stakes of Jewishness so high.

For Progressive Jews, the struggle now and in the foreseeable future is to see if divinely inspired social justice can be reconciled with the real Israel—and, if not, to see what other aspects of Jewish belief and practice might convince the next generation of Progressives not to give up on Jewishness altogether. For Evolutionists, the struggle is to engage and live out Religious Zionist messianism in a world where there is no certainty that the messiah has arrived, much less what the correct course of action is to consolidate the possibility of redemption. For Traditionalists, the struggle is to see how official non-Zionism can coexist with a state they increasingly consider their own and increasingly wish to govern according to their brand of Jewish law.

Finally, for all Jews, Godless or believing, who are skeptical that the nation-state is the highest expression of Jewishness, the struggle of the present is to ascertain what other collective forms of being might provide meaning and richness to make Jewish life worthwhile. Part III of the book will take on that challenge, asking how it might feel to experience the Jews not only as a people, but as a family.

PART III

OF THE JEWISH PEOPLE

III:1

WHAT ARE THE JEWS?

In the five books of Moses—Genesis, Exodus, Leviticus, Numbers, Deuteronomy—there are no "Jews." The first part of the Hebrew Bible refers only to the Children of Israel, divided into twelve tribes, more or less. In the Prophets, we hear about the kingdom of Judah, with its capital in Jerusalem, in contrast to the kingdom of Israel.[1] It is not until the Babylonian exile and the disappearance of the so-called lost tribes that the word *yehudim*, derived from the Hebrew name for members of the tribe of Judah, starts to refer to a larger collective. The book of Nehemiah refers to the people who return from exile to the land of Israel as *yehudim*. The book of Esther, generally considered one of the latest contributions to the Hebrew Bible, consistently refers to the community designated for annihilation by Haman and saved by Esther's intervention as *yehudim*. They are described there as a "people," an entity that, the book specifies, has its own writing and language.*

In the Second Temple period, related words were used in both Greek and Aramaic (*Iudaeon* and *yehudai*).[2] The rabbis, though, preferred the

---

* See Esther 9:9. The book of Esther famously says that King Ahasuerus ruled 127 provinces. Commands of the king go out "to every province in its writing and to every people in its language." The Jews are never said to have their own province, but they are said to have their own writing and language.

term "Israel" to the term *yehudi*, which occurs infrequently in the Mishnah and Talmud. For that matter, medieval rabbis preferred the word "Israel" as a formal designator of who belongs to the community. To this day, Traditionalists writing in rabbinic, legal Hebrew use that term rather than the word "Jews," which American Traditionalists typically use only in English or in the familiar, affectionate Yiddish form, *Yidn*.

Meanwhile, in modern Israel, *yehudi* means "Jew" in everyday speech and is also a legal term of art. Israel's Law of Return grants every *yehudi* the right to immigrate to Israel and become a citizen. It then defines the term as "a person who was born of a Jewish mother, or has converted to Judaism and is not a member of another religion." This legal rule in turn requires further elaboration of what counts as a Jewish mother and what counts as a "conversion" to "Judaism" (not to mention what counts as membership in another religion). To make matters more complicated still, until 2005, the word *yehudi* was used on the Israeli identity card to designate Jewish nationality (*le'om*, which can also be translated as "ethnicity"), in contrast to "Arab" or "Druze" or "Circassian." The category was dropped not to be more inclusive but because Traditionalist cabinet members did not want the word *yehudi* to designate people who were not Jewish under Traditionalist interpretations of Jewish law. (Many of these were immigrants from the former Soviet Union who had been brought to Israel as ethnic Jews but did not count as Jews to the Traditionalists because their mothers were not Jewish.)

It emerges that the word "Jew," often a non-Jewish designation for Jewish people, has been adopted by Jews over time and put to their own purposes. Even the notion that there is a religion of "Judaism" was, it turns out, introduced by Christians in the fourth century in order to create a category in contrast to Christianity.[3] In rabbinic Hebrew, whether in the Middle Ages or today, one never speaks of "Judaism" as an abstraction. One speaks of the Torah, the Law. *Yahadut* is a modern Israeli Hebrew coinage originally intended to translate the English word "Judaism" or its German synonym, *Judaismus*.

So what, then, are the Jews? Who is a Jew? And why does it matter? The answers to these questions are bound up in a complex web of beliefs, ideals, values, and institutions. There can be no single, objective solution, because to use the term "Jew" is to take a stand on what the word ought to mean, not only on what it does mean as a matter of description. "Jew" is what philosophers call an essentially contested concept: a concept whose meaning cannot be ascertained by empirical observation alone because the people who use it are taking a values-based stand on what it means to them.

In this part of the book, I want to explore the vexed question of Jewish peoplehood, recognizing up front that your answer to the question of what the Jewish people *is* will depend to a great degree on what you think the Jewish people *should* be, and for what purpose. God will enter the picture, as will the state of Israel, so the themes of parts I and II of the book will remain highly relevant. Yet I want to go further than we have gone so far, asking not only about the meanings of Jewishness deployed by Jews themselves but by admirers and detractors of the Jews who do not themselves identify as Jewish. I also will consider what contributions Jews as a group are now making or might make to world culture and civilization and what if anything makes those distinctive and valuable.

Ultimately, I hope to uncover some possible answers to forward-looking questions: Would anything be so terrible about a world where there were fewer Jews, or none, provided of course that happened by choice, rather than by coercion or murder? Would it be any sadder than the disappearances of other peoples or ethnicities or languages, which detract from the great diversity of human identity and experience but simultaneously make way for the new forms of identity we are always inventing? In short, I am asking the general question of what are the Jews mostly to provide answers to a highly specific, personal question: Why be a Jew?

PEOPLE AS FAMILY

How, then, should we think about, name, or describe the Jewish collective? The Hebrew Bible does not help much. Not only does it say little about the Jews, as opposed to the Israelites; it also uses the terms *'am*, usually translated "people," and *goy*, usually translated "nation," almost interchangeably.[4] Indeed, in ordinary English, a people and a nation are more or less the same thing. The word "nation," however, may conjure up for some readers the theory of nationalism, according to which nations have special qualities that entitle them to a nation-state of their own.

Consequently, the most neutral way to describe the Jews, the one I have opted for in the subtitle of the book, is as a people. The limitation of the word "people," unfortunately, is that it isn't very specific. Consider that a "people" is often defined broadly as something like "a community of people of shared nationality or race." Defining Jewish peoplehood in terms of nationhood is either banal, if the words mean the same, or else misleading, since it omits a whole necessary argument about the distinctive aspects of nationhood.

As for defining the Jewish people as a race, one difficulty is that Jews have not thought of themselves as a distinct race since World War II.* Another is that Jews belong to multiple ethnicities and races, however you define those contested terms. It is not clear that Ashkenazi Jews of European origin and Mizrahi Jews whose origins lie in Islamic countries belong to the same ethnic group, whether measured by genetics or culture (especially before the two converged in modern Israel). Even apart from this question, the racial and ethnic diversity of Jews in Israel is rapidly increasing as a result of immigration and conversion. The same is true in the United States as a result of marriage, procreation, and adoption. When you add in other groups of people all over the world, especially in Africa, who identify as Jews or Israelites, the diversity of the Jewish people becomes greater still.[5]

To define Jewish peoplehood with more specificity, without using nationality or race, I want to identify the quality of Jewish peoplehood that expresses itself in fellow feeling, mutual concern, and mutual responsibility. A Talmudic aphorism captures these emotional-ethical-affective ties: "All Israelites are mutual guarantors of one another" (*kol yisra'el 'arevim zeh ba-zeh*).[6]

This kind of peoplehood I want to describe will not be exclusively religious or theological. In practice, as we will see, almost no Jews, even

* This is a product both of semiconscious Jewish efforts in the United States to be understood as part of the white race and also of the worry that defining Jews as a race would lead to their being considered an inferior one.

Traditionalists, rely entirely on the formal Jewish legal-religious definition of who is a Jew when they experience sentiments of fellow feeling. The peoplehood will also not be exclusively cultural, because plenty of Jews share almost no overlapping culture with each other.

The Jewish peoplehood that I seek to describe most closely resembles a large, extended *family*. It can include aspects of religion, ethnicity, kinship, and culture, but it goes beyond all of these. It is based on the meaning of the word "family" that is most true to life and inclusive.

The kind of family I have in mind is not fixed or defined by blood ties alone, or even necessarily at all. It is defined by a whole range of different human connections people recognize as creating family. Members of this kind of family can be related by unchosen birth or by chosen relations like marriage, divorce, adoption, fostering, living together, mutual commitment, and connection. Families can bring themselves into existence by love, emotional support, holiday and other gatherings, and by much, much more. They may live together or thousands of miles apart. They may not all know each other, or even know of each other's existence.

If this definition at first sounds too broad, ask yourself: How would you define your own family? Think of all the people you consider family. It's not just biological parents and grandparents and siblings and cousins and in-laws. It may include none of those people, or all of them. It may include those people and their partners, as well as their exes. It can include stepsiblings and half-siblings and adopted siblings, step-parents and adoptive and foster parents, and all *their* family, however they define the term. In the United States, we don't even have simple names for some of these relations. What do I call my ex-wife's husband's kids? What about his mother, who, by the way, acts like a loving bonus grandmother to my kids?

Beyond these kinship ties, chosen and unchosen and semi-chosen, there are many more kinds of family ties. Consider the queer and trans families organized into "houses" in *Paris Is Burning* (1990), the classic documentary of the New York City ball scene. These are families in the deepest sense of the word. They are chosen and also, in a sense, feel like they were destined or fated. Indeed, intentional families are ubiquitous around the world, not restricted to people who experience exclusion from families of origin. Extended clan networks are often intentional in this way. So are religious orders of monks and nuns (whose members, not by coincidence, often call one another Brother, Sister, Father, Mother, and so forth). So are communes. Anthropologists used to refer to relations like these as "fictive" kinship ties, in contrast to supposedly "real" blood ties. That distinction, thankfully, no longer obtains. *All* family relations are both real and also products of our faculty for symbol making.

The Jewish people is like an extended family in this sense. You can be born into it. You can be adopted into it. You can join it in a variety of ways. You can have a close or an ambivalent relationship with it. You can also decide to leave it. It might still be your family of origin, and it might still claim you. But you can, if you choose, disclaim it.

This family conception is a definition of the Jewish people that meets our needs, spiritual and intellectual and practical. It can accommodate fellow feeling as well as division. It acknowledges that it is appropriate for Jews to experience special pain at the death and suffering of fellow Jews, as at the time of the Hamas attacks on Israel, and special pleasure when Jews do something good. It recognizes the familial nature of Jewishness while remembering that families are not defined by genetics alone but by connections that exist in our minds rather than only in our bodies.

At the same time, because of its size, the Jewish people is also more than a family. The scale of a family is different from the scale of a clan or a tribe or a people. If you are a Jew who meets another Jew you did not know previously, you can't be expected to think of that person as family right off the bat, because the degree of intimacy associated with the word "family" has not yet been earned. You may have a lot in common with the person or essentially nothing. You might share biological connections or not. You might share cultural commitments or not. You might share religious beliefs or not. At bottom, all you have in common is that you both think of yourselves as Jews, possibly not even according to the same definition.

Definitions and boundaries of Jewish peoplehood are tricky and sometimes contentious, as I will explore in a moment. For now, let me ask you to complete this thought experiment by asking whether you can name the outer edge of what still counts as your own family. Notice there is no fixed, agreed-on definition of the boundary. It isn't a quantum of genes. Go back far enough, and we're all related genetically. It also isn't only people we know or can name.[7]

Notably, too, family members themselves may not all agree on who is in the family and who is not. If you think closely about it, essentially all our families are like this. Could you list every member of your family? And would that list exactly match everyone else's list? Almost certainly not. The boundaries of families are porous.

Jewish peoplehood is a lot like this inclusive, complex, contested conception of the family. The peoplehood of family cannot be defined without asking how individuals perceive and define themselves. But neither can peoplehood-as-family be defined entirely by self-perception. Considering oneself to be a Jew, a member of the family, is not automatically going to make one a member of the Jewish people in the eyes of all others. Is a bar-mitzvahed, temple-attending Reform Jew, whose father is Jewish and whose mother is not, a Jew? It depends on whom you ask. A messianic Jew, born of two Jewish parents, who accepts Yeshua as his Lord and Savior? Depends again. A member of the Lemba, a Bantu-speaking people in southern Africa who identify as Jews and have some apparent genetic links to ancient Israelites?[8] The House of Israel, a Ghanaian, Akan-speaking group of Sefwis, who don't have a documented genetic relation to other Jews?[9] More disagreement.

Over even relatively short periods of time, the boundaries of the Jewish family-people can change, even in the minds of the most unwavering Traditionalists. Consider the Beta Israel, the official name of the community of Ethiopian Jews, once known pejoratively as Falasha. Today, almost all of them live in Israel after being airlifted there from the late 1970s through the 1990s.

When European Jews encountered the Beta Israel in the early twentieth century, many were skeptical of considering the Ethiopians to be Jewish in any sense. Over the next hundred years, academic scholars, from anthropologists to historians to geneticists, have mostly denied any ancient connection between the Beta Israel and other Jewish communities. They concluded, after research, that the Beta Israel's self-identification as Jews derived from their Christian Ethiopian ancestors, who in the late

Middle Ages embraced the Israelites of the Bible as their model and took on observance of biblical law. (This is a recurring phenomenon in Christianity known to historians of religion as the Judaizing heresy.) Many, perhaps most, important Traditionalist rabbis agreed, noting that the Beta Israel had no knowledge of Hebrew or of rabbinic law.

Yet eventually, the Beta Israel came to be considered Jews by essentially the entire Jewish world. In 1973, Rav Ovadiah Yosef (1920–2013), a hugely influential religious and political figure who was then Sephardi chief rabbi of Israel, ruled that the Beta Israel were Jews who must be rescued and returned to Zion. A rabbinic compromise, hard-won but ultimately effective, called for a modified conversion upon their arrival to Israel. The Knesset enacted special legislation declaring the Beta Israel to be Jews for purposes of the Law of Return. As a result of this embrace, Jews became a multiracial family to a greater degree than they had previously been since the invention of racial classifications.

The point is not to depict the boundaries of Jewish peoplehood as easily or costlessly malleable. Ethiopian Jews continue to experience discrimination in Israel. Some Jews, even today, still quietly question their Jewishness. Beta Israel's unique religious practices have been, to a meaningful degree, marginalized or even destroyed, a cost of "embracing" rabbinic Judaism.

Nevertheless, the point of this example—and the other, more contested ones—is to show that an adequate definition of the Jewish people as family cannot be exhaustive or permanent. Even after we have a workable definition of the Jewish people, there will be debates about who is in and who is out, just as there can be in families. Those debates will in turn be recognizable as part of the structure of Jewish peoplehood, the way they have always been, and the way all groups of humans contest and police the boundaries of their identities.

MY (CRAZY) JEWISH FAMILY

To think of the Jewish people as an oversized family is to invite a series of warm associations with Jewishness. Families love and nurture each other, or are supposed to. Families care what happens to other family members. Above all, families contribute to the way we make sense of our condition as humans. They give us our first models for attachment, compassion, and connection.

But as everyone with any kind of a family knows, all these wonderful aspects of family come with some, shall we say, complexity. For each uplifting feature of family life there can be a corresponding destructive one. Families give us models for favoritism, punishment, unfairness, and even abuse.

As it happens, the book of Genesis is very interested in these pairings of familial good and familial bad. Sarah wants Abraham to have a child and encourages him to father one with her handmaid, Hagar. Then, after Sarah has a child of her own, she encourages Abraham to banish Hagar and her son, Ishmael. Abraham, torn, nevertheless follows her guidance, creating a historic rift between the descendants of Ishmael and of Sarah's son, Isaac. The loving desire to perpetuate the family becomes the cause of its rupture.

Isaac in turn favors Esau, the older of his twins, over Jacob, the younger. His wife Rebecca favors Jacob. The competition between the brothers, fueled by the parents, leads to Jacob's "purchase" of the birthright and his subsequent theft of the blessing Isaac intended for Esau. Jacob has to flee Esau's wrath, and the family is divided permanently. Parental love leads to sibling rivalry and alienation.

In Jacob's own family, things get worse still. Jacob intends to marry Rachel and ends up tricked into marrying her older sister Leah first. He favors Rachel's son Joseph, in recompense for which his other sons sell Joseph into slavery. When famine forces the brothers to Egypt for sustenance, Joseph, unrecognized by his half-brothers, gets his revenge on them and on his father by demanding that his younger full brother, Benjamin, Jacob's beloved last child, be sent to him in Egypt. In this instance, parental love creates near-murderous rage and intergenerational trauma.

These engrossing, dynamically rich tales of the patriarchs and matriarchs are archetypes. They are archetypes of families. They are archetypes meant to explain the origins of the peoplehood of the Israelites, later the Jews. Hence, the stories are *themselves* archetypes of the Jews as family.

In other words, I didn't invent the idea that the Jewish people is like a family. The Bible did.

Acknowledging the pain of the families depicted in the Bible, any account of the Jewish people as a family must similarly acknowledge the multitude of ways a family can inflict pain. Disagreements among Jews can be particularly sharp and devastating because they are, or are felt to be, disputes within family. Those disputes can take on the shapes of sibling rivalry, of resentment of one's parents, or of frustration with one's children. There can be, and often is, a sense that a public dispute among Jews amounts to airing the family's dirty laundry.

To understand further the degree of emotion associated with Jewish conflict, consider that families are where we form our first intense emotional bonds. Family dynamics can often become our most powerful models for other relationships in our lives, whether those are erotic, professional, or based in friendship. Those models can manifest with a vengeance in the course of Jewish conflict. Jewish authority figures may find themselves being treated as instantiations of the father, who might invite respect but also rebellion and rejection. Or the archetype of the Jewish mother may be brought into play, with all the many positive and negative associations she calls up.

This conflictual association between Jewishness and family can operate on several different dimensions simultaneously, all of which cross-cut each other. Consider the modern literary exemplar of Jewish familial conflict: a Philip Roth novel. (It could be almost any Philip Roth novel, but let's call it *Portnoy's Complaint*.) The characters are mainly Jews. They make up a Jewish family. They undergo conflict in the novel. A public readership, much of it made up of Jews, criticizes the author for writing unflatteringly about Jews, thereby adding a second layer of conflict. (Never mind that the Bible's stories of the patriarchs and matriarchs are already public depictions of dysfunctional, conflicting Jewish families.)

In a third layer of conflict, the critics and the author find themselves occupying displaced familial positions, partly because they are Jewish, partly because they are all children born of parents. In yet a fourth layer, the Jews in question begin to argue vociferously about whether the novel has anything to say about the Jews as a people: Does the fictional familial story stand for specifically Jewish types? And of course the novel itself is openly about psychoanalysis and family dynamics and Jewish families and the Jews and Jewish criticism of Jewish families and . . . you get the picture.

Are the Jewish people as a family any more dysfunctional than any other group of people who might be compared to a family? The question is closely related to whether individual Jewish families are crazier than any other kinds of families. In both cases, I think the objective answer is no. All humans can be crazy in culturally specific ways, and Jews are no exception.* Yet it would be hard to find a Jew, myself included, who doesn't secretly sometimes feel that Jewish families are crazier than other families and that the Jews as a people are the craziest family of all.

Why do we feel that way, knowing as we do that there is in fact no fundamental difference between families when it comes to certain kinds of crazy, except maybe how that crazy is expressed? It's because when it comes to family, it's so hard to get outside of your own subject position and look at things from an external point of view. When you're talking to your father or your mother, it's hard not to think of yourself as a son or a daughter. It's challenging to talk to your siblings without thinking of yourself as a sibling. It's almost impossible to talk to your children without thinking of yourself as a parent.

If the Jews are a family, it's going to be hard to speak to them or about them without falling into some familial role or other. Consider the Passover seder, the classic Jewish family get-together and site of loving, contentious struggle. The seder is all about family. Mere attendance puts you into a familial role, since the stated purpose of the ritual is to tell the story of the Exodus to one's children, as the Bible instructs. The

---

* Take the Jewish mother. (No, take her, please.) The negative midcentury stereotype of the Jewish mother seems to be fading, along with the specific cultural circumstances that produced it. It's worth noting that in Europe and the United States in the late nineteenth and early twentieth centuries, the figure of the *yiddishe mama* was typically depicted as loving, caring, and compassionate, not as overbearing or anxious or demanding or smothering. Even Freud had nothing bad to say about Jewish mothers in particular. The point is that the midcentury Jewish mother stereotype had specifically midcentury Jewish cultural characteristics, but those have changed over time, and their perception has changed too.

Haggadah, the Passover script that literally means the "telling" of the story, includes the famous parable about the four sons: one wise, one evil, one quiet, and one who does not know how to ask. It's included in every Haggadah you will ever see, no matter how updated or shortened or deconstructed. I defy anyone, of any faith background or none, to attend a seder and not wonder which son you are, deep down inside. Once you are taking part in the ritual, you will relate to the Jews—in particular to those present—as a family.

The upshot is that when I propose that you think of the Jewish people as a family of Jews, I am asking you to embrace both the love and the crazy, the joyful support and the enraged dysfunction. Part of what makes the Jews the Jews is that there is something familial about Jewish peoplehood. That is, part of what makes the Jews a people is that they relate to each other as family. That can be good and it can be bad. As Rabbi Jay Michaelson, the champion of nondual Judaism, would surely put it: both are true.

WHY NOT A NATION?

So the Jews are a people-family, or so I have been arguing. Why not say, instead or in addition, that the Jews are a nation? And while we're at it, wouldn't it be better for the Jews if they *were* a nation? According to classical Zionism, after all, it wasn't enough just to be a people. The Jews absolutely were and needed to be acknowledged as a nation, an entity deserving and destined for statehood. But today, Jews as a whole are not a nation. To tell the story of how that came to be, we have to go back in time, all the way back to the biblical account of the Israelites' early constitutional history, found in the book of Samuel.

In the Bible story, Samuel, the prophet-judge-leader who gives the book its name, is aging. The children of Israel are concerned that there is no good succession plan in place for when he dies. They approach Samuel and point out that he is getting old and that his sons are not judging the people justly as he long did. Then they demand that he appoint a king over them, "to judge us, like all the nations."[10]

Until this point in the biblical narrative, the Israelites never had a king. Since the death of Joshua, Moses's successor, the Israelites were governed (loosely governed, to be exact) by a series of prophets and judges identified in the book of, you guessed it, Judges. The effects of that weak and intermittent form of government were mixed, according to the biblical narrator, who often comments that "in those days there was no king in Israel, each man did what was right in his own eyes." But between Moses and Samuel, according to the Bible, God never commanded the Israelites to choose a king, nor did he anoint one for them.

Samuel strongly objects to the people's request. In good prophetic fashion, he goes and consults God. God ruefully tells him that by demanding a monarch, the children of Israel "have not rejected you, rather they have rejected me from reigning over them."[11] Samuel then warns the people that the king will take their sons as soldiers and their daughters as perfumers, cooks, and bakers; the king will also seize their fields, vineyards, and olive trees for his courtiers. One day, he promises them, they will cry out to God, who will ignore their cries against the king they demanded. The people refuse to heed Samuel's dire warning. They insist again on a king, "that we also may be like all the nations."[12]

I want to emphasize how this passage captures, in literary form, the idea that the Israelites want to be a nation *like any other*. Those words, and the idea they stood for, affected secular Jewish national thought from the nineteenth century onward.[13] The Bible's ambivalence about that aspiration also resonates: God relents and instructs Samuel to appoint a king. In the biblical narrative, this represents the moment when the Israelites cease to be ruled by God and become subjects of a standard ancient Near Eastern monarchic constitution, yet never quite manage to be a nation like all the others.

As I explained earlier, Zionism was an answer to the so-called Jewish question of what should happen to the Jews once they were formally emancipated and had the capacity to become citizens of European nation-states. Marxists mostly thought that the Jews, conceived as a social class, should cease to have a separate existence, like the bourgeoisie of whom they were an emblem. Liberals mostly thought the Jews should self-define as members of a religion, rather than as a people or even ethnicity, retaining (if they chose) a Progressive version of their faith while becoming full and equal citizens. Some Jewish socialists opted for secular Jewish cultural identity in alliance with other oppressed peoples.

All these responses to the Jewish question somehow wanted Jews to become like other peoples—even the Marxist response, which thought that all distinct nations should eventually cease to exist, not only the Jews. What made Zionism distinctive was that even as it identified the Jews as a nation, it described them as a nation missing the most significant constituent element of nationhood, namely a homeland. Its program therefore called for the Jews to become a nation like any other by acquiring and settling a homeland.

By so doing, Zionism argued, the Jews would lose the distinctive, shameful features of their exilic, diasporic experience. They would lose their idiosyncratic bourgeois economic status by becoming farmers. They would lose the religion that had differentiated them in a way that had all but assured their subordination to Christians and their sense of their own uniqueness. In psychoanalytic terms, they would lose the neurosis derived from the traumatic experience of never fitting into the framework of European nations. Yiddish, the language of that traumatic experience, would be replaced by Hebrew, a language the Zionists imagined as untouched by the weakness of the Diaspora. Zionists even called for the remaking of the Jewish body, which (in terms uncomfortably reminiscent of antisemitism) they sometimes imagined as weak and diseased. The so-called new Jew, like the communist "new man," would be strong, healthy, secure, and self-confident. Above all, he (the pronoun is not an accident) would defend himself by force of arms, not by stratagems or by seeking favor with a royal court.

In all these respects, Zionism imagined that the state of Israel that would eventually emerge would be like any other nation-state. Tel Aviv, built from the ground up as a Jewish city, would be a normal, modern European city of its time, as its Bauhaus architecture was intended to suggest. David Ben-Gurion, Israel's first prime minister, is supposed to have remarked that Israel would be a state like any other when it had its own Jewish prostitutes and thieves conducting their business in Hebrew.[14] Whether the line is apocryphal or not, it perfectly captures the ideology of normalcy to which Zionism from the start aspired.

Seen from this perspective, Zionism functioned as a *deflationary* answer to the question, Who are the Jewish people? Needless to say, the classical Zionists didn't see it that way. In a Europe where Jews were conceived as *less* than a genuine nation, to be a nation like all the others was a promotion in status. In that environment, to be special in any way was to be marginalized and oppressed. In a strand of Christian theology that was dominant at the time (some Christians believe it still), the Jews were chosen by God to survive and to suffer in recognition of the sin of rejecting and murdering Christ. That kind of chosenness was no gift. Accordingly, Zionism wanted Jews *not* to be chosen, but to be normal, exactly like any other group of people who counted as a nation.

What made this conception deflationary was that if the Jews were a nation like all others, they had no special claim to being distinctive or different or more deserving than any other people. As a form of secularism, Zionism had to deny that what made the Jews special was any unique relationship with God. The Bible told the children of Israel that they had not been chosen because they were more numerous than the other nations of the earth or more righteous, but simply because God loved their forefathers.[15] Zionism rejected, in principle, any special love between the nonexistent God and his people. If the classics of Jewish tradition depicted the Jews as chosen, then so did the classical literature of many other national groups emphasize their unique place in history. The Italian nationalists had ancient Rome. French nationalists had "our ancestors, the Gauls." German nationalists had the free tribes of Germania described by the Roman historian Tacitus. The Jews had ancient Israel, no better and no worse, but their own.

Nationalism derived from Romanticism, a complex of ideas that maintained, among many other things, that each individual nation, like each individual human, possessed a specific, individual genius. Seen from that perspective, the deflation of the Jews from being chosen by God did not deny them the possibility of being unique. The Jews could be unique in their own way, like the Italians, French, or Germans, all of whom had their own specific national "genius" according to Romantic nationalism. Nevertheless, for classical Zionists, it was highly desirable that the Jews *not* be different from other nations in the fundamental sense of being uniquely downtrodden. One might go so far as to say that classical Zionists needed to be secularists, indeed atheists, because they believed that the Jews' religious claim to be uniquely chosen by God was the source of their troubles: it led to the Jews being despised by others and simultaneously fed the Jews' defeatism. If God did not exist, then the Jews could not be chosen, for good or ill.

The effect of the Zionist idea that the Jews should be a nation "like all other nations" can be seen today in the frequent complaint of Israelis and Jewish supporters of Israel that the state of Israel is held to a double or higher standard of morality when compared to other nation-states, especially those of the Middle East. Although it might sound otherwise on the surface, this complaint is not merely an attempt to deflect criticism of Israel's liberalism or democracy. It also reflects the frustrated confusion that comes with recognizing that in fact Israel is *not* a nation like other nations, or at least is not treated as such by most of its critics and not a few of its supporters. The reason that Israel is on the minds of so many people around the world who have no concrete national-interest reason to care about it has everything to do with Israel's uniqueness, with the ways it is precisely not treated as a nation like all other nations. Put bluntly, the Zionists' aspiration for the Jews to be a nation like other nations failed, if measured by the way the rest of the world thinks about Israel.

THE HOLOCAUST AND THE FAILURE
OF NORMALCY

Against the odds, Zionism succeeded in creating a Jewish nation-state. How, then, did today's Jews turn out not to be a nation? Put slightly differently, how did the Jews as a whole manage not to become a normal nation, despite the normalizing aims of Jewish nationalism? Our story continues with the context in which the United Nations ultimately proposed the establishment of a state of Israel alongside a state of Palestine in 1947: the aftermath of the Holocaust. In that specific postwar situation, the destruction of European Jewry by Nazi Germany became one of the arguments to justify the creation of a Jewish state. Hitler had attempted to "solve" the Jewish question by murder. That reality, even if incompletely digested by the United Nations in 1947, was clear enough to lead to the conclusion that *something* must be done for the Jews at the national level.

The effect of the invocation of the Holocaust as a justification for creating the state of Israel was to change the older Zionist argument for a Jewish state into something new and different. No longer was it a regular argument for national self-determination. The Jews had been uniquely selected for genocide, went the new argument. It followed that they should be uniquely compensated with a nation-state of their own, notwithstanding their relatively recent return to their historic land and the presence in it of another people, the Palestinians. However strong (or weak) the case for a state of Israel might have been before World War II, the Holocaust made it overwhelming.

Through the ideology and reality of the Holocaust, the justification for Israel's existence got bound up in the history of Jewish uniqueness. After all, Nazi antisemitism drew upon historic Christian antisemitism alongside its various other sources, such as scientific racism, antisemitic anticommunism, antisemitic anticapitalism, and so forth. One need not believe that the Holocaust was the direct continuation of some immutable historical Christian antisemitism to see that the legacy of Christian antisemitism was one source of the Nazi vision. And, crucially, Christian antisemitism was inextricably intermingled with the idea that the Jews were chosen by God, only to be displaced by God and uniquely punished by God and miraculously preserved by God for their sins in murdering and rejecting Christ.

The invention of the idea of genocide by the international lawyer Raphael Lemkin during the war, and its subsequent incorporation into an international treaty, tended to underscore the idea of the Holocaust as a unique crime that had been perpetrated against the Jews. True, Lemkin himself was quick to cite the Armenian genocide as a precursor, and he did not insist that only the Jews had suffered genocide.[16] Yet the very invention of a new kind of crime, with the Holocaust as its legal-conceptual model, emphasized the distinctiveness of the Holocaust. The temporal juxtaposition of the Convention on the Prevention and Punishment of the Crime of Genocide (adopted December 9, 1948) with the establishment of Israel (May 5, 1948) made the association clearer still. By implication, the Jews had suffered a unique crime against humanity and were entitled to unique compensation *from* humanity, represented by the United Nations.

What I am saying is that from the moment that the establishment of the state of Israel came to be associated with the Holocaust, it became essentially impossible for the nations of the world that had acquiesced in Israel's creation to consider it a nation-state like any other. Israel certainly became a nation-state. But it did not become an ordinary nation-state, the kind that would be universally recognized as the national homeland of all the members of the corresponding nation. It became a specific, arguably unique type of morally compensatory nation-state, its origin bound up in the debt that Europe felt it owed the Jews after the Holocaust.

It is worth noting that the Holocaust, coupled with the emergence of Israel as something other than a normal nation-state for all Jews, created further consequences for how Israel is perceived worldwide. If Israel was created (or rather, allowed by the UN to be established) as a response to the immorality of the Holocaust, then Israel had to become, by necessity, an emblem of global morality. This implied, rightly or wrongly, that Israel would be held to a moral standard that would necessarily be distinctive.[17] If Israel was created to be a light unto the nations, then when it failed to live up to that ideal, its failure would inevitably be more conspicuous than the failures of other states.

Israel's emergence in the immediate post-Holocaust context also helps explain why western Europeans continue to hold Israel to the political and moral standards of a western European nation, notwithstanding that those standards developed only in the post–World War II era and that Israel is in the Middle East. The same western Europeans do not hold Arab or Muslim states to western European moral-political standards, either because of implicit racism against them or because of a more defensible political relativism. When Israelis complain that western Europeans expect them to behave just as liberally and democratically as Sweden, they are correct. For western Europeans, the analogue to Israel is precisely western European democracy because, in their view,

Israel was established as a democracy for western European Jews as a solution to the European problem of antisemitism.

A further, related consequence of the western European view of Israel is that as the European left came to condemn European colonialism and imperialism in the 1960s and 1970s, Israel's quasi-colonial creation (as viewed from Europe) itself became a basis for condemnation. From the standpoint of the European left, colonialism now represented a shameful stage in their own national histories that had been left behind. (Never mind that this leaving-behind occurred only as a result of the weakening of the European powers through two world wars and the rise of colonial independence movements.) But unlike the colonies once held outside Europe by even relatively minor western European powers, Israel could not be fully decolonized once the European Jewish population had come to treat it as its homeland, because those Jews had no other country. From this postwar, European left perspective, Israel became an anomaly almost as soon as it was created. It could then be subject to anticolonial criticism that was, in a sense, displaced from anticolonial criticism of their own western European governments that had become passé once the colonies had been shed.

The upshot is that because of the circumstances of its creation, Israel did not become a normal nation-state like any other nation-state. That is, Israel did not achieve global legitimacy as the (normal) nation-state of the (normal) Jewish nation. Instead it became a special case, an instantiation of morally inflected recompense to a people terribly wronged by the Holocaust.

Israel did, however, become a nation-state. But it did not become the nation-state of the Jews as a whole. To the contrary: as we shall now see, Israel's national development shows that whatever may have been true seventy-five years ago, the Jews cannot today be defined as a nation.

THE NATION OF ISRAEL

The crucial fact for understanding Israel's development as a nation-state is that not all the world's Jews emigrated to Israel. To be sure, a significant number did. By choice or coercion, a great many European Jewish refugees who had survived the Holocaust made their way to Israel. So did nearly all the Jews living in Arab countries, who were effectively transferred by governments hostile to Israel in a process that Israel itself treated as proof of the new state's utility as a refuge for Jews subject to antisemitism. But the American Jewish community, by far the largest in the world once the Nazis had killed some two-thirds of the Jews in Europe, stayed put. So did most British Jews, as well as those elsewhere in the Commonwealth, from Canada to Australia to South Africa. So did most Jews living in Latin America. So did the Jews still living in eastern Europe. They had escaped or survived the Holocaust through the protection of the Soviet Union; now they discovered, as the Iron Curtain descended, that they were not permitted to leave the Soviet bloc even if they wanted to move to Israel.

According to the original Zionist picture, all these Jews outside Israel were still members of the Jewish nation. Once Israel came into being, the state defined Jews living outside the country as potential citizens of the national state. They were offered expedited citizenship under a Law of Return that recognized their special status as members of the Jewish nation and was designed to entice them to Israel as much as to protect them from persecution elsewhere.

Yet over time, as Israel grew into a functioning nation-state, it developed its own culture, its own language, and, ultimately, its own sense of contained selfhood. Jews outside Israel who had no intention of moving there did not partake of these. They did not speak modern Israeli Hebrew, a newly evolving national language different from rabbinic or biblical Hebrew. They did not know much about Israeli culture. So long as they stayed in their own countries, they did not take up Israeli citizenship. They were not, in fact, Israelis.

As a result, it gradually became harder and harder to sustain the Zionist-nationalist idea that all Jews everywhere in the world are members of a single nation. Israel's flourishing over seventy-five years created a new national identity: the national identity of the Israeli. That identity, in turn, undercut the notion that the Jews today, including those non-Israeli Jews who live outside the country, are all members of a single nation.

Jewish Israelis today consider themselves Jews, either ethnically or religiously or both. But as Israelis, they acknowledge themselves to be nationally different from Jews living in the United States or Europe or wherever. Their nation is no longer a nation of all the Jews in the world. Their nation is the nation-state of Israel. A Jew can be an Israeli just like a Jew can be an American or a subject of the British Crown or a citizen of the French Republic. Israel is a nation with its own language, culture, and social norms—and of course non-Jewish citizens, themselves Israelis who share its culture to differing degrees. Israelis do not share the national status of being Israeli with Jews anywhere else in the world, except expatriate Israelis.

In other words, if Israel is a nation, and not all Jews belong to it, then the Jews today are not a nation, not even to today's Zionist Israelis. The emergence of an Israeli nationality proves it.

WHO IS A JEW? THE ANATOMY OF A DEBATE

So Israeli national identity does not include all Jews. Yet Israel nevertheless still has something to do with how Jews try to determine who is a member of the Jewish people-family. The government of Israel, as we are about to see, takes stands on who is a Jew in a number of different ways. Jews outside Israel care about what Israel has to say on the matter, even (especially!) when they don't agree with what Israeli institutions think the answer is. The reason Israel's actions and opinions matter for the question of who is a Jew has everything to do with ongoing arguments about Jewish peoplehood and with the afterlife of the Zionist idea of the Jewish nation. To form our own views of the controversy, we need to understand the Israeli debate, past and present, and ask if Israel should continue to fill the role it currently plays.

In the definition of Jewish peoplehood that I'm proposing, no single authority gets or should get the last word on who counts as a Jew. And yet for the last fifty-plus years, a variety of institutional actors have been fighting over exactly the question of who gets to decide—and the main venue for the fight has been the state of Israel. The contours of the debate have become so familiar to the actors who care most about it that the very expression "Who is a Jew?" has come to be used as a shorthand for this recurring struggle. Technically, the parties are fighting over what definition of Jew will be used in Israel and under Israeli law. At a deeper level, however, the debate implicates Jewish identity everywhere, and all the participants understand that.

Let me sketch the existing debate in its Israeli context—without losing sight of the fact that it is, to me, the wrong debate, not the debate we need to have. The state of Israel today deploys the legal definition of Jewishness primarily in two ways: first, in the Law of Return; and second, in family law, which in Israel (following norms created by Ottoman law and continued under the British mandate) varies based on a person's religion.

When the Law of Return was initially conceived by secular Zionists, it was intended to serve the nationalist Zionist goal of ingathering the exiles of the Jewish nation. So when the Law of Return specified a fast track to Israeli citizenship for Jews, the original idea was to include people who belonged to the Jewish nation. Zionists had not settled on a more precise definition because their nationalism did not require them to do so. Consequently, the original Law of Return, enacted in 1950, said only that "every *yehudi* has the right to come to this country as an *oleh* [literally, 'one who goes up,' meaning an immigrant on the citizenship fast-track]."[18]

The casual nationalist-Zionist definition worked fine except in certain highly unusual edge cases, which in turn shed light on what the Zionists had in mind. The most famous is that of Oswald Rufeisen (1922–1998), better known as Brother Daniel. Rufeisen was born to a Jewish family in Poland. Growing up there, he belonged to the Religious Zionist youth movement, Bnei Akiva. When the Germans invaded Poland, he showed extraordinary courage. Posing as a non-Jewish Pole, Rufeisen acted as a translator at a local police station in the town of Mir, then under German occupation. (The town was also the original home of the Mir Yeshiva, now in Jerusalem, that I mentioned in part II.) Rufeisen used the job to warn local Jews of impending deportations. Some two hundred Jews were able to take advantage of his warnings to escape into the forests and join the anti-German partisans there.

When Rufeisen's true identity was discovered by the German authorities, he was hidden and given shelter in a monastery near the police station. While there, Rufeisen experienced a spiritual awakening, underwent baptism, and became a Catholic. He joined the partisans in the forests and after the war was ordained as a priest and became a brother of the Carmelite order.[19] He then sought to emigrate to Israel, where he planned to join the Carmelite monastery of Stella Maris in Haifa. It took until 1959 for the Polish government to allow him to emigrate, which it did only on the condition that he renounce his Polish citizenship.

On arrival in Israel, the now stateless Brother Daniel sought to become a citizen of Israel under the Law of Return. He had a brother who had done exactly that after surviving the war and immigrating to Israel. Yet the Israeli government denied Brother Daniel's request, reasoning that a Catholic—in particular, a Catholic priest—could not be considered a Jew from a "national" point of view. Brother Daniel took his case all the way to Israel's high court, which ultimately upheld the government's position.[20] Brother Daniel was eventually able to become a citizen through the ordinary naturalization process available to non-Jews, rather than the expedited process available under the Law of Return. He lived out his days in Stella Maris.

In retrospect, it might seem strange that the inclusive, nationalist, secular Zionist conception of the Jew led to the exclusion of Brother Daniel, who had so evidently acted in solidarity with his fellow Jews in resisting Nazi German efforts to destroy them and who considered himself part of the Jewish nation. The Traditionalist Jewish position, which was acknowledged and discussed by the justices in their opinions, was that as a matter of Jewish law, Brother Daniel was a Jew. According to medieval Jewish legal authorities, a Jew cannot lose the status of being Jewish by joining another faith: "An Israelite, though he has sinned, is an Israelite."[21] In this instance, the secular Zionist definition of who is a Jew was more restrictive than that of Traditionalist Jewish law.

The secular Zionist reason to reject Brother Daniel's insistence that he was a Jew lay in the nationalist notion that to be a member of the Jewish nation, one must not actively dissociate oneself from that nation. According to this view, the one way that Jews throughout the history of the

Diaspora had been able to disidentify with other Jews was by conversion to Christianity or Islam. Conversion was therefore tantamount to national treason. Secular Zionism was in principle atheist, yet the secular Zionists treated conversion to Christianity not as a religious act but as a national one. That Brother Daniel considered his religious conversion to be perfectly consistent with his national identification as a Jew was confusing and confounding to this version of secular nationalist Zionism.

At the same time, the secular Zionist unwillingness to treat Brother Daniel as a Jew also reflected secular Zionism's failure to get beyond Jewish intuitions—or, if you like, prejudices—about the line between Jews and non-Jews. Even those secular Zionist nationalists who had not formally theorized an answer to the question of who is a Jew found themselves instinctively unable to accept the idea that a Christian was also a Jew. One can see the same intuition at work today in the response of many Jews, whether secular or religious, to Jews for Jesus, a group founded in 1970 that is also loosely affiliated with movements who refer to themselves as messianic Jews. Many Jews refuse to think of Jewish-born Christian believers as Jews, notwithstanding that Jewish legal tradition would acknowledge them to be Jews, albeit Jews whose beliefs are wrong and heretical. The intuition is based on a powerful binary of the Christian and the Jew, coupled with a desire to insist that the two categories do not and cannot overlap.

From the standpoint of secular nationalist Zionism, collective intuitions about who is a Jew might be perfectly legitimate bases for answering the question. After all, nationalism does not necessarily posit that there is any objective definition of who belongs to the nation. So it's possible for the definition to be ascertained by the views of the members of the nation themselves, even if this way of proceeding runs into the logical problem of needing to know who the members are so that their opinions can be taken into account.

Furthermore, to secular Zionists, there is no inherent need to limit the Law of Return to people who are considered Jews under Traditionalist Jewish law, which after all does not define nationhood but religious status. In 1970, the Law of Return was amended so it would extend to "a child and a grandchild of a Jew, the spouse of a Jew, the spouse of a child of a Jew and the spouse of a grandchild of a Jew." This formulation included people whom Traditionalists would not consider Jewish: the non-Jewish spouses of Jews as well as children of Jewish fathers and non-Jewish mothers. At the same time, the amended law *excluded* "a person who has been a Jew and has voluntarily changed his/her religion," reaffirming the rejection of Brother Daniel and repeating the nationalist opposition to including people within the Jewish nation who converted to other religions.[22]

In contrast, Traditionalist Jews would not regard a survey of Jews' intuitions as relevant. They believe in an authoritative God who formally conferred the authority to interpret his law on the rabbis. For them, the question of who is a Jew is a matter of Jewish law. They want the state of Israel's definition of who is a Jew to match the Jewish law definition, because to them, Jewish law is the ultimate source of authority, higher than the law enacted by the state. In the context of the Law of Return, Traditionalist concerns arise in connection with the definition of *yehudi* added in 1970: "a person who was born of a Jewish mother or has become converted to Judaism." For purposes of becoming fast-track citizens of Israel, the law includes anyone converted to Judaism by Progressive rabbis. Traditionalists would prefer the definition of conversion under the Law of Return be restricted to conversion according to halakhah, as they understand the term.[23]

The Traditionalists can live with the definition of who is a Jew under the current Law of Return only insofar as they do not believe that expedited citizenship in the state of Israel is a religious matter at all. That is, their religious beliefs do not extend to the category of Israeli citizenship. Where they have been able to draw the line—and have so far successfully sustained their position by effective politics—is in the realm of the law of marriage.

In Israel, Jews can only be married and divorced under the authority of the Chief Rabbinate of the country, which applies Jewish law as it interprets it. The Chief Rabbinate is a complicated, important institution that deserves a discussion of its own in making sense of how Traditionalist Jewish authorities interact with the state of Israel. Suffice it to say for our purposes that the Rabbinate tries to straddle Religious Zionism and

Traditionalism, without formally committing itself to either. In any case, the Rabbinate defines the legal status of being Jewish to include birth to a Jewish mother or conversion to Judaism according to halakhah. And according to halakhah, Jews may only marry other Jews.*

From this set of legal definitions it follows that a person who is a citizen of Israel and considers himself or herself Jewish but is not considered so according to classical Jewish law cannot, within Israel, marry a person defined as a Jew. There is no civil marriage in Israel, so anyone getting married outside the confines of a state-recognized religious denomination must travel out of the country, marry abroad, and register the marriage on return to Israel. The issue arises most with respect to people whose families came to Israel from the countries of the former Soviet Union in the 1990s and 2000s. Many Jews were married to non-Jews who accompanied them to Israel under the expanded 1970 version of the Law of Return. In consequence, many of their children—those born to non-Jewish mothers—are not considered Jews by the Rabbinate. The only way they could marry Jews within Israel would be to undergo formal conversions recognized by the Rabbinate, namely, Traditionalist or Religious Zionist conversions.

Needless to say, Progressive rabbis outside Israel bitterly resent the Rabbinate's monopoly over who may marry as a Jew in Israel, which tends to invalidate not only Progressive conversions but also, at a symbolic level, all Jewish marriages conducted under the auspices of Progressive rabbis. Adding insult to injury, Traditionalists, especially in Israel, typically refuse to recognize Progressive rabbinic ordination as valid. Many Traditionalists will not even use the Hebrew word *rav* to refer to Progressive rabbis, lest they confer legitimacy on that ordination. Since the majority of American Jews associate themselves with the Reform and Conservative strands of Progressive Judaism, this denial of their rabbis has an

---

* To clarify a bit: Israel's Chief Rabbinate is Orthodox. It uses Orthodox standards of halakhah for defining who is a Jew for those purposes. But the Law of Return as written doesn't give the Chief Rabbinate control over who counts as a Jew for purposes of becoming a citizen under the Law of Return. If this is confusing, it's because the legal reality is highly confusing and confused in a state where religion, nationality, ethnicity, and citizenship all overlap and there is conflict over all of them.

occasional chilling effect on relations between the American Jewish community and Israel.

The simplest way to address the difficulties associated with the Rabbinate's monopoly over Jewish marriage in Israel would be, of course, for the state of Israel to recognize civil marriages or civil unions, which would not have to depend upon the authority of the Rabbinate. But Traditionalists have successfully resisted that possibility. Their argument for preserving the status quo is that civil union in Israel would create confusion between legal marriage and religious marriage. Some Jews who married other Jews civilly might also be religiously married. If so, they would have to be religiously divorced or would retain the status of being married to one another. If they obtained civil divorces and remarried, the result would be that they might be married to one person under religious law and another under civil law. This in turn, warn the Traditionalists, would lead to the Jewish legal problem of bastardy, a legal status that is in practice nearly obsolete but that still exists on the books. In Traditionalist law, being a bastard comes with a permanent prohibition on marrying another Jew unless he or she is also born a bastard.

Never mind that in the United States and elsewhere, where civil marriage exists as an option for Jews, the rabbis have been able to sort out this problem and avoid creating a class of unmarriageable Jewish legal bastards. Never mind that in practice, Israel does recognize civil marriage, provided it takes place outside Israel, in another country. The Rabbinate's hold on marriage is a central reality of Israeli political life. It has proven extremely difficult to break, regardless of its unpopularity among secular Israelis, because the Traditionalist community cares about it so much that its leaders have made its preservation a condition of their joining various governments as coalition partners. In political terms, the Rabbinate's control over marriage, coupled with its control over who counts as a Jew for those purposes, is a side effect of Israel's parliamentary political system.

The effect, I think, of describing the state of the "Who is a Jew?" debate as it currently exists is to suggest just how unproductive it is and how much it is actually a debate about control over political institutions *in Israel*. Consider this paradox: The more time Jews outside Israel spend worrying about whom the state of Israel counts as a Jew, the more they are investing in the secular Zionist narrative that Jews are a nation based in Israel. Yet Israel's persistence as a nation shows that the Jews are *not* a nation.

To make matters more paradoxical still, American Jews' strongest objection to Israel's definition of who is a Jew rests with the fact of Traditionalist religious power and control over the issue within Israel. In other words, the historic success of secular Zionism in making Israel seem central to the question of who is a Jew is being undermined by the failure of secular Zionism to defeat Traditionalist religious control. When it comes to defining who is a Jew, secular Zionism first succeeded—by making Israel into the arbiter—and then failed, by losing control of the definition to Traditionalists. Progressive Jews are suffering from the defeat of secular Zionism at the hands of Traditionalism on the who is a Jew question only because they are so committed to the initial success of Zionism in making Jewish identity into a question that the state of Israel is somehow in a position to define. It seems that the only route for Progressive Jews to care less about whom the state of Israel defines as a Jew would be for them to care less about the state of Israel.

NOT WHO IS A JEW—WHO ARE THE JEWISH PEOPLE?

Let me end my discussion of this aspect of Jewish peoplehood by noticing that no one is exactly certain who the Jewish people are—not even the Traditionalists, who are sure of the Jewish legal definition, but not of much beyond that. On the one hand, Traditionalist discourse sometimes treats Jews who are not religious as though they were barely Jews at all. The basic idea here is that to be a Jew is to embrace and acknowledge God's authority, and to Traditionalists, anyone who does not accept the binding force of Traditionalist Jewish law is not properly accepting the yoke of heaven.* This attitude exists notwithstanding the

---

* Thus, for example, nonreligious Jews are sometimes treated by Traditionalist halakhah as though they were in the category of children who were kidnapped by non-Jews and

Jewish juridical norm that treats everyone born a Jew as a Jew, no matter the person's current beliefs or practices.

On the other hand, some Traditionalists have been struggling with the possibility of a broader conception of Jewishness, one that goes beyond the Jewish legal definition. They rely on a category called *zera' yisra'el*, literally, the seed of Israel. This category encompasses anybody who has Jewish ancestors, even if they are not in the matrilineal line that confers formal Jewish legal status. One iconoclastic contemporary Traditionalist rabbi and politician, Haim Amsalem, has written several volumes on the subject.[24] He argues that people of Jewish origin whose mothers are not Jewish are, in some spiritual sense, part of the greater Jewish people. They therefore ought to be brought into the fold of normative Judaism by conversion. In particular, Amsalem argues for lenient conversion standards to be applied to such potential Jews over and against the stricter standards that prevail among most Traditionalist authorities.

Amsalem was born in 1959 to Moroccan Jewish parents who had moved to Oran, in what was then French Algeria. The family emigrated to Israel when he was a child. He seems to have come to his views mostly through a moral-political intuition. It is not uncommon for Israelis who are technically non-Jews to be conscripted into the IDF, where some inevitably die in the line of duty. Under Traditionalist Jewish law, Jews and non-Jews cannot be buried together in the same burial plot. Some symbolic division must exist between the graves of Jews and non-Jews. The result would be that in some cases, soldiers who died fighting for the state of Israel and who identified as Jews could not be buried in Jewish cemeteries alongside their fellow soldiers. Amsalem, under the influence of a form of Traditionalist identification with the state of Israel's military undertakings, found this situation outrageous. That in turn led him to support conversions of soldiers performed by Religious Zionist rabbis affiliated with the IDF, conversions dismissed by many Traditionalists as inadequately rigorous and therefore illegitimate.

---

did not have access to Jewish identity, knowledge, or education until adulthood. This is supposed to excuse them from being culpable for many of their sins.

From this beginning, Amsalem found himself exploring the notion of the seed of Israel. It led him to an interest in discovering lost tribes of Israel, itself a kind of generationally recurring hobby of a small number of Jews. More important, however, it led Amsalem to the view that becoming formally Jewish should be encouraged and made accessible to all people of Jewish descent.

To be clear, Amsalem is an outlier in contemporary Traditionalist Jewish thought, even a radical outlier. The historical and legal sources he cites, however, are telling. They show that even in the Middle Ages, organized Jewish communities were struggling with questions of belonging. Those included not only conversions to and from Christianity and Islam but also the status of Jewish communities that rejected the authority of rabbinic law, such as the Karaites, who first coalesced in the late eighth or early ninth century in Baghdad and existed uninterruptedly thereafter. (A handful still live today in Israel and Ukraine.) Karaites coexisted alongside rabbinic Jews for much of this long history, sometimes marrying them and sometimes moving back and forth between the two communities. This coexistence demanded a degree of openness and tolerance, even as rabbinic Jewish authorities polemicized against Karaism.

In parallel, today's Traditionalists also must deal with the reality of Jewish communities that do not adhere to the Traditionalist definition of Jewishness. Rejectionism is one available course of action, particularly in Israel, where the political power of the Traditionalists allows it. But there is also the ideological option of expanding notions of Jewishness in the face of the sociological reality of people in Israel, the United States, and beyond who consider themselves Jews and live as Jews but do not qualify as Jews under Traditionalist definitions. The category "seed of Israel" represents one ideological option available even to Traditionalists. It shows that even the Traditionalist definition of who is a Jew may be able to take on board broader conceptions of Jewish familial peoplehood.

If this flexibility is possible for Traditionalists, at least under some conditions, the same also must be true for Progressive and Evolutionist

Jews—and to a greater degree. It should certainly extend to Godless Jews who identify their Jewishness with ethnicity or culture. Jews can understand Jewish peoplehood broadly without fighting over definitional lines, provided the stakes of their understanding do not drive them to winner-take-all arguments about religious or legal authority.

III:2

THE CHOSEN

The most memorable debate I had when I was in law school didn't take place in law school. The debate—really more of a disputation—took place on the Green, a historic park in the middle of New Haven, Connecticut. My interlocutors weren't lawyers, but they were spectacular debaters. They belonged, I know now, to a movement referred to as the "One West Camp," named for the place the group first met, at 1 West 125th Street in Harlem, New York. One Westers are one small subgroup of a larger set of movements known as Black Hebrew Israelites. Like many Black Hebrew Israelites, they believe they, not Jews, are the true descendants of the children of Israel.*

---

* The One Westers made news a few years ago when they indirectly provoked a bizarre encounter at the Lincoln Memorial in which white teenagers wearing MAGA hats confronted a Native American beating a drum. Their views are adjacent to some of those advanced in the film *Hebrews to Negroes: Wake Up Black America!* (2018), which got public attention in 2022 when it was recommended on Twitter by the basketball player Kyrie Irving in a post that led to his suspension. They *aren't* the same group as the better-known African Hebrew Israelites of Jerusalem, who began in Chicago in the 1960s and are now centered in Dimona, Israel. That utterly fascinating group, some of whose members now serve in the IDF and thus profess loyalty to the state of Israel, is the subject of a brilliant book by the scholar John L. Jackson, who has also written deeply about other Black Hebrews. See John L. Jackson Jr., *Thin Description: Ethnography and the African Hebrew Israelites of Jerusalem* (Cambridge, MA: Harvard

I encountered the One Westers for the first time while walking home from class. There were only half a dozen of them, I'm pretty sure, but they were hard to miss. They wore colorful, ancient-style outfits with bandolier-like belts crossed over their chests. They were surrounded by large placards explaining how each of the twelve tribes of Israel corresponded to a different location or group of people in Africa, the Americas, and the Caribbean. They were having animated conversations with passersby. I stopped to listen. I couldn't help myself. I was drawn in.

What got me going was what the One Westers were saying. They were arguing that God loved the children of Israel, his chosen people, more than anyone else on earth. To them this was part of a broader theory of Black supremacy. But that conclusion engaged me less than the method they were using to support their claims. They had proofs from the Bible. Lots of them.

The lead speaker would announce a verse: "Exodus 19:5! Read it!" Then his colleagues would recite it loudly, reading from a well-thumbed copy of what I remember as the King James Version of the Bible. Each time, the biblical passage he chose would powerfully bring home his point: "If ye will obey my voice indeed, and keep my covenant, then ye shall be a peculiar treasure unto me above all people: for all the earth is mine."[1]

This was in the middle of the 1990s. We were in the immediate aftermath of the genocide in Rwanda. The brutal war in the former Yugoslavia was ongoing. My own conception of Jewishness had been painfully challenged by these extreme manifestations of insider-outsider dynamics. Baruch Goldstein, a Jewish doctor born and raised in Brooklyn, had murdered 29 Muslim worshippers and injured 125 more in the mosque at the Tomb of the Patriarchs in Hebron. He was a Modern Orthodox Religious Zionist who had been educated at a high school nearly identical to mine. His actions had shaken my belief structure like no other event in my life, before or since.

In the moment, all I wanted to do was to tell the One Westers that

University Press, 2013); and John L. Jackson Jr., *Harlemworld: Doing Race and Class in Contemporary Black America* (Chicago: University of Chicago Press, 2001).

God didn't love the Israelites most: God loved all humans equally. I had a few verses of my own to back me. The best was Amos 9:7. I asked them to read it out:

> Are ye not as children of the Ethiopians unto me, O children of Israel? saith the LORD. Have not I brought up Israel out of the land of Egypt? and the Philistines from Caphtor, and the Syrians from Kir?

Then I drew my lesson. "You see? God doesn't care more about the Israelites than he cares about any other people!"

The One Westers were ready. They knew that verse well. "What color were the Ethiopians?" they called out. "Black," came the response. "That verse proves the Israelites were Black," the leader explained with a smile of easy victory. "It says the Israelites are 'like the children of Ethiopia.'"

At this point, I should have conceded defeat. True, the One West debaters hadn't exactly addressed my interpretation of the verse from Amos. But they had effectively reinterpreted that verse, deflecting my wish to enlist the Bible for the view that God loves all peoples the same.

The problem—my problem, I guess—was that I was brought up in the tradition of Talmudic debate, where you never leave well enough alone. The One Westers had claimed the Israelites, God's chosen people, were Black, so I came back with another verse. I told them to read out Exodus 11:7. It was the second half of the verse that I wanted: "that you may know that the LORD does make a difference between the Egyptians and Israel." Now I had my own question for them. "What color were the Egyptians?" I demanded to know. In terms of Afrocentrism, there was only one possible answer. And if the Egyptians were Black, and if God differentiated them from the Israelites, what did that say about the Israelites?

Even as the words came out of my mouth, I remember thinking two things. One, I had made what was at best nothing more than a clever debater's point. Two, I hadn't set out to "prove" the Israelites weren't Black. I had wanted to show God's love for all humans. I had now argued something totally orthogonal to what I really wanted to say. In a debate, that's called losing.

The One Westers seemed not to have previously encountered the somewhat perverse argument that Exodus 11:7 refuted the Blackness of the Israelites, maybe because I had invented it on the spot. There was an uncomfortable pause. Then one of them looked me in the eye and said, bluntly, in a Hebrew accent I had not heard before, *"Attah lo yehudi"*— "You are not a Jew." I knew enough not to argue with that one. As I turned and headed home, I could hear them calling after me, almost taunting, a bit louder each time: *"Atah lo yehudi!"*

Leave aside the question of who was a Jew, me or the One Westers, or both, or neither. That belongs to the previous chapter. The reason I'm telling you the story now is to underscore how hard it is to avoid a basic question of Jewish theology, politics, and philosophy. Are the Jews chosen by God? If so, what does that mean? And, in the words of the old joke, couldn't He choose someone else next time?

The idea that the children of Israel are chosen by God is central to the Hebrew Bible and to Jewish consciousness ever since. The book of Deuteronomy puts it succinctly:

For you are a holy people to the Lord your God; the Lord
your God has chosen you for himself to be a treasured people
[*'am segullah*] from among all the peoples on the face of the
earth. Not because you were greater than the other peoples
has God loved you and chosen you, for you are the smallest
of all peoples. But from God's loving you and his keeping the
oath which he swore to your fathers, God took you out with a
strong hand and redeemed you from the house of slavery, from
the hand of Pharaoh king of Egypt.[2]

The basic idea is straightforward. The people of Israel are nothing special and have not done anything special to merit God's choice of them. It is simply an unchangeable fact, based on God's love of their forefathers and by extension of them.

Even in the Bible, being chosen is not an unalloyed good. To the contrary: God took the children of Israel out of Egypt because God loved them, but God also intentionally put them into bondage in Egypt in the first place.[3] A constantly recurring theme of the entire Hebrew Bible, one I emphasized at the end of part II, is that when the children of Israel sin against God, they will be terribly punished for it. The extent of their punishment is connected to their special status as God's beloved people.

The most extreme biblical expression of this dynamic can be found in the book of Hosea. The poetic motif of the entire book, all fourteen chapters, is that Israel is a wayward, unfaithful wife whom God loves but cannot resist punishing even as he (the gender matters) yearns for her return. Enacting the emotional structure depicted in the poetry, Hosea is instructed to marry a woman who betrays him with other lovers, thus placing himself in the empathetic position of God. He suffers terribly, as presumably does his wife. This is not a model of a healthy relationship.

Nevertheless, whether construed in terms of advantages and blessings or distinctive punishments and curses, the idea of Jewish chosenness has persisted. It survived Paul's Christian theology, which flipped chosenness on its head by first universalizing God's love to reach all Christians, then ascribing to the Jews permanent and distinctive punishment for spurning and killing Christ. It survived Islamic theology, which holds that all peoples have their own prophets sent to them by God, and that Moses and the other Jewish prophets (including Jesus) were eventually succeeded and superseded by Muhammad. Although in theory this should have made the Jews into just another nation, it did not, mostly because the Qur'an retold and reimagined many stories that also appeared in the Bible. The Jews came to be seen by Muslims as a "people of the book," entitled to special protection by virtue of their monotheism but also subject to special disabilities and subordinate status.

Jewish chosenness even survived the rise of modern secularism, what Nietzsche (optimistically, in retrospect) called the death of God. Earlier, I described how classical Zionism sought to put an end to the idea of chosenness, only to have it reappear through the historical events of the Holocaust and the course of Israel's historical development. Meanwhile, for modern antisemites, whether non-Jewish or otherwise, Jewish chosenness was often reflected in various pseudoscientific or cultural condemnations of the Jews as uniquely sick, weak, bad, or dangerous.

For philo-Semites, whether Jewish or otherwise, Jews came to be depicted as especially suited to modern life, excelling in science, scholarship, medicine, progressive political activism, the arts, finance, business, and beyond. Not infrequently, philo-Semitic and antisemitic visions of Jewish distinctiveness converged, so that Jewish success in a given domain could be depicted as evidence of conspiratorial Jewish control. The rueful joke that captures this phenomenon depicts a Jew of the 1920s reading *Der Stürmer*, a Nazi propaganda tabloid. Challenged by another Jew about how he could read that filth, the Jew replies, "In every other paper I read that Jews are poor and oppressed and beaten down by pogroms. But in this one they tell me that the Jews control Hollywood, they control Wall Street, they run the Communist International. I feel great!"

The persistence of the idea of Jewish chosenness, like the persistence of the Jewish people itself, therefore calls out for some exploration. The place to begin that exploration is with a caveat: it turns out not to be so unusual for a group of people to think of itself as special or chosen.*

Start with the biblical account of chosenness. In the ancient Near East and beyond, most peoples—in fact most city-states—had specific gods associated with them, gods who had chosen the ancestors who founded the city and stayed with them always. The Bible depicts a number of them, like Chemosh, the god of the Moabites.[4] Athena is the goddess who gave her name to Athens. For Israel to be chosen by the

---

* Even the survival of the Jews, which is sometimes depicted as though it were a kind of evidence of chosenness, is not particularly unusual. Ancient Confucian beliefs thrive today, twenty-five hundred years after Confucius's birth. The Buddha was a rough contemporary of Confucius. Hindu religion is older still. The Han Chinese are alive and well in their hundreds of millions today, over two thousand years after their ascribed birth as a distinct group. The term "Brahmin" was in use three thousand years ago to identify a caste within Hinduism. Christianity is now some two thousand years old. Many ancient peoples have indeed been lost to history. But quite a few have persisted, many of them in vastly greater numbers than the Jews, and not all attached to a single homeland. The idea that Jewish persistence is unique has more to do with theology than with actual history.

God of Israel was therefore not on its own unique, even in the eyes of the prophets. In the passage I tried to use against the One Westers, Amos tells the Israelites that God has even given other peoples their own exoduses.[5] The point of this passage is that even the Exodus from Egypt, which the Bible repeatedly makes the touchstone of God's love of the Israelites, is not a one-off but a familiar worldly phenomenon that has parallels in the lives of neighboring peoples.

Seen in this context, the biblical idea of chosenness was about making the people of Israel distinct *in their relation to the particular God of Israel* (the meaning of *'am segullah*, which literally means a treasured people), not unique when compared to other peoples. What transformed the biblical idea of chosenness into a notion of uniqueness is a separate development in biblical thought, one that was to have substantial global effects later. That was the idea that the God of the Israelites was not merely one god among many, but the only true, real God—and that the other gods were wood and stone.*

Other ancient peoples who considered themselves chosen by their god or gods did not necessarily deny the reality of the existence of other gods who were patrons of other peoples or places. They were content to believe that their god was more powerful or worthy of worship or at any rate appropriate for them to worship. But from the moment that the Israelites began to tell themselves and their neighbors that their God was the single universal God and that other gods had no real existence, the meaning of their chosenness by *that* God—the creator and ruler of heaven and earth—attained a different conceptual status. Their chosenness became not a matter of similarity to other peoples' relationships with their gods but a matter of dissimilarity and uniqueness. If the one unique God had chosen Israel, then Israel was the one unique people.

It is tempting to speculate that antisemitism itself can be traced back to this particular claim of uniqueness. Almost all peoples come in for

---

* In technical terminology, this is the transition from polytheism (worship of many gods) to henotheism (the worship of one particular god associated with a tribe or group without denying the reality of other gods) to monotheism (the denial that other gods exist at all apart from the one true God).

dislike, distrust, stereotypes, and even hatred by their neighbors, especially if they are competitors for land or wealth or trade routes or prestige. Yet you would think there would be something especially irritating about being told by your neighbors not that their god was better than yours but that your god *was no god at all*. The truth is, however, that we have little evidence that this sort of monotheism occasioned particularly virulent antisemitic responses in the ancient world.

In contrast with the denial of other gods, we do know that the Jewish claim to chosenness has featured, in one form or another, in most kinds of antisemitism, past and present. This chosenness, I am suggesting, is a provocation to anyone not so chosen, because it amounts to the claim that the Master of the Universe has chosen me and not you. If God is cosmic, so is the chosenness of the Jewish people.

For Traditionalist believers, there is nothing threatening or morally troubling about this belief. It flows easily and naturally alongside the rest of their conception of God, a conception most Traditionalists see little reason to question. Jewish theology had many centuries to make sense of Jewish suffering, and Traditionalists follow the main line of that theodicy willingly, as I mentioned earlier. It can be traced back to the Hebrew Bible: Follow God's laws and you will be rewarded. Deviate and you will be punished. The same principle can be applied to any of the many misfortunes in Jewish history, all without disrupting the functional concept of chosenness.

To Traditionalists, even the trauma of the Holocaust did not fundamentally disrupt this basic structure of reward and punishment. Traditionalists may debate which sins precipitated the Holocaust, and whose, but that sort of debate is normal in Jewish history in the aftermath of tragedy. God did not destroy the Jewish people utterly, because God had promised not to do so. Anything short of total destruction is, to be callous, part of the divine deal.

It is for this reason that Traditionalists prefer to commemorate the Holocaust not on a special memorial day but on the ninth of the month of Av, the day of fasting and prayer associated with the destruction of the Temple in Jerusalem. Over the centuries, as tragedies multiplied, Jews incorporated their commemoration into the ninth of Av liturgy, each tragedy remembered by its own poetic lament. Although special days of commemoration were sometimes added to the Jewish calendar in the aftermath of particularly devastating tragedies, over time those tended to be subsumed into the ninth of Av. It's not only that the calendar would be too full of fast days if all Jewish communal tragedies got their own individual commemoration. Theologically, all these tragedies had in common a basic pattern of sin, punishment, and inspiration for repentance to future generations. The villains might come and go, but the basic repetitive structure was the same. In the words of the Passover Haggadah, "Not just one [enemy] alone has stood up to destroy us; rather, in every generation they stand up to destroy us; and the Holy One, blessed be He, saves us from their hands."

Traditionalists, then, take Jewish chosenness as a religious fact, and they bear its consequences with proper mourning where required. They tend not to take much pride in the secular accomplishments of individual (mostly secular) Jews, nor do they especially believe that secular Jews are consistently better or more ethical people than non-Jews. They do believe that the Law, properly obeyed, should make for piety and goodness. But Jews who do not accept the authority of God or the yoke of God's commandments should not be expected to prosper more than anyone else and should not in any case be specially praised or honored, considering their failure to perform their true task for which they were put on earth.

Progressive Jews have a much more ambivalent relationship to the idea of chosenness, which is in a certain sense at odds with their egalitarian ideals. The Progressive God loves all humans equally, and the idea of that God singling out one people would seem to undermine the universality of that love. For those Progressives who understand God more metaphorically or spiritually as a unifying principle of order in the universe, it makes little sense to think that such a divine principle prefers some people to others.

In the past, Progressive Jews frequently preserved the notion of chosenness through the idea that the Jews were appointed to be "a light unto the nations," a phrase taken from the book of Isaiah,[6] one of Progressives' favorite sources. For Jews to be a light unto the nations was for them to take on the mission of spreading the prophetic, moral truths of the Hebrew Bible to the world. This formulation subtly preserved the idea that the Jews have a special historical role while downplaying the possibility that this role entailed any unique connection to God. It also put the Jews as a whole into a world-historical role that the Gospel according to Luke assigned to Jesus, namely that of spreading divine revelation to all humans.*

The idea of the Jews as a light unto the nations was by no means restricted to Progressive Jewish thought. It occasionally appeared in classical Zionism—where Ben-Gurion placed it alongside the rather different goal of being a nation like all others—and in Religious Zionism, where the elder Rav Kook made it part of his messianic vision for Israel to be a model state that would inspire others and in turn hasten universal redemption.[7] But the idea was especially fitting for Jewish Progressives because it called for Jews to be model messengers of the divine project of achieving social justice. If Jews fell short in that mission, they could justifiably be chided for failing to live up to their divinely assigned task. If they performed well, their mission would enhance the lives of all humans.

Today's Progressive Jews typically approach the "light unto the nations" version of Jewish chosenness cautiously. Contemporary Progressives mostly think all cultures and societies are equally moral or wise, roughly speaking. To claim a special mission of enlightenment as the distinct role of the Jews smacks of presumptuousness, not to mention condescension. The early Progressive Jewish claim was that the refined essence of prophetic Judaism prefigured not only Christian morals (circa the middle of the nineteenth century) but Western morality in its entirety. Today's Progressive Jewish thought has more modest aspirations. It prefers to think of God's morality as unfolding fitfully but progressively through history, and by no means as the special preserve of the Jews or the ancient Israelites.

That leaves contemporary Progressive Jews in something of a

---

* In Luke, the "light unto the nations" trope from Isaiah is paraphrased as an address to the infant Christ: "Master, now you are dismissing your servant in peace, according to your word; for my eyes have seen your salvation, which you have prepared in the presence of all peoples, a light for revelation to the Gentiles and for glory to your people Israel." Luke 2:29–32. This is also the text of the *Nunc Dimittis*.

quandary with respect to chosenness. Yet collective chosenness is so fundamental to Jewish thought that *something* is needed to fill the gap. I argued earlier that for much of post-1980s Progressive theology, the Holocaust (chosenness as unique genocidal suffering) and the state of Israel (chosenness as unique postgenocidal redemption) came to function as the content of chosenness. For a small number, critique of Israel has subsequently substituted for support of Israel, while still preserving some vestigial version of chosenness. If the Holocaust and Israel eventually can no longer fulfill those roles for younger Progressive Jews, there will need to be a new interpretation or reconfiguration of chosenness to take their place.

I would suggest for this purpose a theology of existential self-chosenness. More easily than most other Jews, Progressive Jews may be able to mount the case that by *choosing* to be Jews and identifying with the divine values of social justice, they are themselves creating the covenantal relationship with the divine. The biblical idea that God chose the people of Israel can be reread or transvalued into the idea that the people of Israel *chose their God*, and choose that same God still. Chosenness can then be reunderstood once again as a divine covenant, in which the human and the divine conjoin freely, voluntarily, and, as it were, equally.

Seen this way, voluntariness constitutes chosenness. One should be able to choose to be a Jew or choose not to be one. The voluntary choice of the individual or the community corresponds to divine choice. This conception differs radically from the idea that Jewishness is something one does not choose but is "thrown into," to borrow the philosopher Martin Heidegger's description of how we are thrown into existence. A Heideggerian chosenness can only be the experience of *being* chosen to be a Jew, not of choosing it. It might well satisfy those Jews who feel, as I sometimes do, that they have no alternative but to engage the Jewishness that shaped their consciousness and lifeworld. But this feeling of being thrown into Jewishness can do little or nothing for Jews who experience themselves as free to be Jews or not to be.

Another version of being chosen rather than choosing Jewishness is associated with Jean-Paul Sartre's famous assertion that the antisemite makes the Jew, and that the Jew therefore has no escape from being a Jew.[8] Sartre, one of the leading figures in existentialism, was writing for a world in which Jewishness was conceived, by non-Jews as well as many Jews, as a social disability. It is certainly true that under the Nazi Nuremberg laws, one could not avoid being categorized as Jewish by insisting on not being a Jew. That followed from the Nuremberg laws' inspiration, namely American Southern Black Codes, which designated a person as Black based on blood quantum, regardless of the person's self-perception.

Nowadays, however, it seems anathema to rely on antisemites—to say nothing of genocidal antisemites who were borrowing from American white supremacists—to provide a definition that we would like to use. If a person asserts that he is not a Jew, it feels ethically strange to insist that he is a Jew nevertheless. If he chooses to "pass" as a non-Jew, no one would be the wiser. And at a deeper level, to be chosen by antisemites is so fundamentally different from being chosen by God that it feels (to me) like a repugnant inversion of the divine covenant to insist that chosenness persists as a consequence of the hatred of Jews.

It follows, I think, that today we should see the appeal of a conception of Jewish chosenness that is essentially voluntary and self-chosen. You should be able to choose not to be a Jew. You should be able to choose to be a Jew.

To see how deep this voluntarism runs in Jewish thought, consider that to the rabbis, becoming a Jew if you were not born one is considered a voluntary act, specifically, *the act of joining the covenant.* According to Maimonides's code of Jewish law, itself based on the Talmud, what it takes to become a Jew is to declare your desire to be a Jew before a rabbinic court. The court reminds you that Jews are subject to oppression. If you say, "I know, and I am not worthy," you are accepted as a Jew "immediately." After you have voluntarily asked to belong and been accepted, the court informs you of basic principles of Jewish belief and of Jewish law, and you are given the chance to change your mind. If you accept what you have been told, the court "should not delay" you, Maimonides states,* but should proceed "immediately" to circumcision (for males) and immersion in a ritual bath (for men and women alike).[9] The essence of the process is neither more nor less than a declaration of intent to belong and acceptance of Jewish beliefs and laws.

The simple, voluntary nature of this process is why I dislike the English-language term "conversion" to describe joining the Jewish people. Far better to speak simply of a person becoming a Jew. The word "conversion," with its Christian origin and associations, implies a transformation that makes someone into a different, new person. None of that is present in the rabbinic conception of becoming a Jew. The process does not require or even recognize a transformative "conversion" experience, like the one Saul of Tarsus experienced on the road to Damascus when he became the Christian Paul. The rabbinic Hebrew word for becoming a Jew, *giyyur*, derives from the biblical Hebrew word for stranger, *ger*, which the rabbis interpreted to refer to someone who becomes a Jew. The idea is that by joining the Jewish community and becoming a Jew, the stranger becomes also fully Jewish. She is still herself, still a person with the same non-Jewish origin. She is not transformed into a new being. Rather, by joining the Jewish people voluntarily, she is a full member of the Jewish people, with the same obligations as other Jews.

If a person not born a Jew can join the covenant and become a member of the chosen people by voluntarily asking to do so, it makes some sense to think that all Jews can become chosen by choosing the covenant themselves. To some Evolutionist Jews, especially in the United States, such a view might seem congenial. Evolutionists often want to soften the exclusivity of chosenness in the light of their moral impulse to human equality. Using allegory, their favored tool of interpretation, they may say that to be chosen by God means to establish a special relationship with God. That relationship need not be unique so long as it is felt to be special. This approach can allow Evolutionists to avoid the apparent collective

---

* Maimonides does not mention the custom of the rabbinic court formally refusing applicants three times before accepting them. The practice is not legally mandatory under the halakhah and indeed arguably contradicts Maimonides's specific dictum that the court should not delay the process but should act "immediately."

narcissism of believing God has chosen only the Jews, even as they repeat the basic principle of chosenness daily in their prayers. They can choose to live "as though" chosen by God, by taking chosenness not to be exclusive.

Nevertheless, for Religious Zionists, who are also Evolutionists, this version of chosenness may not be satisfying. To them, the chosenness of the Jewish people is no allegory. It is, rather, a necessary, concrete condition of the messianic redemption toward which their faith directs them. To Religious Zionists, the chosenness of the Jews leads directly to the state of the Jews. If the people of Israel will fulfill their divine mission, namely the establishment of the state of Israel in the land God gave them, that event will have the cosmic consequence of setting the world aright. Even if they endorse Maimonides's dictum that the days of the messiah are indistinguishable from ours except in virtue of Jewish sovereignty, that outcome is nevertheless divinely blessed, and not by metaphor but by reality.

It emerges that, like so much of the rest of Evolutionist Jewish thought, the future of the concept of chosenness depends on how much Religious Zionism takes over the rest of Evolutionism. To the extent the (spiritual) takeover is completed, Evolutionist Jews may end up embracing their version of chosenness alongside Rav Kook. Their imagined Israel will be, for them, the model of a state that can inspire others. To the extent that some strands of Evolutionist Jewish thought pull back from a full embrace of Religious Zionism, their challenge will be to interpret the divine choice of Israel in terms that reconcile Progressive universalism with Traditionalist particularism. That reconciliation will not be easy, but with the help of allegory, it can surely be achieved.

SECULAR CHOSENNESS AND THE QUESTION OF JEWISH ACCOMPLISHMENT

This review of Jewish versions of chosenness brings me to the troublesome topic of the idea of chosenness in Godless Jewish thought, particularly in the cultural Judaism that I have called (with love, not dismissal) bagels-and-lox Judaism. An atheist worldview cannot, by definition, derive chosenness from a divine origin. So if chosenness is to persist at all—and perhaps it need not—then chosenness must be understood as a distinct product of a distinct Jewish culture.

One of the most common versions of this secular chosenness is Jewish pride in Jews' cultural accomplishments, ascribed, often without much mechanistic explanation, to Jews' unique abilities and talents. At its worst, this perspective expresses itself as crude cultural chauvinism: an accounting of Jewish Nobel laureates followed by "Look how amazing the Jews are!" In its most defensible form, it offers an argument about how Jewish energies and creativity have expressed themselves on the world stage in the two hundred-plus years since Jewish emancipation. It proposes that the Jewish contribution in the realms of science, medicine, law, theory, critique, revolution, and capitalism—to name a few—is unique, distinctive, and disproportionate.

This better form of the argument is not absurd. It *is* exaggerated. To begin with, we need to notice that the evidence for unique Jewish contributions to general culture really only starts with Jewish emancipation.[10] Before that, the history of the Jewish contribution to Western thought and civilization, from ancient Greece and Rome up through the Enlightenment, is not especially remarkable.

By this I do not mean to denigrate the contributions of those premodern Jewish thinkers who managed to make their mark on broader Christian-Islamic civilization, but only to note that they are few and far between, and their influences are for the most part peripheral. Even a giant like Maimonides had little effect on the course of Western thought compared to, say, his exact contemporary Ibn Rushd (1126–1198).*

---

* Abu al-Walid ibn Ahmad ibn Muhammad ibn Rushd, known in Latin as Averroes, was born in Cordoba, like Maimonides, just a few years earlier. Like Maimonides, Ibn Rushd came from a family of jurists and community leaders. He was deeply versed in his own religious legal tradition, about which he wrote books. Like Maimonides, he was a profound philosophical thinker. Like Maimonides, he was a rationalist who allegorized Scripture to bring its meaning into comprehensible relation to Aristotelian philosophical truths. Unlike Maimonides, Ibn Rushd shaped the reception of Greek philosophy in Europe through his writings, particularly his commentaries on all of Aristotle's works that were available to him in Arabic. And although Maimonides was more influential in his lifetime and beyond among the world's Jews than Ibn Rushd was among the world's Muslims, Ibn Rushd shaped medieval Christian philosophy via Thomas Aquinas. Maimonides for the most part directly influenced only Jews.

Benedict de Spinoza (1632–1677), the most important philosopher of Jewish origin in his or maybe any era, is arguably the exception who proves the rule, given that his work was produced in the relative equality and freedom of the Dutch Republic. (The Jewish community of Amsterdam shunned him, but that is another topic.)

In short, the Hebrew Bible influenced Christianity and Islam. Individual Jews, however, did not, for the most part, meaningfully shape the religious or secular thinking of these great civilizations before Jews were emancipated from their subordinate status in Europe. Even Jewish banking and moneylending were probably less important than Florentine banking in shaping the course of European civilizational development.

With emancipation, though, things *did* change. It started slowly, with a number of German Jews emerging in the late eighteenth and early nineteenth centuries as important intellectual (Moses Mendelssohn) and literary (Heinrich Heine) figures. Where things began to speed up was with the movement of eastern European Jews (the so-called Ostjuden) into western Europe in search of economic betterment and cultural opportunity.

Most of these eastern Jews were impoverished and ill-educated due to the economic and social conditions in the East. Even their Jewish education was often rudimentary, limited to basic literacy and the ability to read the Bible and the prayer book. In the poverty of eastern Europe, Talmudic study was the preserve of a small number of exceptionally intelligent and talented men who became rabbis or teachers. Yet within a generation or two, the Ostjuden and the German Jews had produced not hundreds but thousands of important and influential figures in essentially all realms of Western culture. Their contributions, emblematized by Marx, Einstein, and Freud, stand in for those of innumerable other central figures of European culture and thought.

How did it happen? The simplest explanation is that these mostly undereducated Jews possessed an unbounded ambition for learning and knowledge; that these politically repressed Jews possessed grand ideals of social change; and that these economically restricted Jews possessed a boundless capacity for wealth creation. As newly emancipated Germans or as recent immigrants to western Europe, these Jews were not limited by preexisting expectations of social class. In nearly all cases, they had nowhere to go but up, socially or professionally or intellectually.

It is worth noticing that the conditions for this extraordinary process of creativity—which moved to the United States by the end of the first quarter of the twentieth century and boomed there after World War II—coexisted with the general perception that eastern European Jews were a blight on western European society. In popular media and high culture alike they were depicted as thieves, beggars, and prostitutes. In the eugenicist scientific literature of the time, Jews were often characterized as congenitally stupid, infirm, and otherwise diseased. The Nazi brand of antisemitism did not invent the stereotypes it applied to Jews. It amplified prejudices and stereotypes that were widespread in western Europe from the nineteenth century.

So whatever enabled some eastern European Jews to succeed rapidly and remarkably, it did not extend to all European Jews at the time. Nor was it anywhere near enough to save Europe's Jews from the German attempt to take over Europe or the effects of the almost-accomplished Final Solution. What, then, was it, beyond previously bottled-up capacity and ambition, that led to this stunning flourishing of Jewish accomplishment over the course of a century on two continents, or three if you count Israel?

In an absorbing book called *The Jewish Century* (2004), the historian Yuri Slezkine argues that, more or less by chance, eastern European Jews happened to have the skill set necessary for succeeding in modernity. He divides the world into entrepreneurial minorities and food-producing majorities and reasons that since the Jews were already "service nomads" in Europe, they were ideally placed for an era in which the key to success was to be "urban, mobile, literate, articulate, intellectually intricate, physically fastidious, and occupationally flexible."[11]

Slezkine's analysis is brilliant and provocative, like everything he writes. And clearly there was some aspect of the particular cultural modes of repressed eastern European Jews (repressed in all senses) that somehow facilitated the rise of some of them. His analysis also avoids the potentially antisemitic argument that eastern European Jews somehow seized hold of modernity and bent it to their own characteristics.

Yet Slezkine's approach cannot fully explain why a great number of Jews struggled to adapt to modernity, including both those who did not leave eastern Europe and those who emigrated West but did not become successful. Nor can it easily explain the stunning influence of a small number of creative and inventive Jews like Einstein and Freud and Marx, who were not more mobile or urban or flexible than other people, but were, in a word, geniuses: creative minds who perceived or invented what others had not.

One possible direction to explain these two phenomena—the failure of many eastern European Jews to conquer modernity and the outsize influence of a few—is to look at the particularity of Jewish intellectual culture in eastern Europe, the world from which these great thinkers' parents came. That culture was, as I have said, literate but uneducated. Above all things it valued Talmudic genius. If a child was identified as particularly extraordinary, some way would be found to sponsor the child's Talmudic education, even if the parents themselves could not afford it.

I believe it is significant that from the nineteenth century to the present, it is all but unknown for a Jewish genius in the realms of science, scholarship, business, or the arts actually to have undergone the twenty-plus years of full-time Talmudic training that would be necessary to launch a career as a leading Talmudist. The reason, I would speculate, is that while this education sharpens certain aspects of one's intellectual development, it also neglects others. The handful of important academics who underwent this full training have become scholars of, well, Talmud, or allied areas of Jewish scholarship.

The magic combination for Jewish geniuses seems to be separation from the Talmudic intellectual culture of eastern Europe by a generation or two or even three. What remains of that culture in their upbringing has been moved to the background: the recognition, encouragement, and support of youthful ability; the impulse to use argumentation to hone intellectual skill; and the pervasive cultural commitment to developing one's intellectual faculties and capacities to their fullest extent.

To this potent combination must be added a final factor: the drive to succeed, which can be found more frequently among people who are raised in conditions of immigration and immediate postimmigra-tion. The more comfortable one's family of origin has become in its environment, whether through economic accomplishment or cultural acclimatization, the less likely it is for the next generation to possess the drive and work ethic necessary to excel.

The takeaway is that the cycle of accomplishment associated with eastern European Jewish genius is unlikely to persist indefinitely. In the United States, it is already possible to sense and perhaps even measure a decline in Jewish dominance in a range of environments where first-generation, self-made drive and creativity are the leading indicators of success. The sciences are an excellent example. Where Jews once made up a highly disproportionate percentage of important scientists, it is already possible to see a generational shift toward Asian Americans' dispropor-tionate representation. Jews are still substantially overrepresented in the highest echelons of science in proportion to their numbers in the popula-tion. But the number of Jews in those positions is declining relative to the number of Asian Americans. The same is also true of admissions to top universities and to PhD programs in the sciences.*

Jews' disproportionate representation can be expected to continue longer in domains where a deep cultural understanding of norms and customs confers a substantial advantage. In those domains, it also fre-quently took American Jews longer to gain a foothold than in areas where raw talent and drive could be combined to achieve fast success. The prac-tice of corporate law provides an example. Jews did not gain access to partnerships in the most prestigious, powerful, and profitable corporate law firms (known then as "white shoe" firms) until the late 1950s.[12] Even after that, their numbers were relatively small in those firms. It took the rise of "outsider" firms made up mostly of Jewish partners in the 1980s for Jewishness to cease to be a barrier to partnership at the white shoe

---

* College admissions, for its part, has a range of complex sociopolitical dimensions, with advantages given to legacies, athletes, and (until 2023 at least) students who rep-resent diverse constituencies, so this measure is by no means definitive. Nevertheless it is a striking reality that the number of Asian American students admitted to top U.S. universities has risen enormously over the past twenty-five years, while the number of Jewish students admitted seems to have declined.

firms.[13] Today, in contrast, Jewish cultural background may actually confer a mild advantage in the search for employment or partnership at a major corporate law firm, since cultural Jewishness is as much a dominant background cultural norm in many big law firms as a white Anglo-Saxon Protestant background was until the 1980s.

Over time, then, Jewish representation can eventually be expected to decline even in those areas where cultural acclimatization confers some advantage, because the need for drive is still present and because American Jews are further from immigration and therefore are less likely to have the drive. The reason to offer this hypothesis is not in any way to lessen the impressiveness of eastern European–origin Jews' accomplishments in these or other domains. Rather, the historical accidents that led to these outsize accomplishments are time-bound and contingent. They do not inhere in some unchanging features of Jewish culture, much less in "Jewish" genetics. They are changing in real time.

To underscore the point that the accomplishments of Jews over the past century are contingent, consider the case of Israel. Since its establishment in 1948, the country has produced a handful of Nobel laureates in chemistry and economics,* but nowhere near as many as the number of American Jewish Nobel winners in the same period, despite Israel having a Jewish population of roughly comparable size to the United States. Some of this difference can be explained by the global primacy of American universities, but Israeli universities are also excellent and Israelis who teach in them can all speak English.

The major statistical gap suffices to show that genetics cannot explain Jewish accomplishment. More than that, it suggests that Jewish distinctiveness plays out in different ways in different places even in the same time frame. After all, in those same years, Israel produced a number of distinguished Jewish generals, while American Jews produced few general officers of note, and only one of real historical significance.†

---

* The Nobel Peace Prize is a horse of a different color. And Israel's 1966 Nobel laureate in literature, S. Y. Agnon, was born in Poland (in a town that is now in Ukraine) in 1888 and was in that sense a direct product of eastern Europe.

† Admiral Hyman Rickover (1900–1986), credited with creating the U.S. nuclear submarine fleet.

Neither of these observations has anything to do with any inherent Jewish talent or lack of talent at military command. They are the result of Israel's military posture and the fact of near-universal conscription there.

The reason I spent this time on the question of Jewish genius and Jewish success is partly that lots of people are interested in it. Mainly, however, my goal has been to show that any secular account of Jewish uniqueness that is meant to substitute for a religious conception of chosenness is of limited utility if considered over the long historical run. Secular Jews who want to retain some notion of being unique can, if they choose, take pride in a century of remarkable Jewish accomplishments. But a serious look at those accomplishments, and an honest recognition that those accomplishments are already in decline, should quickly correct any belief that they reflect something permanently distinctive about the Jewish people.* Whatever makes Jews or Jewish culture distinctive, it cannot be their success, at least not if we consider the Jewish history before the long twentieth century or after it.

MENSCH OR MONSTER?
STEREOTYPES AND THE JEWS

Beyond pride in outsize accomplishments, the other most common version of secularized chosenness is the idea that Jews particularly reflect certain character traits. A Jew is more likely to be a mensch, say philo-Semites, using the Yiddish word that literally translates as "man" and means a person of integrity and decency, someone you can rely on to do the right thing more often than not. On the other, antisemitic side of the ledger, it is easy to find stereotypes of Jews as particularly greedy

---

* I have not even mentioned the uncomfortable fact that Jews whose ethnic origins lie in the countries of the Middle East have, for the most part, not achieved the same kinds of success on the same scale as the descendants of eastern European Jews. Their cultural experiences were radically different in their countries of ethnic origin. And the great majority of them either emigrated or were forced to emigrate to Israel around the time of the establishment of the state, where they encountered discrimination from European-origin Ashkenazi Jews.

or conniving or self-centered or clannish. (I will get to Jewish neurosis, which may be interpreted positively, negatively, or neutrally.)

No doubt the bases for both positive and negative stereotypes of Jews relate to some real-world aspects of Jewish culture, aspects that may or may not have any measurable effects but capture the imagination. The Jewish mensch is or was once imagined in the United States as a good (male) life partner for a woman, one who does not beat his wife or drink to excess. Sad (and needless) to say, there are and have always been Jewish domestic abusers and Jewish alcoholics. The stereotype never presented itself as anything more than a probabilistic judgment. In any case the truth or falsehood of the generalization would be difficult to ascertain, although perhaps not impossible.[14] The most likely possibility is that cultural norms did play a part in shaping this positive stereotype. In close-knit communities like those of Jewish eastern Europe, strong norms against drinking, for example, can have effects. Conceivably genetics also played a role in the presence or absence of Jewish alcoholism. Yet as Jewish communal solidarity shifted with urbanization and immigration, the norms against drinking (or against spousal abuse, or whatever) may have changed too.

Furthermore, to acknowledge the possibility of some background statistical support for positive Jewish stereotypes is to open the door to recognizing the possibility of similar statistical support for negative Jewish stereotypes. After all, is Jewish financial success—taken on the average, let us say, in the United States—evidence of avarice? It is a double-edged sword to use Jews' experience as economic middlemen or as moneylenders to explain their business success. And what of prominent Jews in finance who turned out to be frauds, like Bernard Madoff? It seems obvious that these should be treated as outlying cases, not evidence for the negative stereotype of the greedy, dishonest Jew.

Of course, pointing out the danger of the view that cultural stereotypes may have some basis in reality is only a cautionary argument against believing the stereotypes. It does not give a substantive reason to disbelieve the stereotypes altogether. Yet the deployment of stereotypes in such extreme ways in connection with Jews does suggest we should be extremely cautious about believing any of them. Which is more likely, that Jews are both superior and inferior, or that Jews are collectively a lot like anybody else, just more likely to be analyzed as a class and to have distinctive characteristics ascribed to them?

Here it is worth noting that antisemitic stereotypes are especially protean. The Jews, it seems, can be everything and its opposite.[15] For example, Jews can be depicted as the ultimate capitalists, and they can be depicted as the ultimate capital-destroying communists. Antisemites have used both stereotypes, sometimes at the same time. Of course, in principle, it's possible that some Jews are greedily seeking to control the world via their wealth while others are trying to control the world by ending capitalism and substituting radical leftist worker control. What is extraordinarily unlikely is that those different (imaginary) Jews are working together in some unified conspiratorial protocol.

A similar nesting of opposites can be found in other antisemitic stereotypes. Jews are described as closed, clannish, and exclusive; they are also condemned as cosmopolitan, rootless, and rejecting of any sense of belonging. Again, the stereotypes could perhaps be reconciled. Some Jews no doubt promote an exclusionary sense of community, and some Jews no doubt embrace a globalized cosmopolitanism that views all human groupings with skepticism and wants us all to be citizens of the world. Neither perspective, however, plausibly describes the great majority of Jews, who fall somewhere in between, believing that partial and parochial affiliations have their place while also believing that we have some bonds and obligations to all humans wherever they might live.

A final example of antisemitic nesting opposites comes from the realm of psychological diagnosis. Haters sometimes say the Jews are neurotic self-questioners and other times that Jews are narcissistically committed to their own superiority. Once again, it is in theory possible that Jews could manifest both sets of symptoms, thinking they are worse than everybody else and also that they are better than everybody else, depending perhaps on the specific area of life being evaluated. Yet it is hard to see how either "diagnosis" could be helpful in specifying Jewish uniqueness if each potentially cancels out the other.

A distinguished psychiatrist who is a close friend of mine (as it happens, not Jewish) once offered me a thoughtful variant on the stereotype of diagnosable Jewish neuroses. His suggestion was admirably free of negative prejudice but also was not, I think, inherently philo-Semitic. He proposed that Jews commonly display a greater degree of "interiority" than people of other ethnic or cultural backgrounds. By interiority, he meant, roughly, the quality of being aware of and in conversation with one's own inner thoughts. To have interiority on this definition is to be internally thoughtful. That thought could be unhealthily ruminative, as in neurosis or obsessive compulsiveness. It could also be healthy, as in the capacity to sit with one's own emotions instead of fleeing from them or erecting defenses against them.

Do Jews experience distinctively great interiority? And if so, why? I admit I found my friend's idea intriguing. On the surface, it seemed to account for a style of self-reflection in which Jews talk about and to themselves, individually and collectively. Perhaps, I thought, it could explain why the Jews are so obsessed with having conversations. It would account for why psychoanalysis first found favor among high-bourgeois Viennese Jews. It might even help explain why Jews have played such a disproportionate role in culture, given that what we call culture is often a record of public conversations.

On further reflection, however, it struck me how disjunct the idea of Jewish interiority was from premodern, Christian critiques of Judaism. According to a recurrent critique that goes back to the apostle Paul, the Hebrew Bible teaches a carnal, bodily religion, whereas Christianity teaches a religion of the spirit. The idea here is that the Hebrew Bible tells the Israelites how to perform God's commandments and tells them what the concrete real-world punishments are for failing to do so. Both the divine commandments and the punishments are of the body, not of the spirit. In contrast, runs the old notion, the Gospels offer a religion where the sole commandment is love and the sole punishment is to be cut off from God's love, which is the definition of damnation. According to the critique of "carnal Israel," Jewishness is all about externality and doing things. Christianity is all about interiority and the search for the elusive inner experiences of faith and love.

It does not matter, for the purposes of this analysis, whether the

Christian critique of carnal Israel is valid or not. What is striking is that for centuries, Jews were condemned by Christians for a *lack* of spiritual interiority. To describe the Jews of the modern world as distinctively in touch with their interiority is to create yet another pair of nested opposites: the Jews distinctively lack interiority and the Jews simultaneously distinctively possess interiority. From this perspective, the idea of Jewish interiority seems more like a stand-in for the idea that Jews like to talk a lot. It is not that Jews or non-Jews or any other group have more or less interiority. It's that Jews, or at least eastern European Jews and their descendants, spend a lot of time talking about their inner experience, the same way they spend a lot of time talking about everything else. That creates the impression of greater interiority but need not reflect any reality of the same.

The lesson I am drawing from this discussion of Jewish stereotypes and Jewish uniqueness is, I hope, more than the banal one that stereotypes are misleading or unhelpful. I am trying to argue that the tendency to seek after Jewish uniqueness as a secularized form of chosenness leads to extremely suspect generalizations. Those stereotypical generalizations can be framed positively or negatively. They can entail the claim that Jews are x and also simultaneously that Jews are not-x. They are, in short, a series of conceptual games, not useful contributions to cultural analysis.

In my view, then, we would do best to recognize secularized cultural claims about Jewish distinctness for what they are, historically speaking: attempts to preserve the old religious notions of Jewish chosenness—both positive and negative—for a nonreligious, secular worldview. Taken as a matter of religious faith, chosenness can hardly be contested. Taken as a set of cultural claims nominally based on observable fact, secularized chosenness is misleading, self-contradictory, and not valuable.

The same, I think, could be said about arguments for Israel's uniqueness, either positive or negative. Israel is not uniquely moral, nor is Israel uniquely immoral. The things Israel does well, ethically speaking, it shares with comparable liberal democracies. The things it does badly are also shared with comparable countries, including liberal democracies that themselves are built in part on legacies of settlement, colonization, imperialism, and discrimination.

The only aspect of the actually existing idea of Israel that makes its nation-state arguably unique is the messianic quality that Religious Zionists ascribe to its emergence. Plenty of other nation-states seek territorial expansion, often based on nationalist arguments about their maximal historical borders. (Think of Russia's claim to Ukraine or China's claim to Taiwan.) Few of them feature constituencies who believe settlement of the land is a divine duty that will lead to messianic redemption. In other words, what makes the state of Israel unique is precisely the religious belief of a meaningful number of its citizens that it is the state of the uniquely chosen people, defined religiously.

Chosenness, it turns out, is a sacred circle. If you begin by believing that the Jewish people are chosen by God, you may well end up believing (under the influence of Religious Zionism) that the state of Israel has a unique sacral character as the fulfillment of the promises God made to the Jewish people. The persistence of the Jewish religious idea of chosenness is itself the cause of Israel's uniqueness: it is (perhaps) the one modern nation-state in which many citizens believe the state is a manifestation of their chosenness. Ultimately, modern Jews' efforts to secularize chosenness have come back to this sacred conception. That belief, it seems, will not die, or in any case not yet.

III:3

THE MARRIAGE PLOT

In the modern world, since Jewish emancipation, few topics have produced more anxiety, moral anguish, and family argument among Jews than marriage between Jews and non-Jews.* It was not always thus. In the Middle Ages, when Jews lived as a minority under nonliberal Christian and Muslim rule, the different religious communities defined the rules of marriage in mutually inconsistent ways, and the status hierarchy imposed by the majority had the last word. The Catholic Church then required anybody being married under its auspices to have been baptized as a Catholic, so for a Jew to marry a Catholic in church required baptism. When, in *Merchant of Venice*, Shylock's daughter Jessica flees her father's home to marry Lorenzo, it goes without saying that she will be baptized first, as indeed Shylock himself is (forcibly) baptized by the end of Shakespeare's play.

---

* I know whereof I speak. Much of this chapter is based on my own experience, as well as the experiences of hundreds of people who have shared their stories with me over several decades during which I became a go-to Jew to discuss the issue as a result of an essay I wrote, "Orthodox Paradox," *New York Times Magazine*, July 22, 2007. I meant the essay as a love letter, albeit an honest one, to the Modern Orthodox community that raised and educated me. That is not how the essay was (mostly) read. Perhaps this time I will do better.

Meanwhile, Jewish rabbinic law did not recognize the legal possibility of marriage between Jews and non-Jews unless the non-Jewish partner formally became a Jew. For a Jew to cause someone to leave Catholicism for Judaism was an act of heresy triable by church courts and punishable by the Christian government.[1] Consequently, such defections were rare. Islamic law, in yet a third configuration, permitted Muslim men to marry Jewish and Christian women but not women who were polytheists, who would have to accept Islam; the same Islamic law prohibited Muslim women from marrying Christian or Jewish men. None of the systems recognized the possibility of civil marriage outside the jurisdiction of religion.

Things began to change with the emergence of a distinctively Protestant set of teachings about marriage. The Catholic Church had considered marriage to be a sacrament under its religious authority. Searching the Bible, some early Protestants concluded there was no scriptural sanction for this belief. They redefined marriage not as a sacrament but as a social institution. It could be performed by a minister in church, but it also took on a civil dimension, under the authority of the state.[2] This made divorce a possibility for Protestantism, as it had not been and still is not for the Catholic Church. Puritans went further, as was their wont: they affirmatively assigned marriage to the state, allowing weddings to be performed by justices of the peace. These developments opened the door to the possibility of state-recognized civil marriage.[3]

Alongside the concept of civil marriage came another Protestant idea that was also secularized into classical liberalism: the idea of marriage as a free choice, a civil contract reflecting the will of both parties. Historically, Judaism, Christianity, and Islam all nominally insisted that the act of marriage must be undertaken voluntarily, without coercion. In practice, however, medieval people of all backgrounds understood marriage to be shaped and often controlled by the couple's families. Liberalism, with its emphasis on the moral centrality of voluntary choice, helped change that perspective. Then came Romanticism, which contributed the idea that a couple marrying should think of themselves as two souls in love, destined to join each other. Romantic love gradually came to be part of the modern Western ideology of marriage, both as a necessary impetus for entering marriage and as a reason for divorcing should that love fade away.

The potent combination of voluntaristic liberalism and Romantic destiny shapes most current Western understandings of marriage. Needless to say, contemporary mainstream Western beliefs about marriage therefore may clash with religious law, whether Catholic or Muslim—or Jewish. If the couple who falls in love and chooses to marry happens to belong to the same religious tradition, there need be no conflict. But, as humans have known as long as they have recognized the emotions of romantic love, that kind of love cannot be entirely cabined to people who share the same religious, racial, ethnic, or class background. In the contemporary world, where people are meant to choose freely and marry the partners they love, a religious tradition that rejects the possibility of their union under its own laws finds itself squarely opposed to broadly held values and beliefs. To deny people who love each other the right to marry defies both liberalism and Romanticism.

The historic success of the movement for marriage equality in the West stands as a powerful confirmation of this analysis. Much of the opposition to same-sex marriage came from religious communities who objected to the validation of gay people's relationships and insisted on a definition of marriage restricted to one man and one woman. (That traditional marriage had, in many times and places, included the possibility of one man being married to several women was mostly ignored in the debate, although the issue of plural marriage is due for a comeback in the near future.*) Ultimately, the religious communities' objections failed to win the day, in the U.S. Supreme Court, in most Western European countries, and in most liberal religious denominations. Civil marriage, liberalism, and Romanticism, all working together, overcame the power of religious tradition.

---

* Already there are powerful constitutional arguments in favor of a right to marry multiple partners. What has held back any movement from actively pursuing the cause is that both political progressives and political conservatives have deep skepticism about polyamory, progressives out of feminist concerns and conservatives out of traditionalist ones. For the history of arguments on the other side, see John Witte Jr., *The Western Case for Monogamy over Polygamy* (New York: Cambridge University Press, 2015).

Different movements within Judaism have addressed the question of marriage between Jews and non-Jews, often called "intermarriage" or "interfaith marriage," differently. For Traditionalist Jews, the topic is a nonstarter. Authoritative rabbinic law denies the validity of the marriage act between a Jewish and a non-Jewish partner.

The Talmud discusses whether the prohibition on a Jewish man marrying or having sex with a non-Jewish woman is biblical or rabbinic. Its main conclusion is that the rabbis prohibited such marital and sexual relations.[4] Beyond this technical issue, at a cultural level, Traditionalists treat marriage to a non-Jew as an act of fundamental self-removal from their community. The communal taboo, in other words, goes beyond even the legal prohibition.

Progressive Jews have come to see marriage differently, although their path has been tortuous and their conclusions are relatively new ones, still subject to ambivalence and development. Reform rabbis from the beginning of the movement until the late twentieth century formally refused to sanction or officiate at marriages between Jews and non-Jews. Notwithstanding the movement's teachings on universal love and its willingness to reject Jewish legal tradition when inconsistent with its theological beliefs, Reform Judaism nevertheless reflected centuries of Jewish taboo against marrying non-Jews. To an important degree, nineteenth-century Reform Judaism in Germany was conceived as a mechanism to keep the Jewish community from disappearing via baptism and marriage to non-Jews. Keeping the prohibition on exogamy intact therefore functioned as a key tool in maintaining the boundaries of the Jewish community, even (or especially) for the Reform movement.

In America, Progressive Jews have tried various options to handle the situation of non-Jews who married Jews and then sought to participate in institutional Progressive Jewish life. Classical rabbinic law considers a Jewish woman's child to be a Jew, regardless of who the father is. In an effort to create a more egalitarian model, one that emphasized practice and choice rather than accidents of birth, both Reform and Reconstructionist Judaism experimented in the late 1960s with a new rule. According to this rule, the children of any Jewish–non-Jewish couple would be considered Jews if they were raised as Jews, regardless of whether the mother or father was the Jewish partner. Simultaneously, the children of any such couple would *not* be considered Jewish if they were not raised as Jews, even if the mother was the Jewish partner. The rule was, in other words, both more and less inclusive of who counted as a Jew than the classical rabbinic rule.[5]

The rule did not last, however. Toward the end of the twentieth century and into the twenty-first, Progressive Jewish attitudes became more fully inclusive. For one thing, practical reality demanded a new perspective. As more and more Progressive Jews married non-Jews, the institutional synagogues associated with Reform and Reconstructionist Judaism had to decide how to attract those Jews—and their spouses— into their communities. Telling such couples that their kids wouldn't be Jewish unless they joined the community was a more coercive, less attractive approach than telling them that their kids were Jews no matter what and that they were welcome to belong. From the standpoint of continued vitality, the shift was also clearly necessary. If Progressive Judaism wanted to maintain its historical role of keeping as many Jews as possible affiliated with Jewish religion, it would be far better to be able to tell the grown children of mixed couples that they were Jewish no matter what than that they were only Jewish if they had been raised Jewish.

At the level of belief, what was required for Progressive Jews was to allow the religious-cultural sentiment against marriage with non-Jews to fade away in the face of the ideals of free choice and Romantic love. If that process sounds easy in theory, the reality was not so, even for many Progressive Jews. The Jewish historical experience of living as a besieged minority created deep and powerful cultural norms that hardened into what you might call cultural instincts: not instincts in the biological sense, but learned, conditioned responses that function as powerfully as instincts. Anthropologists call such culturally conditioned responses taboos. To get a sense of how powerful the taboo against marrying non-Jews has been, even for Progressive Jews, consider that it was, and even remains, easier for many Progressive Jews to embrace gay marriage (among Jews!) than straight marriage between Jews and non-Jews. Among Evolutionist Jews (about whom more in a moment), this hierarchy is actually becoming delineated openly: an increasing number of left-Evolutionists accept some form of gay partnership but insist that it be restricted to Jews.

As the broad cultural success of the gay marriage movement shows, however, it is possible for humans to overcome conditioned responses and taboos around marriage, individually as well as collectively. That is what is in the process of happening in Progressive Jewish circles with respect to marriage between Jews and non-Jews. It is still difficult to find a Progressive rabbi who will say sincerely that she is equally happy to officiate at a wedding between a Jew and a non-Jew as she is at a wedding between two Jews. Such is the power of tradition and instinct, even among open-minded Progressives. But that is changing, slowly, as Progressive Jewish congregations include more and more non-Jewish spouses. Some of those spouses eventually choose to become Jews formally. Others, however, participate in Jewish communal life for many years, effectively performing Jewishness, without feeling the need for any ceremonial marker of their belonging.

From the standpoint of Progressive Jewish thought, the only challenge left is to reframe the acceptance of marriage between Jews and non-Jews as affirmatively positive, rather than as a concession to social reality.[6] Part of this process will interact with the long-standing Progressive Jewish commitment to Jewish continuity. An inclusive attitude can be justified by the bet that the children of such marriages will be more likely to consider themselves Jewish if the Jewish community thinks of their parents' marriage as a good thing, not a bad one. This shift would entail changing the *attitude* of concession to reality as a kind of concession to reality.

More important, however, will be a deeper religious-philosophical exploration of the value of marriage as an interpersonal partnership. Given that Progressive Jews consider universalism and egalitarianism to be basic moral values, I would predict the ultimate success of such a reframing. In the end, contemporary Western thought understands marriage as an expression of freedom, equality, and the realization of selfhood. Progressive Judaism must inevitably embrace these moral and philosophical beliefs as true and find their origins in prophetic teachings of God's love. Ultimately, Progressive Jews can and will disidentify with the strand of Jewish particularism that has historically resisted Jews marrying non-Jews. They will realize—they are already realizing—that the identity of their community can be preserved and even strengthened by declining to police its boundaries so aggressively.

Part of this process, for Progressive Jews, also involves recognizing that the medieval bright line between Jews and non-Jews does not necessarily reflect the realities of ancient Judaism, ancient Israel, or the modern age. The Hebrew Bible prohibits the Israelites from marrying the sons or daughters of the seven nations who lived in the land of Israel on their arrival,[7] but does not otherwise provide a blanket condemnation of the practice. It states that "no Ammonite or Edomite may come into the assembly of God; even the tenth generation of them may not enter the assembly of God forever."[8] But this formulation, which Rabbi Joshua, whom we met earlier in the book, treated as obsolete already in Talmudic times,[9] would seem to permit others not of those two nations to do so.

Moses marries Zipporah, the daughter of Jethro, "a priest of Midian."[10] She becomes a central figure in the Moses narrative.[11] Moses also marries a "Cushite woman."[12] His sister Miriam speaks against him because of it. In response, God appears in a pillar of smoke and tells Miriam and Aaron, Moses's brother, that Moses is his faithful servant to whom he speaks mouth-to-mouth. When the vision ends, Miriam has become "leprous, white as snow." Moses prays to God for her recovery, which is granted after she spends seven days outside the Israelite camp in recognition of her disrespecting Moses's marriage.[13]

Later on in the biblical narrative, King Solomon "loved many foreign women: the daughter of Pharaoh, Moabites, Ammonites, Edomites, Sidonites, Hittites." Some of his seven hundred wives and three hundred concubines, the book of Kings states, belonged to the peoples whom God had prohibited to the Israelites in marriage. To these women, the Bible reports, "Solomon cleaved in love."[14]

These marriages are depicted as a stain on Solomon's previously unspotted character. In his old age, the wives turned his heart after other gods, so that he followed Ashtoret, the goddess of the Sidonians, and Milkom, the god of the Ammonites. He built shrines to Chemosh, the Moabite god, and to Molekh, the Ammonite god, "on the mountain in front of Jerusalem." As a consequence of these sins, says the book of Kings, God decided to take the kingdom of Israel away from Solomon's line, leaving only the kingdom of Judah in the hands of his heirs, because of the merit of his father David. The passage is certainly a serious warning against the danger of marrying non-Jewish women and being drawn to their gods. Solomon's acts are sinful and merit severe generational punishment. Yet they are simultaneously the acts of one of the greatest kings of the Bible and reflect biblical acknowledgment of the constant presence of non-Jewish worship and non-Jewish women in the Israelite milieu.

The book of Ezra, which depicts a community of "people of Israel" who return to the land of Israel after the Babylonian exile, also reflects a deep concern with marriage between Israelites who stayed behind and were never exiled and local peoples (Canaanite, Hittite, Perizite, Jebusite, Ammonite, Moabite, Egyptian, Emorite). Ezra, speaking in the first person, says that by these marriages, "the holy seed has been mixed with the peoples of the lands." That reality causes him to tear his garments and pull the hair from his head and beard and sit stunned in fasting and prayer.[15] Once again, the biblical text condemns marriage with non-Israelite peoples, even as it acknowledges the widespread reality of that phenomenon in the world the book of Ezra describes.

Early rabbinic literature of the post–Second Temple period also reflects the possibility of Jewish–non-Jewish marriage, condemning it without formally prohibiting it.[16] The Talmud, a bit later in Jewish history, is where the technical rulings emerge that both ban marriage to a non-Jew and also classify the offspring of such unions.[17] The strong implication of all these texts is that Jewish communities in late antiquity, like Israelite communities before them, occupied a reality where many Jews and non-Jews were married to each other, even as Jewish religious authorities sought to condemn the unions.

Skipping through the Middle Ages and the early modern period to the period after Jewish emancipation, the conditions of communal interaction around the marriage question once again immediately become complicated. In nineteenth-century Germany, for example, significant numbers of Jews were baptized and yet continued to identify and be identified as Jews, ethnically if not religiously. The consequence was that Jews could marry non-Jews while still insisting on being Jewish in some form. The family of the philosopher Ludwig Wittgenstein was religiously Christian and ethnically Jewish, his grandfather Hermann Wittgenstein having been baptized. According to a family story, one of Hermann's daughters, Emilie, actually had to ask her older brother, Louis, whether the family was of Jewish origin. He answered with the French phrase *pur-sang*, which literally means "pure-blood" and also has the connotation of "beyond all doubt."[18] Whole families could become hybridized this way, or they might be partly religiously Jewish, partly religiously Christian, partly ethnically Jewish, and partly ethnically German by marriage and descent.

This complex situation has repeated itself in the United States. From the moment when substantial numbers of eastern European Jews emigrated to the United States, American Jews were concerned, not to say obsessed, with the issue of marriage to non-Jews. *Abie's Irish Rose* (1922) was a play by Anne Nichols, raised a Baptist in Georgia. It ran on Broadway for a then-record-breaking 2,327 performances. The show featured a Jewish American who marries a Catholic Irish American over the objections of their two fathers. The wedding itself, played for comedy, is repeated multiple times by a priest and a rabbi, who recognize each other from their World War I service and treat each other collegially. In the play's last act, the fathers reconcile with each other and their children.

Critics then and now consider the play ill-written and literarily unimportant. Its popularity reflected the optimistic ideology of the American melting pot, but also the emerging phenomenon of marriage between Jews and non-Jews, which intrigued as well as entertained the audience. In retrospect, the play can be seen as expressing a precursor of contemporary cultural values with respect to marriage. Marriage is depicted as inherently a free choice made by two people who love each other. Views to the contrary are treated as outdated, Old World thinking (this already a century ago). Different religious practices are seen as no bar to compatibility. Contemporary Progressive Jews now mostly agree.

This brings us to Evolutionist Jews, who have not to date really grappled with marriage between Jews and non-Jews but may have to in the near future. To the extent that Evolutionists accept the authority of rabbinic law, they must treat marriage between Jews and non-Jews as invalid from a legal perspective. That might have been the end of the matter were it not for current efforts within left-wing Evolutionism to accommodate gay partnerships. Those efforts, which are in part succeeding, will not be easily restricted to gay couples, but will raise fundamental questions for life partnership between Jews and non-Jews.

The current creative approach among Evolutionist Jewish thinkers around gay marriage has been to design new liturgical rituals and symbolic-but-formal partnership contracts. These enable gay couples to solemnize what is not technically a marriage in Jewish legal terms but is supposed to feel like one in the eyes of contemporary Western society. The Evolutionist thought leader Rabbi Steven Greenberg, whom I introduced in part I, was the first to draft a model partnership contract for gay couples to substitute for the traditional Jewish marriage contract.[19] (His approach followed a suggestion first made for feminist Progressive reasons by the Reform rabbi Rachel Adler.) A growing number of left-Evolutionist rabbis now are prepared to perform partnership-marriage ceremonies built around such contracts.

Innovating in order to facilitate gay marriage within the framework of Jewish law comes from the recognition that gay people should have the same rights and opportunities within normative Judaism as straight people. To Evolutionist Jews, once a moral position is firmly established, the goal is to evolve Jewish law to correspond to it.

At present, the left-Evolutionist rabbis and thinkers who are evolving Jewish law to create opportunities for same-sex marriage do not see the situation of gay Jews as comparable to that of straight Jews who wish to marry non-Jews. Being gay is not a choice, they would almost certainly point out. Marrying a non-Jew is. For a gay person, the only marriage option available in good conscience is to a person of the same gender. A heterosexual Jew, by contrast, may in good conscience marry a Jew of the person's preferred gender. Alternatively, the non-Jewish partner may choose to become Jewish.

This argument is logically sound. It does not, however, fully take account of the liberal-Romantic ideology according to which a couple who fall in love cannot in good conscience do other than marry each other and live together. It does not matter that the nature of their romantic attraction differs from sexual orientation. They are in love, they have chosen one another, and Jewish law, as traditionally interpreted, stands in the way of their union.

Consequently, it seems probable that Evolutionists will eventually be challenged—as Progressive Jews have been—with the arguable immorality of denying a loving couple the opportunity to be joined in a marriage that would be recognized and celebrated by their community. Unlike Progressives, left-Evolutionists will not be able to offer such couples the standard Jewish marriage ceremony. But they might well be able to offer them a partnership contract analogous to the contract adapted for gay unions. Jewish law recognizes the validity of business partnerships between Jews and non-Jews. The same spirit of legal creativity that devised the partnership contract for gay couples could be adopted for the marriage of a Jew and a non-Jew.

The barrier to the partnership contract for Jewish–non-Jewish couples would hence primarily be sociological, not Jewish-legal. Again, at present, the Evolutionist leadership is not open to such an approach. But that could change, especially if the membership in Evolutionist congregations comes to include more Jews who are partnered with non-Jews, and perhaps even their partners themselves. If this possibility shocks some readers, as it no doubt will, recall that the idea of rabbis ordained as Orthodox officiating at gay marriages seemed unthinkable thirty years ago.

CULTURAL JEWS AND MARRIAGE NORMS

If different streams of Judaism are struggling with the marriage question in different ways (or in the case of the Traditionalists, not at all), what about cultural Jews? Is there any good, justifiable reason for practitioners or exponents of bagels-and-lox Judaism to object to Jews and non-Jews marrying each other?

Let me stipulate at the outset that as an empirical matter, many cultural Jews do in fact object when their children announce an intention to marry someone who isn't Jewish. Their arguments are sometimes an ill-expressed version of the taboo, served with a dollop of Jewish guilt: "How can you do this to us?" Sometimes they say that to preserve Jewish culture, Jews really ought to marry other Jews who share the same cultural background. Occasionally one will hear an argument presented as cultural but also to a certain degree religious: citing the Holocaust, the parents may say that marriage to a non-Jew gives Hitler a posthumous victory.* Jewish survival, some cultural Jews might argue, is therefore a moral imperative, not so much an extra divine commandment as a moral consequence of the Holocaust. And, they might conclude, for Jews to marry non-Jews is to undermine the survival of the Jewish people.

Even without Fackenheim's dictum, cultural Jews may find themselves arguing for Jews to marry Jews as a matter of the maintenance of Jewish people, without whom there would (apparently) be no one to perpetuate genuine Jewish culture. This in turn raises important questions: Why, for cultural Jews, is it inherently valuable for the Jewish people to continue to exist? And if the answer is the preservation of Jewish culture, is it true that only Jews can keep Jewish culture alive?

For Jews who believe in God, no matter which version of theology they prefer, the preservation of the Jewish people surely has religious value. At a minimum, God's biblical promise to choose the Israelites, and the covenant between God and Israel that embodies that choice, imply an obligation on the part of the Jews to worship God. God in turn promises to care for the Jewish people, punishing them where necessary, sending them into exile but not destroying them outright. In the theology of the three oaths, there is even a divine promise to the Israelites that their subjugation at the hands of the nations of the world would not be "over-much," usually interpreted to mean "unbearable." The Jewish commitment to self-preservation can thus be understood, in religious terms, as the fulfillment of the commitment by the people of Israel to continue to participate in the divine covenant.

But for Jews who don't believe in God, the preservation of the

---

* Compare Rabbi Emil Fackenheim's 614th commandment, discussed in part I.

Jewish people must be justified in some other, nontheistic terms. Classical Zionism offered an answer based on nationalist Romantic ideas of each people's destiny. Genuine Romantic nationalists valued diversity, at the national level if not at the subnational level. (In fact, their most important predecessor, Johann Gottfried Herder (1744–1803), arguably invented the concept.[20]) They believed that each nation had a distinct unique national genius, and that each nation ought therefore to fulfill its destiny by expressing that genius as best it could. If a given nation failed to do so, that was a tragedy. The failure to self-express would represent a loss for the nation itself, since the whole point of being alive, according to Romanticism, is to self-actualize. But a single nation's failure to self-actualize would also represent a loss for humanity, which would lose the value of that nation's special genius.

It is still possible today to embrace the Romantic nationalist account of why the Jews as a people should continue to exist. Certainly, we continue to value cultural diversity in the broadest sense. When we hear of languages dying because too few people speak them (something that happens every year[21]), we feel sadness and pain at the loss, even if we've never heard of the language before. There is a similarity between this sense of loss and the one we feel when we hear of a species going extinct (another event that occurs much too frequently). We experience, in Romantic terms, the tragedy of the reduction of the gorgeous mosaic of multivariate existence. In these terms, the loss of the Jewish people would be a tragedy because it would impoverish the world's diversity. For Jews who think in Romantic nationalist terms, it would be a particularly great loss, because it would mean that the Jews could no longer attain their destiny of national self-realization.

The elements of this Romantic nationalist worldview that are harder to accept, especially for Jews who don't believe in God, start with the idea that the Jewish people really has some inherent destiny. We are, historically, a long way from the type of nationalism that posits this sort of collective determinism. Israel has unquestionably turned out to be a nation. As I've argued, this development shows that the Jewish people has not turned out to be a nation, but something else. To argue—without God—that the Jewish people has a necessary destiny seems so mystical that it calls out for some theory of *why*. Romantic nationalism offered an answer, but without it the answer is much harder to glimpse.

Then there is the implicit assumption that if a people ceases to exist, its culture dies with it. That is not always true. Consider ancient Greece, which produced literature, philosophy, science, art, architecture, and more. Ancient Greek civilization had a good run among the ancient Greeks. And its ideas, values, and literature have lived on long after the Hellenes (the people, or maybe peoples) who created them ceased to exist as a distinctive group. First Alexander the Great (who was Macedonian) spread Greek civilization throughout his vast empire. Then Greek civilization transfused Roman civilization, which spread even farther afield. Some parts of ancient Greek civilization, especially philosophy, were incorporated into Islamic thought in the Middle Ages. Greek civilization was rediscovered in Europe via the Renaissance (alongside Roman civilization), not that it had ever been entirely forgotten. Eighteenth- and nineteenth-century Britons and Americans came to identify with the Greeks and Romans, which is how the Lincoln Memorial (completed in 1920) and the U.S. Supreme Court building (completed in 1935) came to be surprisingly faithful versions of Greek temples.

It emerges that ancient Greek civilization has persisted without ancient Greeks. True, nineteenth-century Greek nationalists laid claim to ancient Greek heritage as part of their Romantic nationalist project. But as even their supporters (many of them Englishmen enamored of ancient Greece) noted, the connections between ancient Greeks and modern Greeks were attenuated.* The point is that ancient Greek civilization would continue to matter today even if modern Greece had never emerged from the decline of the Ottoman Empire.

There can be little doubt that ancient Israelite civilization, as recorded in the Bible, would similarly continue to exist without the Jews. After all, the Bible and its associated narratives fundamentally shaped Christianity and Islam. Within Christianity, there is a recurrent phenomenon of groups of Christians coming to identify with ancient Israel.

---

* In fact, the degree of connection may be compared to that between ancient Israel and Jewish nationalists of the nineteenth century.

(Two famous examples are the Massachusetts Bay Puritans, who saw themselves as Israelites on a divine "errand into the wilderness,"[22] and the Church of Jesus Christ of Latter-day Saints, which established a durable new Zion in Salt Lake City.[23])

Christians in far-flung times and places have found themselves slipping into what orthodox Christian theology calls the "Judaizing" heresy. That is, they begin to believe that they must obey the commandments of the Hebrew Bible, from which orthodox Christianity considers them to have been liberated by Christ's sacrifice. Such Christians sometimes go so far as to begin to think of themselves as Israelites or Jews, a phenomenon I mentioned in part II in connection with the Ethiopian Beta Israel. This generates a kind of reemergence of certain aspects of Jewish or Israelite identity, even without a role for other Jews in the process.

Admittedly, the influence of late antique and medieval Jewish civilization in a world without Jews would certainly be considerably less. The Mishnah and the Talmud and the midrash and the rest of the vast body of medieval and modern Jewish literature are far less accessible than the Bible. They are far, far less relevant to non-Jewish societies, past or present.

Yet recall that "cultural Jews" rarely advert to this literature either. For them, Jewish culture is usually defined to include ideas and values and attitudes shaped over the past two hundred years, since Jewish emancipation in Europe: critical thinking, argumentation, thirst for knowledge, and the arguably Jewish teachings of Marxism, Freudianism, and so forth. All these practices, ideas, and values would continue to exist without self-identified Jews to perpetuate them.

The upshot is that cultural Jews cannot easily justify the value of perpetuating the Jewish people just to preserve Jewish culture, at least not without God. Even granting Jewish culture its special role in contributing to global civilization, Jewish culture could go on without Jews. Bagels and lox are not themselves of inherent Jewish value. They acquired Jewish meaning because they were eaten by Jews. Like essentially all Jewish cuisine (except maybe matzah, the bread of affliction eaten on Passover), bagels and lox are transient manifestations of non-Jewish foodways that

were adapted and adopted by Jews. Bagels ultimately derive from southern Germany, if linguistic etymology is any guide. And lox is such an
old name for smoked or cured salmon that it is actually proto-Indo-
European, still used in all the living Scandinavian languages as it is in
Yiddish and (increasingly rarely) in English.

Perhaps a slightly different argument could be made by Reconstructionist Jews, those Progressives who do not (necessarily) believe in God
but nevertheless adhere to Jewish practices and liturgy in the fulfillment
of the ideal of "Judaism as a civilization." For Reconstructionists, the
value of Jewish practice lies ultimately in its cultural-spiritual meaning
to them as Jews. They seek to perpetuate Jewish civilizational culture,
understood in their distinctive terms, because they believe that doing so
enhances their own lives, not because of the contribution Jewish civilization is supposed to make to the world at large.

So if Reconstructionist Jewish parents were to advise their child
against marrying someone non-Jewish, a charitable reconstruction of
their intention might run something like this: We in our lives have
found meaning and purpose through engagement with the practices
and rituals of Jewish religious culture, even if we don't exactly believe in
God. To make that kind of civilizational or cultural engagement work,
it helps a lot to have two partners who both participate in and share
that set of traditions and practices. We raised you this way. We believe
that you, too, will continue to benefit from our kind of Reconstructionist engagement with Jewishness. We think that will be harder with a
partner who does not identify as a Jew. So we are not saying that you
must marry a Jew in order to perpetuate the Jewish people and achieve
some greater good. We are, rather, saying that by marrying a Jew, you
will enable yourself to continue in our footsteps. What's more, we think
that is all Jewishness has ever been: a series of people following in their
parents' footsteps.

To this sort of entreaty, the Jew who wants to marry a non-Jew could
make one of several replies. She could say, "My partner is fully committed to joint participation in my culture and rituals, so there is nothing
for you to worry about, Mom and Dad." If that's true, she deserves to

win the argument. (Not that real-world arguments are won and lost in this way, but more on that in a moment.)

Or she could say to her Reconstructionist parents, "I acknowledge the challenge you are describing. I acknowledge the risk that if I marry someone who is not Jewish, it will be more difficult for me to achieve a meaningful, engaged experience of civilizational Judaism. I acknowledge it will be harder for me to pass on that set of experiences to my children. But these are risks I am prepared to take. I will do my best to pass on the version of the tradition that is meaningful to me."

Then would come the kicker: "If I do not manage to create an environment in which my children feel the same kinds of connections to Jewish ritual practice as you and I do, it won't be a tragedy. Jewish practice and culture are wonderful for anyone who, like me or like you, finds them meaningful. But if someone does not find them meaningful, *that's okay*. It's not like we as Reconstructionists believe that there is a God who will be angry or disappointed. There is just the Jewish people, doing some version of what it's always done. If fewer of the Jewish people do so, that's all right with me."

At this point, it's entirely possible that the parents might pull out the last card in their nominally rational argument: the "what if everybody else did it" card. "Surely you see," they might say, "that if all Jews felt as you did, then there would be no Judaism left. And surely the passing away of Jewish civilization would be tragedy."

To this the Jew who seeks to marry a non-Jew might reply, "Yes, *that* would be tragic. But fortunately, not all Jews do feel as I do. Many actually believe in God and perpetuate Jewishness for that reason. Since we don't believe in God, and there isn't much we can do about that, we should not bear the burden of communal preservation that others are prepared to carry."

Alternatively, she might respond, "No, I don't see what would be so tragic if civilizational Judaism ceased to exist. If I believed in God, I might think the end of Jewish civilization represented a violation of the divine will. But the very idea of Judaism as a civilization presumes that Judaism is a civilization like others. Civilizations rise and fall; it's what they do. Reconstructionism is a humanist approach to religion. If there were, as a voluntary matter, no Jews, there would be no humans harmed by there not being any Jews." From the standpoint of Reconstructionism, I do not think there is a powerful answer to be made to this argument. Without God, Jewishness is a civilizational or cultural construct that has inherent value for its participants and for the rest of the world. But it has no supervening need to exist beyond the humans who value it, and who will sustain the Jewish people in whatever way they decide is best.

TRIBALISM AND ITS CONTENTS

Anyone who has ever been anywhere near this kind of marriage argument between Jewish parents and their adult children knows that my stylized model is far from reality. In real life, both sides draw upon religious and rational arguments. But lurking in the near background is a particular affect, the affect I associate with group identity. The parents, in all of my examples, are invoking that group identity in trying to convince their children not to violate the group's solidarity. The talk of God or the Law or Jewish civilization can ring hollow, even among Traditionalist Jews who literally believe in and fear a personal deity whose laws will be violated by their child's marriage to a non-Jew.

What are we to make of the powerful impulses to group identity and solidarity that are felt by many Jews today, regardless of their other beliefs about religion or culture or civilization? From the standpoint of rationalism or cosmopolitan universalism, these impulses are unappealing or even morally wrong. They can be characterized as tribalism, a term that in Western society usually has negative connotations. Tribalism is the word we usually use when we are trying to conjure up the worst aspects of group solidarity. It's the pejorative word we use when we are trying to describe patterns that led Hutus to kill Tutsis in Rwanda or Burmese Buddhists to kill Rohingya Muslims in Myanmar. When we use it to describe Jewish attitudes toward non-Jews, you can be sure we are criticizing those attitudes as crude, premodern, and potentially dangerous. If non-Jews call Jews "tribal," Jews' hackles go up, and they wonder if they are being subjected to antisemitism.

It doesn't take much thought to condemn the kind of tribalism that leads people to kill their neighbors for no reason except that they are different and hated. But is tribalism always so terrible? Is there something inherently harmful about group identification by a combination of birth and culture and myth and belief? In this context, I'm asking the question with respect to marriage between Jews and non-Jews. Yet the question has far greater implications because it goes directly to the fundamental question of Jewishness.

Here's the problem. No matter how you define it, the Jewishness of the Jewish people entails *some* degree of differentiation from other peoples. To that extent, Jewish peoplehood necessarily has a whiff of tribalism associated with it. No matter how hard Progressive Jews have tried to make Judaism into a choice-based religion, it still isn't the same as Christianity or Islam, which as an official matter base membership solely on an act of faith. The ethnic or communal or kinship aspects of Jewishness keep finding their way back into the picture. The very notion of Jews as a people—not a community of the faithful like the Islamic *ummah* or a mystical union of believers like the Catholic Church—implies that there is more than belief at stake, and less. The challenge, put bluntly, is: How can the Jewish people be distinguished from a Jewish tribe?

One possible approach is to find and embrace the good parts of tribalism. Not all kinship-based groups are bad. Families are kinship-based, in part. And while some families are terrible, others can be life-giving and life-affirming. We measure the worth of a family by how it does its job of being a family, not by disqualifying the whole category altogether. As I suggested earlier in part III, families are not *entirely* based on biological kinship, not ever. Neither are tribes. All families bring in members by marriage or other kinds of partnership and by associational acts like adoption. Same for tribes. Biological kinship always coexists with other forms of affiliation. If families aren't always bad, perhaps tribes aren't always bad either.

This much of the argument is not only defensible but plausible. We all know what it's like to feel special bonds to our family. So it doesn't take a great leap of imagination to recognize that we can feel tribal bonds that are analogous, even if less intense or immediate. What is trickier is to embrace aspects of tribalism that are, in an important way, irrational.

Rooting for a sports team, especially a sports team you grew up with, is an example of harmless, irrational affective and emotional adherence that can confer meaning on one's life. Since I'm a Bostonian, the examples come readily to my mind. I root for the Red Sox, the Celtics, the Bruins, and the Patriots just because I do, and because it's a point of solidarity with the people around me. What's more, Bostonians take our support for our teams into the diaspora. You can see lots of us rooting for the Red Sox in games played all over the country, especially in warm places. If the local team is new or doesn't enjoy deep-seated and broad support, it's not unheard of for Boston fans to be louder at away games than the home fans. When I lived in New York, which is only a couple hundred miles from Boston, there was a bar around the corner from me in the West Village that was in all respects a Boston sports bar. You went there to be with other Bostonians doing what we do when we watch our teams play: fretting and arguing and yelling and drinking and second-guessing, a strange but perhaps not unfamilial combination of love and rage mixed together.

A sociologist might say that rooting for a local sports team confers functional advantages on the fans who do it. That's clearly correct in Boston. Very different Bostonians can create instant solidarity by discussing their teams without having to negotiate the potentially perilous territory of class or neighborhood. (Race is a different matter, especially given Boston's shameful history and only slightly better present.) In Boston, people use sports talk as a social equalizer and to grease the wheels of communication, either because we were surrounded by that practice or else have consciously realized its benefits.

That professing allegiance to a sports team creates solidarity does not make that affiliation fully rational. It's one thing to follow sports enough to be able to talk about it, like the weather. It's another to feel—actually feel—joy when your team wins and sadness when it loses. And often enough, if you're a Patriots fan, the experience of supporting the team has come into conflict with the moral values you hold in ordinary life. In the conflict, it's hard not to support the team over what you would ordinarily consider to be right. I know I do. (I will say no more. This book is controversial enough already.[24])

Allegiance to a sports team is a further instance of (relatively) harmless tribalism, based mostly on geography. Of course Jews who want their children to marry other Jews aren't *just* acting like sports fans. They are reflecting a deeper sense of group solidarity, one felt, as it were, in the body. They want their children to belong to the same kinship group as they do in some way partly because they think of their children *as part* of their bodies (whether biological or adopted doesn't matter, as any adoptive parent could tell you).

Tribalism has a lot to do with the body. Many tribes throughout the world and throughout history have used body modification as a primary marker of group identity. To have the tribal marker—a particular kind of scar or tattoo or piercing—is to inscribe tribal membership on and in the body. It is no coincidence that Western Enlightenment culture reacted negatively to such body modifications, which it identified with tribalism. Nor is it surprising that so-called neoprimitives today embrace body modification to express their resistance to hegemonic Western cultural norms that they experience as alienating.[25]

Body modification has been central to Jewish identity from its origins in the Israelite past to the present. The Bible introduces the obligation of male circumcision long before it depicts God giving the commandments to Moses. In the book of Genesis, God commands Abraham, the progenitor of the Israelites, to circumcise himself and his sons and his household. The circumcision, God explains, "shall be a sign of the covenant between you and me." This is not a metaphor. Through circumcision, the covenant is literally inscribed in the flesh as a visible sign.* When Moses fails to circumcise his son, God himself seeks his death. Moses is saved only by the fast thought and action of his wife Zipporah, who circumcises their son with a flint knife and abates the danger.[26]

Christianity, of course, ultimately repudiated physical circumcision. It substituted the metaphorical circumcision of the heart (itself a motif

---

* The ancient Near Eastern cylinder seal is surely relevant here. The infant's penis, like the similarly sized and shaped cylinder, is inscribed with a distinctive pattern that becomes the visible sign of the agreement/covenant, in the way that an inscribed seal would be used to mark an agreement.

found in the Hebrew Bible) as part of its movement toward universalizing Christian faith and superseding the bodily, carnal religion of Israel. The preservation of circumcision for Jews thus became distinctive
in Europe (although not in the Muslim world). As the Jews preserved
circumcision despite background pressures of Christianity, circumcision
came to be the most obviously embodied element of "primitive" Jewish
tribalism.[27]

A few early German Jewish reformers recognized the "barbarism"
(we might say tribalism) of circumcision. They contemplated the possibility of abolishing it along with other aspects of Judaism that fell short
of their ideal of moral-rational faith.[28] Reform Judaism held back from
an outright ban for complex reasons. Most basically, Reform leaders did
not think that those who wished to remain Jews would be prepared to
accept a ban on circumcision, even as Reformers eliminated Hebrew
from the synagogue service and experimented with Sunday worship.
Subsequently, every form of organized Judaism has maintained circumcision, and it has persisted even among the overwhelming majority of
cultural Jews.

Today, some Jews once again are organizing against circumcision,
taking prominent roles in anticircumcision coalitions seeking to effectuate
local bans in the United States. (In Europe, the situation is very different.
Jews and Muslims have come together to resist proposed circumcision
bans in northern European countries.) In the spirit of liberalism, they
reason that even if there were nothing inherently wrong with tribalist
male circumcision, it would require the adult consent of the person being circumcised, and therefore must be banned for people under the age
of eighteen. A further argument invokes medicine to claim that male
circumcision is inherently harmful to male sexual health and functioning. This argument usually also entails cultural comparison. Its exponents maintain that male circumcision is a form of genital mutilation,
comparable to female genital mutilation, which is banned in essentially
all Western countries and many non-Western ones. This perspective is
closer to being a rejection of tribalism, especially because female genital
mutilation is characteristically (perhaps stereotypically) associated with
actual tribal practices in Africa, the Middle East, and parts of Asia.

It is of course possible that attitudes toward male circumcision might change among Jews, reflecting a more universalist and cosmopolitan viewpoint. (The medical arguments against circumcision are much less likely to convince Jews, since they have been debated extensively for a thousand years.) For now, however, the inroads anticircumcision thinking has made seem to be short. This indicates, I think, that the great majority of Jews, including those who think of themselves as enlightened and liberal, are comfortable enough with the tribalism inherent in male circumcision.

They recognize, below the surface, that circumcision cannot really be justified on rational grounds. It is, in the end, a deeply ingrained group practice, one that is also doubtless bound up in the psychosexual phenomenology of fathers and sons. I know plenty of Jews who wince at the thought of circumcision, prefer not to attend circumcision rituals, or feel faint when they do. But mostly, these Jews choose to circumcise their sons, if they have them. Perhaps they cannot precisely say why. The real answer is that they do it because it has always been done, and because it is definitional for their conception of (male) Jewishness.

The persistence of circumcision is, then, surely one of the most powerful indicators of persistent tribalism in Jewish thought and practice. Can it shed light on the question of marriage between Jews and non-Jews? At one level, the answer is yes. Otherwise rational and cosmopolitan Jews who bridle at the thought of their children marrying non-Jews, even without what they would themselves consider a good argument for it, are demonstrating tribalism. This is the same tribalism that those same Jews probably demonstrated in having their sons circumcised. Culturally conditioned instinct is culturally conditioned instinct. Totem is totem. Taboo is taboo.

So a Jewish parent who, without being able to say quite why, embraces circumcision and rejects Jewish marriage to a non-Jew, may be a Jew who is comfortable with a degree of tribalism. That parent's most honest answer to the child who proposes to marry a non-Jew would be, "I just don't want you to. It's against the traditions of the tribe. It's taboo. It doesn't feel right."

Nothing is wrong with this answer. Things get a bit more complicated if the child's response pits romantic love, voluntary choice, and the negative aspects of tribalism against the parents' honest invocation of tribal feeling. What we are then left with is what might be called *default* tribalism: tribalism that remains in effect unless it is overwhelmed or overcome by some other set of powerfully held values. In the case of circumcision, neither the argument from voluntarism nor the argument from medical harm seems to have sufficient weight to convince the great majority of Jews to give up their tribal practice. In the case of marriage to non-Jews, however, the arguments on the other side seem to be more powerful, particularly for Jews who are not Traditionalists or Evolutionists. In the United States, the rate of Jewish marriage to non-Jews has continued to rise consistently, reaching around 50 percent. Israeli Jews nearly always marry other Jews, but some evidence suggests that if they leave Israel, their likelihood of doing so begins to conform to the norms that exist outside Israel.

Nevertheless, it remains improbable that marriages between Jews and non-Jews would eliminate or even substantially reduce the Jewish population worldwide, especially if Jewishness is defined by self-identification and not by Traditionalist Jewish law. For one thing, studies suggest that a substantial and continuously growing number of the children of Jews who marry non-Jews identify as Jews, more than in previous generations. For another, birth rates among Traditionalist Jews remain disproportionately high. Even if some number of the children of Jews cease to identify as Jews, Traditionalists will make up the slack.

The old adage remains true: the one thing that each generation of Jews has in common with every other is the complete confidence that it is the last.

US AND THEM

Not so far beneath the surface of the taboo against Jews marrying non-Jews lies buried the division that haunts the whole topic of Jewish peoplehood: the division between Us and Them. No group of any kind or of any size is free of this specter. Carl Schmitt, a repugnant, antisemitic genius (yes, they exist), asserted that all genuinely political actions and motives can be reduced to the distinction between friends and enemies.[29] Schmitt, who joined the Nazi Party and served as Adolf Hitler's constitutional lawyer (as long as Hitler needed a constitutional lawyer), understood perfectly that, according to Aristotle, humans can be defined as political animals. If to be human is to be political and to be political is to divide the world into ultimate friends and ultimate enemies, then humans are the animal of Us and Them. The thought is horrifying, like most of Schmitt's. It is also just plausible enough to be possibly true.

Suppose Jewish peoplehood entails some division of the world into Us, people who count as Jews, and Them, people who don't. What then? I've struggled with this question as long as I've been able to articulate it. On the one hand, it can't always be morally wrong to divide the world up into Us and Them. All human beings and all human societies do it frequently. Essentially all people consider some such divisions to be appropriate, at least when they are the divisions that those people consider to be relevant and important.

Even empathy itself, that extraordinary virtue and important human faculty, can only exist if I have divided the world into myself and the other people for whom I have empathy. To have empathy for myself is, strictly speaking, a contradiction, or maybe a metaphor intended to teach us something. Ideally, I should care about myself just because I am myself, not because I'm so self-divided that first I must think of myself as someone else and only then feel care for that person.

On the other hand, there are conditions and circumstances in which it feels wrong—ethically and morally wrong—to divide the world into Us and Them. Love seems like one of those domains. Maybe it is even the most important such domain. To love another person most meaningfully, says Aristotle, is to love that person for what is best in the person's character or soul.[30] What makes you a member of an Us or a Them isn't your truest soul, or not usually. Membership comes from who you were born to, or the community you choose, or perhaps what you believe. Those are all important elements of your selfhood and character.

They aren't, however, ultimately what makes you you. To use Aristotle's terminology a last time, in most instances the things that make you part of an Us or a Them seem like accidental aspects of who you are, not your essence.

Love, in its highest form, should be about essence. Yes, as an ordinary human being, I may love someone partly for how the person looks or laughs or sings or thinks or how the person makes me feel. Ideally, however, if I love someone truly, it should be for reasons that transcend these accidental features of the person. I would love the person even if those accidental features changed, because I love the person's soul.

If this is right, even partly, then there is something troubling about saying that I can only love someone if the person is part of my Us, not if the person is part of my Them. I meet someone. We speak. We connect. We go deep, eventually or quickly. We discover things in one another that arouse genuine love of one another's souls. Could we, should we, then say, "Our connection cannot be complete, because we are not part of the same Us"?

In the premodern world, before liberalism or Romanticism, it may have been possible to answer this question by explaining that the truest, highest form of love had nothing to do with marriage. Aristotle was describing loving friendship between men, whom he believed (in the benighted sexist way of the ancient Athenians) were the only sex capable of this kind of true love. For him, marriage fulfilled other functions. In this Aristotle was not alone. Many, probably most civilizations throughout history have conceptualized marriage as fulfilling a range of purposes potentially different from the deepest and truest love between people: functions like household partnership, companionship, familial alliance, procreation, and child rearing. If marriage is seen from this perspective, it is not so strange to say that people should only be married to another if they belong to the same Us. People may love each other even if they don't belong to the same Us, but love and marriage are not the same thing, and indeed are not inherently connected.

To be sure, for as long as we have records of literature, humans have fallen in love and wanted to marry each other, even when they belonged to a different Us. Shakespeare's depiction of Romeo and Juliet's forbidden love was powerful when written precisely because it was not only an invention of love but an artistic depiction of an utterly familiar situation. People fall in love with the wrong partners in the Bible and in ancient Greek epic and drama and in Hindu classics and pre-Islamic Arab poetry and beyond. The common lesson of all those literatures, however, is ordinarily that love and marital partnership cannot invariably go together. The distinction between Us and Them generally wins. That's the tragedy. It's devastating.

To us moderns or postmoderns or whatever it is that we are today, the picture feels and looks different. We believe firmly that *it should be possible* to choose one's love as one's partner. Things might not work out, we know. Contemporary Western society has divorce rates unimagined in the great majority of other societies that have existed throughout history, maybe precisely because we want love and marriage to go together forever. Yet we persist in believing that the confluence of voluntary choice and Romantic attachment ought to be followed. To deny people the opportunity to marry whom they choose and whom they love seems to us inhuman and cruel.

Never mind that there exists a tension, even a contradiction, between our liberal, voluntary idea about the freedom to choose a partner and the Romantic belief that you precisely cannot choose whom you love, because it just happens. We believe both of those things with equal certainty and confidence. We cannot do otherwise, or at least we do not choose to believe otherwise.*

Seen through the lens of our complex, partly contradictory beliefs about love and marriage, it does not feel ethically right to say that we will only marry people who count as our Us. This poses the most fundamental problem for the Jewish taboo against marrying a non-Jew. When our tribalism or our taboos do not contradict our most strongly held

---

* Notice that there is a close parallel between how we today think about love and faith. As liberals, we believe in the right to choose one's faith. Yet at the same time, we understand that faith often feels involuntary, like you cannot will yourself into belief. These ideas are in tension with each other. Welcome to liberalism.

beliefs, we feel comfortable keeping them. When they do, we feel the taboos must go.

If there were a simple answer to this problem, I would give it. I fear there is not. It would be so wonderful to quote my grandmother: "It's as easy to fall in love with a rich girl as a poor girl," and transpose the adage (which, it turns out, isn't Yiddish*) to say, "It's as easy to fall in love with a Jewish girl (or guy) as a non-Jewish girl." But of course, the subtext of the adage is surely that its text is quite wrong. If love were a voluntary choice, it would be true. Jews could restrict their loves (and maybe their acquaintanceships, just to be safe) to other Jews, and then no difficulties would arise. But once we treat love as, to a degree, beyond our control, then we need to acknowledge that we love whom we happen to love. And if we want to be able to choose to marry that person, then we might find ourselves in conflict with the taboo.

The issue is not one of willpower but of ethical values. A Jew can choose not to marry someone who is not Jewish, even if they are in love. The question is whether doing so would violate a core tenet of living well, namely giving that love a chance to manifest itself through an aspirationally lifetime partnership.

For those whose faith in God is clear, the challenge does not necessarily disappear. If God prohibits the union, it does not follow that it cannot go forward. Rather, the marriage can go forward only in outright rebellion against the divine decree or in shamefaced recognition of the sin against God's law. Both stances are painful. And both are possible. Similarly, if God deems us all universally part of the same human race and rejects such differentiation, then the union is blessed, and yet some residual taboo may nevertheless weigh against it. For those whose faith is less resolute, the uncertainty will be more challenging still.

Perhaps the only advice I can give—not that you've asked for it—is that whatever course seems best to you, there is wisdom in empathizing

* See William Makepeace Thackeray, *The History of Pendennis* (1848–1850): "Remember, it is as easy to marry a rich woman as a poor woman." And Thackeray was not the first to say it either. See *The Yale Book of Quotations*, ed. Fred R. Shapiro (New Haven: Yale University Press, 2006), 754.

with those who choose to live otherwise. In the mystical tradition of the Kabbalah, the union of the loving couple is the central metaphor for the mystical union of the godhead; that is, such a union symbolizes the very purpose of existence itself. It is, in this mystical tradition, a transmutation of differences into oneness and wholeness. Its stakes are cosmic. It is not the fate of the Jewish people that rests on its accomplishment. It is the fate of the world as a whole.

III:4

STRUGGLING TOGETHER
WITH GOD

Is there a way to be Jewish today that brings together God, Israel, and Jewish peoplehood and that is available to Jews with very different conceptions of all three? If you've read this far, you won't be surprised to hear that my approach comes wrapped in Maimonides's teaching in his *Guide of the Perplexed* that to make sense of it all, we must both use reason and also simultaneously recognize the limits of our reason. We must think clearly and logically to find truth. We must not commit the error of believing there are definitive proofs for everything, or that everything we cannot prove is necessarily untrue. I cannot prove my answer with perfect and full demonstration. It can be criticized and rejected. If it contains contradictions, they are probably (certainly!) my own. Nevertheless, I owe it to you, my reader, to try. I also owe it to myself.

The answer that resonates for me brings us back to Jacob. Specifically, it brings us back to Jacob on the morning after the all-night struggle in which he saw Elohim face-to-face. On that morning, Jacob saw someone else face-to-face for the first time in many years. It was his brother Esau, whom he had not met since the day he stole Esau's blessing and fled his father's house some twenty years before.[1]

In that period, the book of Genesis recounts, Jacob had worked for his cousin Laban for seven years to earn the right to marry his beloved Rachel and for another seven years after Laban tricked him into marrying Leah instead. After that, Jacob, Leah, Rachel, and Jacob's two other wives, Bilhah and Zilpah, remained in Laban's house long enough for a total of twelve children, eleven boys and a girl, to be born.

When the time came for Jacob and his family to leave Laban, Jacob found he had to engage in yet another act of trickery to get what he believed (and that God told him) was rightfully his. In a kind of repetition compulsion of his initial flight from Esau and his home, Jacob fled again, this time not alone but with his family and livestock. The family went west, heading for Canaan. To get there from Mesopotamia, they would have to pass through the land of Se'ir, the field of Edom, where Esau dwelt.

Jacob feared his brother Esau. When he heard that Esau was coming to meet him with four hundred men, he divided his camp into two, so that half might survive if the other were struck down. To propitiate his brother, he sent him in advance hundreds of sheep and goats, camels and cattle and asses. It was on the brink of a familial showdown that he remained alone at night and met the man or angel or god or God with whom he struggled.[2]

The climactic meeting between the two brothers did not go the way Jacob anticipated. Terrified that Esau would punish him for his past treachery, Jacob arrayed his family before Esau and prostrated himself seven times as a mark of submission. But here is what happened instead, delivered in the famously stripped-down narrative style of the book of Genesis: "Esau ran toward him and embraced him and fell on his neck and kissed him and they cried." In place of confrontation, Jacob found love and reconciliation. When he offered his worldly goods to Esau, his brother replied, "I have much. My brother, may what you have be yours."[3]

I have always been moved by this scene of brotherly love and tears, even more than by Joseph's tears when he reencounters Jacob after many years of absence, in another chapter of the family's painful story.[4] What is so striking is the purity of the forgiveness demonstrated by Esau. Jacob had wronged him, by his lights and their father's. They had struggled mightily with each other. But they were still family. Esau calls Jacob his brother. After years of separation, brothers embrace. They kiss. They cry.

Esau's embrace of Jacob echoes the action of the being or Being who wrestled with Jacob the night before. The Hebrew words for "embrace" and "wrestle" are separated by just one letter of their three-letter roots.[5] The biblical text uses the linguistic parallel to underscore the physical parallel. In the space of a night and a day, Jacob has been embraced in struggle and in love. He has struggled in embrace with God and been embraced by family with whom he has struggled.

Here, for me, lies the entry point for a Jewishness that is both familial *and* oriented toward the divine. To be a Jew, in this sense, is ultimately not, or not only, something one does alone. To be a Jew is also to struggle with God *together*, as a family, embracing one another. Sometimes, when we are very fortunate, we might feel, too, the experience of embracing the divine and being embraced by it.

That is why the word "Israel," the name given to Jacob to memorialize his struggle, is more a collective noun than a personal name for Jacob. It is why we, and the rabbis, and the whole of the Jewish tradition call the individual *Jacob* but call his family the children of *Israel*. In encountering and struggling with God and becoming *Yisra'el*, he who strives with 'El, the individual becomes a people.

In turn, God's covenant joins the people of Israel to God. Indeed, it is precisely the covenant with God that turns the individual descendants of Jacob into the Israelite people. The biblical covenant starts with God's promise to the forefathers to make their children many, like the stars in the sky. Their collective relationship with God is what joins the people of Israel to one another. This covenant is more than a contract. It is, in the Bible and beyond, the strong force that joins God and Israel and the Jewish people.

In the picture I am painting, it is crucially important that God *and* the people *and* individual Jews all figure. Sometimes one must struggle with the divine, or with its absence, alone, like Jacob, and like Rabbi Steven Greenberg's early literary persona Yaakov Levado, "Jacob Alone."[6] Most mysticism and most accounts of religious experience recognize this lonely aspect of the search for transcendent experience. To pray, to meditate, to reason, to reflect: all these begin to occur within the self, within the soul, alone.

But one who always and only struggles alone cannot genuinely partake in the collectivity that is marked by the name Israel. There can be no fully alone, fully private Jewish experience, as there can be no fully alone, fully private language.[7] To be Jewish requires communication and connection with others. To communicate and connect requires others, requires a family, requires people. In the morning, Jacob finds his brother and finds embrace and love. "It is not good for man to be alone."[8] Greenberg, in his career, went from depicting the loneliness of Jacob alone to designing a new ritual of partnership and togetherness, a ritual for creating a nuclear family within the framework of the family-people that is Israel.

Similarly, a nationalism that tries to take God out of the picture and transmute Jewishness into an expression of pure peoplehood will not provide access to experiences of transcendent meaning that make life worth living. To live only for the group's survival is a strategy of evolutionary cooperation. It is not a reason for being that can suffice for thinking humans capable of asking the question, why? For it to be worthwhile for the family of Jews to survive, the humans who make up that family must be joined in acts of meaning making. They must be oriented, somehow, to the divine, understood as that which would transcend mere existence.

Like all humans, Jews need others, need family, to prosper: If we are not for ourselves, who will be for us? But, also like other humans, Jews need to make sure their connection to others is oriented toward something greater, some power capable of helping us imagine love and kindness and compassion: If we are only for ourselves, what are we? God, understood however we may choose, stands for that aspiration to encompassing love that reaches all beings. The nation, I am afraid, loves only itself and its members. At its best, it merely tolerates others.

What we need, therefore, is a Jewishness that enables us, as a people-family, to engage together and alone in the collective and individual experiences of embrace and struggle with and alongside God. By thinking and speaking and feeling and being and, yes, arguing, we fulfill our part of the covenant. By being Jewish, Jews are seeking to fulfill God's will, even if they doubt or disbelieve in God. We are trying to chart a course for what to do and how to live. We as Jews can accomplish that by gathering in our familial and collective settings to try to make sense of our world and our experience.

The first of those settings is, always, the home. Jewishness begins at home with our immediate family. The *Shema'*, the most fundamental element of the Jewish liturgy, drawn from Deuteronomy, enjoins us:

> You shall love the Lord your God with all your heart and
> all your soul and all your might. These words which I command
> you today shall be on your heart. You shall inculcate them to
> your children, and speak of them when you sit in your house
> and when you walk upon the way and when you lie down and
> when you arise.

I remember my father teaching me these words while we walked to the synagogue on the Sabbath, thus doubly fulfilling the biblical commandment. In fact, in my (fallible) memory, I can mark the precise spot where he first taught it to me, about a block from our house, climbing the hill toward the pond.

This love of God is a walking meditation—and a sleeping one, and a rising one, and one for all the moments of our lives. It is a particularly Jewish meditation, because it entails reflecting on words, words that are also laws. That means the meditation can issue forth in debate and disagreement. It means that *debate is itself an expression of loving God.* To disagree is to seek meaning. The meaning sought is the meaning of God's words, the Jews' only remaining evidence of God's will. In that debate, we struggle with one another, with and alongside God. And we do it together, embracing, as a family.

The Sabbath table is a rich weekly setting for teaching and learning and experiencing the struggle with and alongside God together. The family is united by presence and enlivened by discussion. The reason for being there is to acknowledge the rhythm of the week, which mimics and recalls the rhythm of God's acts of creation and rest. On the Jews'

Sabbath, when you pause, you reflect. When you reflect, you talk. There is no fixed agenda, except that some form of Torah is expected. That Torah can lead to or can consist in discussions of values, politics, and Jewish life. Disagreement is normal, because Torah calls for discussing and disagreeing about its own meaning. Together, the Jewish family tries to make sense of the world through the magic of Torah.

The Passover seder, mentioned before as the idealized site of Jewish familial engagement, takes this home-based struggle a step further. It has a fixed topic, Exodus in all its forms. It has a script, one designed to be modified and riffed on and argued about. That script famously boasts of its questions, four for starters. Here disagreement is normative. The Haggadah recounts rabbis' arguments and opinions. It encourages expansion: "The more anyone discusses the Exodus from Egypt, the more praise is deserved." The discursive discussion seems to have no end, and not only because it feels that way if you're hungry. In the Haggadah we find the seder of the Mishnaic rabbis in Benei Berak, which ended only when their students told them it was time for the morning *Shema'*. We find the instruction to invoke the Exodus "all the days of one's life . . . to include the days of the messiah." The endless seder is the endless loop of the Jews' reflection on their existential condition and its relation to the divine. Can we be liberated? From what? Have we been freed? If so, what must we do to free others, and ourselves?

From the home, the family's struggle alongside God moves outward to the synagogue and the study house, which can be one and the same for Jews. (The *shul* is, after all, just the school, put into Yiddish.) Now the broader community is present, not just close relatives and guests.

The rituals of prayer and study evoke, in their own ways, the two most fundamental aspects of Jewish engagement with the divine. We pray together to a God whom we address, but who remains silent and does not answer our prayers in words. Together we try to interpret God's Law, invariably by weighing the suggestions of the many interpreters who have come before us. By continuing that interpretive activity, we become links in the chain of tradition. We respect what those who came before us taught, but we also expand on it by posing disagreements and postulating conflicts and contradictions that need resolving. If our forebears had exhausted their subject, we would have nothing more to say. That, somehow, has never happened in thousands of years of Jewish study, not even once.

The debates of the synagogue and the study hall cannot be contained within their walls. They radiate outward. As the venue expands, so do the topics—and so do the numbers of participants. As the Jewish community argues its way into the public sphere, it further makes itself into a people among other peoples. Here, for the last couple of centuries, the grand questions of peoplehood have dominated, becoming questions of the Jews' place in the world and of the nation postulated and created by Zionism.

In the global era of nationalism and nation-states, the Jews have been arguing about what we are and who we should become. A discussion that began among Jews became one involving many more nations and peoples. From the time Israel began to be conceived as a nation in search of a state, long before 1948, the Palestinian nation came to be foremost among those for whom the debate mattered and who wished to be heard in it. In an important and tragic historical sense, Palestinian nationhood and Israeli nationhood became entwined.

In the wake of this complicated, troubled, troubling entwinement, the old Jewish question has been transformed into the Israel question of today. Neither question was destined to be discussed by Jews only. Yet it is also true that Jews who somehow participate in the Israel or Israel-Palestine conversation today—which means, approximately, all Jews—are doing something slightly different than non-Jews who participate in it. By their words, and by their actions, those Jews are performing their own Jewishness. They are struggling with and alongside God, asking what God has to do with the fate of the Jewish people. That is true of Religious Zionists who insist that God has given them the land. It is equally true of Jewish non-Zionists and anti-Zionists, whether they are Traditionalist, Progressive, or Godless Jews.

The fact that Jews debate Israel as Jews does not tell us which Jews are right in that debate. Nor does it follow from the existence of this debate that all sides are somehow correct. The Jewish tradition is rarely relativist. Jews who are arguing about Israel believe their own positions to be the best. They are, whether directly or indirectly, arguing about what is right. In the broadest sense, they are arguing about what God wants. My own contribution to this debate, in this book, is to show how it has come to dominate large parts of Jewish thought and belief; to notice the conflicts and challenges that development is causing; and to urge all concerned to conduct their Jewish debate in a way that respects the Jewish theology of the land of Israel, a theology ever conscious of the possibility of prideful sin.

If Jewishness is a struggling together with God, in and out of familial and divine embrace, is there anything especially appealing about it? After all, the Jewish people-family today, like the families in the Bible, could be described as troubled and divided to the point of dysfunction. As for God's relationship with the people of Israel, encompassed in the theology of collective sin and collective punishment, it too has its dysfunctional aspect. Just ask the prophet Hosea, commanded by God to love a wayward woman who takes other lovers, "like the love of God for the children of Israel."[9]

To someone approaching the Jews from another perspective, whether Christian or Buddhist or take your pick, the notion of a people-family that strives with God together, that struggles as it embraces and embraces as it struggles, may seem downright perverse. Why not drop all the struggling and liberate yourself by accepting and giving love in its purest and most idealized form? Alternatively, why not recognize the impermanence of attachment and free yourself from the pain of struggle, along with the other recurring pains of this world?

To these reasonable questions, neither I nor the rest of the Jews can give the kind of answer that would end the discussion with an interlocutor saying, "You know what, you're right!" The best I can say is that Jewishness is a way of encountering other humans and the transcendent divine that refuses perfect, permanent solutions. The Jewish family is both loving and troubled, embracing and wrestling, because most real families are like that. The search for ultimate meaning is ongoing and feels as much like a struggle as an embrace because for nearly all humans, nearly all the time, that is how it works.

Holding up the ideals of pure love or pure non-self—of the perfect God-man or the arhat who achieves enlightenment—can be a tremendously powerful way of orienting our lives through aspiration and imitation. It takes just a second to realize that those ways of being must be much more appealing to the vast majority of people than the Jewish way, if you measure by how few Jews there are in the world and how many Christians, Muslims, Buddhists, Hindus, and so forth. There's nothing wrong with that, from a Jewish perspective. The Jews have rarely, if ever, believed that the whole world should become Jewish.

To see what can make being Jewish appealing, it is enough to acknowledge that there are some types of people who could find it meaningful to struggle with God and embrace God; to struggle with one another and embrace one another in that same struggle-embrace. We have a name for those people: those people are Jews. They are not, I think, much like the happy families who are all alike. But they are a family and a people, take them for all in all.

If the God of the Jews loves them and wants them to love him and to love one another—if this God is, in the final analysis, a God of love—then why does the Jewish experience entail so much struggle? Why can't we skip the struggle and go right to the embrace?

One possible answer is that we are human, and as a consequence we love as humans, which means we love partly in struggle. You don't have to read Darwin to realize that humans simultaneously cooperate and compete, love and fight. Seen in these terms, the Jewish way of struggle with God is a way of encountering the divine, designed for humans who are all too human.

Another answer, one that resonates with the Hebrew Bible, is that love itself *inherently* combines wrestling and embrace. The God of the Hebrew Bible loves and struggles. That God, though a God of love, also says he is a God of anger and zeal and vengeance. That God loves all humans equally and yet relates to some people with special love and special rigor that leads to special punishment. The One Westers I met on the New Haven Green weren't wrong in reading the Bible as evincing God's special love for his chosen people. And I wasn't wrong, not entirely, in wanting to read the same Bible as sometimes treating that love as nothing unique to the Israelites.

How could God's love be anything other than pure and uncomplicated? The answer lies in the question of how a universal, transcendent Being could experience emotion at all, as a straightforward reading of the Bible would suggest God does. That question drove Maimonides in the direction of allegory. The earliest rabbis had already observed that the Torah speaks in human language. From this premise, Maimonides could conclude that the actions and emotions ascribed to God are not of the same kind as those we ascribe to mortals. The God of the Bible is a God of metaphor. God no more experiences feelings than does God have an arm that inflicted plagues on the Egyptians.[10]

The power of such allegorical reading remains unquestioned. Yet it is worth noticing that if God's zeal or anger are metaphors, then so is God's love. God's love is a metaphoric representation of the kind of love we humans experience, love that incorporates struggle alongside embrace.

If that's right, it remains possible, conceptually and theologically, to insist that God's love itself inherently encompasses struggles. If so, wrestling and embrace may be twinned aspects of the same reality. Our families and our loves and our complex feelings about them are reflections of a dimly perceived relation with the transcendent divine.

I love my family. I struggle with my family. I love and struggle alongside my family. Together we love and struggle alongside our people-family with a God whose embrace we seek even if it should elude us. In this way, we may be alone and not alone. We may be with God and without. Together, we struggle, we strive, we embrace, we are embraced. If worthy, we may be able.

CONCLUSION:
A JEW FOR ALL THAT

Before we part, return with me, if you will, to the story of Another: Elisha ben Abuyah, the wayward rabbi we met in part I. Elisha is the figure who comes closest to personifying the "bad Jew" in the Talmud, so much so that the rabbis prefer not to utter his name. This particular story, my favorite in the whole sea of the Talmud, describes an encounter between Elisha and his devoted student, Rabbi Meir, a prominent and righteous rabbi.

The narrative begins by describing a strange setting: "The Rabbis taught: It once happened that Another was riding on a horse on the Sabbath, and Rabbi Meir was walking behind him to learn Torah from his mouth."[1] Riding is a violation of the Sabbath laws as taught by the rabbis. So according to the story told by these same rabbis, Elisha, who had already ceased to follow God's law, was violating the Sabbath *while teaching the Law.* If that is not noteworthy enough, Rabbi Meir, a rabbi of undoubted, outstanding piety, was accompanying Elisha in order to learn Torah from a lawbreaker who was in the act of breaking the Torah.[2]

Suddenly, Elisha interrupted his Torah discourse and addressed his disciple: "Meir, turn back. I have calculated by my horse's steps that this is the boundary of the distance one is permitted to walk on the Sabbath." To understand what Another was telling Rabbi Meir, you need to know the background the Talmud assumes: according to the rabbis, on the Sabbath one may only walk two thousand cubits out of town into the countryside, and no further.

Elisha's sudden directive to Rabbi Meir reflects two trains of thought. First, as he rode his horse on the Sabbath in violation of the law, while teaching Torah, Elisha was simultaneously thinking in terms of yet a different Jewish law, the law of the Sabbath boundary, and calculating where it was. Second, Elisha cared so much for his student, Rabbi Meir, and so respected his Sabbath observance, that he broke off their conversation to warn him that if he took another step forward, he would be breaking the Sabbath.

The story is not quite finished. Rabbi Meir, responding to Elisha's solicitude, took the opportunity to make a plea of his own. Elisha had told him, "Turn back." Rabbi Meir rejoined, "You, too, turn back!" As both understood, Rabbi Meir meant that Elisha should turn back from his rejection of the Torah, repent, and return to the rabbinic fold.

Elisha rebuffed his student: "Have I not already told you? I have already heard from behind the [heavenly] curtain: 'Return, wayward children'—except for Another." Elisha was quoting God's message to Jeremiah: "Return, wayward children, and I shall heal your waywardness."[3] And he was quoting, too, the words he had heard in a mystical vision appended to the prophetic promise as a personal message for him. Elisha had heard, directly from Heaven, that there could be no return, no repentance, for him, Elisha ben Abuyah.

The painful yet beautiful exchange between Another and Rabbi Meir is, among other things, a meditation on repentance and return, possibility and impossibility. In Rabbi Meir's view, the gates of repentance are always open. His teacher Elisha, who has not only studied Torah his whole life but is still teaching the Law he now flouts, is a prime candidate to repent and seek God's forgiveness. When Elisha tells him to "turn back," Rabbi Meir seizes on the language of return to urge repentance. Perhaps he is even hinting that, by telling Rabbi Meir to return and follow the law of the Sabbath boundary, Elisha is already engaged in the act of return and repentance himself. Elisha was having none of it. Interpreting the Bible to the last, he was offering a distinction between all Israelites, perhaps all people, who may return to the Lord, and he, Elisha, who could not.

As should by now be evident to readers of this book, a dispute between rabbis is not unusual in the Jewish tradition. It is constitutive of the struggle with or alongside God. Rabbinic dispute—disagreement among Jews about what God truly is or wants or says—is the basic building block out of which the whole Torah is made.

And in the Talmud's account, Elisha was correct about his fate. In the aftermath of the exchange on the country road, Rabbi Meir drags Elisha to a study hall and asks a random child there to recite whatever Bible verse he is memorizing at that moment. Asking a child to "recite your verse" was a form of oracle-cum-bibliomancy practiced by the rabbis to seek supernatural guidance. The child promptly replies with his verse of the day: "There is no peace, saith the Lord, for the wicked."[4]

The supernatural message could not be clearer. Another, the wicked sinner, will have no peace. Rabbi Meir then brings Elisha to a total of thirteen study houses—a bar mitzvah's worth—each time repeating the inquiry. Each different child's verse expresses a different divine denunciation or repudiation of the wicked. There is no coincidence at work. Another is indeed excluded from the world to come.

And yet: the mystical, bibliomantic ritual that confirms Elisha ben Abuyah's assertion of his own abandonment did not cause him to be abandoned by the Law he had ceased to obey. After Elisha died, the Talmud recounts, Elisha's daughter, destitute, sought support from Rabbi Judah the Prince. At first, Rabbi Judah was outraged by the mere thought that a sinner such as Another had any living descendants. But Elisha's daughter told the prince, "Recall his Torah, do not recall his deeds."

The Talmud narrates what happened next: another divine intervention. "Immediately, fire descended [from heaven] and licked the bench of Rabbi Judah." God himself was vindicating Elisha, *the very person whom God had excluded from repentance.* And God was telling the prince that he, too, must vindicate Another. Apprehending the message, and his own misunderstanding, Rabbi Judah wept. He said, "If this is what [comes] to those who become despised through [the Law], how much more so to those who become honored through [the Law]!"[5]

The Mishnah, the great compendium of the Oral Law, identifies Rabbi Judah as its editor. In Rabbi Judah's Mishnah, Elisha's statements are recounted and included under the name of Another. It is, then, not only Rabbi Meir who continued to learn Torah from Another. It is all of us.

What are we to make of the dialectic that judges and excludes Another and simultaneously includes him in the tradition?

One lesson, I believe, is that we would do well not to label those with whom we disagree as bad Jews, even if we think they are disidentifying with the Jewish community. Elisha, so bad in the eyes of the rabbis that he could not be named, never ceased to teach the Torah. Rabbi Meir never ceased to learn from him. And the rabbis never put Elisha under the ban of excommunication.[6]

For his own part, Elisha, even in his state of exclusion from return to God, did not cut himself off from the rabbis. He continued to teach the Law to Rabbi Meir. He acknowledged, in his exchange with Rabbi Meir, the theological reality of sin and repentance. As depicted in the story, Elisha did not deny God's existence or importance. He denied only that he himself could be forgiven by God. In this sense, at least, Another was not excluded from the tradition, nor did he exclude himself.

Finally, Elisha never ceased to struggle with God and God's Law, even after his own experience led him off the prescribed path. Teaching the Torah from within his own nonobservance was Another's idiosyncratic, no doubt painful version of Jacob's struggle with God. That struggle left Jacob injured and limping. And it also left him renamed Israel: he who struggles with God and men and is able.

That struggle-embrace with God lies at the heart of this book. It lies, I have tried to show, at the heart of the Jewish past, the Jewish present, and the hoped-for and possible Jewish future, which we pray to be able to create. It can, I believe, explain and engage and guide the ongoing encounter between God, Israel, and the Jewish people.

The struggle can sometimes be painful. Yet together with the loving embrace, it can, and should, also be joyful, productive, beautiful, transcendent. Struggling with God in this way is a gift: God's gift to Israel, and Israel's unique gift to God. It runs in all directions. The struggle is a covenant and a conflict and a concord all at the same time. It is a blessing, one given and received in love and out of it.

Medieval Jewish books typically ended with a rhymed couplet:

Tam ve-nishlam.
Shevah la-'el bore 'olam.
Perfect and complete.
Praise to God Who creates the world.

Like the struggle itself, like the hobbled Jacob, this book is not, cannot, be perfect. It can never be complete. That is as it should be. Praise to God Who creates the world.

NOTES

Introduction

1. Henry H. Goddard, "Mental Tests and the Immigrant," *Journal of Delinquency* 2, no. 5 (September 1917): 243–77, reported that 83 percent of the Jews in his small sample tested using the Binet measure at Ellis Island were "feebleminded." See Stephen Jay Gould, *The Mismeasure of Man* (New York: W. W. Norton, 1996), 166. One author has denounced the invocation of Goddard by Gould among others as a "myth" and "intellectual fraud" and claimed Goddard only tested immigrants "he *suspected* of being mentally defective." Daniel Seligman, *A Question of Intelligence: The IQ Debate in America* (New York: Carol Publishing, 1992), 129–30. Goddard's actual paper does not support this conclusion. Goddard to the contrary chose his sample "after the government physicians had culled out all mental defectives they recognized as such," although "the very obviously high grade intelligent immigrant was not selected." Goddard did not, to be sure, claim that all Jews were feebleminded. But he set out to test and report on the average immigrant.

2. See, e.g., Ira M. Sheskin and Harriet Hartman, "Denominational Variations Across American Jewish Communities," *Journal for the Scientific Study of Religion* 54, no. 2 (May 2015): 205–21.

3. See Moshe Halbertal, *Maimonides: Life and Thought* (Princeton, NJ: Princeton University Press, 2014), 13.

4. Salo Baron, *A Social and Religious History of the Jews*, vol. 9 (New York: Columbia University Press, 1965), 63.

5. Baron, *A Social and Religious History of the Jews*, 66.

6. Although Bad Jews are apparently out there: There is a play called *Bad Jews* (by Joshua Harmon, 2012) and a book called *Bad Jews: A History of American Jewish*

Politics and Identities (by Emily Tamkin, New York: HarperCollins, 2022). There was even a Los Angeles barbecue restaurant called the Bad Jew, now closed (https://www.thebadjewla.com/).

7. See Babylonian Talmud (hereafter BT) Sanhedrin 44a; also see Ephraim Kanar-fogel, *Brothers from Afar: Rabbinic Approaches to Apostasy and Reversion in Medieval Europe* (Detroit: Wayne State University Press, 2020), which offers an extended study of this principle. See also R. Moshe Feinstein, *Iggerot Moshe* (New York: Rav Moshe Feinstein Foundation, 2011), Even ha-'Ezer 4:83. For a discussion, see David Bashevkin, *Sin.a.gogue* (Boston: Cherry Orchard Books, 2019), 75–85.

8. Matthew 7:1.

9. Deuteronomy 8:17.

10. Proverbs 1:8.

I:1. The God of Black and White

1. Mishnah (hereafter M) Avot 1:1.

2. I know, I know, in Slobodka they wore modern clothes, and at Ner Yisroel, they dress up but not always in black and white. My great-grandfather, may his memory be a blessing, was a *musmakh* of Slobodka. Too much detail spoils the narrative.

3. Other movements within contemporary Jewish life also take tradition seriously, of course. The Reform movement seeks to draw inspiring, universal good from the tradition while leaving behind what seems unjust or irrelevant. The Conservative movement wants to preserve the tradition while simultaneously updating it. Reconstructionism views the tradition as having shaped a civilization that can help guide spiritual and ethical development while not being conceived as explicitly binding. Modern Orthodoxy strives to obey the tradition's laws while embracing social change it deems compatible with Torah. That's why my father dressed like anyone else in our university town and why he and my mother and my friends growing up all comfortably studied liberal arts and sciences at modern universities. But none of these other movements treats the tradition as the be-all and end-all of personal obligation and communal life. None of the others thinks that Truth (with a capital T) may be found solely and entirely in the written and oral Torah contained within the tradition itself.

4. As of 2020, Pew estimated that there were 7.5 million Jews in the United States, of whom 9 percent were Orthodox. The 2020 survey did not break down Orthodoxy into Haredi versus Modern Orthodox. A 2015 Pew analysis, however, estimated that Haredim made up around 62 percent of the Orthodox. Given high Haredi birthrates, that percentage is likely even higher today. "A Portrait of American Orthodox Jews," Pew Research Center, August 26, 2015, https://www.pewresearch.org/religion/2015/08/26/a-portrait-of-american -orthodox-jews.

5. Israel Democracy Institute, "Statistical Report on Ultra-Orthodox Society in Israel," 2020, https://en.idi.org.il/haredi/2020/?chapter=34272. The report

estimates Israel's Haredi population as 1,175,000, "expected to reach 16% of Israel's population by 2030, and to grow to around 2 million people by 2033."

6. According to its website, "8000 students are enrolled in its undergraduate and graduate programs." https://www.bmg.edu/. See also David J. Landes, "How Lakewood, N.J., Is Redefining What It Means to Be Orthodox in America," *Tablet*, June 5, 2013, https://www.tabletmag.com/sections/community/articles /lakewood-redefining-orthodoxy; and Noah Feldman, "Where Jewish Life Thrives in America," *Bloomberg*, October 3, 2013, https://www.bloomberg.com /opinion/articles/2013-10-03/where-jewish-life-thrives-in-america.

7. The Mir's website proudly declares that it is "the largest Yeshiva in the world," with an enrollment that "stands at over 9,000 students." https://themir.org /about/.

8. Exodus 19:5. Deuteronomy 7:6 says, "The Lord your God chose you from among all the peoples on the face of the earth to be a treasured people unto Him."

9. Exodus 19:8.

10. Exodus 19:17.

11. BT Shabbat 88a.

12. BT Shabbat 88a.

13. BT Shabbat 88a.

14. Genesis 1:2.

15. As a child, I was struck by a line in the film *Chariots of Fire* (1981) in which an evangelical Scots minister says that the kingdom of God is not a democracy, thus explaining why the Sabbath may not be broken. It seemed entirely immediate to my religious education and entirely inconsonant with broader social norms of voluntarism and liberty.

16. Deuteronomy 17:11.

17. The most famous exposition of the history of interpretation is Maimonides's introduction to his Commentary on the Mishnah. For a perspective from the boundary of Haredi and Modern Orthodox thought, see Hershel Schachter, *The Transmission of Torah SheBa'al Peh* (New York: Yeshiva University Press, 2017), 109.

18. BT Rosh ha-Shana 25a.

19. BT Rosh ha-Shana 25a.

20. BT Rosh ha-Shana 25a.

21. For a creative analysis that is both serious and lighthearted, see Chaim Saiman, "The Market for Gedolim: A Tale of Supply and Demand," *Lehrhaus*, October 13, 2016, https://thelehrhaus.com/commentary/the-market-for-gedolim-a-tale -of-supply-and-demand/.

22. See *The YIVO Encyclopedia of Jews in Eastern Europe*, q.v. Daas Toyre, https:// yivoencyclopedia.org/article.aspx/Daas_Toyre.

23. The three major views, discussed by all medieval Jewish philosophers, are laid out in Maimonides's *Guide*. See Daniel Rynhold, *An Introduction to Medieval Jewish Philosophy* (London: I. B. Tauris, 2009), 54–60.

24. BT Makkot 23b and in many other rabbinic sources.

25. BT Sanhedrin 56a–b.

26. Yalkut Shimoni 222:1.

27. Leviticus 18:22.

28. Deuteronomy 22:5.

29. BT 'Arakhin 4b.

30. For a comprehensive modern treatment, see 'Idan Ben-Ephraim, *Dor Tahapu-khot* (Jerusalem: 2004). This work was further explored in a lecture by Ronit Irshai, "The Contemporary Discourse on Sex-Reassignment Surgery in Orthodox Jewish Religious Law, as Reflected in *Dor Tahapukhot* (A Generation of Perversions)," presented at the Trans/Gender and Religious Law conference held at Harvard Law School on March 30, 2017.

31. Zalman Rothschild, "Free Exercise's Outer Boundary: The Case of Hasidic Education," *Columbia Law Review Forum* 119 (October 11, 2019): 204.

32. The parliamentary election held on November 1, 2022, led to the creation of the most right-wing government in Israel's history.

33. For one example, see Nehemia Polen, "*Niggun* as Spiritual Practice, with Special Focus on the Writings of Rabbi Kalonymus Shapira, the Rebbe of Piaseczna," in *Contemporary Forms and Uses of Hasidut*, ed. Shlomo Zuckier (New York: Yeshiva University Press, 2022), 257–77.

34. A mystical incantation plays on the name of Rebbe Nachman of Breslov, who moved to the Ukrainian town of Uman and is buried there: Na, Nach, Nachman me-Uman.

35. Hanna Arhirova, "Jewish Pilgrims Gather at Holy Site in Ukraine Despite the Perils of War," Associated Press, September 25, 2022, https://apnews.com /article/russia-ukraine-travel-religion-d403ec92e7b8903911bb72a40e9d51b4.

36. The term appears to have been coined by Eliezer Goldman. Alexander Kaye, "Eliezer Goldman and the Origins of Meta-Halacha," *Modern Judaism* 34, no. 3 (October 2014): 309–33. See, however, Isadore Twersky, "Religion and Law," in *Religion in a Religious Age*, ed. S. D. Goitein (Cambridge, MA: Association for Jewish Studies, 1974), 69.

37. Shaul Stampfer, *Lithuanian Yeshivas of the Nineteenth Century: Creating a Tradition of Learning* (Oxford: Littman Library of Jewish Civilization, 2012), 2, 15.

38. The comparison was noted by R. Aharon Lichtenstein at a question and answer session in Jerusalem with ATID fellows on March 28, 2001: "Rav Chaim of Volozhin says that Torah LiShmah (for its own sake) doesn't mean for the sake of heaven but for the sake of Torah. The equivalent of art for art's sake, or knowledge for knowledge's sake." (Recording and transcription available at ATID.org.) Lichtenstein further elaborated his thoughts in a Hebrew essay published the following month in which he wrote: "The pursuit of Torah for its own sake bestows upon Torah an inherent status of value. Just as the pursuit of 'l'art pour l'art' (art for art's sake) in the nineteenth century expressed a value system in which art occupied a central position, so does the pursuit of

Torah for its own sake reflect a perspective that recognizes Torah as a supreme value . . . This perspective, which held a central place in the philosophy of Rabbi Hayyim of Volozhin, must be ingrained in our consciousness." See Aharon Lichtenstein, "The Way of Yeshiva: Between Alon Shvut and Volozhin," *Alon Shvut Bogrim*, no. 14 (April 2001): 39, 45 (Hebrew). I owe these citations to Menachem Butler, whom I asked if anyone had made the comparison before. Any theory of a source common to both concepts would have to be investigated carefully and judged with extreme caution. Perhaps someday I may have the merit to make that investigation.

39. The artistic theory was, it seems, a product of the French reception of Kant's ideas about pure aesthetic value, simplified and perhaps misunderstood. See John Wilcox, "The Beginnings of l'Art Pour l'Art," *Journal of Aesthetics and Art Criticism* 11, no. 4 (June 1953): 360–77.

40. M Avot 1:3.

41. See Hayyim of Volozhin, *Nefesh ha-Hayyim*, ed. Yissakhar Rubin (Benei Berak: 5749=1988–1989), 209–12, Sha'ar 4, chapters 2–3.

42. Joshua 1:8.

43. BT Berakhot 27b–28a.

44. BT Berakhot 27b–28a.

I:2. The God of Social Justice

1. I believe this identification is made here for the first time. See this partial photograph as proof: https://nmaahc.si.edu/object/nmaahc_2015.129.48. Sister Mary Leoline (Mary Ann Theresa Sommer, 1927–2006) was a Sister of Charity of the Blessed Virgin Mary, based in Kansas City, who made the entire march. Born in California, she served as a teacher and school principal for decades. See https://www.globalsistersreport.org/news/ncr-archives -religious-leaders-refute-orgy-charges-21221; see also http://markdahlin .blogspot.com/2014/01/the-unknown-harding-hero-of-civil.html; https://www .legacy.com/us/obituaries/saltlaketribune/name/mary-ann-sommer-obituary ?id=29033994.

2. Isaiah 58:5–11.

3. BT Shabbat 31a.

4. A koan, according to a leading scholar of the genre, "far from serving as a means to obviate reason, is a highly sophisticated form of scriptural exegesis: the manipulation or 'solution' of a particular *kōan* traditionally demanded an exhaustive knowledge of canonical Buddhist doctrine and classical Zen literature." Robert H. Sharf, "The Zen of Japanese Nationalism," *History of Religions* 33, no. 1 (Aug. 1993): 1, 2.

5. H. H. Ben-Sasson, *A History of the Jewish People* (Cambridge, MA: Harvard University Press, 1976), 788.

6. Jeremiah 7:22–23.

7. Psalms 50:13–15.

8. BT Berakhot 26b.

9. BT Berakhot 26b; cf. BT Menahot 110a.

10. *Guide of the Perplexed* III:32.

11. Gershom G. Scholem, *Major Trends in Jewish Mysticism* (New York: Schocken Books, 1974), 265–68.

12. "Jewish Americans in 2020," Pew Research Center, https://www.pewresearch .org/religion/2021/05/11/jewish-americans-in-2020/.

13. Jill Jacobs, *There Shall Be No Needy: Pursuing Social Justice through Jewish Law and Tradition* (Woodstock, VT: Jewish Lights Publishing, 2010).

14. Menachem Creditor, ed., *None Shall Make Them Afraid: A Rabbis Against Gun Violence Anthology* (N.p.: 2019).

15. BT Shabbat 88a. A version of the same story made its way into the Qur'an, 2:63.

16. See, e.g., Eugene Borowitz, *Choices in Modern Jewish Thought* (West Orange, NJ: Behrman House, 1995), 307–9.

17. For leading examples of this covenant theology, see Judith Plaskow, *Standing Again at Sinai: Judaism from a Feminist Perspective* (San Francisco: HarperSan-Francisco, 1990); Eugene Borowitz, *Renewing the Covenant: A Theology for the Postmodern Jew* (Philadelphia: Jewish Publication Society, 1991).

18. W. Gunther Plaut, *The Rise of Reform Judaism* (Philadelphia: Jewish Publication Society, 1963), 10–11.

19. See Plaut, *The Rise of Reform Judaism*, 31.

20. Jonathan Sarna, *American Judaism: A History* (New Haven: Yale University Press, 2004), 83–84, 194.

21. On Zalman Schachter-Shalomi and the beliefs associated with Havurah and Jewish Renewal, see Shaul Magid, *American Post-Judaism: Identity and Renewal in a Postethnic Society* (Bloomington: Indiana University Press, 2013), 48–56 and passim.

22. See Uriel Heilman, "Conservative Shuls Turning to Musical Instruments to Boost Shabbat Services," Jewish Telegraphic Agency," April 8, 2015, https:// www.jta.org/2015/04/08/united-states/conservative-shuls-turning-to-musical -instruments-to-boost-shabbat-services. For an account of the history of the issue, see Rabbis Elie Kaplan Sapitz and Elliott N. Dorf, "Musical Instruments and Recorded Music as Part of Shabbat and Festival Worship," Voting Draft (2010), 7, cbi18.org. (In 1940, Rabbi Boaz Cohen unofficially forbade use of the organ on the Sabbath; in 1959, the Committee on Jewish Laws and Standards stated without analysis that it did "not consider the use of the organ as hal-akhically prohibited at services"; in 1963, writing on behalf of the Committee, Rabbi Ben Zion Bokser called the organ "legitimate"; and in 1970, the Com-mittee formally permitted instruments other than the organ.)

23. On neo-Hasidism, see Arthur Green, "Neo-Hasidism and Our Theological Struggles," *Ra'ayonot* 4, no. 3 (1984): 11–17; Yaakov Ariel, "From Neo-Hasidism to Outreach Yeshivot: The Origins of the Movements of Renewal and Return to Tradition," in Boaz Huss, ed., *Kabbalah and Contemporary Spiritual Revival* (Beer Sheva: Ben-Gurion University of the Negev, 2011), 17–37; Shaul Magid, "Between Paradigm Shift Judaism and Neo-Hasidism: The New Metaphy-sics of Jewish Renewal," *Tikkun* 30, no. 1 (2015): 11–15; Shaul Magid, *Piety*

and Rebellion: Essays in Hasidism (Boston: Academic Studies Press, 209), xi–xli. On Modern Orthodox neo-Hasidism, see Shai Secunda, "Wild Things: The New Neo-Hasidism and Modern Orthodoxy," *Jewish Review of Books* (Winter 2022), and David J. Landes, "Didan Notzach: Toward a Hasidic Modern Orthodoxy," in *Contemporary Forms and Uses of Hasidut*, ed. Shlomo Zuckier (New York: Yeshiva University Press, 2022), 371–418.

24. See Jay Michaelson, *Everything Is God: The Radical Path of Nondual Judaism* (Boulder, CO: Trumpeter Books, 2009). On Jews and Buddhism, see the classic, oft-reprinted Rodger Kamenetz, *The Jew in the Lotus: A Poet's Rediscovery of Jewish Identity in Buddhist India* (San Francisco: HarperSanFrancisco, 1994).

25. Or maybe the problem is that mysticism seems disjunct from social justice. As Michaelson puts it, "Let's not pretend that the heart's yearnings about God have anything to say about how the world should be." *Everything Is God*, 199.

I:3. The God Whose Law Evolves

1. Rabbi Regina Jonas was ordained privately in Berlin in 1935. She died at Auschwitz-Birkenau in 1944. On her life, see Elisa Klapheck, *Fräulein Rabbiner Jonas: The Story of the First Woman Rabbi*, trans. Toby Axelrod (San Francisco: Jossey-Bass, 2004). See also Jonathan D. Sarna, "From Antoinette Brown Blackwell to Sally Priesand: An Historical Perspective on the Emergence of Women in the American Rabbinate," in Gary P. Zola, ed., *Women Rabbis: Exploration and Celebration* (Cincinnati: American Jewish Archives, 1996), 43–53; *The Sacred Calling: Four Decades of Women in the Rabbinate*, eds. Rebecca Einstein Schorr, Alysa Mendelson Graf, and Renee Edelman (New York: CCAR, 2016).

2. The qualification is given in the United States by a feminist Orthodox institution called Nishmat. See https://www.yoatzot.org/about-us/602/.

3. See https://www.ou.org/assets/Responses-of-Rabbinic-Panel.pdf.

4. A video of the panel can be found at https://vimeo.com/310039157. The comments I am describing by Rabbi Rahel Berkovits can be heard beginning at 1:13.

5. Berkovits then added an argument about the difference between Traditionalism and Modern Orthodoxy: "So I feel [that] where we are in the modern world should be relevant to this discussion. I am pained because I feel like this reliance on *gedolim* and what is said to me feels like an ultra-Orthodox understanding of halakhah and not what I understand to be the dynamic function of halakhah that I thought was Modern Orthodoxy . . . I feel possibly we are coming to this in very different ways that are linked to our understanding of the divine in this world."

6. Deuteronomy 30:12.

7. BT Bava Metzia 59b.

8. II Kings 2 tells the tale.

9. Deuteronomy 21:18–21.

10. BT Sanhedrin 68b.

11. BT Sanhedrin 71a.
12. The case of the rebellious son isn't the only time the Talmud offers a version of this formula. The Talmud uses a parallel form of morally inflected reasoning to reread the biblical law that says a whole city of Israelites who have become idolaters must be put to the sword (Deuteronomy 13:13–18; BT Sanhedrin 71a). It does something similar with the biblical case of the leprous house (Leviticus 14:33–53; BT Sanhedrin 71a); with Ezekiel's parable of the dry bones (BT Sanhedrin 92b); and even with the existence of the biblical character Job (BT Bava Batra 15a).
13. Yaakov Levado (Steven Greenberg), "Gayness and God," *Tikkun* (Fall 1993), https://www.eshelonline.org/gayness-and-god/. I am intrigued by the possible influence on the essay of Tony Kushner's masterpiece, *Angels in America: A Gay Fantasia on National Themes*, whose two parts premiered in 1991 and 1992, respectively, and which first appeared on Broadway in 1993. Kushner refers to the story of Jacob and the angel several times, most crucially in the climactic scene in which Prior Walter, advised by Hannah Pitt, detains the Angel who visits him, telling her he will not release her unless she blesses him.
14. Yaakov Levado (Greenberg), "Gayness and God."
15. Steven Greenberg, *Wrestling with God and Men: Homosexuality in the Jewish Tradition* (Madison: University of Wisconsin Press, 2004).
16. See, e.g., BT Pesahim 50b; BT Sanhedrin 105b.
17. BT Bava Metzia 59b.
18. BT Bava Metzia 59b.

I:4. Jews Without God

1. Isaac Deutscher, *The Non-Jewish Jew: And Other Essays* (Oxford: Oxford University Press, 1967, 2017), 25.
2. "Four entered the orchard," the famous text reads. "One looked and died. One looked and was injured. One looked and cut the shoots. And one ascended safely and descended safely." Tosefta Hagigah 2:2; BT Hagigah 14b–15a.
3. Exodus 20:12; Deuteronomy 5:16.
4. BT Hagigah 15b.
5. BT Hagigah 15b.
6. Jacob Gordin, *Elisha ben Abuyah* (New York: Dai Internazionale Bibliotheque, 1906); Milton Steinberg, *As a Driven Leaf* (Behrman House, 1939); Yochi Brandes, *The Orchard* (Jerusalem: Gefen Publishing House, 2018). See also David Golinkin, "Sources and Observations," in Milton Steinberg, *As a Driven Leaf* (Jerusalem: Yediot Aharonot, 2015), 455–93 (Hebrew).
7. For sources on the General Jewish Labour Bund (1897–1920), see Jack Jacobs and Gertrud Pickhan, "The General Jewish Workers' Bund," *Oxford Bibliographies* (2020), https://www.oxfordbibliographies.com/display/document/obo-9780199840731/obo-9780199840731-0199.xml.
8. On the complex topic of Jewish emancipation, see David Sorkin, *Jewish Emancipation: A History Across Five Centuries* (Princeton, NJ: Princeton University Press, 2019).

9. Astonishingly, there is even a religious kibbutz movement, which aspired and aspires to reconcile socialism, Zionism, and Evolutionist Jewish practice. It is truly tiny, as you might imagine, but especially instructive for all that. See Aryei Fishman, *Judaism and Modernization on the Religious Kibbutz* (Cambridge: Cambridge University Press, 1992). Professor Fishman was extremely kind to me when I was a boy.

10. In France, things are a bit different. Official French republicanism, an ideology going back to the French Revolution, is formally secular. And it is also humanistic insofar as it tends to deny particularist identities other than the identity "French," which in truth it tends to treat as basically the same as "human." So in theory, French Jewish Republicans should be part of mainstream French republicanism. Yet somehow, nevertheless, their Jewishness does come up, and not infrequently.

11. West Virginia v. Barnette, 319 U.S. 624, 646 (1943) (Frankfurter, J., dissenting).

12. *Guide of the Perplexed* I:32.

I:5. The Struggle

1. Jeremiah 23:29.

2. BT Sanhedrin 34a.

II:1. The Idea of Israel

1. There is controversy among linguists on whether modern, "revived" Hebrew is or is not a new language. See Ghil'ad Zuckerman, *Yisra'elit Safah Yafah* [Israeli—A Beautiful Language] (Tel Aviv: Am Oved, 2008).

2. I was re-fascinated by these years later when I read Nadia Abu El-Haj, *Facts on the Ground: Archaeological Practice and Territorial Self-Fashioning in Israeli Society* (Chicago: University of Chicago Press, 2001).

3. John Kifner, "Israel's New Violent Tactic Takes Toll on Both Sides," *New York Times*, January 22, 1988, https://www.nytimes.com/1988/01/22/world/israel-s-new-violent-tactic-takes-toll-on-both-sides.html. For a denial (issued three years later), see "Rabin Denies Giving Orders to Break Bones of Palestinians," Jewish Telegraphic Agency, July 6, 1990 ("Troops were ordered to storm the rioters 'beating them with fists and batons, not to punish them but to hurt them and force them to cease their assault,' Rabin said"), https://www.jta.org/archive/rabin-denies-giving-orders-to-break-bones-of-palestinians.

4. The term was popularized by Max Weber, who had borrowed it from Friedrich Schiller. See Richard Jenkins, "Disenchantment, Enchantment, and Re-Enchantment: Max Weber at the Millennium," *Max Weber Studies* 1, no. 1 (November 2000): 11.

5. This helps explain why Walter Benjamin, the literary theorist and Marxist philosopher, was so enamored of messianism, as was (in a different way) his Zionist friend and counterpart, the towering scholar of Jewish mysticism Gershom Scholem. Each was following one of the two paths of the displacement of historical Jewish messianism, the one Marxist, the other Zionist.

6. See Hasan Kayalı, *Arabs and Young Turks: Ottomanism, Arabism, and Islamism*

in the Ottoman Empire, 1908–1918 (Berkeley: University of California Press, 1997).

7. Frank Giles, "Who Can Blame Israel," *Sunday Times*, June 15, 1969, 12: FRANK GILES: Do you think the emergence of the Palestinian fighting forces, the Fedayeen, is an important new factor in the Middle East? GOLDA MEIR: Important, no. A new factor, yes. There was no such thing as Palestinians. When was there an independent Palestinian people with a Palestinian state? It was either southern Syria before the first world war and then it was a Palestine including Jordan. It was not as though there was a Palestinian people in Palestine considering itself as a Palestinian people and we came and threw them out and took their country from them. They did not exist.

8. He continued:
   > Only those sand fields or stone mountains that would require the investment of hard labour and great expense to make them good for planting remain uncultivated and that's because the Arabs do not like working too much in the present for a distant future. Therefore, it is very difficult to find good land for cattle. And not only peasants, but also rich landowners, are not selling good land so easily . . . We who live abroad are accustomed to believing that the Arabs are all wild desert people who, like donkeys, neither see nor understand what is happening around them. But this is a grave mistake. The Arab, like all the Semites, is sharp minded and shrewd. All the townships of Syria and Eretz Yisra'el are full of Arab merchants who know how to exploit the masses and keep track of everyone with whom they deal—the same as in Europe.

   Ahad Ha'am, "Truth from the Land of Israel," *Hamelitz*, June 19–30, 1891, https://benyehuda.org/read/1153. A translation of the entire essay can be found in Alan Dowty, "Much Ado About Little: Ahad Ha'am's 'Truth from Eretz Yisrael,' Zionism, and the Arabs," *Israel Studies* 5, no. 2 (Fall 2000): 154–81.

9. Hillel Cohen, *Year Zero of the Arab-Israeli Conflict 1929* (Waltham, MA: Brandeis University Press, 2015).

10. Caroline Elkins, *Legacy of Violence: A History of the British Empire* (New York: Alfred A. Knopf, 2021).

11. Benny Morris, *The Birth of the Palestinian Refugee Problem, 1947–1949* (Cambridge: Cambridge University Press, 1987), 63. See also the updated edition, *The Birth of the Palestinian Refugee Problem Revisited, 1947–1949* (Cambridge: Cambridge University Press, 2004).

12. Benny Morris, "My Military Jail-Time in Israel," *Quillette*, October 5, 2020, https://quillette.com/2020/10/05/my-military-jail-time-in-israel/.

13. Avi Shlaim, *Collusion Across the Jordan: King Abdullah, the Zionist Movement, and the Partition of Palestine* (Oxford: Oxford University Press, 1988); Ilan Pappé, *The Ethnic Cleansing of Palestine* (Oxford: Oneworld, 2006).

14. Ari Shavit, "Survival of the Fittest," *Haaretz*, January 9, 2004. Part I: https://web.archive.org/web/20080515210330/http://www.haaretz.com/hasen/pages/ShArt.jhtml?itemNo=380986&contrassID=2; Part II: https://web.archive

.org/web/20080607060238/http://www.haaretz.com/hasen/pages/ShArt
.jhtml?itemNo=380984.

15. Shavit, "Survival of the Fittest."

16. This line of comparison has recently begun to receive serious historical engage-
ment. See Arie M. Dubnov and Laura Robson, eds., *Partitions: A Transnational
History of Twentieth-Century Territorial Separatism* (Palo Alto, CA: Stanford
University Press, 2019); Faisal Devji, *Muslim Zion: Pakistan as a Political Ideal*
(Cambridge, MA: Harvard University Press, 2013).

II:2. Israel in the Jewish Spirit

1. UAHC, "On the State of Israel" (1950), https://urj.org/what-we-believe
/resolutions/state-israel.

2. For a detailed discussion, see Peter Novick, *The Holocaust in American Life* (Boston: Houghton Mifflin, 1999), especially 148–51 (arguing that 1967 "marked an
important stage in [American Jews'] changing relationship to the Holocaust,"
while "it was the Yom Kippur War of October 1973 that was decisive in con-
verting many to this worldview" of a "centering of the Holocaust in American
Jewish consciousness").

3. Rachel Donadio, "The Story of 'Night,'" *New York Times*, January 20, 2008,
https://www.nytimes.com/2008/01/20/books/review/Donadio-t.html.

4. See Noah Feldman, *Scorpions: The Battles and Triumphs of FDR's Great Supreme
Court Justices* (New York: Twelve, 2010), 275–84.

5. Cf. Novick, *The Holocaust in American Life*, 152–61.

6. Kovner's pamphlet, sometimes called his Ghetto Manifesto, "Let Us Not Go
Like Sheep to the Slaughter," was delivered as a speech to his colleagues in the
Vilna Ghetto, and is usually dated to January 1, 1942. Cf. Isaiah 53:7; Jeremiah
12:3; Psalms 54:23.

7. Emil Fackenheim, *To Mend the World: Foundations of Post-Holocaust Jewish
Thought* (Bloomington: Indiana University Press, 1994), 213.

8. BT Mo'ed Katan 28a.

9. Teresa Watanabe, "Doubting the Story of Exodus," *Los Angeles Times*, April
13, 2001, https://www.latimes.com/archives/la-xpm-2001-apr-13-mn-50481
-story.html.

10. It has been argued that this point of view was not actually held by early Zionists, including Herzl, who might be understood as seeking a subnational
autonomous entity within an imperial framework. See Dmitry Shumsky,
*Beyond the Nation-State: The Zionist Political Imagination from Pinsker to Ben-
Gurion* (New Haven: Yale University Press, 2018).

11. See the declassified Kissinger State Department briefing, October 23, 1973,
chrome-extension://efaidnbmnnnibpcajpcglclefindmkaj/https://nsarchive2
.gwu.edu/NSAEBB/NSAEBB98/octwar-63.pdf; and see "Kissinger Denies
Delaying Weapons Airlifts to Israel During 1973 Yom Kippur War," *Times of
Israel*, May 30, 2023, https://www.timesofisrael.com/kissinger-denies-delaying
-weapons-airlifts-to-israel-during-1973-yom-kippur-war/.

12. The neat fit of Progressive Jewish support for African American civil rights

became more complicated as the Black Power movement began to express both skepticism of Jewish power structures and also an anti-imperialist critique of Israel.

13. For an early observation of "Holocaust and redemption theology," see Jacob Neusner, *The Jewish War Against the Jews: Reflections on Golah, Shoah, and Torah* (New York: Ktav, 1984), 70–71. On Neusner's account, see Magid, *American Post-Judaism*, 204–6.

14. Adam Popescu, "U.S. Holocaust Museums Are Updating Content and Context," *New York Times*, October 8, 2021, https://www.nytimes.com/2021/10 /08/arts/design/us-holocaust-museums.html. Boston's Holocaust Museum is scheduled to open in 2026; Orlando's is scheduled for groundbreaking in 2024.

15. See Edward T. Linenthal, *Preserving Memory: The Struggle to Create America's Holocaust Museum* (New York: Viking, 1995), 114–32, https://www.ushmm.org /information/exhibitions/museum-exhibitions/permanent/last-chapter.

16. See https://www.ushmm.org/information/exhibitions/museum-exhibitions/per manent/last-chapter.

17. See, for example, the section of the website titled "The Middle East Conflict, Antisemitism and the Holocaust," https://www.yadvashem.org/holocaust /holocaust-antisemitism.html.

18. Ka'adan v. Israel Land Administration, HCJ 6698/95 (2000), available in translation at https://versa.cardozo.yu.edu/opinions/ka%E2%80%99adan-v -israel-land-administration. The reality was more complicated.

19. Thomas L. Friedman, "The Israel We Knew Is Gone," *New York Times*, November 4, 2022, https://www.nytimes.com/2022/11/04/opinion/israel-netanyahu .html.

20. On Kahane, and on Black Power's influence on him, see Shaul Magid, *Meir Kahane: The Public Life and Political Thought of an American Jewish Radical* (Princeton, NJ: Princeton University Press, 2021), 83, 85, 101; Jacob S. Dorman, "Dreams Defended and Deferred: The Brooklyn Schools Crisis of 1968 and Black Power's Influence on Rabbi Meir Kahane," *American Jewish History* 100, no. 3 (2016): 411-37.

21. See Judy Maltz, "The Lawyer for Jewish Terrorists Who Started Out by Stealing Rabin's Car Emblem," *Haaretz*, January 4, 2016, https://www.haaretz.com /israel-news/2016–01–04/ty-article/.premium/jewish-terrorisms-star-lawyer /0000017f-eda1-da6f-a77f-fdaff1f00000.

22. Peter Beinart, "The Failure of the American Jewish Establishment," *New York Review of Books*, June 10, 2010.

23. Menachem Creditor and Amanda Berman, eds., *Fault Lines: Exploring the Complicated Place of Progressive American Jewish Zionism* (N.p.: 2021).

24. "A Threshold Crossed," Human Rights Watch, April 27, 2021, https://www .hrw.org/report/2021/04/27/threshold-crossed/israeli-authorities-and-crimes -apartheid-and-persecution.

25. "A Regime of Jewish Supremacy from the Jordan River to the Mediterranean Sea: This Is Apartheid," B'Tselem, January 12, 2021, https://www.btselem.org /publications/fulltext/202101_this_is_apartheid.

26. "Israel's Apartheid Against Palestinians," Amnesty International, February 2022, https://www.amnesty.org/en/latest/campaigns/2022/02/israels-system-of-apartheid/.

27. "In Support of Boycott, Divest, Sanctions and a Free Palestine," *Harvard Crimson*, April 29, 2022, https://www.thecrimson.com/article/2022/4/29/editorial-bds/.

28. Atalia Omer, *Days of Awe: Reimagining Jewishness in Solidarity with Palestinians* (Chicago: University of Chicago Press, 2019).

II:3. Israel at the Center

1. On Kook, see Yehudah Mirsky, *Rav Kook: Mystic in a Time of Revolution* (New Haven: Yale University Press, 2014).

2. See David Cohen, "Introduction," in Avraham Yitzhak Kook, *Orot ha-Kodesh*, vol. 1 (Jerusalem: Mosad HaRav Kook, 1963), 21. For a helpful discussion of this passage, see Shlomo Fischer, "Post-Kookism and Neo-Hasidut," in *Contemporary Forms and Uses of Hasidut*, ed. Shlomo Zuckier (New York: Yeshiva University Press, 2022), 308–9.

3. See the classic essay by Ze'ev Jabotinsky, "The Iron Wall," (1923), https://www.jewishvirtuallibrary.org/quot-the-iron-wall-quot.

4. For a useful overview, see Eliezer Don-Yehiya, "The Book and the Sword: The Nationalist Yeshivot and Political Radicalism in Israel," in *Accounting for Fundamentalisms: The Dynamic Character of Movements*, ed. Martin E. Marty and R. Scott Appleby (Chicago: University of Chicago Press, 1994), 264–302.

5. The classic starting place is Gershom Scholem, *The Messianic Idea in Judaism and Other Studies in Jewish Mysticism* (New York: Schocken Books, 1971).

6. See Maimonides, *Mishneh Torah*, Hilkhot Melakhim 11:1.

7. The Gaon of Vilna, for example, arguably considered Messiah son of Joseph to be an era rather than a man, which is not quite the same as a collective messiah. This view is presented by one of his students in *Kol Hator* 1:2. See Joel David Bakst, *The Secret Doctrine of the Gaon of Vilna: Mashiach ben Yoseph and the Messianic Role of Torah, Kabbalah, and Science* (Manitou Springs, CO: City of Luz Publications, 2008), 171.

8. See BT Sukkot 52b; Abraham Isaac Ha-Kohen Kook, *The Misped [Eulogy] in Jerusalem* (1904), delivered on the occasion of the passing of Theodor Herzl at the age of forty-four. See also Benny Lau, "Statehood and Spirit: Rabbi Abraham Isaac HaCohen Kook," *Jerusalem Post*, August 28, 2019, https://www.jpost.com/magazine/statehood-and-spirit-599950.

9. Thus, for example, there has been at various times an argument over whether the state of Israel should be described in the liturgy as "the beginning of the blossoming of our redemption," in the formulation of the state of Israel's first Ashkenazi chief rabbi, Rabbi Isaac Herzog. See Tracy Frydberg, "Mystery of Who Wrote the 'Prayer for the State of Israel' Is Finally Solved, *Times of Israel*, April 18, 2018, https://www.timesofisrael.com/mystery-over-who-wrote-the-prayer-for-the-state-of-israel-is-finally-solved/. Some have reasoned that the formula should be tweaked to reflect that the process of

redemption is potential rather than definitively underway. (Thus: "that [the state] *should become* the beginning of the blossoming of our redemption.")

10. Jeremy Sharon, "Smotrich Handed Sweeping Powers over West Bank, Control over Settlement Planning," *Times of Israel*, February 23, 2023, https://www.timesofisrael.com/smotrich-handed-sweeping-powers-over-west-bank-control-over-settlement-planning/.

11. The originator may have been the influential Israeli geographer David Benvenisti (1897–1993), father of the activist Meron Benvenisti and grandfather of the international law scholar Eyal Benvenisti.

12. Joseph B. Soloveitchik, *Kol Dodi Dofek: Listen, My Beloved Knocks* (Brooklyn, NY: KTAV Publishing House, 2006), https://www.torahmusings.com/2011/06/rav-soloveitchik-and-the-jacobs-affair/.

13. Chaim Saiman, "How Zionism Is Reconstructing American Orthodoxy," *Tradition* 51, no. 4 (2019): 92, 94.

14. Tzvi Lev, "Prayer for IDF Soldiers to Now Include Police as Well," *Arutz Sheva*, July 18, 2018, https://www.israelnationalnews.com/news/248609.

15. See "Prayer for Missing Israeli Soldiers," *Jewish Virtual Library*, https://www.jewishvirtuallibrary.org/prayer-for-missing-israeli-soldiers.

16. He has taken up the topic in his most recent book. See Daniel Boyarin, *The No-State Solution: A Jewish Manifesto* (New Haven: Yale University Press, 2023).

II:4. Israel Without Zionism

1. For the interview (in Hebrew), see Yaniv Kalif, "The Spread of the Corona Virus in Israel: Health Minister Ya'akov Liztman in an Exclusive Interbview with Yaniv Kalif," Hamal News, March 19, 2020, https://www.hamal.co.il/post/-M2mfwikR1Z2RY5n4CDk.

2. See Rabbi Abraham Isaac Kook, *Letters of the Re'ayah*, vol. 3 (Machon Har Beracha), 88.

3. See, in this context, Tzvi Hirsch Kalischer, *Derishat Ziyyon* (1862).

4. BT Ketubot 111a.

5. See Yirmiyahu Cohen, *I Will Await Him* (Natruna Publishers, 2018). See also Shmuel Silberman, "A Controversial Halakhic Case Against the State of Israel," *Lehrhaus*, January 3, 2019, https://thelehrhaus.com/culture/a-controversial-halakhic-case-against-the-state-of-israel/.

6. On Teitelbaum, see Shaul Magid, "The Satmar Are Anti-Zionist. Should We Care?" *Tablet*, May 21, 2020, https://www.tabletmag.com/sections/belief/articles/satmar-anti-zionist.

7. On the Hazon Ish, see Benjamin Brown, *The Hazon Ish: Halakhist, Believer and Leader of the Haredi Revolution* (Hebrew) (Jerusalem: Magnes Press, 2011).

8. Tom Segev, *A State at Any Cost: The Life of David Ben-Gurion* (New York: Farrar, Straus and Giroux, 2019), 474–75.

9. See Richard Primus, "Black and Blue: The Road to Haredi Zionism" (A.B. thesis, Harvard College, 1992), on file with the author and available in Harvard University archives, http://id.lib.harvard.edu/alma/990026024640203941/catalog.

10. Samuel Heilman and Menachem Friedman, *The Rebbe: The Life and Afterlife of Menachem Mendel Schneerson* (Princeton, NJ: Princeton University Press, 2012).

11. See Babylonian Talmud, Berakhot 34b; Maimonides, *Mishneh Torah*, Hilkhot Melakhim 12:2.

12. Both were based in Brooklyn: Williamsburg for Satmar and Crown Heights for Chabad. Their followers even fought some gang-like street battles in the early 1980s. Kenneth A. Briggs, "2 Hasidic Groups in Brooklyn Involved in Complex Conflict," *New York Times*, June 21, 1983, https://www.nytimes.com/1983/06/21 /nyregion/2-hasidic-groups-in-brooklyn-involved-in-complex-conflict.html.

13. More than ten other, less precise replicas exist around the world. Only the one in Kfar Chabad is said to have been built "on the Rebbe's instructions." See "How Many 770s Are There?" Anash.org, September 10, 2020, https://anash.org/how -many-770s-are-there/.

14. See https://www.chabad.org/library/article_cdo/aid/306097/jewish/A-Soldiers -Blessing.htm; https://www.chabad.org/therebbe/article_cdo/aid/1202/jewish /The-Rebbe-Said-Thank-You.htm.

15. See, e.g., Joseph Telushkin, *Rebbe: The Life and Teachings of Menachem M. Schneerson, the Most Influential Rabbi in Modern History* (New York: Harper-Collins, 2014), 249–68.

16. M. Safra and Yaakov Hanon, *Just Imagine! COVID-19* (Beitar Illit: Tfutza Publications, 2021).

17. Cf. Genesis 45:26.

18. On the founding in 1982 by a group including Roman (also called Romem) Aldubi, see https://www.jgive.co.il/new/en/ils/charity-organizations/1535.

19. See https://www.odyosefchai.co.il/.

20. See https://www.btselem.org/sites/default/files/sites/default/files2/update_june _1.1989.pdf ("May 29—Several dozen civilians, apparently students at the Joseph's Tomb Yeshiva, at Nablus, arrived at the village of Kifl Haret near Ariel. They fired in all directions, killed Ibtisam Abdul Rachman Buzia, aged 16, and injured two villagers, one of them severely. They also caused much damage to property, and shot at livestock. Two donkeys were killed and one wounded. The police detained suspects.").

21. The yeshiva was not disbanded, ultimately. In 2020 the Israeli government said it would pay retrospective compensation to the yeshiva. "State to Pay NIS 400,000 Compensation to Yeshiva Seized by Military in West Bank," *Times of Israel*, November 16, 2020, https://www.timesofisrael.com/state-to-pay-nis -400000-compensation-to-yeshiva-seized-by-military-in-west-bank/.

22. For a report of Ginsburgh's followers singing him the "Long live" song, see "A Group of Rabbi Berland's Hasidim Are Going Over to the Sect of Rabbi Ginsburgh and Joined in the Singing of 'Long Live Our Master the King Messiah Forever,'" April 8, 2013 (in Hebrew), on the blog *Be-'olamam shel haredim*, https://bshch.blogspot.com/2013/04/blog-post_6214.html?m=1. See also Noah Feldman, "Violence in the Name of the Messiah," *Bloomberg*, November 1, 2015, https://www.bloomberg.com/opinion/articles/2015-11-01 /violence-in-the-name-of-the-messiah.

23. Assaf Harel, "'The Eternal Nation Does Not Fear a Long Road': An Ethnography of Jewish Settlers in Israel/Palestine" (Doctoral dissertation, Rutgers University, 2015), 306.

24. Harel, "The Eternal Nation Does Not Fear a Long Road."

25. Yitzhak Shapira and Yosef Elitzur, *Torat ha-Melekh: Berurei Halakhah be-ʿInyenei Malkhut u-Milhamot: Dinei Nefashot bein Yisrael la-ʿAmmim* (Lev ha-Shomron: Yeshivat Od Yosef Chai, 2009). Yitzhak Shapira was Ginsburgh's successor as head of the yeshiva.

26. Shapira and Elitzur, *Torat ha-Melekh*. The metaphysical dimension is equally shocking. The authors write, "In a perfected situation, there would be no prohibition on the killing of a non-Jew, because the existence of a non-Jew who does not fulfill the basic commandments is not legitimate." Behind this position lies a mystical view that the soul of the non-Jew has less value than the Jewish soul. Indeed, the authors opine that a Jew may kill an innocent non-Jew to preserve his own life, although he may not kill an innocent Jew for the same purpose.

27. Yonah Jeremy Bob, "High Court: No Basis to Indict Torat Hamelech Authors for Incitement," *Jerusalem Post*, December 9, 2015, https://www.jpost.com/israel-news/high-court-no-basis-to-indict-torat-hamelech-authors-for-incitement-436795.

28. Noah Feldman, "Virtual Reality and Dangerous Fantasy in Jerusalem," *Bloomberg*, December 4, 2016, https://www.bloomberg.com/opinion/articles/2016-12-04/virtual-reality-and-dangerous-fantasy-in-jerusalem?sref=EBhNhdBZ.

II:5. Israel as Struggle and the Question of Sin

1. Deuteronomy 8:12–20.

2. Philip Roth, *Operation Shylock: A Confession* (New York: Vintage International, 1993), 126.

3. Its origins can be found already in an essay by the scholar brothers Daniel and Jonathan Boyarin published in 1993, the same year as *Operation Shylock*, titled "Diaspora: Generation and the Ground of Jewish Identity," *Critical Inquiry* 19, no. 4 (Summer 1993): 693–725. They wrote, "We want to propose a privileging of Diaspora, a dissociation of ethnicities and political hegemonies as the only structure that even begins to make possible a maintenance of cultural identity in a world grown thoroughly and inextricably interdependent. Indeed, we would suggest the Diaspora, and not monotheism, may be the most important contribution that Judaism has to make to the world."

4. This kind of Diasporism has come to be explicitly opposed to Zionism. In 2007, the writer Melanie Kaye/Kantrowitz put it this way: "Diasporism takes root in the Jewish Socialist Labor Bund's principle of doikayt—hereness—the right to be, and to fight for justice, wherever we are . . . Doikayt is about wanting to be citizens, to have rights, to not worry about being shipped off at any moment where someone else thinks you do or don't belong . . . I name this commitment Diasporism." Melanie Kaye/Kantrowitz, *The Colors of Jews: Racial Politics and Radical Diasporism* (Bloomington: Indiana University Press, 2007). For a more recent es-

say revisiting the work, see Jacob Plitman, "On an Emerging Diasporism," *Jewish Currents*, April 16, 2018, https://jewishcurrents.org/on-an-emerging-diasporism.

5. Judith Butler, *Parting Ways: Jewishness and the Critique of Zionism* (New York: Columbia University Press, 2012), 15.

6. Reinhold Niebuhr, *The Irony of American History* (Chicago: University of Chicago Press, 2008), 42.

7. See Noah Feldman, *The Arab Winter: A Tragedy* (Princeton, NJ: Princeton University Press, 2020), 113–17.

8. Maimonides, *Mishneh Torah*, Hilkhot De'ot 1:7; cf. *Mishneh Torah*, Hilkhot Teshuvah 6:3.

III:1. What Are the Jews?

1. The Hebrew word *yehudim*, Judeans, is used to refer to citizens of Judah in several places in the Prophets. For example, 2 Kings 16:6 reports that the king of the Arameans drove the Judeans out of the city of Eilat and that Aramaeans dwell there "to this day."

2. As in the marriage contract of Babatha, daughter of Simeon, which dates to 128 CE, and refers to marriage according to "the law of Moses and *yehudai*." See Center for Online Judaic Studies, "Babatha's Ketubah: An Early Marriage Contract," http://cojs.org/babatha-s_ketubah-_an_early_marriage_contract/. Compare the rabbinic Jewish marriage contract formula, "according to the laws of Moses and Israel."

3. Daniel Boyarin, *Judaism: The Genealogy of a Modern Notion* (New Brunswick, NJ: Rutgers University Press, 2018).

4. Compare "You shall be unto me a kingdom of priests and a holy nation (*goy kadosh*)," Exodus 19:6, to "You are a holy people (*'am kadosh*) to the Lord," Deuteronomy 7:6, 14:2, and 14:21. It is not even clear that "nation" is a good translation of *goy*, implying as it does (from its Latin root) some aspect of nativity or birth. The Vulgate, the Latin translation of the Bible, uses both *populus* and *natio* to translate the Hebrew *goy*, again almost interchangeably.

5. See, for example, Nathan P. Devir, *New Children of Israel: Emerging Jewish Communities in an Era of Globalization* (Salt Lake City: University of Utah Press, 2017).

6. BT Shevu'ot 39a.

7. The idea of family I am propounding differs from Ludwig Wittgenstein's famous account of "family resemblance." He was comparing the similarity between a class of things, say games, with "the various resemblances between members of a family: build, features, color of eyes, gait, temperament, etc. etc." Wittgenstein, *Philosophical Investigations*, trans. G. E. M. Anscombe (Oxford: Blackwell, 1952), § 67. Wittgenstein's idea may be helpful in that he uses the term "family resemblance" to account for phenomena that are roughly similar even where we cannot specify an exact formal relationship between them. Yet notice that Wittgenstein's use of the term "family" invokes genetically influenced traits, implying common biological descent. The Jewish family I am describing may not have these sorts of resemblances insofar as its members

may not be genetically related to each other and therefore may not look all that similar, either literally or metaphorically.

8. A. B. Spurdle and T. Jenkins, "The Origins of the Lemba 'Black Jews' of Southern Africa: Evidence from p12F2 and Other Y-Chromosome Markers," *American Journal of Human Genetics* 59, no. 5 (November 1996): 1126, https://www .ncbi.nlm.nih.gov/pmc/articles/PMC1914832/#:~:text=The%20Lemba%20 are%20a%20southern,and%20origins%20of%20the%20Lemba.

9. See Devir, *New Children of Israel.*

10. I Samuel 8:5.

11. I Samuel 8:7.

12. I Samuel 8:20.

13. This fascinating passage came to play a significant role in early modern European debates about monarchy and democracy. See Eric Nelson, *The Hebrew Republic: Jewish Sources and the Transformation of European Political Thought* (Cambridge, MA: Harvard University Press, 2011), 24–56.

14. James Loeffler, "Should American Jews Speak Hebrew?" *Tablet*, July 30, 2019, https://www.tabletmag.com/sections/arts-letters/articles/ben-gurion-hebrew -revolution.

15. Deuteronomy 7:6–8.

16. Philippe Sands, *East West Street* (New York: Alfred A. Knopf, 2016), 152–53.

17. Although this formulation was formally secular, it resonated with the history of Christian thought. Chosen specially by God, the Jews were, according to the Hebrew Bible itself, subject to a special moral standard of divine judgment. Christian theology continued to subject Jews to a special standard based on their unique historical crimes against Christ. Europeans of Christian heritage, consciously or otherwise, may therefore have seen the Jewish state in terms of the Jews' theological-historical uniqueness, which came with a higher divine standard of judgment.

18. The Law of Return, 1950; see https://www.knesset.gov.il/laws/special/eng /return.htm.

19. "The Story of the Jewish Community in Mir: We Remember Oswald," https:// www.yadvashem.org/yv/en/exhibitions/communities/mir/rufeisen.asp.

20. HCJ 72/62 Rufeisen v. Minister of the Interior, 16 PD 2428 [1962]. An English translation was published in Asher F. Landau, ed., *Selected Judgments of the Supreme Court of Israel* (London: Routledge, 1971), 1–34.

21. BT Sanhedrin 44a.

22. Dan Ernst, "The Meaning and Liberal Justifications of Israel's Law of Return," *Israel Law Review* 42 (2009): 564–65.

23. In 2021, Israel's High Court held that such Progressive conversions could even occur within Israel. Previously, they had only been recognized if they occurred outside Israel. Patrick Kingsley, "Israel Court Says Converts to Non-Orthodox Judaism Can Claim Citizenship," *New York Times*, March 1, 2021, https:// www.nytimes.com/2021/03/01/world/middleeast/israel-jewish-converts -citizenship.html.

24. Haim Amsalem, *Zera' Yisra'el: Hikrei Halakhah be-Dinei Gerim*, two vols.

(Jerusalem: Mekhon Nidhei Yisra'el, 2010, 2014); Haim Amsalem, ed., *Mekor Yisra'el: Leket Teshuvot u-Fesakim ve-Hora'ot le-Ma'aseh be-'Inyenei Gerim ve-Giyyur mi-Gedolei Yisra'el Rishonim va-Aharonim Asher 'Aleihem Mushtat Sefer Zera' Yisra'el*, 2 vols. (Jerusalem: Mekhon Nidhei Yisra'el, 2010).

III:2. The Chosen

1. Exodus 19:5.
2. Deuteronomy 7:6–8.
3. See., e.g., Genesis 15:13 ("He said to Abram: Know that your seed will be strangers in a land that is not theirs and shall be enslaved to them; and they shall oppress them for 400 years").
4. Numbers 21:29; Jeremiah 48:46.
5. I am using an English plural, not one from Greek or Latin. On the plural question, including a reference to *The California Book of Exoduses*, see Keith Paul Bishop, "A New Book of Exodus," *California Corporate and Securities Law Blog*, October 11, 2021, https://www.calcorporatelaw.com/a-new-book -of-exodus.
6. Isaiah 42:6, 49:6; and cf. Isaiah 60:3.
7. See Michael Brenner, "A State Like Any Other State or a Light Unto the Nations?" *Israel Studies* 23, no. 3, Israel at 70; Vision & Reality (2018): 3–10.
8. Jean-Paul Sartre, *Réflexions sur la question juive* (Paris: Editions Morihien, 1946). The essay was first written in 1944.
9. Maimonides, *Mishneh Torah*, Hilkhot Issurei Bi'ah 14:1–5.
10. Jewish legal emancipation is often dated to the late eighteenth to early nineteenth centuries but in fact began fitfully before that. See Sorkin, *Jewish Emancipation*.
11. Yuri Slezkine, *The Jewish Century* (Princeton, NJ: Princeton University Press, 2019), 1.
12. Cravath Swaine & Moore named its first Jewish partner in 1958; see Jerold S. Auerbach, "Don't Call Us. We'll Call You," *New York Times*, April 13, 1976, https://www.nytimes.com/1976/04/13/archives/dont-call-us-well-call-you .html; Davis Polk and Wardwell in 1961; see David Margolick, "At the Bar," *New York Times*, November 11, 1988, https://www.nytimes.com/1988/11/11 /us/the-law-at-the-bar.html.
13. Such as Wachtell, Lipton, Rosen & Katz, which was founded in 1965 and rose to prominence in the 1980s and 1990s after partner Martin Lipton invented the poison pill defense against corporate takeovers. Roy Strom, "Twitter's Poison Pill Began with Marty Lipton's Valuable Memo," *Bloomberg Law*, April 21, 2022, https://news.bloomberglaw.com/business-and-practice/twitters-poison -pill-began-with-lawyers-most-valuable-memo.
14. In a series of studies, Deborah Hasin of Columbia University, an epidemiologist of clinical psychiatry, has suggested that the ADH1b*2 allele, which seems to appear disproportionally among Jews and affects alcohol metabolite administration in the liver, may partially account for lower rates of alcoholism found among at least some Jews. But the same body of research, conducted in Israel over decades, also showed that cultural norms were highly significant

in determining alcohol dependence and abuse patterns even among populations with similar manifestation of the allele. Thus, for example, immigrants
from the former Soviet Union had higher alcohol use rates than genetically
indistinguishable Israeli-born Jews. And younger Israelis had higher drinking
rates than older Israelis, reflecting substantial changes in the national culture
with respect to alcohol use. See Deborah S. Hasin, "Alcohol and Nicotine Use
Disorders in Israel," NYSPI/Columbia University, http://www.columbia.edu
/~dsh2/Israel%20genetics.htm.

15. For a magisterial account of antisemitic ideas over three thousand years, see
David Nirenberg, *Anti-Judaism: The Western Tradition* (New York: W. W. Norton, 2013).

III:3. The Marriage Plot

1. Jacob Rader Marcus and Marc Saperstein, *The Jews in Christian Europe* (Cincinnati: Hebrew Union College Press, 2015), 141.
2. John Witte Jr., *Church, State, and Family: Reconciling Traditional Teachings and
Modern Liberties* (Cambridge: Cambridge University Press, 2019), 81–83.
3. Witte, *Church, State, and Family*, 218.
4. BT Avodah Zarah 36b.
5. Resolution, "Status of Children of Mixed Marriages," Central Conference of
American Rabbis, March 15, 1983, https://www.ccarnet.org/ccar-resolutions
/status-of-children-of-mixed-marriages-1983/.
6. For the concession view, see, e.g., https://www.reformjudaism.org.uk/reform
-judaism-1000-words-intermarriage/.
7. Deuteronomy 7:3.
8. Deuteronomy 23:4.
9. BT Berakhot 28a. Rabbi Joshua's view prevailed over the stricter view of Rabban Gamliel.
10. Exodus 2:18.
11. Exodus 4:24–26.
12. Numbers 12:1.
13. Numbers 12:5–16.
14. See 1 Kings 11:2–13.
15. Ezra 9:1–15; see also Nehemiah 13:23–24, where the *yehudim* have married
women of Ashdod, Ammon, and Moab, such that "of their children half speak
Ashdodite and do not know how to speak Judean, but according to the language
of each people."
16. See Mekhilta de-Rabbi Shimon b. Yohai on Exodus 34:17: "Thus, if one eats of
their sacrifices, he will marry from amongst their daughters, and they will lead
him astray and he will worship idols." Cited in Jordan D. Rosenblum, "From
Their Bread to Their Bed: Commensality, Intermarriage, and Idolatry in Tan-
naitic Literature," *Journal of Jewish Studies* 61, no. 1 (2010): 23.
17. BT Kiddushin 68a–b.
18. Ray Monk, *Ludwig Wittgenstein: The Duty of Genius* (London: Vintage, 1991), 20.
19. Josefin Dolsten, "Small but Growing Number of US Orthodox Rabbis Of-

ficiating Same-Sex Weddings," *Times of Israel*, November 6, 2020, https://www.timesofisrael.com/small-but-growing-number-of-us-orthodox-rabbis-officiating-same-sex-weddings/.

20. Herder's role in embracing and theorizing diversity was noticed by Isaiah Berlin. See Berlin, *Vico and Herder: Two Studies in the History of Ideas* (New York: Viking, 1977), 154–55; see also Fred Dallmayr, "Truth and Diversity: Some Lessons from Herder," *Journal of Speculative Philosophy* 11, no. 2 (1997): 101–24.

21. One estimate by a group organized to combat language extinction puts the current rate at nine per year. See the Language Conservancy, "The Loss of Our Languages," https://languageconservancy.org/language-loss/.

22. Perry Miller, *Errand into the Wilderness* (Cambridge, MA: Belknap Press, 1984).

23. The Mormons', and particularly Joseph Smith's, belief that they were establishing a new Zion is extensively documented. See, for example, Richard H. Jackson, "The Mormon Village: Genesis and Antecedents of the City of Zion Plan," *BYU Studies Quarterly* 17, no. 2 (Winter 1977): 224–25.

24. On my second thoughts, see Noah Feldman, "Aaron Hernandez and the Dark Side of 'Boston Strong,'" *Bloomberg Opinion*, April 15, 2015, https://www.bloomberg.com/opinion/articles/2015-04-15/aaron-hernandez-and-the-dark-side-of-boston-strong-?sref=EBhNhdBZ.

25. See Michael Frederick Atkinson and Kevin Young, "Flesh Journeys: Neo Primitives and the Contemporary Rediscovery of Radical Body Modification," *Deviant Behavior* 22, no. 2 (2001): 117–46.

26. Exodus 4:24–27.

27. Compare Jonathan Boyarin and Daniel Boyarin, "Self-Exposure as Theory: The Double Mark of the Male Jew," in *Rhetorics of Self-Making*, ed. Debbora Battaglia (Berkeley: University of California Press, 1995), 16–42.

28. For context, see the chapter titled "The Circumcision Controversy in Classical Reform in Historical Context," in Judith Bleich, *Defenders of the Faith: Studies in Nineteenth- and Twentieth-Century Orthodoxy and Reform* (Boston: Academic Studies Press, 2020), 85–107, especially p. 95 n. 32 on the German reformer Rabbi Samuel Holdheim (1802–1860).

29. Carl Schmitt, *The Concept of the Political*, trans. George Schwab (Chicago: University of Chicago Press, 2007), 26.

30. *Nicomachean Ethics*, book 8, chap. 3.

III:4. Struggling Together with God

1. Genesis 31:30.
2. Genesis 32:4–33.
3. Genesis 33:4–9.
4. Genesis 46:29.
5. AVK—to wrestle or struggle. HBK—to embrace. Compare *va-ye'avek* (Genesis 32:25) with *va-yehabbek(ehu)* (Genesis 33:4). Some commentators associate Jacob's nighttime wrestling partner with Esau.
6. Or the "Lonely Man of Faith" of Rabbi Joseph B. Soloveitchik, *Tradition* 7:2 (Summer 1965), to whom Greenberg was subtly alluding.

7. Yes, I have in mind Wittgenstein's argument against private language. See Ludwig Wittgenstein, *Philosophical Investigations*, 2nd ed. (Oxford: Blackwell Publishers, 1958, 1992), sec. 269 et seq.

8. Genesis 2:18.

9. Hosea 3:1.

10. Exodus 9:3.

Conclusion: A Jew for All That

1. BT Hagigah 15a.

2. And although the Talmud later contemplates the question of why it is permitted to learn from a rabbi who has gone sour, in this story the ongoing master-student relationship between Another and Rabbi Meir goes unremarked.

3. Jeremiah 3:22; see also Jeremiah 3:14.

4. Isaiah 48:22.

5. BT Hagigah 15b.

6. Consider, in contrast, that the rabbis did impose the ban on the great sage Rabbi Eliezer in the aftermath of the oven episode discussed in part I. Rabbi Eliezer's fault was to be right about the true meaning of the Law and to insist on his rightness even to the point of threatening the rabbis' authority. That subjected him to discipline. It also subjected the rabbis in turn to the consequences of punishing one of their number whose powers extended to unwittingly killing the prince of his day through his own prayers. Rabbi Eliezer, beloved of God, was the furthest thing from a bad Jew. Nevertheless, his pious challenge to rabbinic authority merited punishment more than Elisha's violation of the Law.

ACKNOWLEDGMENTS

How do you write acknowledgments for a book you've been thinking about your whole life? Underinclusively, that's how. A complete list would include not only my parents and brothers and partners and kids and relatives and all my teachers (Jewish and non-Jewish alike) but also my friends and friends' parents and the students with whom I've discussed the ideas in this book since long before I knew there would be a book. Many of you will find traces of yourselves in these pages, and I hope you will all know how grateful I am, even when I have not followed the path you would have wished for me.

I would like to thank a number of people who carefully read the manuscript and commented on it, including: Michael Alexander, Julia Allison, Gary J. Bass, Peter Baugher, Michael Bohnen, Shmuley Boteach, Brandon Broukhim, Idan Dershowitz, Rabea Eghbariah, Joshua Freundel, Jill Goldenziel, Lila Kagedan, Shaul Magid, Jay Moses, Nate Orbach, Nitsan Plitman, Chaim Saiman, and Avi Siegal. I had important conversations specifically about the book with each of them as well as with Zohar Atkins, Lawrence Bacow, Yishai Blank, Gabriella Blum, Daniel Boyarin, Jordan Cotler, Jason Ferguson, Tamar Gendler, Starielle Hope, Susan Kahn, Katie Ebner Landy, Benay Lappe, Daniel Libenson, Jess Magic, Miryam Segal, Jonah Steinberg, and Baya Voce. Over the years I have been influenced by what must be thousands of conversations about Jewish subjects with Hans Agrawal, Eli Aizenman, Avishay Ben Sasson-Gordis, Jonathan Baron, Seth Berman, Homi Bhabha, Menachem Butler, Shaye Cohen, Isaac Corré, Idan Dershowitz, Ezra Feldman, Penny Hollander Feldman, Roy Feldman, Simon Feldman, Peter Galison, Alan Garber, Shoshana Razel Gordon, Stephen Greenblatt, Moshe Halbertal, Mishy Harman, Jay Harris, Jonathan Jarashow, Joseph and Meg Koerner, Sarah Levine, Jed Lewinsohn, Jonathan Lewinsohn, Jay Michaelson, Tamara Morsel-Eisenberg, Nader Mousavizadeh, Eric Nelson, Darren Orbach, Marty Peretz, Richard Primus, Samuel Rascoff, Zalman Rothschild, Michal and Moshe Safdie, Philip Schreiber, Eliot Schwab, Daniel I. Schwartz, Jonah Steinberg, Prudence Steiner, David Stern, Gregg Stern, Rafi Stern, Jeannie Suk-Gersen, E. Parker Waller Jr., Tali Farhadian Weinstein, Leon Wieseltier, Hirschy and Elkie Zarchy, Daniel Zuckerman, and many, many, many others.

My debt to my teachers of Jewish subjects, both at the Maimonides School and Harvard, especially the late Isadore Twersky and the very much alive Bernard Septimus, is incalculable. They deserve credit for anything I have written here that might happen to seem correct to them but must be absolved from any blame for the much (all?) that they would reject on grounds intellectual, spiritual, temperamental, and otherwise.

The participants in the Jewish Law and Legal Theory Reading Group at Harvard Law School (also known as the *haburah*) have contributed so much to my thinking over the last dozen years that they collectively deserve special recognition. Menachem Butler, my co-conspirator and co-convener, has had an enormous effect on my knowledge of and thinking about things Jewish in that time. My appreciation for his unique qualities is unbounded. The Julis-Rabinowitz Program in Jewish and Israeli Law, skillfully run by Susan Kahn, has supported our efforts as well as my own research, and for that I am also deeply grateful. Charles Berlin's unmatched Judaica collection at Harvard has provided us with every source we could imagine and many we could not.

Shannon Whalen-Lipko continues to manage my professional life with such skill and grace that I cannot imagine any of it without her. Alex Star, the editor writers dream of, once again showed his brilliance in guiding me through another subject on which he seemed to know everything. Andrew Wylie, the agent who needs no introduction, was genuinely tolerant of my desire to write this book and find an audience for it.

Without the encouragement of my fiancée, Julia Allison, I don't think I would have written the book. I certainly wouldn't have written *this* book. Her beneficent influence is present in many dimensions here, seen and unseen, as it is in my life.

This book is dedicated to the memory of Rabbi Ben-Zion Gold (1923–2016), who was born in Radom, Poland, survived the Holocaust, and was for many decades the director and spiritual leader of the Harvard Hillel. There he officiated at my parents' wedding. There he held me as my *sandak*, or godfather. There, over the years, he gave me wise guidance, always with a smile and usually with an ironic twinkle in his eye. His pluralism, his love of Jews and Jewishness, his intellectual range, and his seriousness of purpose left their mark on the institution he did so much to shape, and that so profoundly shaped me.

INDEX

Exodus, in Hebrew Bible, 27–28, 289,
290–91, 294
extremism, of Ginsburgh, 234
Ezra, in Hebrew Bible, 321

Fackenheim, Emil, 157–58, 325,
325*n*
faith, 10–11, 93, 104, 105, 137, 340*n*;
of Traditionalist Jews, 47, 79,
89–90
family, 14–15, 261–63, 268, 332,
351–52, 375*n7*; Jewishness
as, 264–65, 266–67, 347;
Traditionalist Jews relation
to, 27
Feldman, Dovid, 230–31
female Jewish law adviser (*yo'etzet
halakhah*), 69
feminism, Jewish religious, 70
Fiddler on the Roof (film), 38
"final solution to the Jewish question"
(*die Endlösung der Judenfrage*),
100*n*
first intifada, 128, 172, 236
France, 8, 367*n10*
Frank, Anne, 153
Frankfurter, Felix, 109–110
Freud, Sigmund, 101*n*, 140
Freudian psychology, 101
Friedman, Thomas L., 173
Fundamentalism Project, University
of Chicago, 24*n†*

Gamliel (Rabban), 31–32, 44–45,
93
Gaon, of Vilna, 371*n7*
gay marriage, 316, 318–19, 323,
324
"Gayness and God" (essay), 85
gay people, 35, 84–85
gay rights, 174

Gaza, Israeli occupation of, 128
gedolim (great ones), 32–33, 46, 72,
219–20, 232–33
gender, 26, 33–34, 35
General Jewish Labor Federation
(Bund), 98
generational conflict, of Progressive
Jews, 176–78
Genesis, in Hebrew Bible, 83, 85,
115–17, 248, 265, 344–45
genetics, 262–63, 309
geniuses, 305, 308
genocide, 273; *see also* Holocaust
Gen X, 176–77, 178
Gen Z, 177–78, 178
Germany, 51–52
Giles, Frank, 368*n7*
Ginsburgh, Yitzchak, 234–41
God, 24, 82, 91, 116–18, 122,
157*n†*; authority of, 29–30, 72,
94, 118; chosenness by, 294,
300–301, 376*n17*; covenants with,
27–29, 58–59, 345, 346–47; in
Evolutionism, 92, 94; Godless
Jews and, 96, 111, 112–13, 121;
historical materialism relation to,
104; Israelites and, 27–28, 57–58;
Israel (nation-state) relation to,
198*n*; Jewish beliefs and, 6, 10–11,
12; Jewish religious feminism
and, 70; Kabbalah and, 120–21;
love of, 351–52; nationalism
relation to, 346; peoplehood
and, 14–15; Progressivism and,
54–55, 56, 58, 65, 119, 156;
Protestant Christianity and, 59;
Reconstructionism and, 330–31;
in Reform Judaism, 52; sacrifice
relation to, 53; social justice of,
49–50, 182; struggle with, 15,
118–20, 345–48, 349–51, 356–57;
Torah relation to, 22, 30, 75–76;
Traditionalist Jews and, 23, 25,

A Note About the Author

Noah Feldman is the Felix Frankfurter Professor of Law and chair of the Society of Fellows at Harvard University, where he is also founding director of the Julis-Rabinowitz Program on Jewish and Israeli Law. A leading public intellectual, he is a contributing writer for Bloomberg Opinion and the author of ten books, including *Divided by God* and *The Fall and Rise of the Islamic State*.